Contents

Foreword

The primary aim of the International Maritime Solid Bulk Cargoes (IMSBC) Code, which replaces the Code of Safe Practice for Solid Bulk Cargoes (BC Code), is to facilitate the safe stowage and shipment of solid bulk cargoes by providing information on the dangers associated with the shipment of certain types of solid bulk cargoes and instructions on the procedures to be adopted when the shipment of solid bulk cargoes is contemplated. The IMSBC Code, adopted on 4 December 2008 by resolution MSC.268(85), may be applied from 1 January 2009 on a voluntary basis, anticipating its envisaged official entry into force on 1 January 2011, from which date it will be mandatory under the provision of the SOLAS Convention.

In order to keep pace with the expansion and progress of industry, in recent years, the BC Code underwent many changes, in both layout and content, before being superseded by the IMSBC Code. The new Code includes:

- Fully updated individual schedules for solid bulk cargoes
- New individual schedules for such cargoes as direct reduced iron fines, chopped rubber and plastic insulation and granulated tyre rubber
- New provisions about an alternative form of sulphur
- References to the text of SOLAS 1974 as it has most recently been amended
- Updated information from the 2008 edition of the IMDG Code

This publication presents additional information to supplement the IMSBC Code, such as the Code of Practice for the Safe Loading and Unloading of Bulk Carriers (BLU Code) and Recommendations on the safe use of pesticides in ships applicable to the fumigation of cargo holds. It also includes a directory of contact names and addresses of offices of designated national competent authorities responsible for the safe carriage of grain and solid bulk cargoes. *IMSBC Code and supplement* is commended to Administrations, shipowners, shippers and masters and all others concerned with the standards to be applied in the safe stowage and shipment of solid bulk cargoes, excluding grain.

IMSBC Code

International Maritime Solid Bulk Cargoes Code

Contents

Resolution MSC.268(85)
(adopted on 4 December 2008)

Adoption of the International Maritime Solid Bulk Cargoes (IMSBC) Code

THE MARITIME SAFETY COMMITTEE,

RECALLING Article 28(b) of the Convention on the International Maritime Organization concerning the functions of the Committee,

NOTING the adoption by the Committee of resolution MSC.193(79) on the Code of Safe Practice for Solid Bulk Cargoes, 2004,

RECOGNIZING the need to provide a mandatory application of the agreed international standards for the carriage of solid bulk cargoes by sea,

NOTING ALSO resolution MSC.269(85) by which it adopted amendments to chapters VI and VII of the International Convention for the Safety of Life at Sea (SOLAS) 1974, as amended (hereinafter referred to as "the Convention"), to make the provisions of the International Maritime Solid Bulk Cargoes (IMSBC) Code mandatory under the Convention,

HAVING CONSIDERED, at its eighty-fifth session, the text of the proposed International Maritime Solid Bulk Cargoes (IMSBC) Code,

1.   ADOPTS the International Maritime Solid Bulk Cargoes (IMSBC) Code, the text of which is set out in the annex to the present resolution;

2.   NOTES that, under the aforementioned amendments to chapter VI of the Convention, future amendments to the IMSBC Code shall be adopted, brought into force and shall take effect in accordance with the provisions of article VIII of the Convention concerning the amendments procedures applicable to the Annex to the Convention other than chapter I thereof;

3.   INVITES Contracting Governments to the Convention to note that the IMSBC Code will take effect on 1 January 2011 upon entry into force of amendments to chapters VI and VII of the Convention;

4.   AGREES that Contracting Governments to the Convention may apply the IMSBC Code in whole or in part on a voluntary basis as from 1 January 2009;

5.   REQUESTS the Secretary-General to transmit certified copies of this resolution and its annex to all Contracting Governments to the Convention;

6.   FURTHER REQUESTS the Secretary-General to transmit copies of this resolution and its annex to all Members of the Organization which are not Contracting Governments to the Convention;

7.   RESOLVES that the annexed IMSBC Code supersedes the Code of Safe Practice for Solid Bulk Cargoes, 2004, adopted by resolution MSC.193(79).

Foreword

The International Convention for the Safety of Life at Sea, 1974 (SOLAS Convention), as amended, deals with various aspects of maritime safety and contains, in parts A and B of chapter VI and part A-1 of chapter VII, the mandatory provisions governing the carriage of solid bulk cargoes and the carriage of dangerous goods in solid form in bulk, respectively. These provisions are amplified in the International Maritime Solid Bulk Cargoes Code (IMSBC Code).

Detailed fire protection arrangements for ships carrying solid bulk cargoes are incorporated into chapter II-2 of the SOLAS Convention by regulations 10 and 19. Attention is drawn to regulation II-2/19.4 of the SOLAS Convention as amended. This provides for an appropriate document as evidence of compliance of construction and equipment with the requirements of regulation II-2/19 to be issued to ships constructed on or after 1 July 2002 and carrying dangerous goods in solid form in bulk as defined in regulation VII/7 of the Convention, except class 6.2 and class 7.

For:

  - cargo ships of 500 gross tonnage or over constructed on or after 1 September 1984 but before 1 July 2002; or
  - cargo ships of less than 500 gross tonnage constructed on or after 1 February 1992 but before 1 July 2002,

the requirements of regulation II-2/54 of SOLAS, 1974, as amended by resolutions MSC.1(XLV), MSC.6(48), MSC.13(57), MSC.22(59), MSC.24(60), MSC.27(61), MSC.31(63) and MSC.57(67), apply (see SOLAS regulation II-2/1.2).

For cargo ships of less than 500 gross tonnage constructed on or after 1 September 1984 and before 1 February 1992, it is recommended that Contracting Parties extend such application to these cargo ships as far as possible.

The problems involved in the carriage of bulk cargoes were recognized by the delegates to the 1960 International Conference on Safety of Life at Sea, but at that time it was not possible to frame detailed requirements, except for the carriage of grain. The Conference did recommend, however, in paragraph 55 of Annex D to the Convention, that an internationally acceptable code of safe practice for the shipment of bulk cargoes should be drawn up under the sponsorship of the International Maritime Organization (IMO). This work was undertaken by the Organization's Sub-Committee on Containers and Cargoes, and several editions of the Code of Safe Practice for Solid Bulk Cargoes (BC Code) have been published, since the first edition in 1965. The Sub-Committee was expanded to include dangerous goods and is now called the Sub-Committee on Dangerous Goods, Solid Cargoes and Containers (DSC Sub-Committee).

The prime hazards associated with the shipment of solid bulk cargoes are those relating to structural damage due to improper cargo distribution, loss or reduction of stability during a voyage and chemical reactions of cargoes. Therefore the primary aim of this Code is to facilitate the safe stowage and shipment of solid bulk cargoes by providing information on the dangers associated with the shipment of certain types of solid bulk cargoes and instructions on the procedures to be adopted when the shipment of solid bulk cargoes is contemplated. The requirements for the transport of grain are covered by the International Code for the Safe Carriage of Grain in Bulk (International Grain Code, 1991).

The IMSBC Code that was adopted by resolution MSC.268(85) was recommended to Governments for adoption or for use as the basis for national regulations in pursuance of their obligations under regulation of the SOLAS Convention, as amended. The Code is mandatory under the provision of the SOLAS Convention from 1 January 2011. However, some parts of the Code continue to be recommendatory or informative. It needs to be emphasized that, in the context of the language of the Code: the words "shall", "should" and "may", when used in the Code, mean that the relevant provisions are "mandatory", "recommendatory" and "optional", respectively. Observance of the Code harmonizes the practices and procedures to be followed and the appropriate precautions to be taken in the loading, trimming, carriage and discharge of solid bulk cargoes when transported by sea, ensuring compliance with the mandatory provisions of the SOLAS Convention.

The Code has undergone many changes, both in layout and content, in order to keep pace with the expansion and progress of industry. The Maritime Safety Committee (MSC) is authorized by the Organization's Assembly to adopt amendments to the Code, thus enabling the IMO to respond promptly to developments in transport.

The MSC, at its eighty-fifth session, agreed that, in order to facilitate the safe transport of solid bulk cargoes, the provisions of the Code may be applied as from 1 January 2009 on a voluntary basis, pending their official entry into force on 1 January 2011 without any transitional period. This is described in resolution MSC.268(85).

Section 1

General provisions

1.1 Introductory note

1.1.1 It should be noted that other international and national regulations exist and that those regulations may recognize all or part of the provisions of this Code. In addition, port authorities and other bodies and organizations should recognize the Code and may use it as a basis for their storage and handling by-laws within loading and discharge areas.

1.2 Cargoes listed in this Code

1.2.1 Typical cargoes currently shipped in bulk, together with advice on their properties and methods of handling, are given in the schedules for individual cargoes. However, these schedules are not exhaustive and the properties attributed to the cargoes are given only for guidance. Consequently, before loading, it is essential to obtain current valid information from the shipper on the physical and chemical properties of the cargoes presented for shipment. The shipper shall provide appropriate information about the cargo to be shipped (see section 4.2).

1.2.2 Where a solid bulk cargo is specifically listed in appendix 1 to this Code (individual schedules for solid bulk cargoes), it shall be transported in accordance with the provisions in its schedule in addition to the provisions in sections 1 to 10 and 11.1.1 of this Code. The master shall consider to consult the authorities at the ports of loading and discharge, as necessary, concerning the requirements which may be in force and applicable for the carriage.

1.3 Cargoes not listed in this Code

1.3.1 If a solid cargo which is not listed in appendix 1 to this Code is proposed for carriage in bulk, the shipper shall, prior to loading, provide the competent authority of the port of loading with the characteristics and properties of the cargo in accordance with section 4 of this Code. Based on the information received, the competent authority will assess the acceptability of the cargo for safe shipment.

1.3.1.1 When it is assessed that the solid bulk cargo proposed for carriage may present hazards as those defined by Group A or B of this Code as defined in 1.7, advice is to be sought from the competent authorities of the port of unloading and of the flag State. The three competent authorities will set the preliminary suitable conditions for the carriage of this cargo.

1.3.1.2 When it is assessed that the solid bulk cargo proposed for carriage presents no specific hazards for transportation, the carriage of this cargo shall be authorized. The competent authorities of the port of unloading and of the flag State shall be advised of that authorization.

1.3.2 The competent authority of the port of loading shall provide to the master a certificate stating the characteristics of the cargo and the required conditions for carriage and handling of this shipment. The competent authority of the port of loading shall also submit an application to the Organization, within one year from the issue of the certificate, to incorporate this solid bulk cargo into appendix 1 of this Code. The format of this application shall be as outlined in subsection 1.3.3.

1.3.3 Format for the properties of cargoes not listed in this Code and conditions of the carriage

TENTATIVE BULK CARGO SHIPPING NAME (In capital letters)

Description (Describe the cargo)

Characteristics (Fill the following table)

Angle of repose	Bulk density (kg/m^3)	Stowage factor (m^3/t)
Size	**Class**	**Group**

Hazard (Clarify the hazard of carriage of the cargo)

(Determine the following types of requirements. If no requirement is necessary, write "No special requirements")

Stowage & segregation

Hold cleanliness

Weather precautions

Loading

Precautions

Ventilation

Carriage

Discharge

Clean-up

(Specify the emergency procedures for the cargo, if necessary)

Emergency procedures

Special emergency equipment to be carried
Emergency procedures **Emergency action in the event of fire** **Medical First Aid**

1.4 Application and implementation of this Code

1.4.1 The provisions contained in this Code apply to all ships to which the SOLAS Convention, as amended, applies and that are carrying solid bulk cargoes as defined in regulation 1-1 of part A of chapter VI of the Convention.

1.4.2 Although this Code is legally treated as a mandatory instrument under the SOLAS Convention, the following provisions of this Code remain recommendatory or informative:

Section 11 Security provisions (except subsection 11.1.1);

Section 12 Stowage factor conversion tables;

Section 13 References to related information and recommendations;

Appendices other than appendix 1, Individual schedules of solid bulk cargoes; and

The texts in the sections for "Description", "Characteristics", "Hazard" and "Emergency procedures" of individual schedules of solid bulk cargoes in appendix 1.

1.4.3 In certain parts of this Code, a particular action is prescribed, but the responsibility for carrying out the action has not been specifically assigned to any particular person. Such responsibility may vary according to the laws and customs of different countries and the international conventions into which these countries have entered. For the purpose of this Code, it is not necessary to make this assignment, but only to identify the action itself. It remains the prerogative of each Government to assign this responsibility.

1.5 Exemptions and equivalent measures

1.5.1 Where this Code requires that a particular provision for the transport of solid bulk cargoes shall be complied with, a competent authority or competent authorities (port State of departure, port State of arrival or flag State) may authorize any other provision by exemption if satisfied that such provision is at least as effective and safe as that required by this Code. Acceptance of an exemption authorized under this section by a competent authority not party to it is subject to the discretion of that competent authority. Accordingly, prior to any shipment covered by the exemption, the recipient of the exemption shall notify other competent authorities concerned.

1.5.2 A competent authority or competent authorities which have taken the initiative with respect to the exemption:

.1 shall send a copy of such exemption to the Organization, which shall bring it to the attention of the Contracting Parties to SOLAS; and

.2 shall take action to amend this Code to include the provisions covered by the exemption, as appropriate.

1.5.3 The period of validity of the exemption shall be not more than five years from the date of authorization. An exemption that is not covered under 1.5.2.2 may be renewed in accordance with the provisions of this section.

1.5.4 A copy of the exemption or an electronic copy thereof shall be maintained on board each ship transporting solid bulk cargoes in accordance with the exemption, as appropriate.

1.5.5 Contact information for the main designated national competent authorities concerned is given in the separate document issued by the Organization.

1.6   Conventions

Parts A and B of chapter VI and part A-1 of chapter VII of the SOLAS Convention, as amended, deal with the carriage of solid bulk cargoes and the carriage of dangerous goods in solid form in bulk, respectively, and are reproduced in full. This extract incorporates amendments envisaged to enter into force from 1 January 2011.

CHAPTER VI
Carriage of cargoes

Part A
General provisions

Regulation 1
Application

1   This chapter applies to the carriage of cargoes (except liquids in bulk, gases in bulk and those aspects of carriage covered by other chapters) which, owing to their particular hazards to ships or persons on board, may require special precautions in all ships to which the present regulations apply and in cargo ships of less than 500 gross tonnage. However, for cargo ships of less than 500 gross tonnage, the Administration, if it considers that the sheltered nature and conditions of voyage are such as to render the application of any specific requirements of part A or B of this chapter unreasonable or unnecessary, may take other effective measures to ensure the required safety for these ships.

2   To supplement the provisions of parts A and B of this chapter, each Contracting Government shall ensure that appropriate information on cargo and its stowage and securing is provided, specifying, in particular, precautions necessary for the safe carriage of such cargoes.*

Regulation 1-1
Definitions

For the purpose of this chapter, unless expressly provided otherwise:

1   *IMSBC Code* means the International Maritime Solid Bulk Cargoes (IMSBC) Code adopted by the Maritime Safety Committee of the Organization by resolution MSC.268(85), as may be amended by the Organization, provided that such amendments are adopted, brought into force and take effect in accordance with the provisions of article VIII of the present Convention concerning the amendment procedures applicable to the annex other than chapter I.

2   *Solid bulk cargo* means any cargo, other than liquid or gas, consisting of a combination of particles, granules or any larger pieces of material generally uniform in composition, which is loaded directly into the cargo spaces of a ship without any intermediate form of containment.

Regulation 1-2
Requirements for the carriage of solid bulk cargoes other than grain

1   The carriage of solid bulk cargoes other than grain shall be in compliance with the relevant provisions of the IMSBC Code.

---

* Refer to:
.1 the Code of Safe Practice for Cargo Stowage and Securing adopted by the Organization by resolution A.714(17), as amended; and
.2 the Code of Safe Practice for Ships Carrying Timber Deck Cargoes adopted by the Organization by resolution A.715(17), as amended; MSC/Circ.525, Guidance note on precautions to be taken by the masters of ships of below 100 metres in length engaged in the carriage of logs; and MSC/Circ.548, Guidance note on precautions to be taken by masters of ships engaged in the carriage of timber cargoes.

Regulation 2
Cargo information

1   The shipper shall provide the master or his representative with appropriate information on the cargo sufficiently in advance of loading to enable the precautions which may be necessary for proper stowage and safe carriage of the cargo to be put into effect. Such information* shall be confirmed in writing† and by appropriate shipping documents prior to loading the cargo on the ship.

2   The cargo information shall include:

.1   in the case of general cargo, and of cargo carried in cargo units, a general description of the cargo, the gross mass of the cargo or of the cargo units, and any relevant special properties of the cargo. For the purpose of this regulation the cargo information required in sub-chapter 1.9 of the Code of Safe Practice for Cargo Stowage and Securing, adopted by the Organization by resolution A.714(17), as may be amended, shall be provided. Any such amendment to sub-chapter 1.9 shall be adopted, brought into force and take effect in accordance with the provisions of article VIII of the present Convention concerning the amendment procedures applicable to the annex other than chapter I;

.2   in the case of solid bulk cargo, information as required by section 4 of the IMSBC Code.

3   Prior to loading cargo units on board ships, the shipper shall ensure that the gross mass of such units is in accordance with the gross mass declared on the shipping documents.

Regulation 3
Oxygen analysis and gas detection equipment

1   When transporting a solid bulk cargo which is liable to emit a toxic or flammable gas, or cause oxygen depletion in the cargo space, an appropriate instrument for measuring the concentration of gas or oxygen in the air shall be provided together with detailed instructions for its use. Such an instrument shall be to the satisfaction of the Administration.

2   The Administration shall take steps to ensure that crews of ships are trained in the use of such instruments.

Regulation 4
The use of pesticides in ships‡

Appropriate precautions shall be taken in the use of pesticides in ships, in particular for the purposes of fumigation.

Regulation 5
Stowage and securing

1   Cargo, cargo units§ and cargo transport units¶ carried on or under deck shall be so loaded, stowed and secured as to prevent as far as is practicable, throughout the voyage, damage or hazard to the ship and the persons on board, and loss of cargo overboard.

2   Cargo, cargo units and cargo transport units shall be so packed and secured within the unit as to prevent, throughout the voyage, damage or hazard to the ship and the persons on board.

---

* Refer to the Form for cargo information (MSC/Circ.663).

† Reference to documents in this regulation does not preclude the use of electronic data processing (EDP) and electronic data interchange (EDI) transmission techniques as an aid to paper documentation.

‡ Refer to:
  .1 The Recommendations on the safe use of pesticides in ships (MSC/Circ.612, as amended);
  .2 The Recommendations on the safe use of pesticides in ships applicable to the fumigation of cargo holds (MSC.1/Circ.1264) (see the supplement of this publication); and
  .3 The Recommendations on the safe use of pesticides in ships applicable to the fumigation of cargo transport units (MSC.1/Circ.1265), as appropriate.

§ Refer to the Code of Safe Practice for Cargo Stowage and Securing, adopted by the Organization by resolution A.714(17), as amended.

¶ Refer to the International Maritime Dangerous Goods (IMDG) Code, adopted by the Organization by resolution MSC.122(75).

3   Appropriate precautions shall be taken during loading and transport of heavy cargoes or cargoes with abnormal physical dimensions to ensure that no structural damage to the ship occurs and to maintain adequate stability throughout the voyage.

4   Appropriate precautions shall be taken during loading and transport of cargo units and cargo transport units on board ro–ro ships, especially with regard to the securing arrangements on board such ships and on the cargo units and cargo transport units and with regard to the strength of the securing points and lashings.

5   Freight containers shall not be loaded to more than the maximum gross weight indicated on the Safety Approval Plate under the International Convention for Safe Containers (CSC), as amended.

6   All cargoes, other than solid and liquid bulk cargoes, cargo units and cargo transport units, shall be loaded, stowed and secured throughout the voyage in accordance with the Cargo Securing Manual approved by the Administration. In ships with ro–ro spaces, as defined in regulation II-2/3.41, all securing of such cargoes, cargo units, and cargo transport units, in accordance with the Cargo Securing Manual, shall be completed before the ship leaves the berth. The Cargo Securing Manual shall be drawn up to a standard at least equivalent to relevant guidelines developed by the Organization.*

Regulation 5-1
Material safety data sheets

1   Ships carrying MARPOL Annex I cargoes, as defined in Appendix I to Annex I of the Protocol of 1978 relating to the International Convention for the Prevention of Pollution from Ships, 1973, and marine fuel oils shall be provided with a material safety data sheet prior to the loading of such cargoes based on the recommendations developed by the Organization.

Part B
Special provisions for solid bulk cargoes

Regulation 6
Acceptability for shipment

1   Prior to loading a solid bulk cargo, the master shall be in possession of comprehensive information on the ship's stability and on the distribution of cargo for the standard loading conditions. The method of providing such information shall be to the satisfaction of the Administration.†

Regulation 7
Loading, unloading and stowage of solid bulk cargoes‡

1   For the purpose of this regulation, terminal representative means a person appointed by the terminal or other facility, where the ship is loading or unloading, who has responsibility for operations conducted by that terminal or facility with regard to the particular ship.

2   To enable the master to prevent excessive stresses in the ship's structure, the ship shall be provided with a booklet, which shall be written in a language with which the ship's officers responsible for cargo operations are familiar. If this language is not English, the ship shall be provided with a booklet written also in the English language. The booklet shall, as a minimum, include:

   .1   stability data, as required by regulation II-1/5-1;

   .2   ballasting and deballasting rates and capacities;

---

* Refer to the Guidelines on the preparation of the Cargo Securing Manual (MSC/Circ.745).

† Refer to:
   .1 SOLAS regulation II-1/5-1 on Stability information to be supplied to the master; and
   .2 the Recommendation on a severe wind and rolling criterion (weather criterion) for the intact stability of passenger and cargo ships of 24 metres in length and over adopted by the Organization by resolution A.562(14).

‡ Refer to the Code of Practice for the Safe Loading and Unloading of Bulk Carriers (BLU Code) adopted by the Organization by resolution A.862(20), as amended (see the supplement of this publication).

.3   maximum allowable load per unit surface area of the tanktop plating;

.4   maximum allowable load per hold;

.5   general loading and unloading instructions with regard to the strength of the ship's structure including any limitations on the most adverse operating conditions during loading, unloading, ballasting operations and the voyage;

.6   any special restrictions such as limitations on the most adverse operating conditions imposed by the Administration or organization recognized by it, if applicable; and

.7   where strength calculations are required, maximum permissible forces and moments on the ship's hull during loading, unloading and the voyage.

3   Before a solid bulk cargo is loaded or unloaded, the master and the terminal representative shall agree on a plan* which shall ensure that the permissible forces and moments on the ship are not exceeded during loading or unloading, and shall include the sequence, quantity and rate of loading or unloading, taking into consideration the speed of loading or unloading, the number of pours and the deballasting or ballasting capability of the ship. The plan and any subsequent amendments thereto shall be lodged with the appropriate authority of the port State.

4   The master and terminal representative shall ensure that loading and unloading operations are conducted in accordance with the agreed plan.

5   If during loading or unloading any of the limits of the ship referred to in paragraph 2 are exceeded or are likely to become so if the loading or unloading continues, the master has the right to suspend operation and the obligation to notify accordingly the appropriate authority of the port State with which the plan has been lodged. The master and the terminal representative shall ensure that corrective action is taken. When unloading cargo, the master and terminal representative shall ensure that the unloading method does not damage the ship's structure.

6   The master shall ensure that ship's personnel continuously monitor cargo operations. Where possible, the ship's draught shall be checked regularly during loading or unloading to confirm the tonnage figures supplied. Each draught and tonnage observation shall be recorded in a cargo log-book. If significant deviations from the agreed plan are detected, cargo or ballast operations or both shall be adjusted to ensure that the deviations are corrected.

CHAPTER VII
Carriage of dangerous goods

Part A-1
Carriage of dangerous goods in solid form in bulk

Regulation 7
Definitions

Dangerous goods in solid form in bulk means any material, other than liquid or gas, consisting of a combination of particles, granules or any larger pieces of material, generally uniform in composition, which is covered by the IMDG Code and is loaded directly into the cargo spaces of a ship without any intermediate form of containment, and includes such materials loaded in a barge on a barge-carrying ship.

Regulation 7-1
Application†

1   Unless expressly provided otherwise, this part applies to the carriage of dangerous goods in solid form in bulk in all ships to which the present regulations apply and in cargo ships of less than 500 gross tonnage.

---

* Refer to the Code of Practice for the Safe Loading and Unloading of Bulk Carriers (BLU Code) adopted by the Organization by resolution A.862(20), as amended (see the supplement of this publication).

† Refer to regulation II-2/19, which contains special requirements for ship carrying dangerous goods.

2   The carriage of dangerous goods in solid form in bulk is prohibited except in accordance with the provisions of this part.

3   To supplement the provisions of this part, each Contracting Government shall issue, or cause to be issued, instructions on emergency response and medical first aid relevant to incidents involving dangerous goods in solid form in bulk, taking into account the guidelines developed by the Organization.*

Regulation 7-2
Documents

1   In all documents relating to the carriage of dangerous goods in solid form in bulk by sea, the bulk cargo shipping name of the goods shall be used (trade names alone shall not be used).

2   Each ship carrying dangerous goods in solid form in bulk shall have a special list or manifest setting forth the dangerous goods on board and the location thereof. A detailed stowage plan, which identifies by class and sets out the location of all dangerous goods on board, may be used in place of such a special list or manifest. A copy of one of these documents shall be made available before departure to the person or organization designated by the port State authority.

Regulation 7-3
Stowage and segregation requirements

1   Dangerous goods in solid form in bulk shall be loaded and stowed safely and appropriately in accordance with the nature of the goods. Incompatible goods shall be segregated from one another.

2   Dangerous goods in solid form in bulk, which are liable to spontaneous heating or combustion, shall not be carried unless adequate precautions have been taken to minimize the likelihood of the outbreak of fire.

3   Dangerous goods in solid form in bulk, which give off dangerous vapours, shall be stowed in a well-ventilated cargo space.

Regulation 7-4
Reporting of incidents involving dangerous goods

1   When an incident takes place involving the loss or likely loss overboard of dangerous goods in solid form in bulk into the sea, the master, or other person having charge of the ship, shall report the particulars of such an incident without delay and to the fullest extent possible to the nearest coastal State. The report shall be drawn up based on general principles and guidelines developed by the Organization.†

2   In the event of the ship referred to in paragraph 1 being abandoned, or in the event of a report from such a ship being incomplete or unobtainable, the company, as defined in regulation IX/1.2, shall, to the fullest extent possible, assume the obligations placed upon the master by this regulation.

Regulation 7-5
Requirements for the carriage of dangerous goods in solid form in bulk

1   The carriage of dangerous goods in solid form in bulk shall be in compliance with the relevant provisions of the IMSBC Code, as defined in regulation VI/1-1.1.

1.7   Definitions

For the purpose of this Code, unless expressly provided otherwise, the following definitions shall apply:

1.7.1   *Angle of repose* means the maximum slope angle of non-cohesive (i.e., free-flowing) granular material. It is measured as the angle between a horizontal plane and the cone slope of such material.

---

* Refer to the *Medical First Aid Guide for Use in Accidents involving Dangerous Goods (MFAG)* (MSC/Circ.857).

† Refer to the General principles for ship reporting systems and ship reporting requirements, including Guidelines for reporting incidents involving dangerous goods, harmful substances and/or marine pollutants, adopted by the Organization by resolution A.851(20).

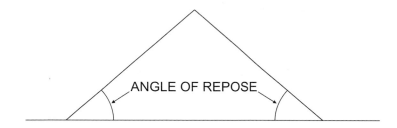

1.7.2   *Bulk Cargo Shipping Name (BCSN)* identifies a bulk cargo during transport by sea. When a cargo is listed in this Code, the Bulk Cargo Shipping Name of the cargo is identified by capital letters in the individual schedules or in the index. When the cargo is a dangerous good, as defined in the IMDG Code, as defined in regulation VII/1.1 of the SOLAS Convention, the Proper Shipping Name of that cargo is the Bulk Cargo Shipping Name.

1.7.3   *Bulk density* means the weight of solids, air and water per unit volume. Bulk density is expressed in kilograms per cubic metre (kg/m^3), in general. The void spaces in the cargo may be filled with air and water.

1.7.4   *Cargo space* means any space in a ship designated for carriage of cargoes.

1.7.5   *Cargoes which may liquefy* means cargoes which contain a certain proportion of fine particles and a certain amount of moisture. They may liquefy if shipped with a moisture content in excess of their transportable moisture limit.

1.7.6   *Cohesive material* means materials other than non-cohesive materials.

1.7.7   *Competent authority* means any national regulatory body or authority designated or otherwise recognized as such for any purpose in connection with this Code.

1.7.8   *Concentrates* means materials obtained from a natural ore by a process of enrichment or beneficiation by physical or chemical separation and removal of unwanted constituents.

1.7.9   *Consignment* means a solid bulk cargo presented by a shipper for transport.

1.7.10   *Flow moisture point* means the percentage moisture content (wet mass basis) at which a flow state develops under the prescribed method of test in a representative sample of the material (see paragraph 1 of appendix 2).

1.7.11   *Flow state* means a state occurring when a mass of granular material is saturated with liquid to an extent that, under the influence of prevailing external forces such as vibration, impaction or ship's motion, it loses its internal shear strength and behaves as a liquid.

1.7.12   *Group A* consists of cargoes which may liquefy if shipped at a moisture content in excess of their transportable moisture limit.

1.7.13   *Group B* consists of cargoes which possess a chemical hazard which could give rise to a dangerous situation on a ship.

1.7.14   *Group C* consists of cargoes which are neither liable to liquefy (Group A) nor to possess chemical hazards (Group B).

1.7.15   *High-density solid bulk cargo* means a solid bulk cargo with a stowage factor of 0.56 m^3/t or less.

1.7.16   *IMDG Code* means the International Maritime Dangerous Goods (IMDG) Code adopted by the Maritime Safety Committee of the Organization by resolution MSC.122(75), as may be amended by the Organization.

1.7.17   *Incompatible materials* means materials that may react dangerously when mixed. They are subject to the segregation requirements of subsection 9.3 and the schedules for individual cargoes classified in Group B.

1.7.18 *International Ship and Port Facility Security (ISPS) Code* means the International Code for the Security of Ships and of Port Facilities, consisting of part A (the provisions of which shall be treated as mandatory) and part B (the provisions of which shall be treated as recommendatory), as adopted, on 12 December 2002, by resolution 2 of the Conference of Contracting Governments to the International Convention for the Safety of Life at Sea, 1974, as may be amended by the Organization.

1.7.19 *Materials hazardous only in bulk (MHB)* means materials which may possess chemical hazards when carried in bulk other than materials classified as dangerous goods in the IMDG Code.

1.7.20 *Moisture content* means that portion of a representative sample consisting of water, ice or other liquid expressed as a percentage of the total wet mass of that sample.

1.7.21 *Moisture migration* means the movement of moisture contained in a cargo by settling and consolidation of the cargo due to vibration and ship's motion. Water is progressively displaced, which may result in some portions or all of the cargo developing a flow state.

1.7.22 *Non-cohesive material* means dry materials that readily shift due to sliding during transport, as listed in appendix 3, paragraph 1, "Properties of solid bulk cargoes".

1.7.23 *Representative test sample* means a sample of sufficient quantity for the purpose of testing the physical and chemical properties of the consignment to meet specified requirements.

1.7.24 *Shipper* means any person by whom or in whose name, or on whose behalf, a contract of carriage of goods by sea has been concluded with a carrier, or any person by whom or in whose name, or on whose behalf, the goods are actually delivered to the carrier in relation to the contract of carriage by sea.

1.7.25 *Solid bulk cargo* means any cargo, other than a liquid or a gas, consisting of a combination of particles, granules or any larger pieces of material generally uniform in composition which is loaded directly into the cargo spaces of a ship without any intermediate form of containment.

1.7.26 *Stowage factor* means the figure which expresses the number of cubic metres which one tonne of cargo will occupy.

1.7.27 *Transportable moisture limit (TML)* of a cargo which may liquefy means the maximum moisture content of the cargo which is considered safe for carriage in ships not complying with the special provisions of subsection 7.3.2. It is determined by the test procedures, approved by a competent authority, such as those specified in paragraph 1 of appendix 2.

1.7.28 *Trimming* means any levelling of a cargo within a cargo space, either partial or total.

1.7.29 *Ventilation* means exchange of air from outside to inside a cargo space.

    .1   *Continuous ventilation* means ventilation that is operating at all times.

    .2   *Mechanical ventilation* means power-generated ventilation.

    .3   *Natural ventilation* means ventilation that is not power-generated.

    .4   *Surface ventilation* means ventilation of the space above the cargo.

Section 2

General loading, carriage and unloading precautions

2.1   Cargo distribution

2.1.1   General

A number of accidents have occurred as a result of improper loading and unloading of solid bulk cargoes. It shall be noted that solid bulk cargoes have to be properly distributed throughout the ship to provide adequate stability and to ensure that the ship's structure is never overstressed. Furthermore, the shipper shall provide the master with adequate information about the cargo, as specified in section 4, to ensure that the ship is properly loaded.*

2.1.2   To prevent the structure being overstressed

A general cargo ship is normally constructed to carry cargoes in the range of 1.39 to 1.67 cubic metres per tonne when loaded to full bale and deadweight capacities. When loading a high-density solid bulk cargo, particular attention shall be paid to the distribution of weights to avoid excessive stresses, taking into account that the loading conditions may be different from those found normally and that improper distribution of such cargo may be capable of stressing either the structure under the load or the entire hull. To set out exact rules for the distribution of loading is not practicable for all ships because the structural arrangements of each vessel may vary greatly. The information on proper distribution of cargo may be provided in the ship's stability information booklet or may be obtained by the use of loading calculators, if available.

2.1.3   To aid stability

2.1.3.1   Having regard to regulation II-1/22.1 of the SOLAS Convention, a stability information booklet shall be provided aboard all ships subject to the Convention. The master shall be able to calculate the stability for the anticipated worst conditions during the voyage, as well as that on departure, and demonstrate that the stability is adequate.

2.1.3.2   Shifting divisions and bins, of adequate strength, shall be erected whenever solid bulk cargoes which are suspected of readily shifting are carried in 'tween-deck cargo spaces or in only partially filled cargo spaces.

2.1.3.3   As far as practicable, high-density cargoes shall be loaded in the lower hold cargo spaces in preference to 'tween-deck cargo spaces.

2.1.3.4   When it is necessary to carry high-density cargoes in 'tween-decks or higher cargo spaces, due consideration shall be paid to ensure that the deck area is not overstressed and that the ship's stability is not reduced below the minimum acceptable level specified in the ship's stability data.

---

* Also refer to the Code of Practice for the Safe Loading and Unloading of Bulk Carriers, adopted by the Organization by resolution A.862(20), as amended (see the supplement of this publication).

2.2 Loading and unloading

2.2.1 Cargo spaces shall be inspected and prepared for the particular cargo which is to be loaded.*

2.2.2 Due consideration shall be paid to bilge wells and strainer plates, for which special preparation is necessary, to facilitate drainage and to prevent entry of the cargoes into the bilge system.

2.2.3 Bilge lines, sounding pipes and other service lines within the cargo space shall be in good order.

2.2.4 Because of the velocity at which some high-density solid bulk cargoes are loaded, special care may be necessary to protect cargo space fittings from damage. To sound bilges after the completion of loading may be effective to detect damage on cargo space fittings.

2.2.5 As far as practicable, ventilation systems shall be shut down or screened and air conditioning systems placed on recirculation during loading or discharge, to minimize dust ingress into the living quarters or other interior spaces.

2.2.6 Due consideration shall be paid to minimize the extent to which dust may come into contact with moving parts of deck machinery and external navigational aids.

---

* Refer to the *Guidance to ships' crews and terminal personnel for bulk carrier inspections*, adopted by the Organization by resolution A.866(20).

Section 3

Safety of personnel and ship

3.1 General requirements

3.1.1 Prior to and during loading, carriage and discharge of a solid bulk cargo, all necessary safety precautions shall be observed.

3.1.2 A copy of the instructions on emergency response and medical first aid* relevant to incidents involving dangerous goods in solid form in bulk shall be on board.

3.2 Poisoning, corrosive and asphyxiation hazards

3.2.1 Some solid bulk cargoes are susceptible to oxidation, which may result in oxygen depletion, emission of toxic gases or fumes and self-heating. Some cargoes are not liable to oxidize but may emit toxic fumes, particularly when wet. There are also cargoes which, when wetted, are corrosive to skin, eyes and mucous membranes or to the ship's structure. When these cargoes are carried, particular attention shall be paid to protection of personnel and the need for special precautions to be taken prior to loading and after unloading.

3.2.2 Appropriate attention shall be paid that cargo spaces and adjacent spaces may be depleted in oxygen or may contain toxic or asphyxiating gases, and that an empty cargo space or tank which has remained closed for some time may have insufficient oxygen to support life.

3.2.3 Many solid bulk cargoes are liable to cause oxygen depletion in a cargo space or tank. These include, but are not limited to, most vegetable products and forest products, ferrous metals, metal sulphide concentrates and coal cargoes.

3.2.4 Prior to entry into an enclosed space aboard a ship, appropriate procedures shall be followed, taking into account the recommendations developed by the Organization.† It is to be noted that, after a cargo space or tank has been tested and generally found to be safe for entry, small areas may exist where oxygen is deficient or toxic fumes are still present.

3.2.5 When carrying a solid bulk cargo that is liable to emit a toxic or flammable gas, and/or cause oxygen depletion in the cargo space, the appropriate instrument(s) for measuring the concentration of gas and oxygen in the cargo space shall be provided.

3.2.6 Emergency entry into a cargo space shall be undertaken only by trained personnel wearing self-contained breathing apparatus and protective clothing and always under the supervision of a responsible officer.

---

* Refer to the *Medical First Aid Guide for Use in Accidents Involving Dangerous Goods (MFAG)* (MSC/Circ.857).

† Refer to the Recommendations for entering enclosed spaces aboard ships, adopted by the Organization by resolution A.864(20), as amended (see the supplement of this publication).

3.3 Health hazards due to dust

To minimize the chronic and acute risks associated with exposure to the dust of some solid bulk cargoes, the need for a high standard of personal hygiene of those exposed to the dust cannot be overemphasized. Precautions, including the use of appropriate breathing protection, protective clothing, protective skin creams, adequate personal washing and laundering of outer clothing, shall be taken as necessary.

3.4 Flammable atmosphere

3.4.1 Dust of some solid bulk cargoes may constitute an explosion hazard, especially while loading, unloading and cleaning. This risk can be minimized by ventilating to prevent the formation of a dust-laden atmosphere and by hosing down rather than sweeping.

3.4.2 Some cargoes may emit flammable gases in sufficient quantities to constitute a fire or explosion hazard. Where this is indicated in the cargo schedule in this Code or by the cargo information provided by the shipper, the cargo spaces shall be effectively ventilated as necessary. The atmosphere in the cargo spaces shall be monitored by means of an appropriate gas detector. Due consideration shall be paid to the ventilation and monitoring of the atmosphere in the enclosed spaces adjacent to the cargo spaces.

3.5 Ventilation

3.5.1 Unless expressly provided otherwise, when cargoes which may emit toxic gases are carried, the cargo spaces shall be provided with mechanical or natural ventilation; and, when cargoes which may emit flammable gases are carried, the cargo spaces shall be provided with mechanical ventilation.

3.5.2 If maintaining ventilation would endanger the ship or the cargo, it may be interrupted unless this would produce a risk of explosion.

3.5.3 When continuous ventilation is required by the schedule for the cargo in this Code or by the cargo information provided by the shipper, ventilation shall be maintained while the cargo is on board, unless a situation develops where ventilation would endanger the ship.

3.5.4 Ventilation openings shall be provided in holds intended for the carriage of cargoes that require continuous ventilation. Such openings shall comply with the requirements of the Load Line Convention, as amended, for openings not fitted with means of closure.

3.5.5 Ventilation shall be such that any escaping hazardous gases, vapours or dust cannot enter the accommodation or other interior spaces in hazardous concentrations. Due consideration shall be given to prevent escaping hazardous gases, vapours or dust from reaching enclosed work areas. Adequate precautions shall be taken to protect the personnel in these work areas.

3.5.6 When a cargo may heat spontaneously, ventilation other than surface ventilation shall not be applied. On no account shall air be directed into the body of the cargo.

3.6 Cargo under in-transit fumigation

Fumigation shall be performed based on the recommendations developed by the Organization.*

---

* Refer to the Recommendations on the safe use of pesticides in ships applicable to the fumigation of cargo holds (MSC.1/Circ.1264) (see the supplement of this publication).

Section 4

Assessment of acceptability of consignments for safe shipment

4.1 Identification and classification

4.1.1 Each solid bulk cargo in this Code has been assigned a Bulk Cargo Shipping Name (BCSN). When a solid bulk cargo is carried by sea it shall be identified in the transport documentation by the BCSN. The BCSN shall be supplemented with the United Nations (UN) number when the cargo is dangerous goods.

4.1.2 If waste cargoes are being transported for disposal, or for processing for disposal, the name of the cargoes shall be preceded by the word "WASTE".

4.1.3 Correct identification of a solid bulk cargo facilitates identification of the conditions necessary to safely carry the cargo and the emergency procedures, if applicable.

4.1.4 Solid bulk cargoes shall be classified, where appropriate, in accordance with the UN *Manual of Tests and Criteria*, part III. The various properties of a solid bulk cargo required by this Code shall be determined, as appropriate to that cargo, in accordance with the test procedures approved by a competent authority in the country of origin, when such test procedures exist. In the absence of such test procedures, those properties of a solid bulk cargo shall be determined, as appropriate to that cargo, in accordance with the test procedures prescribed in appendix 2 to this Code.

4.2 Provision of information

4.2.1 The shipper shall provide the master or his representative with appropriate information on the cargo sufficiently in advance of loading to enable the precautions which may be necessary for proper stowage and safe carriage of the cargo to be put into effect.

4.2.2 Cargo information shall be confirmed in writing and by appropriate shipping documents prior to loading. The cargo information shall include:

.1 the BCSN when the cargo is listed in this Code. Secondary names may be used in addition to the BCSN;

.2 the cargo group (A and B, A, B or C);

.3 the IMO Class of the cargo, if applicable;

.4 the UN number, preceded by letters "UN" for the cargo, if applicable;

.5 the total quantity of the cargo offered;

.6 the stowage factor;

.7 the need for trimming and the trimming procedures, as necessary;

.8 the likelihood of shifting, including angle of repose, if applicable;

.9 additional information in the form of a certificate on the moisture content of the cargo and its transportable moisture limit in the case of a concentrate or other cargo which may liquefy;

.10 likelihood of formation of a wet base (see subsection 7.2.3 of this Code);

.11 toxic or flammable gases which may be generated by cargo, if applicable;

.12 flammability, toxicity, corrosiveness and propensity to oxygen depletion of the cargo, if applicable;

.13 self-heating properties of the cargo, and the need for trimming, if applicable;

.14 properties on emission of flammable gases in contact with water, if applicable;

.15 radioactive properties, if applicable; and

.16 any other information required by national authorities.

4.2.3 Information provided by the shipper shall be accompanied by a declaration. An example of a cargo declaration form is set out below. Another form may be used for cargo declaration. As an aid to paper documentation, Electronic Data Processing (EDP) or Electronic Data Interchange (EDI) techniques may be used.

FORM FOR CARGO INFORMATION
for solid bulk cargoes

BCSN	
Shipper	Transport document number
Consignee	Carrier
Name/means of transport Port/place of departure	Instructions or other matters
Port/place of destination	
General description of the cargo (Type of material/particle size)	Gross mass (kg/tonnes)
Specifications of bulk cargo, if applicable: Stowage factor: Angle of repose, if applicable: Trimming procedures: Chemical properties if potential hazard*: * e.g., Class & UN No. or "MHB"	
Group of the cargo ☐ Group A and B* ☐ Group A* ☐ Group B ☐ Group C * For cargoes which may liquefy (Group A and Group A and B cargoes)	Transportable moisture limit Moisture content at shipment
Relevant special properties of the cargo (e.g., highly soluble in water)	Additional certificate(s)* ☐ Certificate of moisture content and transportable moisture limit ☐ Weathering certificate ☐ Exemption certificate ☐ Other (specify) * If required
DECLARATION I hereby declare that the consignment is fully and accurately described and that the given test results and other specifications are correct to the best of my knowledge and belief and can be considered as representative for the cargo to be loaded.	Name/status, company/organization of signatory Place and date Signature on behalf of shipper

4.3 Certificates of test

4.3.1 To obtain the information required in 4.2.1, the shipper shall arrange for the cargo to be properly sampled and tested. The shipper shall provide the ship's master or his representative with the appropriate certificates of test, if required in this Code.

4.3.2 When a concentrate or other cargo which may liquefy is carried, the shipper shall provide the ship's master or his representative with a signed certificate of the TML, and a signed certificate or declaration of the moisture content. The certificate of TML shall contain, or be accompanied by, the result of the test for determining the TML. The declaration of moisture content shall contain, or be accompanied by, a statement by the shipper that the moisture content is, to the best of his knowledge and belief, the average moisture content of the cargo at the time the declaration is presented to the master.

4.3.3 When a concentrate or other cargo which may liquefy is to be loaded into more than one cargo space of a ship, the certificate or the declaration of moisture content shall certify the moisture content of each type of finely grained material loaded into each cargo space. Notwithstanding this requirement, if sampling according to internationally or nationally accepted standard procedures indicates that the moisture content is uniform throughout the consignment, then one certificate or declaration of average moisture content for all cargo spaces is acceptable.

4.3.4 Where certification is required by the individual schedules for cargoes possessing chemical hazards, the certificate shall contain, or be accompanied by, a statement from the shipper that the chemical characteristics of the cargo are, to the best of his knowledge, those present at the time of the ship's loading.

4.4 Sampling procedures

4.4.1 Physical property tests on the consignment are meaningless unless they are conducted prior to loading on truly representative test samples.

4.4.2 Sampling shall be conducted only by persons who have been suitably trained in sampling procedures and who are under the supervision of someone who is fully aware of the properties of the consignment and also the applicable principles and practices of sampling.

4.4.3 Prior to taking samples, and within the limits of practicability, a visual inspection of the consignment which is to form the ship's cargo shall be carried out. Any substantial portions of material which appear to be contaminated or significantly different in characteristics or moisture content from the bulk of the consignment shall be sampled and analysed separately. Depending upon the results obtained in these tests, it may be necessary to reject those particular portions as unfit for shipment.

4.4.4 Representative samples shall be obtained by employing techniques which take the following factors into account:

.1 the type of material;

.2 the particle size distribution;

.3 composition of the material and its variability;

.4 the manner in which the material is stored, in stockpiles, rail wagons or other containers, and transferred or loaded by material-handling systems such as conveyors, loading chutes, crane grabs, etc.;

.5 the chemical hazards (toxicity, corrosivity, etc.);

.6 the characteristics which have to be determined: moisture content, TML, bulk density/ stowage factor, angle of repose, etc.;

.7 variations in moisture distribution throughout the consignment which may occur due to weather conditions, natural drainage, e.g., to lower levels of stockpiles or containers, or other forms of moisture migration; and

.8 variations which may occur following freezing of the material.

4.4.5 Throughout the sampling procedures, utmost care shall be taken to prevent changes in quality and characteristics. Samples shall be immediately placed in suitable sealed containers which are properly marked.

4.4.6 Unless expressly provided otherwise, sampling for the test required by this Code shall follow an internationally or nationally accepted standard procedure.

4.5 Interval between sampling/testing and loading for TML and moisture content determination

4.5.1 A test to determine the TML of a solid bulk cargo shall be conducted within six months to the date of loading the cargo. Notwithstanding this provision, where the composition or characteristics of the cargo are variable for any reason, a test to determine the TML shall be conducted again after it is reasonably assumed that such variation has taken place.

4.5.2 Sampling and testing for moisture content shall be conducted as near as practicable to the time of loading. If there has been significant rain or snow between the time of testing and loading, check tests shall be conducted to ensure that the moisture content of the cargo is still less than its TML. The interval between sampling/testing and loading shall never be more than seven days.

4.5.3 Samples of frozen cargo shall be tested for the TML or the moisture content after the free moisture has completely thawed.

4.6 Sampling procedures for concentrate stockpiles

4.6.1 It is not practicable to specify a single method of sampling for all consignments since the character of the material and the form in which it is available will affect the selection of the procedure to be used. In the absence of internationally or nationally accepted standard sampling procedures, the following sampling procedures for concentrate stockpiles may be used to determine the moisture content and the TML of mineral concentrates. These procedures are not intended to replace sampling procedures, such as the use of automatic sampling, that achieve equal or superior accuracy of either moisture content or TML.

4.6.2 Sub-samples are taken in a reasonably uniform pattern, where possible from a levelled stockpile.

4.6.3 A plan of the stockpile is drawn and divided into areas, each of which contains approximately 125 t, 250 t or 500 t, depending on the amount of concentrate to be shipped. Such a plan will indicate the number of sub-samples required and where each is to be taken. Each sub-sample taken is drawn from approximately 50 cm below the surface of the designated area.

4.6.4 The number of sub-samples and sample size are given by the competent authority or determined in accordance with the following scale:

Consignments of not more than 15,000 t:
One 200 g sub-sample is taken for each 125 t to be shipped.

Consignments of more than 15,000 but not more than 60,000 t:
One 200 g sub-sample is taken for each 250 t to be shipped.

Consignments of more than 60,000 t:
One 200 g sub-sample is taken for each 500 t to be shipped.

4.6.5 Sub-samples for moisture content determination are placed in sealed containers (such as plastic bags, cans or small metallic drums) immediately on withdrawal for conveyance to the testing laboratory, where they are thoroughly mixed in order to obtain a fully representative sample. Where testing facilities are not available at the testing site, such mixing is done under controlled conditions at the stockpile and the representative sample is placed in a sealed container and shipped to the test laboratory.

4.6.6 Basic procedural steps include:

.1 identification of the consignment to be sampled;

.2 determination of the number of individual sub-samples and representative samples, as described in 4.6.4, which are required;

.3 determination of the positions from which to obtain sub-samples and the method of combining such sub-samples to arrive at a representative sample;

.4 gathering of individual sub-samples and placing them in sealed containers;

.5 thorough mixing of sub-samples to obtain the representative sample; and

.6 placing the representative sample in a sealed container if it has to be shipped to a test laboratory.

4.7 Examples of standardized sampling procedures, for information

ISO 3082:1998	Iron ores – Sampling and sample preparation procedures
ISO 1988:1975	Hard coal – Sampling
ASTMD 2234-99	Standard Practice for Collection of a Gross Sample of Coal

Australian Standards

AS 4264.1	Coal and Coke – Sampling: Part 1: Higher rank coal – sampling procedures
AS 1141 – Series	Methods for sampling and testing aggregates
BS 1017:1989	Methods of sampling coal and coke
BS 1017	British Standard Part 1: 1989 methods of sampling of coal
BS 1017	British Standard Part 2: 1994 methods of sampling of coal

Canadian Standard Sampling Procedure for Concentrate Stockpiles

European Communities Method of Sampling for the Control of Fertilizers

JIS M 8100	Japanese General Rules for Methods of Sampling Bulk Materials
JIS M 8100:1992	Particulate cargoes – General Rules for Methods of Sampling

Polish Standard Sampling Procedure for:

Iron and Manganese Ores – Ref. No. PN-67/H-04000

Non-ferrous Metals – Ref. No. PN-70/H-04900

Russian Federation Standard Sampling Procedure for the Determination of Moisture Content in Ore Concentrates.

4.8 Documentation required on board the ship carrying dangerous goods

4.8.1 Each ship carrying dangerous goods in solid form in bulk shall have a special list or manifest setting forth the dangerous goods on board and the location thereof, in accordance with SOLAS regulation VII/7-2.2. A detailed stowage plan, which identifies by class and sets out the location of all dangerous goods on board, may be used in place of such a special list or manifest.

4.8.2 When dangerous goods in solid form in bulk are carried, appropriate instructions on emergency response to incidents involving the cargoes shall be on board.

4.8.3 Cargo ships of 500 gross tonnage and over constructed on or after 1 September 1984 and cargo ships of less than 500 gross tonnage constructed on or after 1 February 1992, subject to SOLAS regulation II-2/19.4 (or II-2/54.3), shall have a document of compliance when carrying dangerous goods in solid form in bulk, except class 6.2 and class 7.

Section 5

Trimming procedures

5.1 General provisions for trimming

5.1.1 Trimming a cargo reduces the likelihood of the cargo shifting and minimizes the air entering the cargo. Air entering the cargo could lead to spontaneous heating. To minimize these risks, cargoes shall be trimmed reasonably level, as necessary.

5.1.2 Cargo spaces shall be as full as practicable without resulting in excessive loading on the bottom structure or 'tween-deck to prevent sliding of a solid bulk cargo. Due consideration shall be given to the amount of a solid bulk cargo in each cargo space, taking into account the possibility of shifting and longitudinal moments and forces of the ship. Cargo shall be spread as widely as practicable to the boundary of the cargo space. Alternate hold loading restrictions, as required by SOLAS chapter XII, may also need to be taken into account.

5.1.3 The master has the right to require that the cargo be trimmed level, where there is any concern regarding stability based upon the information available, taking into account the characteristics of the ship and the intended voyage.

5.2 Special provisions for multi-deck ships

5.2.1 When a solid bulk cargo is loaded only in lower cargo spaces, it shall be trimmed sufficiently to equalize the mass distribution on the bottom structure.

5.2.2 When solid bulk cargoes are carried in 'tween-decks, the hatchways of such 'tween-decks shall be closed in those cases where the loading information indicates an unacceptable level of stress of the bottom structure if the hatchways are left open. The cargo shall be trimmed reasonably level and shall either extend from side to side or be secured by additional longitudinal divisions of sufficient strength. The safe load-carrying capacity of the 'tween-decks shall be observed to ensure that the deck structure is not overloaded.

5.2.3 If coal cargoes are carried in 'tween decks, the hatchways of such 'tween-decks shall be tightly sealed to prevent air moving up through the body of the cargo in the 'tween decks.

5.3 Special provisions for cohesive bulk cargoes

5.3.1 All damp cargoes and some dry ones possess cohesion. For cohesive cargoes, the general provisions in subsection 5.1 shall apply.

5.3.2 The angle of repose is not an indicator of the stability of a cohesive bulk cargo and it is not included in the individual schedules for cohesive cargoes.

5.4 Special provisions for non-cohesive bulk cargoes

5.4.1 Non-cohesive bulk cargoes are those listed in paragraph 1 in appendix 3 and any other cargo not listed in the appendix, exhibiting the properties of a non-cohesive material.

5.4.2 For trimming purposes, solid bulk cargoes can be categorized as cohesive or non-cohesive. The angle of repose is a characteristic of non-cohesive bulk cargoes which is indicative of cargo stability and has been included in the individual schedules for non-cohesive cargoes. The angle of repose of the cargoes shall establish which provisions of this section apply. Methods for determining the angle of repose are given in section 6.

5.4.3 Non-cohesive bulk cargoes having an angle of repose less than or equal to 30°

These cargoes, which flow freely like grain, shall be carried according to the provisions applicable to the stowage of grain cargoes.* The bulk density of the cargo shall be taken into account when determining:

.1 the scantlings and securing arrangements of divisions and bin bulkheads; and

.2 the stability effect of free cargo surfaces.

5.4.4 Non-cohesive bulk cargoes having an angle of repose greater than 30° to 35° inclusive

These cargoes shall be trimmed according to the following criteria:

.1 the unevenness of the cargo surface measured as the vertical distance (Δh) between the highest and lowest levels of the cargo surface shall not exceed $B/10$, where B is the beam of the ship in metres, with a maximum allowable $\Delta h = 1.5$ m; or

.2 loading is carried out using trimming equipment approved by the competent authority.

5.4.5 Non-cohesive bulk cargoes having an angle of repose greater than 35°

These cargoes shall be trimmed according to the following criteria:

.1 the unevenness of the cargo surface measured as the vertical distance (Δh) between the highest and lowest levels of the cargo surface shall not exceed $B/10$, where B is the beam of the ship in metres, with a maximum allowable $\Delta h = 2$ m; or

.2 loading is carried out using trimming equipment approved by the competent authority.

---

* Reference is made to chapter VI of the SOLAS Convention, and the International Code for the Safe Carriage of Grain in Bulk adopted by the Maritime Safety Committee of the Organization by resolution MSC.23(59).

Section 6

Methods of determining the angle of repose

6.1 General

An angle of repose of a non-cohesive solid bulk material shall be measured by a method approved by the appropriate authority as required by section 4.1.4 of this Code.

6.2 Recommended test methods

There are various methods in use to determine the angle of repose for non-cohesive solid bulk materials. The recommended test methods are listed below:

6.2.1 Tilting box method

This laboratory test method is suitable for non-cohesive granular materials with a grain size not greater than 10 mm. A full description of the equipment and procedure is given in subsection 2.1 of appendix 2.

6.2.2 Shipboard test method

In the absence of a tilting box apparatus, an alternative procedure for determining the approximate angle of repose is given in subsection 2.2 of appendix 2.

Section 7

Cargoes that may liquefy

7.1 Introduction

7.1.1 The purpose of this section is to bring to the attention of masters and others with responsibilities for the loading and carriage of bulk cargoes the risks associated with liquefaction and the precautions to minimize the risk. Such cargoes may appear to be in a relatively dry granular state when loaded, and yet may contain sufficient moisture to become fluid under the stimulus of compaction and the vibration which occurs during a voyage.

7.1.2 A ship's motion may cause a cargo to shift sufficiently to capsize the vessel. Cargo shift can be divided into two types, namely, sliding failure or liquefaction consequence. Trimming the cargo in accordance with section 5 can prevent sliding failure.

7.1.3 Some cargoes which may liquefy may also heat spontaneously.

7.2 Conditions for hazards

7.2.1 Group A cargoes contain a certain proportion of small particles and a certain amount of moisture. Group A cargoes may liquefy during a voyage even when they are cohesive and trimmed level. Liquefaction can result in cargo shift. This phenomenon may be described as follows:

.1 the volume of the spaces between the particles reduces as the cargo is compacted owing to the ship motion, etc.;

.2 the reduction in space between cargo particles causes an increase in water pressure in the space; and

.3 the increase in water pressure reduces the friction between cargo particles, resulting in a reduction in the shear strength of the cargo.

7.2.2 Liquefaction does not occur when one of the following conditions is satisfied:

.1 the cargo contains very small particles. In this case, particle movement is restricted by cohesion and the water pressure in spaces between cargo particles does not increase;

.2 the cargo consists of large particles or lumps. Water passes through the spaces between the particles and there is no increase in the water pressure. Cargoes which consist entirely of large particles will not liquefy;

.3 the cargo contains a high percentage of air and low moisture content. Any increase in the water pressure is inhibited. Dry cargoes are not liable to liquefy.

7.2.3 A cargo shift caused by liquefaction may occur when the moisture content exceeds the TML. Some cargoes are susceptible to moisture migration and may develop a dangerous wet base even if the average moisture content is less than the TML. Although the cargo surface may appear dry, undetected liquefaction may take place, resulting in shifting of the cargo. Cargoes with high moisture content are prone to sliding, particularly when the cargo is shallow and subject to large heel angles.

7.2.4 In the resulting viscous fluid state cargo may flow to one side of the ship with a roll but not completely return with a roll the other way. Consequently the ship may progressively reach a dangerous heel and capsize quite suddenly.

7.3 Provisions for cargoes that may liquefy

7.3.1 General

7.3.1.1 Concentrates or other cargoes which may liquefy shall only be accepted for loading when the actual moisture content of the cargo is less than its TML. Notwithstanding this provision, such cargoes may be accepted for loading on specially constructed or fitted cargo ships even when their moisture content exceeds the TML.

7.3.1.2 Cargoes which contain liquids other than packaged canned goods or the like shall not be stowed in the same cargo space above or adjacent to these solid bulk cargoes.

7.3.1.3 Adequate measures shall be taken to prevent liquids entering the cargo space in which these solid bulk cargoes are stowed during the voyage.

7.3.1.4 Masters shall be cautioned about the possible danger of using water to cool these cargoes while the ship is at sea. Introducing water may bring the moisture content of these cargoes to a flow state. When necessary, due regard shall be paid to apply water in the form of a spray.

7.3.2 Specially constructed or fitted cargo ships

7.3.2.1 Cargoes having a moisture content in excess of the TML shall only be carried in specially constructed cargo ships or in specially fitted cargo ships.

7.3.2.2 Specially constructed cargo ships shall have permanent structural boundaries, so arranged as to confine any shift of cargo to an acceptable limit. The ship concerned shall carry evidence of approval by the Administration.

7.3.2.3 Specially fitted cargo ships shall be fitted with specially designed portable divisions to confine any shift of cargo to an acceptable limit. Specially fitted cargo ships shall be in compliance with the following requirements:

    .1 The design and positioning of such special arrangements shall adequately provide not only the restraint of the immense forces generated by the flow movement of high-density bulk cargoes, but also for the need to reduce to an acceptable safe level the potential heeling movements arising out of a transverse cargo flow across the cargo space. Divisions provided to meet these requirements shall not be constructed of wood.

    .2 The elements of the ship's structure bounding such cargo shall be strengthened, as necessary.

    .3 The plan of special arrangements and details of the stability conditions on which the design has been based shall have been approved by the Administration. The ship concerned shall carry evidence of approval by the Administration.

7.3.2.4 A submission made to an Administration for approval of such a ship shall include:

    .1 relevant structural drawings, including scaled longitudinal and transverse sections;

    .2 stability calculations, taking into account loading arrangements and possible cargo shift, showing the distribution of cargo and liquids in tanks, and of cargo which may become fluid; and

    .3 any other information which may assist the Administration in the assessment of the submission.

Section 8

Test procedures for cargoes that may liquefy

8.1 General

For a Group A cargo, the actual moisture content and transportable moisture limit shall be determined in accordance with a procedure determined by the appropriate authority as required by section 4.1.4 of this Code, unless the cargo is carried in a specially constructed or fitted ship.

8.2 Test procedures for measurement of moisture content

There are recognized international and national methods for determining moisture content for various materials. Reference is made to paragraph 1.1.4.4 of appendix 2.

8.3 Methods for determining transportable moisture limit

The recommended methods for determining transportable moisture limit are given in appendix 2.

8.4 Complementary test procedure for determining the possibility of liquefaction

A ship's master may carry out a check test for approximately determining the possibility of flow on board ship or at the dockside by the following auxiliary method:

Half fill a cylindrical can or similar container (0.5 to 1 litre capacity) with a sample of the material. Take the can in one hand and bring it down sharply to strike a hard surface such as a solid table from a height of about 0.2 m. Repeat the procedure 25 times at one- or two-second intervals. Examine the surface for free moisture or fluid conditions. If free moisture or a fluid condition appears, arrangements should be made to have additional laboratory tests conducted on the material before it is accepted for loading.

Section 9

Materials possessing chemical hazards

9.1 General

Solid bulk cargoes which may possess a chemical hazard during transport, because of their chemical nature or properties, are in Group B. Some of these materials are classified as dangerous goods and others are materials hazardous only in bulk (MHB). It is essential to obtain current, valid information about the physical and chemical properties of the cargoes to be shipped in bulk, prior to loading.

9.2 Hazard classification

9.2.1 The classification of materials possessing chemical hazards and intended to be shipped in bulk under the requirements of this Code shall be in accordance with 9.2.2 and 9.2.3.

9.2.2 Classification of dangerous goods

SOLAS regulation VII/7 defines dangerous goods in solid form in bulk. For the purpose of this Code, dangerous goods shall be classified in accordance with part 2 of the IMDG Code.

9.2.2.1 *Class 4.1: Flammable solids*

The materials in this class are readily combustible solids and solids which may cause fire through friction.

9.2.2.2 *Class 4.2: Substances liable to spontaneous combustion*

The materials in this class are materials, other than pyrophoric materials, which, in contact with air without energy supply, are liable to self-heating.

9.2.2.3 *Class 4.3: Substances which, in contact with water, emit flammable gases*

The materials in this class are solids which, by interaction with water, are liable to become spontaneously flammable or to give off flammable gases in dangerous quantities.

9.2.2.4 *Class 5.1: Oxidizing substances*

The materials in this class are materials that, while in themselves not necessarily combustible, may, generally by yielding oxygen, cause, or contribute to, the combustion of other material.

9.2.2.5 *Class 6.1: Toxic substances*

The materials in this class are materials liable either to cause death or serious injury or to harm human health if swallowed or inhaled, or by skin contact.

9.2.2.6 *Class 7: Radioactive material*

The materials in this class are any materials containing radionuclides where both the activity concentration and the total activity in the consignment exceed the values specified in 2.7.2.2.1 to 2.7.2.2.6 of the IMDG Code.

9.2.2.7 *Class 8: Corrosive substances*

The materials in this class are materials which, by chemical action, will cause severe damage when in contact with living tissue or will materially damage, or even destroy, other goods or the means of transport.

9.2.2.8 *Class 9: Miscellaneous dangerous substances and articles*

The materials in this class are materials and articles which, during transport, present a danger not covered by other classes.

9.2.3 Materials hazardous only in bulk (MHB)

These are materials which may possess chemical hazards when transported in bulk other than materials classified as dangerous goods in the IMDG Code.

9.3 Stowage and segregation requirements

9.3.1 General requirements

9.3.1.1 The potential hazards of the cargoes in Group B and falling within the classification of 9.2.2 and 9.2.3 entail the need for segregation of incompatible cargoes. Segregation shall also take account of any identified subsidiary risk.

9.3.1.2 In addition to general segregation as between whole classes of materials, there may be a need to segregate a particular material from others. In the case of segregation from combustible materials, this shall be understood not to include packaging material, ceiling or dunnage; the latter shall, in these circumstances, be kept to a minimum.

9.3.1.3 For the purpose of segregating incompatible materials, the words "hold" and "compartment" are deemed to mean a cargo space enclosed by steel bulkheads or shell plating and by steel decks. The boundaries of such a space shall be resistant to fire and liquid.

9.3.1.4 When two or more different solid bulk cargoes of Group B are to be carried, the segregation between them shall be in accordance with 9.3.4.

9.3.1.5 Where different grades of a solid bulk cargo are carried in the same cargo space, the most stringent segregation provisions applicable to any of the different grades shall apply to all of them.

9.3.1.6 When solid bulk cargoes of Group B and dangerous goods in packaged form are to be carried, the segregation between them shall be in accordance with 9.3.3.

9.3.1.7 Incompatible materials shall not be handled simultaneously. Upon completion of loading one cargo, the hatch covers of every cargo space shall be closed and the decks cleaned of residue before the loading of other material is commenced. When discharging, the same procedures shall be followed.

9.3.1.8 To avoid contamination, all foodstuffs shall be stowed:

   .1   "separated from" a material which is indicated as toxic;

   .2   "separated by a complete compartment or hold from" all infectious materials;

   .3   "separated from" radioactive materials; and

   .4   "away from" corrosive materials.

The terms are defined in 9.3.3 and 9.3.4, as appropriate.

9.3.1.9 Materials which may evolve toxic gases in sufficient quantities to affect health shall not be stowed in those spaces from where such gases may penetrate into living quarters or ventilation systems connecting to living quarters.

9.3.1.10 Materials which present corrosive hazards of such intensity as to affect either human tissue or the ship's structure shall only be loaded after adequate precautions and protective measures have been taken.

9.3.1.11 After discharge of toxic or oxidizing cargoes, the spaces used for their carriage shall be inspected for contamination before being used for other cargoes. A space which has been contaminated shall be properly cleaned and examined before being used for other cargoes.

9.3.1.12 After discharge of cargoes, a close inspection shall be made for any residue, which shall be removed before the ship is presented for other cargoes.

9.3.1.13 For cargoes for which in case of an emergency the hatches shall be opened, these hatches shall be kept free to be capable of being opened up.

9.3.2 Special requirements

9.3.2.1 *Materials of classes 4.1, 4.2 and 4.3*

9.3.2.1.1 Materials of these classes shall be kept as cool and dry as reasonably practicable and, unless expressly provided otherwise in this Code, shall be stowed "away from" all sources of heat or ignition.

9.3.2.1.2 Electrical fittings and cables shall be in good condition and properly safeguarded against short circuits and sparking. Where a bulkhead is required to be suitable for segregation purposes, cable and conduit penetrations of the decks and bulkheads shall be sealed against the passage of gas and vapour.

9.3.2.1.3 Cargoes liable to give off vapours or gases which can form an explosive mixture with air shall be stowed in a mechanically ventilated space.

9.3.2.1.4 Prohibition of smoking in dangerous areas shall be enforced, and clearly legible "NO SMOKING" signs shall be displayed.

9.3.2.2 *Materials of class 5.1*

9.3.2.2.1 Cargoes of this class shall be kept as cool and dry as reasonably practicable and, unless expressly provided otherwise in this Code, shall be stowed "away from" all sources of heat or ignition. They shall also be stowed "separated from" other combustible materials.

9.3.2.2.2 Before loading cargoes of this class, particular attention shall be paid to the cleaning of the cargo spaces into which they will be loaded. As far as reasonably practicable, non-combustible securing and protecting materials shall be used and only a minimum of dry wooden dunnage shall be used.

9.3.2.2.3 Precautions shall be taken to avoid the penetration of oxidizing materials into other cargo spaces, bilges and other spaces which may contain a combustible material.

9.3.2.3 *Materials of class 7*

9.3.2.3.1 Cargo spaces used for the transport of Low Specific Activity Materials (LSA-I) and Surface Contaminated Objects (SCO-I) shall not be used for other cargoes until decontaminated by a qualified person so that the non-fixed contamination on any surface, when averaged over an area of 300 cm^2, does not exceed the following levels:

4 Bq/cm^2 (10^{-4} μCi/cm^2)   for beta and gamma emitters and the low-toxicity alpha emitters; natural uranium; natural thorium; uranium-235 or uranium-238; thorium-232; thorium-228 and thorium-230 when contained in ores, physical or chemical concentrates; radionuclides with a half-life of less than 10 days; and

0.4 Bq/cm^2 (10^{-5} μCi/cm^2)   for all other alpha emitters.

9.3.2.4 *Materials of class 8 or materials having similar properties*

9.3.2.4.1 These cargoes shall be kept as dry as reasonably practicable.

9.3.2.4.2 Prior to loading these cargoes, attention shall be paid to the cleaning of the cargo spaces into which they will be loaded, particularly to ensure that these spaces are dry.

9.3.2.4.3 Penetration of these materials into other cargo spaces, bilges, wells and between the ceiling boards shall be prevented.

9.3.2.4.4 Particular attention shall be paid to the cleaning of the cargo spaces after unloading, as residues of these cargoes may be highly corrosive to the ship's structure. Hosing down of the cargo spaces followed by careful drying shall be considered.

9.3.3 Segregation between bulk materials possessing chemical hazards and dangerous goods in packaged form

9.3.3.1 Unless otherwise required in this section or in the individual schedules, segregation between solid bulk cargoes of Group B and dangerous goods in packaged form shall be in accordance with the following table.

The Dangerous Goods List of the IMDG Code shall be consulted for additional requirements with regard to stowage and segregation of packaged dangerous goods.

Bulk cargo (classified as dangerous goods)	Class/ Division	Dangerous goods in packaged form															
		1.1 1.2 1.5	1.3	1.4	2.1	2.2 2.3	3	4.1	4.2	4.3	5.1	5.2	6.1	6.2	7	8	9
Flammable solids	4.1	4	3	2	2	2	2	X	1	X	1	2	X	3	2	1	X
Substances liable to spontaneous combustion	4.2	4	3	2	2	2	2	1	X	1	2	2	1	3	2	1	X
Substances which, in contact with water, emit flammable gases	4.3	4	4	2	1	X	2	X	1	X	2	2	X	2	2	1	X
Oxidizing substances (agents)	5.1	4	4	2	2	X	2	1	2	2	X	2	1	3	1	2	X
Toxic substances	6.1	2	2	X	X	X	X	X	1	X	1	1	X	1	X	X	X
Radioactive materials	7	2	2	2	2	2	2	2	2	2	1	2	X	3	X	2	X
Corrosive substances	8	4	2	2	1	X	1	1	1	1	2	2	X	3	2	X	X
Miscellaneous dangerous substances and articles	9	X	X	X	X	X	X	X	X	X	X	X	X	X	X	X	X
Materials hazardous only in bulk (MHB)	MHB	X	X	X	X	X	X	X	X	X	X	X	X	3	X	X	X

Numbers relate to the following segregation terms:

1 "Away from":
Effectively segregated so that incompatible materials cannot interact dangerously in the event of an accident but may be carried in the same hold or compartment or on deck provided a minimum horizontal separation of 3 metres, projected vertically, is provided.

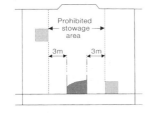

2 "Separated from":
In different holds when stowed under deck. Provided an intervening deck is resistant to fire and liquid, a vertical separation, i.e., in different compartments, may be accepted as equivalent to this segregation.

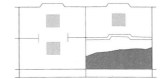

3 "Separated by a complete compartment or hold from":
Means either a vertical or a horizontal separation. If the
decks are not resistant to fire and liquid, then only
a longitudinal separation, i.e., by an intervening complete
compartment, is acceptable.

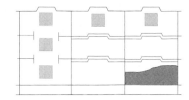

4 "Separated longitudinally by an intervening complete
compartment or hold from":
Vertical separation alone does not meet this requirement.

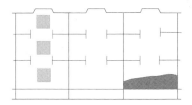

X Segregation, if any, is shown in the Dangerous Goods List of the IMDG Code or in the individual
schedules in this Code.

Legend

Reference bulk material

Packages containing incompatible goods

Deck resistant to liquid and fire

NOTE: Vertical lines represent transverse watertight bulkheads between cargo spaces.

9.3.4 Segregation between solid bulk cargoes possessing chemical hazards

Unless otherwise required in this section or in the individual schedules for cargoes of Group B,
segregation between solid bulk cargoes possessing chemical hazards shall be according to the
following table:

	Solid bulk materials									
	Class/division	4.1	4.2	4.3	5.1	6.1	7	8	9	MHB
Flammable solids	4.1	X								
Substances liable to spontaneous combustion	4.2	2	X							
Substances which, in contact with water, emit flammable gases	4.3	3	3	X						
Oxidizing substances	5.1	3	3	3	X					
Toxic substances	6.1	X	X	X	2	X				
Radioactive materials	7	2	2	2	2	2	X			
Corrosive substances	8	2	2	2	2	X	2	X		
Miscellaneous dangerous substances and articles	9	X	X	X	X	X	2	X	X	
Materials hazardous only in bulk (MHB)	MHB	X	X	X	X	X	2	X	X	X

Numbers relate to the following segregation terms:

2   "Separated from":
    In different holds when stowed under deck. Provided an
    intervening deck is resistant to fire and liquid, a vertical
    separation, i.e., in different compartments, may be
    accepted as equivalent to this segregation.

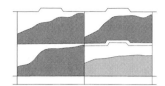

3   "Separated by a complete compartment or hold from":
    Either a vertical or a horizontal separation. If the decks
    are not resistant to fire and liquid, then only a longitudinal
    separation, i.e., by an intervening complete compartment,
    is acceptable.

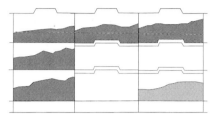

X   Segregation, if any, is shown in the individual schedules in this Code.

Legend

Reference bulk material

Incompatible bulk material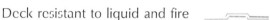

Deck resistant to liquid and fire

NOTE: Vertical lines represent transverse watertight bulkheads between cargo spaces.

Section 10

Carriage of solid wastes in bulk

10.1 Preamble

10.1.1 The transboundary movement of wastes represents a threat to human health and to the environment.

10.1.2 Wastes shall be carried in accordance with the relevant international recommendations and conventions and in particular, where it concerns transport in bulk by sea, with the provisions of this Code.

10.2 Definitions

10.2.1 *Wastes*, for the purpose of this section, means solid bulk cargoes containing or contaminated with one or more constituents which are subject to the provisions of this Code applicable to cargoes of classes 4.1, 4.2, 4.3, 5.1, 6.1, 8 or 9 for which no direct use is envisaged but which are carried for dumping, incineration or other methods of disposal.

10.2.2 *Transboundary movement of waste* means any shipment of wastes from an area under the national jurisdiction of one country to or through an area under the national jurisdiction of another country, or to or through an area not under the national jurisdiction of any country provided at least two countries are involved in the movement.

10.3 Applicability

10.3.1 The provisions of this section are applicable to the transport of wastes in bulk by ships and shall be considered in conjunction with all other provisions of this Code.

10.3.2 Solid cargoes containing or contaminated with radioactive materials shall be subject to the provisions applicable to the transport of radioactive materials and shall not be considered as wastes for the purposes of this section.

10.4 Transboundary movements under the Basel Convention*

Transboundary movement of wastes shall be permitted to commence only when:

.1 notification has been sent by the competent authority of the country of origin, or by the generator or exporter through the channel of the competent authority of the country of origin, to the country of final destination; and

.2 the competent authority of the country of origin, having received the written consent of the country of final destination stating that the wastes will be safely incinerated or treated by other methods of disposal, has given authorization for the movement.

---

* Basel Convention on the Control of Transboundary Movements of Hazardous Wastes and their Disposal (1989).

10.5 Documentation

In addition to the required documentation for the transport of solid bulk cargoes, all transboundary movements of wastes shall be accompanied by a waste movement document from the point at which a transboundary movement commences to the point of disposal. This document shall be available at all times to the competent authorities and to all persons involved in the management of waste transport operations.

10.6 Classification of wastes

10.6.1 A waste containing only one constituent which is a cargo subject to the provisions of this Code applicable to cargoes of classes 4.1, 4.2, 4.3, 5.1, 6.1, 8 or 9 shall be regarded as being that particular cargo. If the concentration of the constituent is such that the waste continues to present a hazard inherent in the constituent itself, it shall be classified as the class applicable to that constituent.

10.6.2 A waste containing two or more constituents which are cargoes subject to the provisions of this Code applicable to cargoes of classes 4.1, 4.2, 4.3, 5.1, 6.1, 8 or 9 shall be classified under the applicable class in accordance with their dangerous characteristics and properties as described in 10.6.3 and 10.6.4.

10.6.3 The classification according to dangerous characteristics and properties shall be carried out as follows:

.1 determination of the physical and chemical characteristics and physiological properties by measurement or calculation followed by classification according to the criteria applicable to the constituents; or

.2 if the determination is not practicable, the waste shall be classified according to the constituent presenting the predominant hazard.

10.6.4 In determining the predominant hazard, the following criteria shall be taken into account:

.1 if one or more constituents fall within a certain class and the waste presents a hazard inherent in these constituents, the waste shall be included in that class; or

.2 if there are constituents falling under two or more classes, the classification of the waste shall take into account the order of precedence applicable to cargoes with multiple hazards set out in the IMDG Code.

10.7 Stowage and handling of wastes

Wastes shall be stowed and handled in accordance with the provisions of sections 1 to 9 of this Code and with any additional provisions included in the individual schedules for cargoes in Group B applicable to the constituents presenting the hazards.

10.8 Segregation

Wastes shall be segregated in accordance with the provisions of 9.3.3 and 9.3.4, as appropriate.

10.9 Accident procedures

In the event that, during transport, a waste will constitute a danger for the carrying ship or the environment, the master shall immediately inform the competent authorities of the countries of origin and destination and receive advice on the action to be taken.

Section 11

Security provisions

Introductory note

The provisions of this section address the security of bulk cargoes in transport by sea. It should be borne in mind that some substances shipped as bulk cargo may, through their intrinsic nature, or when shipped in combination with other substances, be used as constituents for, or enhance the effect of, weapons used in the commission of unlawful acts. (It should also be borne in mind that ships used to carry bulk cargoes may also be used as a means to transport unauthorized weapons, incendiary devices or explosives, irrespective of the nature of the cargo carried.) National competent authorities may apply additional security provisions, which should be considered when offering or transporting bulk cargoes. The provisions of this chapter remain recommendatory except subsection 11.1.1.

11.1   General provisions for companies, ships and port facilities

11.1.1   The relevant provisions of chapter XI-2 of SOLAS 74, as amended, and of part A of the ISPS Code shall apply to companies, ships and port facilities both engaged in the handling and transport of solid bulk cargoes and to which regulation XI-2 of SOLAS 74, as amended, applies, taking into account the guidance given in part B of the ISPS Code.

11.1.2   Due regard should be given to the security-related provisions of the ILO/IMO Code of practice on security in ports and the IMDG Code, as appropriate.

11.1.3   Any shore-based company personnel, ship-based personnel and port facility personnel engaged in the handling and transport of bulk cargoes should be aware of any security requirements for such cargoes, in addition to those specified in the ISPS Code, and commensurate with their responsibilities.

11.1.4   The training of the company security officer, shore-based company personnel having specific security duties, port facility security officer and port facility personnel having specific duties, engaged in the handling and transport of bulk cargoes, should also include elements of security awareness related to the nature of those cargoes, for example where such cargoes are materials hazardous only in bulk.

11.1.5   All shipboard personnel and port facility personnel who are not mentioned in subsection 11.1.4 and are engaged in the transport of bulk cargoes should be familiar with the provisions of the relevant security plans related to those cargoes, commensurate with their responsibilities.

11.2   General provisions for shore-side personnel

11.2.1   For the purpose of this subsection, "shore-side personnel" covers individuals such as those who:

-   prepare transport documents for bulk cargoes;

-   offer bulk cargoes for transport;

-   accept bulk cargoes for transport;

-   handle bulk cargoes;

- prepare bulk cargoes' loading/stowage plans;

- load/unload bulk cargoes into/from ships; and

- enforce or survey or inspect for compliance with applicable rules and regulations; or

- are otherwise involved in the handling and transport of bulk cargoes as determined by the competent authority.

However, the provisions of subsection 11.2 do not apply to:

- the company security officer and appropriate shore-based personnel mentioned in section A/13.1 of the ISPS Code;

- the ship security officer and the shipboard personnel mentioned in sections A/13.2 and A/13.3 of the ISPS Code; and

- the port facility security officer, the appropriate port facility security personnel and the port facility personnel having specific security duties mentioned in sections A/18.1 and A/18.2 of the ISPS Code.

For the training of those officers and personnel, refer to the ISPS Code.

11.2.2   Shore-side personnel engaged in transport by sea of bulk cargoes should consider security provisions for the transport of bulk cargoes commensurate with their responsibilities.

11.2.3   Security training

11.2.3.1   The training of shore-side personnel should also include elements of security awareness, the need to control access to cargoes and ships, and general guidance on the types of bulk cargoes of security significance.

11.2.3.2   Security awareness training should address the nature of security risks, recognizing security risks, methods to address and reduce risks and actions to be taken in the event of a security breach. It should include awareness of security plans (if appropriate, refer to subsection 11.3), commensurate with the responsibilities of individuals and their part in implementing security plans.

11.2.3.3   Such training should be provided or verified upon employment in a position involving transport of bulk cargoes by sea and should be periodically supplemented with retraining.

11.2.3.4   Records of all security training undertaken should be kept by the employer and made available to the employee if requested.

11.3   Provisions for high-consequence solid bulk cargoes

11.3.1   For the purposes of this subsection, high-consequence solid bulk cargoes with high potential security implications are those which have the potential for misuse in an unlawful act and which may, as a result, produce serious consequences such as mass casualties or mass destruction, for example, class 5.1 ammonium nitrate UN 1942 and ammonium nitrate fertilizers UN 2067.

11.3.2   The provisions of this subsection do not apply to ships and to port facilities (see the ISPS Code for ship security plan and for port security plan).

11.3.3   Consignors and others engaged in the transport of solid bulk cargoes with high potential security implications should adopt, implement and comply with a security plan that addresses at least the elements specified in subsection 11.3.4.

11.3.4   The security plan should comprise at least the following elements:

.1   specific allocation of responsibilities for security to competent and qualified persons with appropriate authority to carry out their responsibilities;

.2   records of bulk cargoes with high potential security implications or types of bulk cargoes with high potential security implications transported;

.3   review of current operations and assessment of vulnerabilities, including intermodal transfer, temporary transit storage, handling and distribution, as appropriate;

.4   clear statements of measures, including training, policies (including response to higher threat conditions, new employee/employment verification, etc.), operating practices (e.g., choice/use of routes, where known, control of access to ships, bulk cargo storage and loading areas, proximity to vulnerable infrastructure, etc.), equipment and resources that are to be used to reduce security risks;

.5   effective and up-to-date procedures for reporting and dealing with security threats, breaches of security or security-related incidents;

.6   procedures for the evaluation and testing of security plans and procedures for periodic review and update of the plans;

.7   measures to ensure the security of transport information contained in the plan; and

.8   measures to ensure that the distribution of transport information is limited as far as possible.

Section 12

Stowage factor conversion tables

12.1   Cubic metres per metric tonne to cubic feet per long ton (2240 lb, 1016 kg)

Factor: 1 m^3/t = 35.87 ft^3/ton (rounded to the nearest hundredth of a ft^3/ton)

m^3/t	0.00	0.01	0.02	0.03	0.04	0.05	0.06	0.07	0.08	0.09
0.0	–	0.36	0.72	1.08	1.43	1.79	2.15	2.51	2.87	3.23
0.1	3.59	3.95	4.30	4.66	5.02	5.38	5.74	6.10	6.46	6.82
0.2	7.17	7.53	7.89	8.25	8.61	8.97	9.33	9.68	10.04	10.40
0.3	10.76	11.12	11.48	11.84	12.20	12.55	12.91	13.27	13.63	13.99
0.4	14.35	14.71	15.07	15.42	15.78	16.14	16.50	16.86	17.22	17.58
0.5	17.94	18.29	18.65	19.01	19.37	19.73	20.09	20.45	20.80	21.16
0.6	21.52	21.88	22.24	22.60	22.96	23.32	23.67	24.03	24.39	24.75
0.7	25.11	25.47	25.83	26.19	26.54	26.90	27.26	27.62	27.98	28.34
0.8	28.70	29.05	29.41	29.77	30.13	30.49	30.85	31.21	31.57	31.92
0.9	32.28	32.64	33.00	33.36	33.72	34.08	34.44	34.79	35.15	35.51
1.0	35.87	36.23	36.59	36.95	37.31	37.66	38.02	38.38	38.74	39.10
1.1	39.46	39.82	40.17	40.53	40.89	41.25	41.61	41.97	42.33	42.69
1.2	43.04	43.40	43.76	44.12	44.48	44.84	45.20	45.56	45.91	46.27
1.3	46.63	46.90	47.35	47.71	48.07	48.43	48.78	49.14	49.50	49.86
1.4	50.22	50.58	50.94	51.29	51.65	52.01	52.37	52.73	53.09	53.45
1.5	53.81	54.16	54.52	54.88	55.24	55.60	55.96	56.32	56.67	57.03
1.6	57.39	57.75	58.11	58.47	58.83	59.19	59.54	59.90	60.26	60.62

ft^3/ton

12.2 Cubic feet per long ton (ft³/ton) (2240 lb, 1016 kg) to cubic metres per metric tonne (m³/t) (2204 lb, 1000 kg)

Factor: 1 ft³/ton = 0.02788 m³/t (rounded to the nearest ten-thousandth of a m³/t)

ft³/ton	0	1	2	3	4	5	6	7	8	9
0	–	0.0279	0.0558	0.0836	0.1115	0.1394	0.1673	0.1952	0.2230	0.2509
10	0.2788	0.3067	0.3346	0.3624	0.3903	0.4182	0.4461	0.4740	0.5018	0.5297
20	0.5576	0.5855	0.6134	0.6412	0.6691	0.6970	0.7249	0.7528	0.7806	0.8085
30	0.8364	0.8643	0.8922	0.9200	0.9479	0.9758	1.0037	1.0316	1.0594	1.0873
40	1.1152	1.1431	1.1710	1.1988	1.2267	1.2546	1.2825	1.3104	1.3382	1.3661
50	1.3940	1.4219	1.4498	1.4776	1.5055	1.5334	1.5613	1.5892	1.6170	1.6449
60	1.6728	1.7007	1.7286	1.7564	1.7843	1.8122	1.8401	1.8680	1.8958	1.9237
70	1.9516	1.9795	2.0074	2.0352	2.0631	2.0910	2.1189	2.1468	2.1746	2.2025
80	2.2304	2.2583	2.2862	2.3140	2.3419	2.3698	2.3977	2.4256	2.4534	2.4818
90	2.5092	2.5371	2.5650	2.5928	2.6207	2.6486	2.6765	2.7044	2.7322	2.7601
100	2.7880	2.8159	2.8438	2.8716	2.8995	2.9274	2.9553	2.9832	3.0110	3.0389

m³/t

Section 13

References to related information and recommendations

13.1 General

This section lists the references to the IMO instruments relevant to the requirements in this Code. It should be noted that this listing is not exhaustive.

13.2 Reference list*

The references to the subsections in this Code, references to the relevant IMO instruments and subjects are in the following tables. Column 1 contains the references to the subsection numbers in this Code. Column 2 contains the references to the relevant IMO Instruments. Column 3 identifies the relevant subjects.

Reference to subsections in this Code (1)	Reference to the relevant IMO instruments (2)	Subject (3)
13.2.1	**Dangerous goods and classification**	
9.2	IMDG Code (SOLAS VII/1.1) SOLAS VII/1.2	Classification of dangerous goods
13.2.2	**Stability**	
2.1.3	SOLAS II-1/22	Stability information
2.1.3	SOLAS VI/6.1	Stability information
2.1.3	SOLAS VI/7.2.1	Stability information
2.1.3	SOLAS VI/7.4	Loading and trimming of bulk cargoes
2.1.3	SOLAS XII/8	Stability information
13.2.3	**Fire-extinguishing arrangements**	
General Group B	SOLAS II-2/10.7	Fire-extinguishing arrangements in cargo spaces
General	FSS Code chapter 9	Fixed fire detection and fire alarm systems
General	FSS Code chapter 10	Sample extraction smoke detection systems
Group B	SOLAS II-2/19	Special requirements for ships carrying dangerous goods
Groups A, B and C	MSC/Circ.1146	List of solid bulk cargoes for which a fixed gas fire-extinguishing system may be exempted

---

* A reference to a provision in the SOLAS Convention is given in the form chapter/regulation. For example, "SOLAS regulation II-1/22" means regulation 22 in chapter II-1 of the Convention.

Reference to subsections in this Code (1)	Reference to the relevant IMO instruments (2)	Subject (3)
13.2.4 Ventilation		
General Group B	International Convention on Load Lines 1966, Annex I, regulation 19	Ventilation openings
General Group B	SOLAS II-2/9.7	Ventilation systems
General Group B	SOLAS II-2/19.3.4	Ventilation for ships carrying dangerous goods
13.2.5 Personnel protection		
General Group B	IMO/WHO/ILO *Medical First Aid Guide for Use in Accidents Involving Dangerous Goods (MFAG)*	First aid measures
General Group B	SOLAS II-2/10.10 and FSS Code chapter 3	Fire-fighter's outfits
General Group B	SOLAS II-2/19.3.6.1 and FSS Code chapter 3	Protective clothing
General Group B	SOLAS II-2/19.3.6.2 and FSS Code chapter 3	Self-contained breathing apparatus
13.2.6 Gas detection		
General	SOLAS VI/3	Oxygen analysis and gas detection equipment
General	Recommendations on the safe use of pesticides in ships applicable to the fumigation of cargo holds (MSC.1/Circ.1264), section 3	Gas detection equipment for fumigation
13.2.7 Minimum information/documentation		
4.8.3	SOLAS II-2/19.4	Document of compliance for carriage of dangerous goods
4.2	SOLAS VI/2	Cargo information
4.2	SOLAS XII/10 SOLAS XII/8	Density of bulk cargoes Cargo restrictions and other information
4.2	SOLAS VI/7.2	Stability and other information on ships
4.2	SOLAS VII/7-2	Documentation for solid bulk dangerous goods
13.2.8 Insulation of machinery space boundaries		
Group B	SOLAS II-2/3.2, 3.4, 3.10	Definitions of "A", "B" and "C" class divisions
Group B	SOLAS II-2/9.2	Fire integrity of bulkheads and decks
Group B	SOLAS II-2/19.3.8	Insulation standard ("A-60")
13.2.9 Fumigation		
3.6	Recommendations on the safe use of pesticides in ships applicable to the fumigation of cargo holds (MSC.1/Circ.1264), section 3	Fumigation, application of fumigation, fumigants, safety precautions
3.6	SOLAS VI/4	Use of pesticides in ships

Reference to subsections in this Code (1)	Reference to the relevant IMO instruments (2)	Subject (3)
13.2.10 *Segregation*		
9.3	SOLAS VII/7-3	Stowage and segregation requirement
9.3.3	IMDG Code, chapter 7.2.6	Segregation between bulk cargoes possessing chemical hazards and dangerous goods in packaged form
13.2.11 *Transport of solid wastes in bulk*		
10.4	Basel Convention on the Control of Transboundary Movements of Hazardous Wastes and their Disposal (1989)	Permitted transboundary movement of wastes
10.6	IMDG Code, chapter 7.8.4	Classification of wastes
13.2.12 *Entering enclosed spaces*		
3.2.4	Resolution A.864(20), 5 December 1997	Recommendations for entering enclosed spaces aboard ships
13.2.13 *Avoidance of excessive stresses*		
2.1.2	SOLAS XII/5 and 6	Structural strength
2.1.2	SOLAS XII/11	Loading instrument

Appendix 1

Individual schedules of solid bulk cargoes

ALFALFA

Description

Material derived from dried alfalfa grass. Shipped in the form of meal, pellets, etc.

Characteristics

Angle of repose	Bulk density (kg/m³)	Stowage factor (m³/t)
Not applicable	508 to 719	1.39 to 1.97
Size	**Class**	**Group**
Fine powder	Not applicable	C

Hazard

No special hazards.

This cargo is non-combustible or has a low fire-risk.

[handwritten margin notes: A – liable to liquefy / B – Posses a chemical hazard / C – Neither A nor B / Page 17 => 1.7.12 – 1.7.14]

Stowage & segregation

No special requirements.

Hold cleanliness

No special requirements.

Weather precautions

This cargo shall be kept as dry as practicable. This cargo shall not be handled during precipitation. During handling of this cargo, all non-working hatches of the cargo spaces into which this cargo is loaded or to be loaded shall be closed.

Loading

Trim in accordance with the relevant provisions required under sections 4 and 5 of the Code.

Prior to loading of this cargo, a certificate shall be provided by a competent authority or shipper stating that the material as shipped does not meet the requirements for seed cake. Shipments which do meet the oil and moisture criteria for SEED CAKE shall comply with the requirements for SEED CAKE (a) UN 1386, SEED CAKE (b) UN 1386 or SEED CAKE UN 2217.

Precautions

No special requirements.

Ventilation

No special requirements.

Carriage

No special requirements.

Discharge

No special requirements.

Clean-up

No special requirements.

ALUMINA

Description

Alumina is a fine, white odourless powder with little or no moisture. Insoluble in organic liquids. Moisture content: 0% to 5%. If wet, alumina is unpumpable. This cargo is insoluble in water.

Characteristics

Angle of repose	Bulk density (kg/m^3)	Stowage factor (m^3/t)
Not applicable	781 to 1087	0.92 to 1.28
Size	**Class**	**Group**
Fine powder	Not applicable	C

Hazard

Alumina dust is very abrasive and penetrating. Irritating to eyes and mucous membranes.

This cargo is non-combustible or has a low fire-risk.

Stowage & segregation

No special requirements.

Hold cleanliness

No special requirements.

Weather precautions

This cargo shall be kept as dry as practicable. This cargo shall not be handled during precipitation. During handling of this cargo, all non-working hatches of the cargo spaces into which this cargo is loaded or to be loaded shall be closed.

Loading

Trim in accordance with the relevant provisions required under sections 4 and 5 of the Code.

Precautions

Bilge wells shall be clean, dry and covered as appropriate, to prevent ingress of the cargo. Appropriate precautions shall be taken to protect machinery and accommodation spaces from the dust of the cargo. Bilge wells of the cargo spaces shall be protected from ingress of the cargo. Due consideration shall be paid to protect equipment from the dust of the cargo. Persons who may be exposed to the dust of the cargo shall wear goggles or other equivalent dust eye-protection and dust filter masks. Those persons shall wear protective clothing, as necessary.

Ventilation

No special requirements.

Carriage

No special requirements.

Discharge

No special requirements.

Clean-up

The water used for the cleaning of the cargo spaces, after discharge of this cargo, shall not be pumped by the fixed bilge pumps. A portable pump shall be used, as necessary, to clear the cargo spaces of the water.

ALUMINA, CALCINED

Description

Light to dark grey in colour. No moisture content. This cargo is insoluble in water.

Characteristics

Angle of repose	Bulk density (kg/m³)	Stowage factor (m³/t)
Not applicable	1639	0.61

Size	Class	Group
Small particles and lumps	Not applicable	C

Hazard

No special hazards.

This cargo is non-combustible or has a low fire-risk.

Stowage & segregation

No special requirements.

Hold cleanliness

No special requirements.

Weather precautions

This cargo shall be kept as dry as practicable. This cargo shall not be handled during precipitation. During handling of this cargo, all non-working hatches of the cargo spaces into which this cargo is loaded or to be loaded shall be closed.

Loading

Trim in accordance with the relevant provisions required under sections 4 and 5 of the Code.

Precautions

Appropriate precautions shall be taken to protect machinery and accommodation spaces from the dust of the cargo. Bilge wells of the cargo spaces shall be protected from ingress of the cargo. Due consideration shall be paid to protect equipment from the dust of the cargo. Persons who may be exposed to the dust of the cargo shall wear protective clothing, goggles or other equivalent dust eye-protection and dust filter masks, as necessary.

Ventilation

No special requirements.

Carriage

No special requirements.

Discharge

No special requirements.

Clean-up

The water used for the cleaning of the cargo spaces, after discharge of this cargo, shall not be pumped by the fixed bilge pumps. A portable pump shall be used, as necessary, to clear the cargo spaces of the water.

ALUMINA SILICA

Description

White, consists of alumina and silica crystals. Low moisture content (1% to 5%).

Lumps 60%.

Coarse grained powder – 40%. This cargo is insoluble in water.

Characteristics

Angle of repose	Bulk density (kg/m³)	Stowage factor (m³/t)
Not applicable	1429	0.70
Size	**Class**	**Group**
Not applicable	Not applicable	C

Hazard

No special hazards.

This cargo is non-combustible or has a low fire-risk.

Stowage & segregation

No special requirements.

Hold cleanliness

No special requirements.

Weather precautions

This cargo shall be kept as dry as practicable. This cargo shall not be handled during precipitation. During handling of this cargo, all non-working hatches of the cargo spaces into which this cargo is loaded or to be loaded shall be closed.

Loading

Trim in accordance with the relevant provisions required under sections 4 and 5 of the Code.

Precautions

Appropriate precautions shall be taken to protect machinery and accommodation spaces from the dust of the cargo. Bilge wells of the cargo spaces shall be protected from ingress of the cargo. Due consideration shall be paid to protect equipment from the dust of the cargo. Persons who may be exposed to the dust of the cargo shall wear protective clothing, goggles or other equivalent dust eye-protection and dust filter masks, as necessary.

Ventilation

No special requirements.

Carriage

No special requirements.

Discharge

No special requirements.

Clean-up

The water used for the cleaning of the cargo spaces, after discharge of this cargo, shall not be pumped by the fixed bilge pumps. A portable pump shall be used, as necessary, to clear the cargo spaces of the water.

ALUMINA SILICA, pellets

Description
White to off-white. No moisture content.

Characteristics

Angle of repose	Bulk density (kg/m^3)	Stowage factor (m^3/t)
Not applicable	1190 to 1282	0.78 to 0.84
Size	**Class**	**Group**
Length: 6.4 mm to 25.4 mm Diameter: 6.4 mm	Not applicable	C

Hazard
No special hazards.

This cargo is non-combustible or has a low fire-risk.

Stowage & segregation
No special requirements.

Hold cleanliness
No special requirements.

Weather precautions
This cargo shall be kept as dry as practicable. This cargo shall not be handled during precipitation. During handling of this cargo, all non-working hatches of the cargo spaces into which this cargo is loaded or to be loaded shall be closed.

Loading
Trim in accordance with the relevant provisions required under sections 4 and 5 of the Code.

Precautions
Appropriate precautions shall be taken to protect machinery and accommodation spaces from the dust of the cargo. Bilge wells of the cargo spaces shall be protected from ingress of the cargo. Due consideration shall be paid to protect equipment from the dust of the cargo. Persons who may be exposed to the dust of the cargo shall wear protective clothing, goggles or other equivalent dust eye-protection and dust filter masks, as necessary.

Ventilation
No special requirements.

Carriage
No special requirements.

Discharge
No special requirements.

Clean-up
No special requirements.

ALUMINIUM FERROSILICON POWDER UN 1395

Description
Fine powder or briquettes.

Characteristics

Angle of repose	Bulk density (kg/m^3)		Stowage factor (m^3/t)
Not applicable	–		–
Size	**Class**	**Subsidiary risk**	**Group**
Not applicable	4.3	6.1	B

Hazard
In contact with water may evolve hydrogen, a flammable gas which may form an explosive mixture in air. Impurities may, under similar conditions, produce phosphine and arsine, which are highly toxic gases.

This cargo is non-combustible or has a low fire-risk.

Stowage & segregation
"Separated from" foodstuffs and all class 8 liquids.

Hold cleanliness
Clean and dry as relevant to the hazards of the cargo.

Weather precautions
This cargo shall be kept as dry as practicable. This cargo shall not be handled during precipitation. During handling of this cargo, all non-working hatches of the cargo spaces into which this cargo is loaded or to be loaded shall be closed.

Loading
Trim in accordance with the relevant provisions required under sections 4 and 5 of the Code.

Precautions
Prior to loading this cargo, a certificate shall be provided by the manufacturer or shipper stating that the material was stored under cover, but exposed to the weather in the particle size to be shipped, for not less than 3 days prior to shipment. The bulkheads between the cargo spaces and the engine-room shall be gastight and shall be inspected and approved by the competent authority. During handling of this cargo, "NO SMOKING" signs shall be posted on decks and in areas adjacent to cargo spaces and no naked lights shall be permitted in these areas. At least two sets of self-contained breathing apparatus, in addition to those required by SOLAS regulation II-2/10.10, shall be provided on board.

Ventilation
Continuous mechanical ventilation shall be conducted during the voyage for the cargo spaces carrying this cargo. If maintaining ventilation endangers the ship or the cargo, it may be interrupted unless there is a risk of explosion or other danger due to interruption of the ventilation. In any case, mechanical ventilation shall be maintained for a reasonable period prior to discharge.

ALUMINIUM FERROSILICON POWDER UN 1395 *(concluded)*

Carriage

For quantitative measurements of hydrogen, phosphine and arsine and silane, suitable detectors for each gas or combination of gases shall be on board while this cargo is carried. The detectors shall be of certified safe type for use in explosive atmosphere. The concentrations of these gases in the cargo spaces carrying this cargo shall be measured regularly, during the voyage, and the results of the measurements shall be recorded and kept on board.

Discharge

No special requirements.

Clean-up

After discharge of this cargo, the cargo spaces shall be swept clean twice. Water shall not be used for cleaning of the cargo space which has contained this cargo, because of danger of gas.

Emergency procedures

Special emergency equipment to be carried   Self-contained breathing apparatus.
Emergency procedures   Wear self-contained breathing apparatus.   **Emergency action in the event of fire**   Batten down and use CO_2 if available. **Do not use water.**   **Medical First Aid**   Refer to the *Medical First Aid Guide (MFAG)*, as amended.

ALUMINIUM NITRATE UN 1438

Description
Colourless or white crystals. Soluble in water.

Characteristics

Angle of repose	Bulk density (kg/m^3)	Stowage factor (m^3/t)
Not applicable	–	–
Size	**Class**	**Group**
Not applicable	5.1	B

Hazard
If involved in a fire will greatly intensify the burning of combustible materials and yield toxic nitrous fumes. Although non-combustible, mixtures with combustible material are easily ignited and may burn fiercely.

Stowage & segregation
"Separated from" foodstuffs.

Hold cleanliness
Clean and dry as relevant to the hazards of the cargo.

Weather precautions
This cargo shall be kept as dry as practicable. This cargo shall not be handled during precipitation. During handling of this cargo, all non-working hatches of the cargo spaces into which this cargo is loaded or to be loaded shall be closed.

Loading
Trim in accordance with the relevant provisions required under sections 4 and 5 of the Code.

Precautions
Due regard shall be paid to prevent contact of the cargo and combustible materials.

Ventilation
No special requirements.

Carriage
No special requirements.

Discharge
No special requirements.

Clean-up
No special requirements.

ALUMINIUM NITRATE UN 1438 *(concluded)*

Emergency procedures

Special emergency equipment to be carried

Protective clothing (gloves, overalls, headgear).
Self-contained breathing apparatus.
Spray nozzles.

Emergency procedures

Wear protective clothing and self-contained breathing apparatus.

Emergency action in the event of fire

Use copious quantities of water, which is best applied in the form of a spray to avoid disturbing the surface of the material. The material may fuse or melt; in which condition application of water may result in extensive scattering of the molten materials. Exclusion of air or the use of CO_2 will not control the fire. Due consideration should be given to the effect on the stability of the ship due to accumulated water.

Medical First Aid

Refer to the *Medical First Aid Guide (MFAG)*, as amended.

ALUMINIUM SILICON POWDER, UNCOATED UN 1398

Description
Powder

Characteristics

Angle of repose	Bulk density (kg/m³)	Stowage factor (m³/t)
Not applicable	–	–
Size	**Class**	**Group**
Not applicable	4.3	B

Hazard
In contact with water may evolve hydrogen, a flammable gas which may form explosive mixtures with air. Impurities may, under similar circumstances, produce phosphine and arsine, which are highly toxic gases. May also evolve silanes, which are toxic and may ignite spontaneously.

This cargo is non-combustible or has a low fire-risk.

Stowage & segregation
"Separated from" foodstuffs and all class 8 liquids.

Hold cleanliness
Clean and dry as relevant to the hazards of the cargo.

Weather precautions
This cargo shall be kept as dry as practicable before loading, during loading and during voyage. This cargo shall not be loaded during precipitation. During loading of this cargo, all non-working hatches of the cargo spaces to which this cargo is loaded or to be loaded shall be closed.

Loading
Trim in accordance with the relevant provisions required under sections 4 and 5 of the Code.

Precautions
Prior to loading this cargo, a certificate shall be provided by the manufacturer or shipper stating that the material was stored under cover, but exposed to the weather in the particle size to be shipped, for not less than 3 days prior to shipment. The bulkheads between the cargo spaces and the engine-room shall be gastight and shall be inspected and approved by the competent authority. During handling of this cargo, "NO SMOKING" signs shall be posted on decks and in areas adjacent to cargo spaces and no naked lights shall be permitted in these areas. This cargo shall be loaded in cargo spaces fitted with mechanical ventilation having at least two separate fans. The total ventilation shall be at least six air changes per hour, based on the empty space. At least two sets of self-contained breathing apparatus, in addition to those required by SOLAS regulation II-2/10.10, shall be provided on board.

Ventilation
Continuous mechanical ventilation shall be conducted during the voyage for the cargo spaces carrying this cargo. If maintaining ventilation endangers the ship or the cargo, it may be interrupted unless there is a risk of explosion or other danger due to interruption of the ventilation. In any case, mechanical ventilation shall be maintained for a reasonable period prior to discharge. Ventilation shall be arranged such that any escaping gases are minimized from reaching living quarters on or under the deck.

ALUMINIUM SILICON POWDER, UNCOATED UN 1398 *(concluded)*

Carriage

For quantitative measurements of hydrogen, phosphine, arsine, suitable detectors for each gas or combination of gases shall be on board while this cargo is carried. The detectors shall be of certified safe type for use in explosive atmosphere. The concentrations of these gases in the cargo spaces carrying this cargo shall be measured regularly, during the voyage, and the results of the measurements shall be recorded and kept on board.

Discharge

No special requirements.

Clean-up

After discharge of this cargo, the cargo spaces shall be swept clean twice.

Water shall not be used for cleaning of the cargo space which has contained this cargo, because of danger of gas.

Emergency procedures

Special emergency equipment to be carried
Self-contained breathing apparatus.
Emergency procedures   Wear self-contained breathing apparatus.   **Emergency action in the event of fire**   Batten down and use CO_2 if available. **Do not use water.**   **Medical First Aid**   Refer to the *Medical First Aid Guide (MFAG)*, as amended.

ALUMINIUM SMELTING BY-PRODUCTS or
ALUMINIUM REMELTING BY-PRODUCTS UN 3170

Description

Aluminium smelting by-products are wastes from the aluminium manufacturing process. Grey or black powder or lumps with some metallic inclusions. The term encompasses various different waste materials, which include but are not limited to:

ALUMINIUM DROSS   **SPENT CATHODES**
ALUMINIUM SALT SLAGS   **SPENT POTLINER**
ALUMINIUM SKIMMINGS

Characteristics

Angle of repose	Bulk density (kg/m^3)	Stowage factor (m^3/t)
Not applicable	1220	0.82
Size	**Class**	**Group**
Not applicable	4.3	B

Hazard

Contact with water may cause heating with possible evolution of flammable and toxic gases such as hydrogen, ammonia and acetylene.

This cargo is non-combustible or has a low fire-risk.

Fire is unlikely but may follow an explosion of flammable gas and will be difficult to extinguish. In port, flooding may be considered, but due consideration should be given to stability.

Stowage & segregation

"Separated from" foodstuffs and all class 8 liquids.

Hold cleanliness

Clean and dry as relevant to the hazards of the cargo.

Weather precautions

This cargo shall be kept as dry as practicable. This cargo shall not be handled during precipitation. During handling of this cargo, all non-working hatches of the cargo spaces into which this cargo is loaded or to be loaded shall be closed.

Loading

Trim in accordance with the relevant provisions required under sections 4 and 5 of the Code.

Precautions

Prior to loading this cargo, a certificate shall be provided by the manufacturer or shipper stating that, after manufacture, the material was stored under cover, but exposed to the weather in the particle size to be shipped, for not less than 3 days prior to shipment. Whilst the ship is alongside and the hatches of the cargo spaces containing this cargo are closed, the mechanical ventilation shall be operated continuously as weather permits. During handling of this cargo, "NO SMOKING" signs shall be posted on decks and in areas adjacent to cargo spaces and no naked lights shall be permitted in these areas. At least two self-contained breathing apparatus, in addition to those required by SOLAS regulation II-2/10.10, shall be provided on board. Bulkheads between the cargo spaces and the engine-room shall be gastight. Inadvertent pumping through machinery spaces shall be avoided.

ALUMINIUM SMELTING BY-PRODUCTS or
ALUMINIUM REMELTING BY-PRODUCTS UN 3170 *(concluded)*

Ventilation

Continuous mechanical ventilation shall be conducted during the voyage for the cargo spaces carrying this cargo. If maintaining ventilation endangers the ship or the cargo, it may be interrupted unless there is a risk of explosion or other danger due to interruption of the ventilation. In any case, mechanical ventilation shall be maintained for a reasonable period prior to discharge. Ventilation shall be arranged such that any escaping gases are minimized from reaching living quarters on or under the deck.

Carriage

For quantitative measurements of hydrogen, ammonia and acetylene, suitable detectors for each gas or combination of gases shall be on board while this cargo is carried. The detectors shall be of certified safe type for use in explosive atmosphere. The concentrations of these gases in the cargo spaces carrying this cargo shall be measured regularly, during voyage, and the results of the measurements shall be recorded and kept on board.

Discharge

No special requirements.

Clean-up

Water shall not be used for cleaning of the cargo space which has contained this cargo, because of danger of gas.

Emergency procedures

Special emergency equipment to be carried
Nil
Emergency procedures Nil **Emergency action in the event of fire** Batten down and use CO_2 if available. **Do not use water.** If this proves ineffective, endeavour to stop fire from spreading and head for the nearest suitable port. **Medical First Aid** Refer to the *Medical First Aid Guide (MFAG)*, as amended.

AMMONIUM NITRATE UN 1942
with not more than 0.2% total combustible material, including any organic substance, calculated as carbon to the exclusion of any other added substance

Description

White crystals, prills or granules. Wholly or partly soluble in water. Supporter of combustion. Hygroscopic.

Characteristics

Angle of repose	Bulk density (kg/m³)	Stowage factor (m³/t)
27° to 42°	1000	1.00
Size	**Class**	**Group**
1 to 4 mm	5.1	B

Hazard

A major fire aboard a ship carrying these materials may involve a risk of explosion in the event of contamination (e.g., by fuel oil) or strong confinement. An adjacent detonation may also involve a risk of explosion. If heated strongly, this cargo decomposes, giving off toxic gases and gases which support combustion.

Ammonium nitrate dust might be irritating to skin and mucous membranes.

This cargo is hygroscopic and will cake if wet.

Stowage & segregation

There should be no sources of heat or ignition in the cargo space.

"Separated by a complete compartment or hold from" combustible materials (particularly liquids), chlorates, chlorides, chlorites, hypochlorites, nitrites, permanganates and fibrous materials (e.g., cotton, jute, sisal, etc.).

"Separated from" all other goods.

If the bulkhead between the cargo space and the engine-room is not insulated to class A-60 standard, this cargo shall be stowed "away from" the bulkhead.

Hold cleanliness

Clean and dry as relevant to the hazards of the cargo.

Weather precautions

This cargo shall be kept as dry as practicable. This cargo shall not be handled during precipitation. During handling of this cargo, all non-working hatches of the cargo spaces into which this cargo is loaded or to be loaded shall be closed.

Loading

Trim in accordance with the relevant provisions required under sections 4 and 5 of the Code.

Prior to loading, the following provisions shall be complied with:

- This cargo shall not be accepted for loading when the temperature of the cargo is above 40°C.

- Prior to loading, the shipper shall provide the master with a certificate signed by the shipper stating that all the relevant conditions of the cargo required by this Code, including this individual schedule, have been met.

AMMONIUM NITRATE UN 1942
with not more than 0.2% total combustible material, including any organic substance, calculated as carbon to the exclusion of any other added substance *(continued)*

- The fuel tanks situated under the cargo spaces to be used for the transport of this cargo shall be pressure tested to ensure that there is no leakage of manholes and piping systems leading to the tanks.

- All electrical equipment, other than those of approved intrinsically safe type, in the cargo spaces to be used for this cargo shall be electrically disconnected from the power source, by appropriate means other than a fuse, at a point external to the space. This situation shall be maintained while the cargo is on board.

- Due consideration shall be paid to the possible need to open hatches in case of fire to provide maximum ventilation and to apply water in an emergency, and the consequent risk to the stability of the ship through fluidization of the cargo.

During loading, the following provisions shall be complied with:

- Smoking shall not be allowed on deck and in the cargo spaces and "NO SMOKING" signs shall be displayed while this cargo is on board.

- Bunkering of fuel oil shall not be allowed. Pumping of fuel oil in spaces adjacent to the cargo spaces for this cargo, other than the engine-room, shall not be allowed.

- As far as reasonably practicable, combustible securing and protecting materials shall not be used. When wooden dunnage is necessary, only a minimum shall be used.

Precautions

This cargo shall only be accepted for loading when the competent authority is satisfied in regard to the resistance to detonation of this material based on the test.* Prior to loading, the shipper shall provide the master with a certificate stating that the resistance to detonation of this material is in compliance with this requirement. The master and officers shall note that a fixed gas fire-extinguishing system is ineffective on the fire involving this cargo and that applying water may be necessary. Pressure on the fire mains shall be maintained for fire-fighting and fire hoses shall be laid out or be in position and ready for immediate use during loading and discharging of this cargo. No welding, burning, cutting or other operations involving the use of fire, open flame, spark- or arc-producing equipment shall be carried out in the vicinity of the cargo spaces containing this cargo except in an emergency. Precautions shall be taken to avoid the penetration of this cargo into other cargo spaces, bilges and other enclosed spaces. Smoking shall not be allowed on deck and in the cargo spaces and "NO SMOKING" signs shall be displayed on deck whenever this cargo is on board. The hatches of the cargo spaces, whenever this material is on board, shall be kept free to be capable of being opened in case of an emergency. When the bulkhead between the cargo space and the engine-room is not insulated to class A-60 standard, this cargo shall not be accepted for loading unless the competent authority approves that the arrangement is equivalent.

Appropriate precautions shall be taken to protect machinery and accommodation spaces from the dust of the cargo. Bilge wells of the cargo spaces shall be protected from ingress of the cargo. Due consideration shall be paid to protect equipment from the dust of the cargo. Persons who may be exposed to the dust of the cargo shall wear goggles or other equivalent dust eye-protection and dust filter masks. Those persons shall wear protective clothing, as necessary.

Ventilation

The cargo spaces carrying this cargo shall not be ventilated during voyage.

---

* Reference is made to section 5 of appendix 2 to this Code.

AMMONIUM NITRATE UN 1942
with not more than 0.2% total combustible material, including any organic substance, calculated as carbon to the exclusion of any other added substance *(concluded)*

Carriage

Hatches of the cargo spaces carrying this cargo shall be weathertight to prevent the ingress of water.

Discharge

If this cargo has hardened, it shall be trimmed to avoid the formation of overhangs, as necessary. Bunkering or pumping of fuel oil shall not be allowed.

Clean-up

After discharge of this cargo, the bilge wells and the scuppers of the cargo spaces shall be checked and any blockage in the bilge wells and the scuppers shall be removed.

Emergency procedures

Special emergency equipment to be carried

Protective clothing (boots, gloves, coveralls, and headgear).
Self-contained breathing apparatus.

Emergency procedures

Wear protective clothing and self-contained breathing apparatus.

Emergency action in the event of fire

Fire in a cargo space containing this material: Open hatches to provide maximum ventilation. Ship's fixed gas fire extinguishing will be inadequate. Use copious quantities of water. Flooding of the cargo space may be considered but due consideration should be given to stability.

Fire in an adjacent cargo space: Open hatches to provide maximum ventilation. Heat transferred from fire in an adjacent space can cause the material to decompose with consequent evolution of toxic fumes. Dividing bulkheads should be cooled.

Medical First Aid

Refer to the *Medical First Aid Guide (MFAG)*, as amended.

AMMONIUM NITRATE BASED FERTILIZER UN 2067

Description

Crystals, granules or prills. Wholly or partly soluble in water. Hygroscopic.

Ammonium nitrate-based fertilizers classified as UN 2067 are uniform mixtures containing ammonium nitrate as the main ingredient within the following composition limits:

.1 not less than 90% ammonium nitrate with not more than 0.2% total combustible/organic material calculated as carbon and with added matter, if any, which is inorganic and inert towards ammonium nitrate; or

.2 less than 90% but more than 70% ammonium nitrate with other inorganic materials or more than 80% but less than 90% ammonium nitrate mixed with calcium carbonate and/or dolomite and not more than 0.4% total combustible/organic material calculated as carbon; or

.3 ammonium nitrate-based fertilizers containing mixtures of ammonium nitrate and ammonium sulphate with more than 45% but less than 70% ammonium nitrate and not more than 0.4% total combustible organic material calculated as carbon such that the sum of the percentage compositions of ammonium nitrate and ammonium sulphate exceeds 70%.

Notes:

1 All nitrate ions for which there is present in the mixture a molecular equivalent of ammonium ions should be calculated as ammonium nitrate.

2 The transport of ammonium nitrate materials which are liable to self-heating sufficient to initiate decomposition is prohibited.

3 This entry may only be used for substances that do not exhibit explosive properties of class 1 when tested in accordance to Test Series 1 and 2 of class 1 (see UN *Manual of Tests and Criteria*, part I).

Characteristics

Angle of repose	Bulk density (kg/m^3)	Stowage factor (m^3/t)
27° to 42°	900 to 1200	0.83 to 1.11
Size	**Class**	**Group**
1 to 5 mm	5.1	B

Hazard

Supports combustion. A major fire aboard a ship carrying these substances may involve a risk of explosion in the event of contamination (e.g., by fuel oil) or strong confinement. An adjacent detonation may involve a risk of explosion.

If heated strongly decomposes, risk of toxic fumes and gases which support combustion, in the cargo space and on deck.

Fertilizer dust might be irritating to skin and mucous membranes.

This cargo is hygroscopic and will cake if wet.

Stowage & segregation

"Separated by a complete compartment or hold from" combustible materials (particularly liquid), bromates, chlorates, chlorites, hypochlorites, nitrites, perchlorates, permanganates, powdered metals and vegetable fibres (e.g., cotton, jute, sisal, etc.).

"Separated from" all other goods.

"Separated from" sources of heat or ignition (*see also* **Loading**);

Not to be stowed immediately adjacent to any tank or double bottom containing fuel oil heated to more than 50°C.

If the bulkhead between the cargo space and the engine-room is not insulated to class A-60 standard, this cargo shall be stowed "away from" the bulkhead.

AMMONIUM NITRATE BASED FERTILIZER UN 2067 *(continued)*

Hold cleanliness
Clean and dry as relevant to the hazards of the cargo.

Weather precautions
This cargo shall be kept as dry as practicable. This cargo shall not be handled during precipitation. During handling of this cargo, all non-working hatches of the cargo spaces into which this cargo is loaded or to be loaded shall be closed.

Loading
Trim in accordance with the relevant provisions required under sections 4 and 5 of the Code.

Prior to loading, the following provisions shall be complied with:

- This cargo shall not be accepted for loading when the temperature of the cargo is above 40°C.

- Prior to loading, the shipper shall provide the master with a certificate signed by the shipper stating that all the relevant conditions of the cargo required by this Code, including this individual schedule, have been met.

- The fuel tanks situated under the cargo spaces to be used for the transport of this cargo shall be pressure tested to ensure that there is no leakage of manholes and piping systems leading to the tanks.

- All electrical equipment, other than those of approved intrinsically safe type, in the cargo spaces to be used for this cargo shall be electrically disconnected from the power source, by appropriate means other than a fuse, at a point external to the space. This situation shall be maintained while the cargo is on board.

- Due consideration shall be paid to the possible need to open hatches in case of fire to provide maximum ventilation and to apply water in an emergency and the consequent risk to the stability of the ship through fluidization of the cargo.

During loading, the following provisions shall be complied with:

- Bunkering of fuel oil shall not be allowed. Pumping of fuel oil in spaces adjacent to the cargo spaces for this cargo, other than the engine-room, shall not be allowed.

- As far as reasonably practicable, combustible securing and protecting materials shall not be used. When wooden dunnage is necessary, only a minimum shall be used.

Precautions
This cargo shall only be accepted for loading when the competent authority is satisfied in regard to the resistance to detonation of this material based on the test.* Prior to loading, the shipper shall provide the master with a certificate stating that the resistance to detonation of this material is in compliance with this requirement. Pressure on the fire mains shall be maintained for fire-fighting and fire hoses shall be laid out or be in position and ready for immediate use during loading and discharging of this cargo. No welding, burning, cutting or other operations involving the use of fire, open flame, spark- or arc-producing equipment shall be carried out in the vicinity of the cargo spaces containing this cargo except in an emergency. Smoking shall not be allowed on deck and in the cargo spaces and "NO SMOKING" signs shall be displayed on deck whenever this cargo is on board. Precautions shall be taken to avoid the penetration of this cargo into other cargo spaces, bilges and other enclosed spaces. The hatches of the cargo spaces, whenever this material is on board, shall be kept free to be capable of being opened in case of an emergency.

---

* Reference is made to section 5 of appendix 2 to this Code.

AMMONIUM NITRATE BASED FERTILIZER UN 2067 *(concluded)*

Appropriate precautions shall be taken to protect machinery and accommodation spaces from the dust of the cargo. Bilge wells of the cargo spaces shall be protected from ingress of the cargo. Due consideration shall be paid to protect equipment from the dust of the cargo. Persons who may be exposed to the dust of the cargo shall wear goggles or other equivalent dust eye-protection and dust filter masks. Those persons shall wear protective clothing, as necessary.

Ventilation
The cargo spaces carrying this cargo shall not be ventilated during voyage.

Carriage
Hatches of the cargo spaces carrying this cargo shall be weathertight to prevent the ingress of water. The temperature of this cargo shall be monitored and recorded daily during the voyage to detect decomposition resulting in spontaneous heating and oxygen depletion.

Discharge
Bunkering or pumping of fuel oil shall not be allowed. If this cargo has hardened, it shall be trimmed to avoid the formation of overhangs, as necessary.

Clean-up
After discharge of this cargo, the bilge wells and the scuppers of the cargo spaces shall be checked and any blockage in the bilge wells and the scuppers shall be removed.

Emergency procedures

Special emergency equipment to be carried

Protective clothing (boots, gloves, coveralls, and headgear).

Self-contained breathing apparatus.

Emergency procedures

Wear protective clothing and self-contained breathing apparatus.

Emergency action in the event of fire

Fire in a cargo space containing this material: Open hatches to provide maximum ventilation. Ship's fixed fire-fighting installation will be inadequate. Use copious quantities of water. Flooding of the cargo space may be considered but due consideration should be given to stability.

Fire in an adjacent cargo space: Open hatches to provide maximum ventilation. Heat transferred from fire in an adjacent space can cause the material to decompose with consequent evolution of toxic fumes. Dividing bulkheads should be cooled.

Medical First Aid

Refer to the *Medical First Aid Guide (MFAG)*, as amended.

AMMONIUM NITRATE BASED FERTILIZER UN 2071

Description

Usually granules. Wholly or partly soluble in water. Hygroscopic.

Ammonium nitrate based fertilizers classified as UN 2071 are uniform ammonium nitrate based fertilizer mixtures of nitrogen, phosphate or potash, containing not more than 70% ammonium nitrate and not more than 0.4% total combustible organic material calculated as carbon or with not more than 45% ammonium nitrate and unrestricted combustible material. Fertilizers within these composition limits are not subject to the provisions of this schedule when shown by a trough test (see UN *Manual of Tests and Criteria*, part III, subsection 38.2) that they are not liable to self-sustaining decomposition.

Notes:

1   All nitrate ions for which there is present in the mixture a molecular equivalent of ammonium ions should be calculated as ammonium nitrate.

2   The transport of ammonium nitrate materials which are liable to self-heating sufficient to initiate a decomposition is prohibited.

3   The NPK proportions for a fertilizer should not be used as a guide to its ability to undergo self-sustaining decomposition as this depends on the chemical species present (refer to UN *Manual of Tests and Criteria*, part III, subsection 38.2).

Characteristics

Angle of repose	Bulk density (kg/m^3)	Stowage factor (m^3/t)
27° to 42°	900 to 1200	0.83 to 1.11
Size	**Class**	**Group**
1 to 5 mm	9	B

Hazard

These mixtures may be subject to self-sustaining decomposition if heated. The temperature in such a reaction can reach 500°C. Decomposition, once initiated, may spread throughout the remainder, producing gases which are toxic. None of these mixtures is subject to the explosion hazard.

Fertilizer dust might be irritating to skin and mucous membranes.

This cargo is hygroscopic and will cake if wet.

Stowage & segregation

"Separated by a complete compartment or hold from" combustible materials (particularly liquid), bromates, chlorates, chlorites, hypochlorites, nitrites, perchlorates, permanganates, powdered metals and vegetable fibres (e.g., cotton, jute, sisal, etc.).

"Separated from" all other goods.

"Separated from" sources of heat or ignition (*see also* **Loading**).

Not to be stowed immediately adjacent to any tank or double bottom containing fuel oil heated to more than 50°C.

If the bulkhead between the cargo space and the engine-room is not insulated to class A-60 standard, "away from" the bulkhead.

Hold cleanliness

Clean and dry as relevant to the hazards of the cargo.

AMMONIUM NITRATE BASED FERTILIZER UN 2071 *(continued)*

Weather precautions

This cargo shall be kept as dry as practicable. This cargo shall not be handled during precipitation. During handling of this cargo, all non-working hatches of the cargo spaces into which this cargo is loaded or to be loaded shall be closed.

Loading

Trim in accordance with the relevant provisions required under sections 4 and 5 of the Code.

Prior to loading, the following provisions shall be complied with:

- All electrical equipment, other than that of approved intrinsically safe type, in the cargo spaces to be used for this cargo shall be electrically disconnected from the power source, by appropriate means other than fuse, at a point external to the space. This situation shall be maintained while the cargo is on board.

- Due consideration shall be paid to the possible need to open hatches in case of fire to provide maximum ventilation and to apply water in an emergency and the consequent risk to the stability of the ship through fluidization of the cargo.

- In addition, if decomposition occurs, the residue left after decomposition may have only half the mass of the original cargo. Due consideration shall be paid to the effect of the loss of mass on the stability of the ship.

During loading, the following provisions shall be complied with:

- Bunkering of fuel oil shall not be allowed. Pumping of fuel oil in spaces adjacent to the cargo spaces for this cargo, other than the engine-room, shall not be allowed.

Precautions

This cargo shall only be accepted for loading when, as a result of testing in the trough test, its liability to self-sustaining decomposition shows decomposition rate not greater than 0.25 m/h. Pressure on the fire mains shall be maintained for fire-fighting and fire hoses shall be laid out or be in position and ready for immediate use during loading and discharging of this cargo. No welding, burning, cutting or other operations involving the use of fire, open flame, spark- or arc-producing equipment shall be carried out in the vicinity of the cargo spaces containing this cargo except in an emergency. Smoking shall not be allowed on deck and in the cargo spaces and "NO SMOKING" signs shall be displayed on deck whenever this cargo is on board. Precautions shall be taken to avoid the penetration of this cargo into other cargo spaces, bilges and other enclosed spaces. The hatches of the cargo spaces, whenever this material is on board, shall be kept free to be capable of being opened in case of an emergency.

Appropriate precautions shall be taken to protect machinery and accommodation spaces from the dust of the cargo. Bilge wells of the cargo spaces shall be protected from ingress of the cargo. Due consideration shall be paid to protect equipment from the dust of the cargo. Persons who may be exposed to the dust of the cargo shall wear goggles or other equivalent dust eye-protection and dust filter masks. Those persons shall wear protective clothing, as necessary.

Ventilation

The cargo spaces carrying this cargo shall not be ventilated during voyage.

Carriage

Hatches of the cargo spaces carrying this cargo shall be weathertight to prevent the ingress of water.

The temperature of this cargo shall be monitored and recorded daily during the voyage to detect decomposition resulting in spontaneous heating and oxygen depletion.

AMMONIUM NITRATE BASED FERTILIZER UN 2071 *(concluded)*

Discharge

Bunkering or pumping of fuel oil shall not be allowed. If this cargo has hardened, it shall be trimmed to avoid the formation of overhangs, as necessary.

Clean-up

After discharge of this cargo, the bilge wells and the scuppers of the cargo spaces shall be checked and any blockage in the bilge wells and the scuppers shall be removed.

Emergency procedures

Special emergency equipment to be carried

Protective clothing (boots, gloves, coveralls, and headgear).

Self-contained breathing apparatus.

Emergency procedures

Wear protective clothing and self-contained breathing apparatus.

Emergency action in the event of fire

Fire in a cargo space containing this material: Open hatches to provide maximum ventilation. Ship's fixed fire-fighting installation will be inadequate. Use copious quantities of water. Flooding of the cargo space may be considered but due consideration should be given to stability.

Fire in an adjacent cargo space: Open hatches to provide maximum ventilation. Heat transferred from fire in an adjacent space can cause the material to decompose with consequent evolution of toxic fumes. Dividing bulkheads should be cooled.

Medical First Aid

Refer to the *Medical First Aid Guide (MFAG)*, as amended.

AMMONIUM NITRATE BASED FERTILIZER (non-hazardous)

Description

Crystals, granules or prills non-cohesive when dry. Wholly or partly soluble in water.

Ammonium nitrate based fertilizers transported in conditions mentioned in this schedule are uniform mixtures containing ammonium nitrate as the main ingredient within the following composition limits:

.1 not more than 70% ammonium nitrate with other inorganic materials;

.2 not more than 80% ammonium nitrate mixed with calcium carbonate and/or dolomite and not more than 0.4% total combustible organic material calculated as carbon;

.3 nitrogen type ammonium nitrate based fertilizers containing mixtures of ammonium nitrate and ammonium sulphate with not more than 45% ammonium nitrate and not more than 0.4% total combustible organic material calculated as carbon; and

.4 uniform ammonium nitrate based fertilizer mixtures of nitrogen, phosphate or potash, containing not more than 70% ammonium nitrate and not more than 0.4% total combustible organic material calculated as carbon or with not more than 45% ammonium nitrate and unrestricted combustible material. Fertilizers within these composition limits are not subject to the provisions of this schedule when shown by a trough test (see UN *Manual of Tests and Criteria*, part III, subsection 38.2) that they are liable to self-sustaining decomposition or if they contain an excess of nitrate greater than 10% by mass.

Notes:

1 All nitrate ions for which there is present in the mixture a molecular equivalent of ammonium ions should be calculated as ammonium nitrate.

2 The transport of ammonium nitrate materials which are liable to self-heating sufficient to initiate decomposition is prohibited.

3 The NPK proportions for a fertilizer should not be used as a guide to its ability to undergo self-sustaining decomposition as this depends on the chemical species present (refer to UN *Manual of Tests and Criteria*, part III, subsection 38.2).

4 This schedule may only be used for substances that do not exhibit explosive properties of class 1 when tested in accordance to Test Series 1 and 2 of class 1 (see UN *Manual of Tests and Criteria*, part I).

5 This schedule may only be used if the chemical or physical properties of an ammonium nitrate based fertilizer are such that, when tested, it does not meet the established defining criteria of any class.

Characteristics

Angle of repose	Bulk density (kg/m³)	Stowage factor (m³/t)
27° to 42°	1000 to 1200	0.83 to 1.00
Size	**Class**	**Group**
1 to 4 mm	Not applicable	C

Hazard

This cargo is non-combustible or with a low fire-risk.

Even though this cargo is classified as non-hazardous, it will behave in the same way as the ammonium nitrate based fertilizers classified in class 9 under UN 2071 when heated strongly, by decomposing and giving off toxic gases.

The speed of the decomposition reaction is lower, but there will be a risk of toxic fumes in the cargo space and on deck if the cargo is strongly heated.

Fertilizer dust might be irritating to skin and mucous membranes.

This cargo is hygroscopic and will cake if wet.

AMMONIUM NITRATE BASED FERTILIZER (non-hazardous) *(continued)*

Stowage & segregation

The compatibility of non-hazardous ammonium nitrate based fertilizers with other materials which may be stowed in the same cargo space should be considered before loading.

"Separated from" sources of heat or ignition (*see also* **Loading**).

Not to be stowed immediately adjacent to any tank or double bottom containing fuel oil heated to more than 50°C.

Fertilizers of this type should be stowed out of direct contact with a metal engine-room boundary. This may be done, for example, by using flame-retardant bags containing inert materials or by any equivalent barrier approved by the competent authority. This requirement need not apply to short international voyages.

Hold cleanliness

Clean and dry as relevant to the hazards of the cargo.

Weather precautions

This cargo shall be kept as dry as practicable. This cargo shall not be handled during precipitation. During handling of this cargo, all non-working hatches of the cargo spaces into which this cargo is loaded or to be loaded shall be closed.

Loading

Trim in accordance with the relevant provisions required under sections 4 and 5 of the Code.

Prior to loading, the following provisions shall be complied with:

- All electrical equipment, other than that of approved intrinsically safe type, in the cargo spaces to be used for this cargo shall be electrically disconnected from the power source, by appropriate means other than a fuse, at a point external to the space. This situation shall be maintained while the cargo is on board.

- Due consideration shall be paid to the possible need to open hatches in case of fire to provide maximum ventilation and to apply water in an emergency and the consequent risk to the stability of the ship through fluidization of the cargo.

- In addition, if decomposition occurs, the residue left after decomposition may have only half the mass of the original cargo. Due consideration shall be paid to the effect of the loss of mass on the stability of the ship.

During loading, the following provisions shall be complied with:

- Bunkering of fuel oil shall not be allowed. Pumping of fuel oil in spaces adjacent to the cargo spaces for this cargo, other than the engine-room, shall not be allowed.

Precautions

No welding, burning, cutting or other operations involving the use of fire, open flame, spark- or arc-producing equipment shall be carried out in the vicinity of the cargo spaces containing this cargo except in an emergency. Smoking shall not be allowed on deck and in the cargo spaces and "NO SMOKING" signs shall be displayed on deck whenever this cargo is on board. The hatches of the cargo spaces, whenever this material is on board, shall be kept free to be capable of being opened in case of an emergency.

Appropriate precautions shall be taken to protect machinery and accommodation spaces from the dust of the cargo. Bilge wells of the cargo spaces shall be protected from ingress of the cargo. Due consideration shall be paid to protect equipment from the dust of the cargo. Persons who may be exposed to the dust of the cargo shall wear goggles or other equivalent dust eye-protection and dust filter masks. Those persons shall wear protective clothing, as necessary.

AMMONIUM NITRATE BASED FERTILIZER (non-hazardous) *(concluded)*

Ventilation

The cargo spaces carrying this cargo shall not be ventilated during voyage.

Carriage

Hatches of the cargo spaces carrying this cargo shall be weathertight to prevent the ingress of water.

The temperature of this cargo shall be monitored and recorded daily during the voyage to detect decomposition resulting in spontaneous heating and oxygen depletion.

Discharge

Bunkering or pumping of fuel oil shall not be allowed. If this cargo has hardened, it shall be trimmed to avoid the formation of overhangs, as necessary.

Clean-up

After discharge of this cargo, the bilge wells and the scuppers of the cargo spaces shall be checked and any blockage in the bilge wells and the scuppers shall be removed.

Emergency procedures

Special emergency equipment to be carried

Protective clothing (boots, gloves, coveralls, and headgear).
Self-contained breathing apparatus.

Emergency procedures

Wear protective clothing and self-contained breathing apparatus.

Emergency action in the event of fire

Fire in a cargo space containing this material: Open hatches to provide maximum ventilation. Ship's fixed fire-fighting installation will be inadequate. Use copious quantities of water. Flooding of the cargo space may be considered but due consideration should be given to stability.

Fire in an adjacent cargo space: Open hatches to provide maximum ventilation. Heat transferred from fire in an adjacent space can cause the material to decompose with consequent evolution of toxic fumes. Dividing bulkheads should be cooled.

Medical First Aid

Refer to the *Medical First Aid Guide (MFAG)*, as amended.

AMMONIUM SULPHATE

Description
Brownish-grey to white crystals. Soluble in water. Free-flowing. Absorbs moisture. Moisture content 0.04% to 0.5%. Ammonia odour. Subject to natural loss in weight.

Characteristics

Angle of repose	Bulk density (kg/m^3)	Stowage factor (m^3/t)
28° to 35°	943 to 1052	0.95 to 1.06
Size	**Class**	**Group**
2 mm to 4 mm	Not applicable	C

Hazard
Dust may cause skin and eye irritation. Harmful if swallowed. Even though this cargo is classified as non-hazardous, it may cause heavy corrosion of framing, side shell, bulkhead, etc., if sweating of cargo space occurs.

This cargo is non-combustible or has a low fire-risk.

Stowage & segregation
No special requirements.

Hold cleanliness
Clean and dry as relevant to the hazards of the cargo.

Weather precautions
This cargo shall be kept as dry as practicable. This cargo shall not be handled during precipitation. During handling of this cargo, all non-working hatches of the cargo spaces into which this cargo is loaded or to be loaded shall be closed.

Loading
Avoid generating dust when loading. During loading, due consideration shall be paid to minimize dust generation. Trim in accordance with the relevant provisions required under sections 4 and 5 of the Code.

Precautions
Appropriate precautions shall be taken to protect machinery and accommodation spaces from the dust of the cargo. Bilge wells of the cargo spaces shall be protected from ingress of the cargo. Due consideration shall be paid to protect equipment from the dust of the cargo. Persons who may be exposed to the dust of the cargo shall wear goggles or other equivalent dust eye-protection and dust filter masks. Those persons shall wear protective clothing, as necessary.

Ventilation
The cargo spaces carrying this cargo shall not be ventilated during voyage.

Carriage
No special requirements.

Discharge
If this cargo has hardened, it shall be trimmed to avoid the formation of overhangs, as necessary.

Clean-up
After discharge of this cargo, the cargo spaces shall be thoroughly cleaned and washed out to remove all traces of the cargo and dried, except in the case that the cargo to be loaded subsequent to discharge is AMMONIUM SULPHATE.

ANTIMONY ORE AND RESIDUE

Description
Lead-grey mineral, subject to black tarnish.

Characteristics

Angle of repose	Bulk density (kg/m³)	Stowage factor (m³/t)
Not applicable	2381 to 2941	0.34 to 0.42
Size	**Class**	**Group**
Not applicable	Not applicable	C

Hazard
This cargo is non-combustible or has a low fire-risk.

If involved in a fire, dangerous fumes of antimony and sulphur oxides can evolve.

Stowage & segregation
No special requirements.

Hold cleanliness
No special requirements.

Weather precautions
No special requirements.

Loading
Trim in accordance with the relevant provisions required under sections 4 and 5 of the Code.

As the density of the cargo is extremely high, the tanktop may be overstressed unless the cargo is evenly spread across the tanktop to equalize the weight distribution. Due consideration shall be paid to ensure that the tanktop is not overstressed during voyage and during loading by a pile of the cargo.

Precautions
Appropriate precautions shall be taken to protect machinery and accommodation spaces from the dust of the cargo. Bilge wells of the cargo spaces shall be protected from ingress of the cargo. Due consideration shall be paid to protect equipment from the dust of the cargo. Persons who may be exposed to the dust of the cargo shall wear protective clothing, goggles or other equivalent dust eye-protection and dust filter masks, as necessary.

Ventilation
No special requirements.

Carriage
No special requirements.

Discharge
No special requirements.

Clean-up
No special requirements.

BARIUM NITRATE UN 1446

Description

Glossy white crystals or powder. Soluble in water.

Characteristics

Angle of repose	Bulk density (kg/m³)		Stowage factor (m³/t)
Not applicable	–		–
Size	**Class**	**Subsidiary risk**	**Group**
Fine powder	5.1	6.1	B

Hazard

Toxic if swallowed or by dust inhalation. If involved in a fire mixture with combustible materials is readily ignited and may burn fiercely.

Stowage & segregation

"Separated from" foodstuffs.

Hold cleanliness

Clean and dry as relevant to the hazards of the cargo.

Weather precautions

No special requirements.

Loading

Trim in accordance with the relevant provisions required under sections 4 and 5 of the Code.

Precautions

Appropriate precautions shall be taken to protect machinery and accommodation spaces from the dust of the cargo. Bilge wells of the cargo spaces shall be protected from ingress of the cargo. Due consideration shall be paid to protect equipment from the dust of the cargo. Persons who may be exposed to the dust of the cargo shall wear goggles or other equivalent dust eye-protection and dust filter masks. Those persons shall wear protective clothing, as necessary.

Bilge wells shall be clean, dry and covered as appropriate, to prevent ingress of the cargo.

Ventilation

Surface ventilation only, either natural or mechanical, shall be conducted, as necessary, during the voyage for this cargo.

Carriage

No special requirements.

Discharge

No special requirements.

Clean-up

No special requirements.

BARIUM NITRATE UN 1446 *(concluded)*

Emergency procedures

Special emergency equipment to be carried

Protective clothing (gloves, boots, overalls, headgear). Self-contained breathing apparatus. Spray nozzles.

Emergency procedures

Wear protective clothing and self-contained breathing apparatus.

Emergency action in the event of fire

Use copious amounts of water, which is best applied in the form of a spray to avoid disturbing the surface of the material. The material may fuse or melt, in which condition application of water may result in excessive scattering of molten materials. Exclusion of air or the use of CO_2 will not control the fire. Due consideration should be given to the stability of the ship due to the effect of accumulated water.

Medical First Aid

Refer to the *Medical First Aid Guide (MFAG)*, as amended.

BARYTES

Description

Crystalline ore mineral. A sulphate of barium. Moisture 1% to 6%.

Characteristics

Angle of repose	Bulk density (kg/m³)	Stowage factor (m³/t)
Not applicable	2941	0.34
Size	**Class**	**Group**
80% lumps: 6.4 to 101.6 mm 20% fines: less than 6.4 mm	Not applicable	C

Hazard

No special hazards.

This cargo is non-combustible or has a low fire-risk.

Stowage & segregation

No special requirements.

Hold cleanliness

No special requirements.

Weather precautions

No special requirements.

Loading

Trim in accordance with the relevant provisions required under sections 4 and 5 of the Code.

As the density of the cargo is extremely high, the tanktop may be overstressed unless the cargo is evenly spread across the tanktop to equalize the weight distribution. Due consideration shall be paid to ensure that the tanktop is not overstressed during voyage and during loading by a pile of the cargo.

Precautions

Appropriate precautions shall be taken to protect machinery and accommodation spaces from the dust of the cargo. Bilge wells of the cargo spaces shall be protected from ingress of the cargo. Due consideration shall be paid to protect equipment from the dust of the cargo. Persons who may be exposed to the dust of the cargo shall wear protective clothing, goggles or other equivalent dust eye-protection and dust filter masks, as necessary.

Ventilation

No special requirements.

Carriage

No special requirements.

Discharge

No special requirements.

Clean-up

No special requirements.

BAUXITE

Description
A brownish-yellow clay-like and earthy mineral. Moisture content: 0% to 10%. Insoluble in water.

Characteristics

Angle of repose	Bulk density (kg/m^3)	Stowage factor (m^3/t)
Not applicable	1190 to 1389	0.72 to 0.84
Size	**Class**	**Group**
70% to 90% lumps: 2.5 mm to 500 mm 10% to 30% powder	Not applicable	C

Hazard
No special hazards.

This cargo is non-combustible or has a low fire-risk.

Stowage & segregation
No special requirements.

Hold cleanliness
No special requirements.

Weather precautions
No special requirements.

Loading
Trim in accordance with the relevant provisions required under sections 4 and 5 of the Code.

Precautions
Bilge wells shall be clean, dry and covered as appropriate, to prevent ingress of the cargo.

Ventilation
No special requirements.

Carriage
No special requirements.

Discharge
No special requirements.

Clean-up
No special requirements.

BIOSLUDGE

Description

Heat-dried activated sludge. Very fine granular product. Moisture: 3% to 5%. Black speckled colour.

Characteristics

Angle of repose	Bulk density (kg/m^3)	Stowage factor (m^3/t)
Not applicable	654	1.53
Size	**Class**	**Group**
Not applicable	Not applicable	C

Hazard

No special hazards.

This cargo is non-combustible or has a low fire-risk.

Stowage & segregation

No special requirements.

Hold cleanliness

No special requirements.

Weather precautions

No special requirements.

Loading

Trim in accordance with the relevant provisions required under sections 4 and 5 of the Code.

Precautions

Appropriate precautions shall be taken to protect machinery and accommodation spaces from the dust of the cargo. Bilge wells of the cargo spaces shall be protected from ingress of the cargo. Due consideration shall be paid to protect equipment from the dust of the cargo. Persons who may be exposed to the dust of the cargo shall wear protective clothing, goggles or other equivalent dust eye-protection and dust filter masks, as necessary.

Ventilation

No special requirements.

Carriage

No special requirements.

Discharge

No special requirements.

Clean-up

No special requirements.

BORAX (PENTAHYDRATE CRUDE)

Description

A chemical compound of boracic acid and soda. Free-flowing powder or granules. Grey colour. Dusty.

Characteristics

Angle of repose	Bulk density (kg/m³)	Stowage factor (m³/t)
Not applicable	1087	0.92
Size	**Class**	**Group**
Up to 2.36 mm	Not applicable	C

Hazard

No special hazards.

This cargo is non-combustible or has a low fire-risk.

This cargo is hygroscopic and will cake if wet.

Stowage & segregation

No special requirements.

Hold cleanliness

No special requirements.

Weather precautions

This cargo shall be kept as dry as practicable. This cargo shall not be handled during precipitation. During handling of this cargo, all non-working hatches of the cargo spaces into which this cargo is loaded or to be loaded shall be closed.

Loading

Trim in accordance with the relevant provisions required under sections 4 and 5 of the Code.

Precautions

Appropriate precautions shall be taken to protect machinery and accommodation spaces from the dust of the cargo. Bilge wells of the cargo spaces shall be protected from ingress of the cargo. Due consideration shall be paid to protect equipment from the dust of the cargo. Persons who may be exposed to the dust of the cargo shall wear protective clothing, goggles or other equivalent dust eye-protection and dust filter masks, as necessary.

Ventilation

No special requirements.

Carriage

No special requirements.

Discharge

If this cargo has hardened, it shall be trimmed to avoid the formation of overhangs, as necessary.

Clean-up

No special requirements.

BORAX, ANHYDROUS
(crude or refined)

Description

Crude is normally of yellow-white appearance. When highly refined, becomes white crystalline. Dusty and hygroscopic.

Characteristics

Angle of repose	Bulk density (kg/m^3)	Stowage factor (m^3/t)
35°	1282	0.78
Size	**Class**	**Group**
Granules less than 1.4 mm	Not applicable	C

Hazard

Dust is very abrasive and irritating, but not toxic, if inhaled.

This cargo is non-combustible or has a low fire-risk.

This cargo is hygroscopic and will cake if wet.

Stowage & segregation

No special requirements.

Hold cleanliness

No special requirements.

Weather precautions

No special requirements.

Loading

Trim in accordance with the relevant provisions required under sections 4 and 5 of the Code.

Precautions

Appropriate precautions shall be taken to protect machinery and accommodation spaces from the dust of the cargo. Bilge wells of the cargo spaces shall be protected from ingress of the cargo. Due consideration shall be paid to protect equipment from the dust of the cargo. Persons who may be exposed to the dust of the cargo shall wear goggles or other equivalent dust eye-protection and dust filter masks. Those persons shall wear protective clothing, as necessary.

Ventilation

No special requirements.

Carriage

No special requirements.

Discharge

If this cargo has hardened, it shall be trimmed to avoid the formation of overhangs, as necessary.

Clean-up

No special requirements.

BROWN COAL BRIQUETTES

Description

Brown coal (lignite) briquettes are manufactured by pressing dried brown coal particles into compressed blocks.

Characteristics

Angle of repose	Bulk density (kg/m³)	Stowage factor (m³/t)
Not applicable	750	1.34
Size	**Class**	**Group**
Mainly up to 50 mm	MHB	B

Hazard

Briquettes are easily ignited, liable to spontaneous combustion and will deplete oxygen in cargo space.

Stowage & segregation

Refer to the appendix to this schedule.

Hold cleanliness

Clean and dry as relevant to the hazards of the cargo. Previous cargo battens shall be removed from the cargo spaces.

Weather precautions

No special requirements.

Loading

Refer to the appendix to this schedule.

Precautions

Appropriate precautions shall be taken to protect machinery and accommodation spaces from the dust of the cargo. Bilge wells of the cargo spaces shall be protected from ingress of the cargo. Due consideration shall be paid to protect equipment from the dust of the cargo. Persons who may be exposed to the dust of the cargo shall wear protective clothing, goggles or other equivalent dust eye-protection and dust filter masks, as necessary.

Ventilation

The cargo spaces carrying this cargo shall not be ventilated during voyage. *Refer to the appendix to this schedule.*

Carriage

Refer to the appendix to this schedule.

Discharge

Refer to the appendix to this schedule.

Clean-up

After discharge of this cargo, the bilge wells and the scuppers of the cargo spaces shall be checked and any blockage in the bilge wells and the scuppers shall be removed.

BROWN COAL BRIQUETTES *(continued)*

Emergency procedures

<table>
<tr><td align="center">

Special emergency equipment to be carried
Nil

</td></tr>
<tr><td align="center">

Emergency procedures
Nil

Emergency action in the event of fire
Batten down. Exclusion of air may be sufficient to control fire. **Do not use water.**
Seek expert advice and consider heading for the nearest suitable port.

Medical First Aid
Refer to the *Medical First Aid Guide (MFAG)*, as amended.

</td></tr>
</table>

Remarks

The use of CO_2 or inert gas, if available, should be withheld until fire is apparent.

Appendix

BROWN COAL BRIQUETTES

Hazard

1   This cargo is easily ignited, liable to heat spontaneously and deplete oxygen in the cargo space.

2   This cargo is subject to oxidation, leading to depletion of oxygen and an increase in carbon dioxide in the cargo space (see also section 3).

3   This cargo is liable to heat spontaneously and may ignite spontaneously in the cargo space. When spontaneous heating occurs, flammable and toxic gases, including carbon monoxide, may be produced. Carbon monoxide is an odourless gas, slightly lighter than air, and has flammable limits in air of 12% to 75% by volume. It is toxic by inhalation, with an affinity for blood haemoglobin over 200 times that of oxygen. The recommended threshold limit value (TLV) for carbon monoxide exposure is 50 ppm.

Stowage & segregation

1   Boundaries of cargo spaces where these cargoes are carried shall be resistant to fire and liquids.

2   This cargo shall be "separated from" goods of classes 1 (division 1.4), 2, 3, 4 and 5 in packaged form (see IMDG Code) and "separated from" solid bulk material of classes 4 and 5.1.

3   Stowage of goods of class 5.1 in packaged form or solid bulk materials of class 5.1 above or below this cargo shall be prohibited.

4   This cargo shall be "separated longitudinally by an intervening complete compartment or hold from" goods of class 1 other than division 1.4.

5   This cargo shall not be stowed adjacent to hot areas.

Note: For interpretation of these terms, see section 9.

BROWN COAL BRIQUETTES *(appendix, continued)*

Loading

1   Prior to loading, the shipper, or their appointed agent, shall provide in writing to the master the characteristics of the cargo and the recommended safe handling procedures for loading and transport of the cargo. As a minimum, the cargo's contract specifications for moisture content, sulphur content and size shall be stated.

2   This cargo shall be stored for 7 days prior to loading. This substantially reduces the risk of spontaneous combustion in subsequent transport, storage and handling.

3   Before loading this cargo, the master shall ensure the following:

   3.1   weather-deck enclosures to the cargo space have been inspected to ensure their integrity. Such closures are closed and sealed;

   3.2   all electrical cables and components situated in cargo spaces and adjacent enclosed spaces are free from defects. Such cables and electrical components are safe to be used in a flammable and/or dusty atmosphere or positively isolated. The provisions of this clause need not apply to engine-rooms where the engine-room is separated from the cargo space by a gastight bulkhead with no direct access.

4   Smoking and the use of naked flames shall not be permitted in the cargo areas and adjacent spaces and appropriate warning notices shall be posted in conspicuous places. Burning, cutting, chipping, welding or other sources of ignition shall not be permitted in the vicinity of cargo spaces or in other adjacent spaces.

5   This cargo shall not be dropped more than one metre during loading, to minimize the production of dust and fines.

6   Individual cargo spaces shall be loaded without interruption, where possible. Hot spots may develop in a cargo space that has been kept open for more than six days (or less in weather over 30°C).

7   Prior to departure, the master shall be satisfied that the surface of the material has been trimmed reasonably level to the boundaries of the cargo space to avoid the formation of gas pockets and to prevent air from permeating the body of the briquettes. Casing leading into the cargo space shall be adequately sealed. The shipper shall ensure that the master receives the necessary co-operation from the loading terminal.

8   Individual cargo spaces shall be closed and sealed as soon as practicable after the cargo has been loaded into each cargo space.

Precautions

1   The ship shall be suitably fitted and carry on board appropriate instruments for measuring the following without requiring entry into the cargo space:

   1.1   concentration of methane in the atmosphere above the cargo and opening cargo space enclosures;

   1.2   concentration of oxygen in the atmosphere above the cargo;

   1.3   concentration of carbon monoxide in the atmosphere above the cargo;

   1.4   pH value of cargo hold bilge samples.

   These instruments shall be regularly serviced and calibrated. Ship personnel shall be trained in the use of such instruments.

2   It is recommended that means be provided for monitoring the temperature of the cargo in the range of 0°C to 100°C to enable the measurement of temperature of the cargo during the voyage without requiring entry into the cargo space.

Carriage

1   As far as practicable, any gases which may be emitted from the cargo shall not be allowed to accumulate in adjacent enclosed spaces, such as store-rooms, carpenter's shop, passageways, tunnels, etc. Such spaces shall be adequately ventilated and regularly monitored for methane, oxygen and carbon monoxide.

BROWN COAL BRIQUETTES *(appendix, continued)*

2   Under no circumstances, except in emergency, shall the hatches be opened or the cargo space be ventilated or entered during the voyage.

3   The atmosphere in the space above the cargo in each cargo space shall be regularly monitored for the concentrations of methane, oxygen and carbon monoxide.

4   The frequency of the monitoring shall be determined based upon the information provided by the shipper and the information obtained through the analysis of the atmosphere in the cargo space. The monitoring shall be conducted at least daily and as close as practical to the same time of day. The results of monitoring shall be recorded. The shipper may request more frequent monitoring, particularly if there is evidence of significant self-heating during the voyage.

5   The following issues shall be taken into account:

    5.1   The oxygen level in the sealed cargo space will fall from an initial 21% over a period of days to stabilize at levels of the order of 6 to 15%. If the oxygen level does not fall below 20%, or rapidly increases after an initial fall, it is possible that the cargo space is inadequately sealed and is at risk of spontaneous combustion.

    5.2   Carbon monoxide levels will build up to concentrations which fluctuate in the 200 to 2000 parts per million (ppm) range in a safe, well-sealed cargo space. A rapid increase of approximately 1000 ppm in carbon monoxide levels in this cargo over a 24-hour period is a possible indicator of spontaneous combustion, particularly if accompanied by an increase in methane levels.

    5.3   The methane composition in briquette cargo is normally low, less than 5 ppm, and does not constitute a hazard. However, a sudden and continuing rise in methane levels, to concentrations above 10 ppm, is an indicator of the occurrence of spontaneous combustion in the hold.

    5.4   The temperature in this cargo in a well-sealed cargo space normally remains at 5 to 10°C above seawater temperature, the increase being due to normal diurnal breathing of small quantities of air into the cargo space. Checking of the cargo space seals to minimize air leakage is essential. A rapid increase in temperature of approximately 20°C over 24 hours is evidence of spontaneous combustion.

6   Regular hold bilge testing shall be systematically carried out. If the pH monitoring indicates that a corrosion risk exists, the master shall ensure that all bilges are kept dry during the voyage in order to avoid possible accumulation of acids on tanktops and in the bilge system.

7   When the behaviour of the cargo during the voyage differs from that specified in the cargo information, the master shall report such differences to the shipper. Such reports will enable the shipper to maintain records on the behaviour of this cargo, so that the information being provided to the master can be reviewed in the light of the transport experience.

8   When the master is concerned that the cargo is showing any signs of self-heating or spontaneous combustion, such as an increase in the concentration of methane or carbon monoxide or an increase in temperature, as described above, the following actions shall be taken:

    8.1   Consult with the ship's agent at the loading port. The company's designated person ashore shall be advised immediately.

    8.2   Check the seal of the cargo space and re-seal the cargo space, as necessary.

    8.3   Do not enter the cargo space and do not open the hatches, unless the master considers access is necessary for the safety of the ship or safety of life. When any ship's personnel have entered into a cargo space, re-seal the cargo space immediately after the personnel vacate the cargo space.

    8.4   Increase the frequency of monitoring the gas composition, and temperature when practicable, of the cargo.

BROWN COAL BRIQUETTES *(appendix, continued)*

8.5 Send the following information, as soon as possible, to the ship's owner or agent at the loading port to obtain expert advice:

.1 the number of cargo spaces involved;

.2 monitoring results of the carbon monoxide, methane and oxygen concentrations;

.3 if available, temperature of the cargo, location and method used to obtain results;

.4 the time the gas analyses were taken (monitoring routine);

.5 the quantity of the cargo in the cargo space(s) involved;

.6 the description of the cargo as per the shipper's declaration, and any special precautions indicated on the declaration;

.7 the date of loading, and Estimated Time of Arrival (ETA) at the intended discharge port (which shall be specified); and

.8 any other comments or observations the master may consider relevant.

Discharge

Prior to, and during, discharge:

1 The cargo space shall be kept closed until just before the commencement of discharge of that space. The cargo may be sprayed with a fine water spray to reduce dust.

2 Personnel shall not enter the cargo space without having tested the atmosphere above the cargo. The personnel entering into a cargo space in which the atmosphere contains oxygen levels below 21% shall wear self-contained breathing apparatus. Carbon dioxide and carbon monoxide gas levels shall also be tested prior to entry into the cargo spaces. The recommended threshold limit value (TLV) for carbon monoxide is 50 ppm.

3 During discharge, attention shall be paid to the cargo for signs of hot spots (i.e., steaming). If a hot spot is detected, the area shall be sprayed with fine water spray and the hot spot shall be removed immediately to prevent spreading. The hot-spot cargo shall be spread out on the wharf away from the remainder of the cargo.

4 Prior to suspending the discharge of this cargo for more than eight hours, the hatch covers and all other ventilation for the cargo space shall be closed.

Procedures for gas monitoring of brown coal briquette cargoes

1 Observations

1.1 Carbon monoxide monitoring, when conducted in accordance with the following procedures, will provide a reliable early indication of self-heating within this cargo. This allows preventive action to be considered without delay. A sudden rapid rise in carbon monoxide detected within a cargo space, particularly if accompanied by an increase in methane levels, is a conclusive indication that self-heating is taking place.

1.2 All vessels engaged in the carriage of this cargo shall carry on board an instrument for measuring methane, oxygen and carbon monoxide gas concentrations, to enable the monitoring of the atmosphere within the cargo space. This instrument shall be regularly serviced and calibrated in accordance with the manufacturer's instructions. Care shall be exercised in interpreting methane measurements carried out in the low oxygen concentrations often found in unventilated cargo holds. The catalytic sensors normally used for the detection of methane rely on the presence of sufficient oxygen for accurate measurement. This phenomenon does not affect the measurement of carbon monoxide, or measurement of methane by infrared sensor. Further guidance may be obtained from the instrument manufacturer.

BROWN COAL BRIQUETTES *(appendix, continued)*

2   Sampling and measurement procedure

2.1   Equipment

2.1.1   An instrument which is capable of measuring methane, oxygen and carbon monoxide concentrations shall be provided on board a ship carrying this cargo. The instrument shall be fitted with an aspirator, flexible connection and a length of spark-proof metal tubing to enable a representative sample to be obtained from within the square of the hatch.

2.1.2   When recommended by the manufacturer, a suitable filter shall be used to protect the instrument against the ingress of moisture. The presence of even a small amount of water will compromise the accuracy of the measurement.

2.2   Siting of sampling points

2.2.1   In order to obtain meaningful information about the behaviour of this cargo in a cargo space, gas measurements shall be made via one sample point per cargo space. To ensure flexibility of measurement in adverse weather, however, two sample points shall be provided per cargo space, one on the port side and one on the starboard side of the hatch cover or hatch coaming (refer to the diagram of gas sampling point). Measurement from either of these locations is satisfactory.

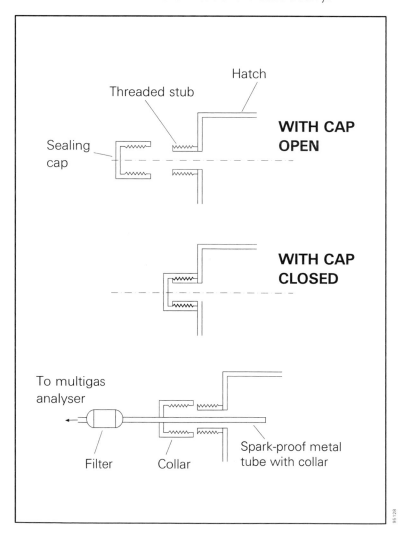

Diagram of gas sampling point

BROWN COAL BRIQUETTES *(appendix, concluded)*

2.2.2   Each sample point shall comprise a hole of diameter approximately 12 mm positioned as near to the top of the hatch coaming as possible. It shall be sealed with a sealing cap to prevent ingress of water and air. It is essential this cap be securely replaced after each measurement to maintain a tight seal.

2.2.3   The provision of any sample point shall not compromise the seaworthiness of the vessel.

2.3   *Measurement*

The explanation on procedures for measurement is as follows:

.1   remove the sealing cap, insert the rigid tube into the sampling point and tighten the integral cap to ensure an adequate seal;

.2   connect the instrument to the sampling tube;

.3   draw a sample of the atmosphere through the tube, using the aspirator, until steady readings are obtained;

.4   log the results on a form which records cargo hold, date and time for each measurement; and

.5   put back the sealing cap.

CALCIUM NITRATE UN 1454

Description

White deliquescent solid, soluble in water. The provisions of this Code should not apply to the commercial grades of calcium nitrate fertilizers consisting mainly of a double salt (calcium nitrate and ammonium nitrate) and containing not more than 10% ammonium nitrate and at least 12% water of crystallization.

Characteristics

Angle of repose	Bulk density (kg/m³)	Stowage factor (m³/t)
Not applicable	893 to 1099	0.91 to 1.12
Size	**Class**	**Group**
Not applicable	5.1	B

Hazard

Non-combustible materials. If involved in a fire, will greatly intensify the burning of combustible materials. Although non-combustible, mixtures with combustible material are easily ignited and may burn fiercely.

This cargo is hygroscopic and will cake if wet.

This cargo is harmful if swallowed

Stowage & segregation

"Separated from" foodstuffs.

Hold cleanliness

Clean and dry as relevant to the hazards of the cargo.

Weather precautions

This cargo shall be kept as dry as practicable. This cargo shall not be handled during precipitation. During handling of this cargo, all non-working hatches of the cargo spaces into which this cargo is loaded or to be loaded shall be closed.

Loading

Appropriate measures shall be taken to prevent the cargo from contact with combustible materials.

Trim in accordance with the relevant provisions required under sections 4 and 5 of the Code.

Precautions

Bilge wells shall be clean, dry and covered as appropriate, to prevent ingress of the cargo.

Ventilation

The cargo spaces carrying this cargo shall not be ventilated during voyage.

Carriage

No special requirements.

Discharge

If this cargo has hardened, it shall be trimmed to avoid the formation of overhangs, as necessary.

Clean-up

No special requirements.

CALCIUM NITRATE UN 1454 *(concluded)*

Emergency procedures

Special emergency equipment to be carried

Protective clothing (gloves, boots, coveralls, headgear). Self-contained breathing apparatus. Spray nozzles.

Emergency procedures

Wear protective clothing and self-contained breathing apparatus.

Emergency action in the event of fire

Use copious quantities of water, which is best applied in the form of a spray to avoid disturbing the surface of the material. The material may fuse or melt, in which condition application of water may result in extensive scattering of the molten materials. Exclusion of air or the use of CO_2 will not control the fire. Due consideration should be given to the stability of the ship due to the effect of accumulated water.

Medical First Aid

Refer to the *Medical First Aid Guide (MFAG)*, as amended.

CALCIUM NITRATE FERTILIZER

Description

Granules mainly of a double salt (calcium nitrate and ammonium nitrate) and containing not more than 15.5% total nitrogen and at least 12% water. Refer to the schedule for CALCIUM NITRATE UN 1454 where the total nitrogen content exceeds 15.5%, or where the water content is less than 12%.

Characteristics

Angle of repose	Bulk density (kg/m³)	Stowage factor (m³/t)
34°	1053 to 1111	0.90 to 0.95
Size	**Class**	**Group**
1 mm to 4 mm	Not applicable	C

Hazard

No special hazards.

This cargo is non-combustible or has a low fire-risk.

Stowage & segregation

"Separated from" foodstuffs.

Hold cleanliness

Clean and dry as relevant to the hazards of the cargo.

Weather precautions

This cargo shall be kept as dry as practicable. This cargo shall not be handled during precipitation. During handling of this cargo, all non-working hatches of the cargo spaces into which this cargo is loaded or to be loaded shall be closed.

Loading

Trim in accordance with the relevant provisions required under sections 4 and 5 of the Code.

Precautions

No special requirements.

Ventilation

The cargo spaces carrying this cargo shall not be ventilated during voyage.

Carriage

No special requirements.

Discharge

No special requirements.

Clean-up

No special requirements.

CARBORUNDUM

Description
A hard black crystalline compound of carbon and silicon. Odourless. No moisture content.

Characteristics

Angle of repose	Bulk density (kg/m³)	Stowage factor (m³/t)
Not applicable	1786	0.56
Size	**Class**	**Group**
75% lumps: under 203.2 mm 25% lumps: under 12.7 mm	Not applicable	C

Hazard
Slightly toxic by inhalation.

This cargo is non-combustible or has a low fire-risk.

Stowage & segregation
No special requirements.

Hold cleanliness
No special requirements.

Weather precautions
No special requirements.

Loading
Trim in accordance with the relevant provisions required under sections 4 and 5 of the Code.

Precautions
Protect machinery, accommodation and equipment from dust. Personnel involved in cargo handling should wear protective clothing and dust filter masks.

Ventilation
No special requirements.

Carriage
No special requirements.

Discharge
No special requirements.

Clean-up
No special requirements.

CASTOR BEANS or
CASTOR MEAL or
CASTOR POMACE or
CASTOR FLAKE UN 2969

Description
The beans from which castor oil is obtained.

Characteristics

Angle of repose	Bulk density (kg/m³)	Stowage factor (m³/t)
Not applicable	–	–
Size	**Class**	**Group**
Not applicable	9	B

Hazard
Contain a powerful allergen which, by inhalation of dust or by skin contact with crushed bean products, can give rise to severe irritation of the skin, eyes, and mucous membranes in some persons. They are also toxic by ingestion.

Stowage & segregation
"Separated from" foodstuffs and oxidizing materials (goods in packages and solid bulk materials).

Hold cleanliness
No special requirements.

Weather precautions
No special requirements.

Loading
Trim in accordance with the relevant provisions required under sections 4 and 5 of the Code.

Precautions
Due consideration shall be paid to prevent dust entering living quarters and working areas. Castor meal, castor pomace and castor flakes shall not be carried in bulk.

Appropriate precautions shall be taken to protect machinery and accommodation spaces from the dust of the cargo. Bilge wells of the cargo spaces shall be protected from ingress of the cargo. Due consideration shall be paid to protect equipment from the dust of the cargo. Persons who may be exposed to the dust of the cargo shall wear goggles or other equivalent dust eye-protection and dust filter masks. Those persons shall wear protective clothing, as necessary.

Ventilation
Surface ventilation only, either natural or mechanical, shall be conducted, as necessary, during the voyage for this cargo.

Carriage
No special requirements.

Discharge
No special requirements.

CASTOR BEANS or CASTOR MEAL or CASTOR POMACE or CASTOR FLAKE UN 2969 *(concluded)*

Clean-up

After discharge of this cargo, the cargo spaces shall be thoroughly cleaned and washed out to remove all traces of the cargo.

Emergency procedures

<table>
<tr><td>

Special emergency equipment to be carried

Protective clothing (gloves, boots, coveralls, headgear). Self-contained breathing apparatus. Spray nozzles.

</td></tr>
<tr><td>

Emergency procedures

Wear protective clothing and self-contained breathing apparatus.

Emergency action in the event of fire

Batten down. Use ship's fixed fire-fighting installation if available. Exclusion of air may be sufficient to control fire.

Medical First Aid

Refer to the *Medical First Aid Guide (MFAG)*, as amended.

</td></tr>
</table>

CEMENT

Description

Cement is a finely ground powder which becomes almost fluid in nature when aerated or significantly disturbed, thereby creating a very minimal angle of repose. After loading is completed, de-aeration occurs almost immediately and the product settles into a stable mass. Cement dust can be a major concern during loading and discharge if the vessel is not specially designed as a cement carrier or shore equipment is not fitted with special dust control equipment.

Characteristics

Angle of repose	Bulk density (kg/m³)	Stowage factor (m³/t)
Not applicable	1000 to 1493	0.67 to 1.00
Size	**Class**	**Group**
Up to 0.1 mm	Not applicable	C

Hazard

It may shift when aerated.

This cargo is non-combustible or has a low fire-risk.

Stowage & segregation

No special requirements.

Hold cleanliness

Clean and dry as relevant to the hazards of the cargo.

Weather precautions

This cargo shall be kept as dry as practicable. This cargo shall not be handled during precipitation. During handling of this cargo, all non-working hatches of the cargo spaces into which this cargo is loaded or to be loaded shall be closed.

Loading

The ship shall be kept upright during loading of this cargo. This cargo shall be so trimmed to the boundaries of the cargo space that the angle of the surface of the cargo with the horizontal plane does not exceed 25°. Both the specific gravity and the flow characteristics of this cargo are dependent on the volume of air in the cargo. The volume of air in this cargo may be up to 12%. This cargo shows fluid state prior to settlement. The ship carrying this cargo shall not depart until the cargo has settled. After the settlement, shifting of the cargo is not liable to occur unless the angle of the surface with the horizontal plane exceeds 30°.

Precautions

Appropriate precautions shall be taken to protect machinery and accommodation spaces from the dust of the cargo. Bilge wells of the cargo spaces shall be protected from ingress of the cargo. Due consideration shall be paid to protect equipment from the dust of the cargo. Persons who may be exposed to the dust of the cargo shall wear protective clothing, goggles or other equivalent dust eye-protection and dust filter masks, as necessary. Bilge wells shall be clean, dry and covered as appropriate, to prevent ingress of the cargo.

Ventilation

The cargo spaces carrying this cargo shall not be ventilated during voyage.

CEMENT *(concluded)*

Carriage

After the completion of loading of this cargo, the hatches of the cargo spaces shall be sealed, as necessary. All vents and access ways to the cargo spaces shall be shut during the voyage. Bilges in the cargo spaces carrying this cargo shall not be pumped unless special precautions are taken.

Discharge

No special requirements.

Clean-up

In the case that the residues of this cargo are to be washed out, the cargo spaces and the other structures and equipment which may have been in contact with this cargo or its dust shall be thoroughly swept prior to washing out. Particular attention shall be paid to bilge wells and framework in the cargo spaces. The fixed bilge pumps shall not be used to pump the cargo spaces, because this cargo may make the bilge systems inoperative.

CEMENT CLINKERS

Description

Cement is formed by burning limestone with clay. This burning produces rough cinder lumps that are later crushed to a fine powder to produce cement. The rough cinder lumps are called clinkers and are shipped in this form to avoid the difficulties of carrying cement powder.

Characteristics

Angle of repose	Bulk density (kg/m³)	Stowage factor (m³/t)
Not applicable	1190 to 1639	0.61 to 0.84
Size	**Class**	**Group**
0 mm to 40 mm	Not applicable	C

Hazard

No special hazards.

This cargo is non-combustible or has a low fire-risk.

Stowage & segregation

No special requirements.

Hold cleanliness

Clean and dry as relevant to the hazards of the cargo.

Weather precautions

This cargo shall be kept as dry as practicable. This cargo shall not be handled during precipitation. During handling of this cargo, all non-working hatches of the cargo spaces into which this cargo is loaded or to be loaded shall be closed.

Loading

Trim in accordance with the relevant provisions required under sections 4 and 5 of the Code.

Precautions

Appropriate precautions shall be taken to protect machinery and accommodation spaces from the dust of the cargo. Bilge wells of the cargo spaces shall be protected from ingress of the cargo. Due consideration shall be paid to protect equipment from the dust of the cargo. Persons who may be exposed to the dust of the cargo shall wear protective clothing, goggles or other equivalent dust eye-protection and dust filter masks, as necessary. Bilge wells shall be clean, dry and covered as appropriate, to prevent ingress of the cargo.

Ventilation

The cargo spaces carrying this cargo shall not be ventilated during voyage.

Carriage

After the completion of loading of this cargo, the hatches of the cargo spaces shall be sealed. All vents and access ways to the cargo spaces shall be shut during the voyage. Bilges in the cargo spaces carrying this cargo shall not be pumped unless special precautions are taken.

Discharge

No special requirements.

CEMENT CLINKERS *(concluded)*

Clean-up

In the case that the residues of this cargo are to be washed out, the cargo spaces and the other structures and equipment which may have been in contact with this cargo or its dust shall be thoroughly swept prior to washing out.

CHAMOTTE

Description

Burned clay. Grey. Shipped in the form of fine crushed stone. Used by zinc smelters and in manufacture of firebrick (road metal). Dusty.

Characteristics

Angle of repose	Bulk density (kg/m³)	Stowage factor (m³/t)
Not applicable	667	1.50
Size	**Class**	**Group**
Up to 10 mm	Not applicable	C

Hazard

No special hazards.

This cargo is non-combustible or has a low fire-risk.

Stowage & segregation

No special requirements.

Hold cleanliness

No special requirements.

Weather precautions

No special requirements.

Loading

Trim in accordance with the relevant provisions required under sections 4 and 5 of the Code.

Precautions

Appropriate precautions shall be taken to protect machinery and accommodation spaces from the dust of the cargo. Bilge wells of the cargo spaces shall be protected from ingress of the cargo. Due consideration shall be paid to protect equipment from the dust of the cargo. Persons who may be exposed to the dust of the cargo shall wear protective clothing, goggles or other equivalent dust eye-protection and dust filter masks, as necessary.

Ventilation

No special requirements.

Carriage

No special requirements.

Discharge

No special requirements.

Clean-up

No special requirements.

CHARCOAL

Description
Wood burnt at a high temperature with as little exposure to air as possible. Very dusty, light cargo. Can absorb moisture to about 18 to 70% of its weight. Black powder or granules.

Characteristics

Angle of repose	Bulk density (kg/m³)	Stowage factor (m³/t)
Not applicable	199	5.02
Size	**Class**	**Group**
–	MHB	B

Hazard
May ignite spontaneously. Contact with water may cause self-heating. Liable to cause oxygen depletion in the cargo space. Hot charcoal screenings in excess of 55°C should not be loaded.

Stowage & segregation
Segregation as required for class 4.1 materials. "Separated from" oily materials.

Hold cleanliness
Clean and dry as relevant to the hazards of the cargo.

Weather precautions
This cargo shall be kept as dry as practicable. This cargo shall not be handled during precipitation. During handling of this cargo, all non-working hatches of the cargo spaces into which this cargo is loaded or to be loaded shall be closed.

Loading
Trim in accordance with the relevant provisions required under sections 4 and 5 of the Code.

Precautions
Charcoal in class 4.2 shall not be carried in bulk. This cargo shall be exposed to the weather for not less than 13 days prior to shipment. Prior to loading, the manufacturer or shipper shall give the master a certificate stating that the cargo is not class 4.2 in accordance with the result of the test approved by the competent authority.* The certificate shall also state that this cargo has been weathered for not less than 13 days. This cargo shall only be accepted for loading when the actual moisture content of the cargo is not more than 10%.

Appropriate precautions shall be taken to protect machinery and accommodation spaces from the dust of the cargo. Bilge wells of the cargo spaces shall be protected from ingress of the cargo. Due consideration shall be paid to protect equipment from the dust of the cargo. Persons who may be exposed to the dust of the cargo shall wear protective clothing, goggles or other equivalent dust eye-protection and dust filter masks, as necessary.

Ventilation
No special requirements.

---

* Reference is made to section 6 of appendix 2 to this Code.

CHARCOAL *(concluded)*

Carriage
No special requirements.

Discharge
No special requirements.

Clean-up
No special requirements.

Emergency procedures

Special emergency equipment to be carried
Nil
Emergency procedures Nil **Emergency action in the event of fire** Batten down; use ship's fixed fire-fighting installation if fitted. Exclusion of air may be sufficient to control fire. **Medical First Aid** Refer to the *Medical First Aid Guide (MFAG)*, as amended.

CHOPPED RUBBER AND PLASTIC INSULATION

Description
Plastic and rubber insulation material, clean and free from other materials, in granular form.

Characteristics

Angle of repose	Bulk density (kg/m³)	Stowage factor (m³/t)
Not applicable	500 to 570	1.76 to 1.97
Size	**Class**	**Group**
Granular 1 to 4 mm	Not applicable	C

Hazard
No special hazards.

This cargo is non-combustible or has a low fire-risk.

Stowage & segregation
No special requirements.

Hold cleanliness
No special requirements.

Weather precautions
No special requirements.

Loading
Trim in accordance with the relevant provisions required under sections 4 and 5 of the Code.

Precautions
During handling and carriage, no hot work, burning and smoking shall be permitted in the vicinity of the cargo spaces containing this cargo. Prior to shipment, a certificate shall be given to the master by the shipper stating that this cargo consists of clean plastic and rubber material only. When the planned interval between the commencement of loading and the completion of discharge of this cargo exceeds 5 days, the cargo shall not be accepted for loading unless the cargo is to be carried in cargo spaces fitted with a fixed gas fire-extinguishing system. The administration may, if it considers that the planned voyage does not exceed 5 days from the commencement of loading to the completion of discharge, exempt from the requirements of a fitted fixed gas fire-extinguishing system in the cargo spaces for the carriage of this cargo.

Ventilation
No special requirements.

Carriage
No special requirements.

Discharge
No special requirements.

Clean-up
No special requirements.

CHROME PELLETS

Description

Pellets. Moisture: up to 2% maximum.

Characteristics

Angle of repose	Bulk density (kg/m³)	Stowage factor (m³/t)
Not applicable	1667	0.6
Size	**Class**	**Group**
8 to 25 mm	Not applicable	C

Hazard

No special hazards.

This cargo is non-combustible or has a low fire-risk.

Stowage & segregation

No special requirements.

Hold cleanliness

No special requirements.

Weather precautions

No special requirements.

Loading

Trim in accordance with the relevant provisions required under sections 4 and 5 of the Code.

Precautions

No special requirements.

Ventilation

No special requirements.

Carriage

No special requirements.

Discharge

No special requirements.

Clean-up

No special requirements.

CHROMITE ORE

Description
Concentrates or lumpy, dark grey in colour.

Characteristics

Angle of repose	Bulk density (kg/m³)	Stowage factor (m³/t)
Not applicable	2222 to 3030	0.33 to 0.45
Size	**Class**	**Group**
Up to 254 mm	Not applicable	C

Hazard
Toxic by dust inhalation.

This cargo is non-combustible or has a low fire-risk.

Stowage & segregation
No special requirements.

Hold cleanliness
No special requirements.

Weather precautions
No special requirements.

Loading
Trim in accordance with the relevant provisions required under sections 4 and 5 of the Code.

As the density of the cargo is extremely high, the tanktop may be overstressed unless the cargo is evenly spread across the tanktop to equalize the weight distribution. Due consideration shall be paid to ensure that the tanktop is not overstressed during voyage and during loading by a pile of the cargo.

Precautions
Appropriate precautions shall be taken to protect machinery and accommodation spaces from the dust of the cargo. Bilge wells of the cargo spaces shall be protected from ingress of the cargo. Due consideration shall be paid to protect equipment from the dust of the cargo. Persons who may be exposed to the dust of the cargo shall wear goggles or other equivalent dust eye-protection and dust filter masks. Those persons shall wear protective clothing, as necessary.

Ventilation
No special requirements.

Carriage
No special requirements.

Discharge
No special requirements.

Clean-up
No special requirements.

CLAY

Description

Clay is usually light to dark grey and comprises 10% soft lumps and 90% soft grains. The material is usually moist but not wet to the touch. Moisture is up to 25%.

Characteristics

Angle of repose	Bulk density (kg/m³)	Stowage factor (m³/t)
Not applicable	746 to 1515	0.66 to 1.34
Size	**Class**	**Group**
Up to 150 mm	Not applicable	C

Hazard

No special hazards.

This cargo is non-combustible or has a low fire-risk.

Stowage & segregation

No special requirements.

Hold cleanliness

No special requirements.

Weather precautions

This cargo shall be kept as dry as practicable. This cargo shall not be handled during precipitation. During handling of this cargo, all non-working hatches of the cargo spaces into which this cargo is loaded or to be loaded shall be closed.

Loading

Trim in accordance with the relevant provisions required under sections 4 and 5 of the Code.

Precautions

The moisture content of this cargo shall be kept as low as practicable to prevent the cargo becoming glutinous and handling of the cargo becoming extremely difficult.

Ventilation

No special requirements.

Carriage

No special requirements.

Discharge

No special requirements.

Clean-up

Prior to washing out the residues of this cargo, the bilge wells of the cargo spaces shall be cleaned.

COAL
(See also the appendix to this schedule)

Description
Coal (bituminous and anthracite) is a natural, solid, combustible material consisting of amorphous carbon and hydrocarbons.

Characteristics

Angle of repose	Bulk density (kg/m³)	Stowage factor (m³/t)
Not applicable	654 to 1266	0.79 to 1.53
Size	**Class**	**Group**
Up to 50 mm	MHB	B (and A)

Hazard
Coal may create flammable atmospheres, may heat spontaneously, may deplete the oxygen concentration, may corrode metal structures. Can liquefy if predominantly fine 75% less than 5 mm coal.

Stowage & segregation
Refer to the appendix to this schedule.

Hold cleanliness
Clean and dry as relevant to the hazards of the cargo.

Weather precautions
When a cargo may liquefy during voyage in case that the moisture content of the cargo is in excess of its TML and the cargo is carried in a ship other than a specially constructed or fitted cargo ship complying with the requirements in subsection 7.3.2 of this Code, the following provisions shall be complied with:

.1 the moisture content of the cargo shall be kept less than its TML during voyage;

.2 unless expressly provided otherwise in this individual schedule, the cargo shall not be handled during precipitation;

.3 unless expressly provided otherwise in this individual schedule, during handling of the cargo, all non-working hatches of the cargo spaces into which the cargo is loaded or to be loaded shall be closed;

.4 the cargo may be handled during precipitation provided that the actual moisture content of the cargo is sufficiently less than its TML so that the actual moisture content is not liable to be increased beyond the TML by the precipitation; and

.5 the cargo in a cargo space may be discharged during precipitation provided that the total amount of the cargo in the cargo space is to be discharged in the port.

Loading
Trim in accordance with the relevant provisions required under sections 4 and 5 of the Code.

Without reasonable trimming, vertical cracks into the body of the coal may form, permitting oxygen circulation and possible self-heating.

Precautions
Bilge wells shall be clean, dry and covered as appropriate, to prevent ingress of the cargo. *Refer to the appendix to this schedule.*

COAL *(continued)*

Ventilation
Refer to **Special precautions** *in the appendix to this schedule.*

Carriage
Refer to the appendix to this schedule.

Discharge
No special requirements.

Clean-up
No special requirements.

Emergency procedures

Special emergency equipment to be carried Nil
Emergency procedures Nil **Emergency action in the event of fire** Batten down. Exclusion of air may be sufficient to control the fire. **Do not use water.** Seek expert advice and consider heading to the nearest port. **Medical First Aid** Refer to the *Medical First Aid Guide (MFAG)*, as amended.

Remarks
The use of CO_2 or inert gas, if available, should be withheld until fire is apparent.

Appendix

COAL

Properties and characteristics

1. Coals may emit methane, a flammable gas. A methane/air mixture containing between 5% and 16% methane constitutes an explosive atmosphere which can be ignited by sparks or naked flame, e.g., electrical or frictional sparks, a match or lighted cigarette. Methane is lighter than air and may, therefore, accumulate in the upper region of the cargo space or other enclosed spaces. If the cargo space boundaries are not tight, methane can seep through into spaces adjacent to the cargo space.

2. Coals may be subject to oxidation, leading to depletion of oxygen and an increase in carbon dioxide or carbon monoxide concentrations in the cargo space. Carbon monoxide is an odourless gas, slightly lighter than air, and has flammable limits in air of 12% to 75% by volume. It is toxic by inhalation, with an affinity for blood haemoglobin over 200 times that of oxygen.

3. Some coals may heat spontaneously and the spontaneous heating may lead to spontaneous combustion in the cargo space. Flammable and toxic gases, including carbon monoxide, may be produced.

COAL *(appendix, continued)*

4   Some coals may be liable to react with water and produce acids which may cause corrosion. Flammable and toxic gases, including hydrogen, may be produced. Hydrogen is an odourless gas, much lighter than air, and has flammable limits in air of 4% to 75% by volume.

Segregation and stowage requirements

1   Unless expressly provided otherwise, boundaries of cargo spaces where this cargo is carried shall be resistant to fire and liquids.

2   This cargo shall be "separated from" goods of classes 1 (division 1.4), 2, 3, 4 and 5 in packaged form (see IMDG Code) and "separated from" solid bulk materials of classes 4 and 5.1.

3   Stowage of goods of class 5.1 in packaged form or solid bulk materials of class 5.1 above or below this cargo shall be prohibited.

4   The master shall ensure that this cargo is not stowed adjacent to hot areas.

5   This cargo shall be "separated longitudinally by an intervening complete compartment or hold from" goods of class 1 other than division 1.4.

Note: For interpretation of these terms, see section 9.

General requirements for all types of these cargoes

1   Prior to loading, the shipper or his appointed agent shall provide in writing to the master the characteristics of the cargo and the recommended safe handling procedures for loading and transport of the cargo. As a minimum, the cargo's contract specifications for moisture content, sulphur content and size shall be stated, and especially whether the cargo may be liable to emit methane or self-heat.

2   Before loading, the master shall ensure the following:

2.1   All cargo spaces and bilge wells are clean and dry. Any residue of waste material or previous cargo is removed, including removable cargo battens; and

2.2   All electrical cables and components situated in cargo spaces and adjacent enclosed spaces are free from defects. Such cables and electrical components are safe for use in an explosive atmosphere or positively isolated. The provisions of this clause need not apply to engine-rooms where the engine-room is separated from the cargo space by a gastight bulkhead with no direct access.

3   The ship shall be suitably fitted and carry on board appropriate instruments for measuring the following without requiring entry in the cargo space:

3.1   concentration of methane in the atmosphere;

3.2   concentration of oxygen in the atmosphere;

3.3   concentration of carbon monoxide in the atmosphere; and

3.4   pH value of cargo space bilge samples.

4   These instruments shall be regularly serviced and calibrated. Ship personnel shall be trained in the use of such instruments. Details of gas measurement procedures are given at the end of this appendix.

5   It is recommended that means be provided for measuring the temperature of the cargo in the range 0°C to 100°C to enable the measurement of temperature of the cargo while being loaded and during voyage without requiring entry into the cargo space.

6   Smoking and the use of naked flames shall not be permitted in the cargo areas and adjacent spaces and appropriate warning notices shall be posted in conspicuous places. Burning, cutting, chipping, welding or other sources of ignition shall not be permitted in the vicinity of cargo spaces or in other adjacent spaces, unless the space has been properly ventilated and the methane gas measurements indicate it is safe to do so.

COAL (appendix, continued)

7 Prior to departure, the master shall be satisfied that the surface of the material has been trimmed reasonably level to the boundaries of the cargo space to avoid the formation of gas pockets and to prevent air from permeating the body of the briquettes. Casings leading into the cargo space shall be adequately sealed. The shipper shall ensure that the master receives the necessary co-operation from the loading terminal.

8 The atmosphere in the space above the cargo in each space shall be regularly monitored for the concentration of methane, oxygen and carbon monoxide. Details of gas monitoring procedures are given at the end of this appendix. The results of monitoring shall be recorded. The frequency of the monitoring shall be determined based upon the information provided by the shipper and the information obtained through the analysis of the atmosphere in the cargo space.

9 Unless expressly provided otherwise, surface ventilation shall be conducted in all cargo spaces carrying this cargo for the first 24 hours after departure from the loading port. During this period, the atmosphere in the cargo spaces shall be monitored once from one sample point per cargo space and, for the purpose of the gas monitoring, the ventilation shall be stopped for an appropriate period prior to the gas monitoring.

10 When the methane concentrations monitored within 24 hours after departure are at an acceptably low level, the ventilation openings shall be closed and the atmosphere in the cargo spaces shall be monitored. When the methane concentrations monitored within 24 hours after departure are not at an acceptably low level, surface ventilation shall be maintained, except for an appropriate period for gas monitoring, and the atmosphere in the cargo spaces shall be monitored. This procedure shall be followed until the methane concentrations become acceptably low level. In any event, the atmosphere in the cargo spaces shall be monitored on a daily basis.

11 When significant concentrations of methane are subsequently observed in unventilated cargo spaces, the appropriate special precautions for coals emitting methane shall apply.

12 The master shall ensure, as far as practicable, that any gases which may be emitted from this cargo do not accumulate in adjacent enclosed spaces.

13 The master shall ensure that enclosed working spaces such as storerooms, carpenter's shop, passageways, tunnels, etc., are regularly monitored for the presence of methane, oxygen and carbon monoxide. Such spaces shall be adequately ventilated.

14 Regular hold bilge testing shall be systematically carried out during voyage carrying this cargo. If the pH monitoring indicates that a corrosion risk exists, bilges shall be frequently pumped out during the voyage in order to avoid possible accumulation of acids on tanktops and in the bilge system.

15 If the behaviour of the cargo during the voyage differs from that specified in the cargo declaration, the master shall report such differences to the shipper. Such reports will enable the shipper to maintain records on the behaviour of the coal cargoes, so that the information provided to the master can be reviewed in the light of transport experience.

Special precautions
1   Coals emitting methane

When the shipper has informed that the cargo is liable to emit methane or analysis of the atmosphere in the cargo space indicates the presence of methane in excess of 20% of the Lower Explosion Limit (LEL), the following additional precautions shall be taken:

.1 Adequate surface ventilation shall be maintained, except for an appropriate period for the purpose of gas monitoring.

.2 Care shall be taken to remove any accumulated gases prior to operation of the hatch covers or other openings for any reason, including discharging. Care shall be taken to operate hatch covers of the cargo spaces and other openings to avoid creating sparks. Smoking and the use of naked flame shall be prohibited.

COAL *(appendix, continued)*

.3 Personnel shall not be permitted to enter the cargo space or enclosed adjacent spaces unless the space has been ventilated and the atmosphere tested and found to be gas-free and to have sufficient oxygen to support life. Notwithstanding these provisions, emergency entry into the cargo space may be permitted without ventilation, testing the atmosphere or both, provided that the entry into the cargo space is undertaken only by trained personnel wearing self-contained breathing apparatus under the supervision of a responsible officer and special precautions are observed to ensure that no source of ignition is carried into the space.

.4 The master shall ensure that enclosed working spaces such as storerooms, carpenter's shops, passageways, tunnels, etc., are regularly monitored for the presence of methane. Such spaces shall be adequately ventilated and, in the case of mechanical ventilation, only equipment safe for use in an explosive atmosphere shall be used.

2 Self-heating coals

When the shipper informed that the cargo is likely to self-heat or analysis of the atmosphere in the cargo space indicates an increasing concentration of carbon monoxide, then the following additional precautions shall be taken:

.1 The cargo spaces shall be closed immediately after completion of loading in each cargo space. The hatch covers may also be additionally sealed with a suitable sealing tape. Only natural surface ventilation shall be permitted and ventilation shall be limited to the absolute minimum time necessary to remove methane which may have accumulated.

.2 Personnel shall not enter the cargo space during voyage, unless they are wearing self-contained breathing apparatus and access is critical to safety of life and the safety of the ship.

.3 Prior to loading, temperature of this cargo shall be monitored. This cargo shall only be accepted for loading when the temperature of the cargo is not higher than 55°C.

.4 When the carbon monoxide level is increasing steadily, a potential self-heating may be developing. In such a case, the cargo space shall be completely closed and all ventilation ceased, and the master shall seek expert advice immediately. Water shall not be used for cooling material or fighting coal cargo fires at sea, but may be used for cooling the boundaries of the cargo space.

.5 When the carbon monoxide level in any cargo space reaches 50 ppm or exhibits a steady rise over three consecutive days, a self-heating condition may be developing and the master shall inform the shipper and the company of, at least, the following information if an accurate assessment of the situation is to be achieved:

.5.1 identity of the cargo spaces involved; monitoring results covering carbon monoxide, methane and oxygen concentrations;

.5.2 if available, temperature of the cargo, location and method used to obtain results;

.5.3 time gas sample taken (monitoring routine);

.5.4 time ventilators opened/closed;

.5.5 quantity of coal in hold(s) involved;

.5.6 type of coal as per cargo information, and any special precautions indicated on information;

.5.7 date loaded, and ETA at intended discharge port (which shall be specified); and

.5.8 comments or observations from the ship's master.

COAL *(appendix, continued)*

3 Gravity-fed self-unloading bulk carrier

3.1 A gravity-fed self-unloading bulk carrier means a vessel that has gravity fed systems from the bottom of cargo holds, using gates that may be opened or closed to feed the cargo onto conveyor belts. Such belts run in a fore-and-aft direction underneath the holds; from there the cargo is carried by means of conveyor systems to the deck and discharged onto shore with a self-unloading boom that can extend over the shore and has a conveyor belt. This is not applicable for the vessels with unloading systems such as cranes and grabs.

3.2 When this cargo is carried on a gravity-fed self-unloading bulk carrier, the following requirements of this appendix need not apply:

– paragraph 1 of "Segregation and stowage requirements"; and

– paragraph 9 of "General requirements for all types of these cargoes".

3.3 Loaded voyage procedures for atmospheric monitoring of cargoes

3.3.1 Bulk coal cargo safety procedures

3.3.1.1 These requirements apply when these cargoes are to be carried on a gravity-fed self-unloading bulk carrier. It is recommended that a document, such as a flow chart, describing cargo operations and carriage procedures for these cargoes be provided to the ship by the vessel's operator.

3.4 Ventilation

3.4.1 When ventilating, it shall be ensured that excess air does not ingress excessively into the body of the cargo of coal as this may eventually promote self-heating.

3.4.2 Due to the presence of non-airtight unloading gates at the bottom of the cargo hoppers just above the tunnels, the following methods of ventilation shall be used:

– if methane is detected in the tunnel, it shall be "positive-pressure" ventilated (more supply than exhaust in the tunnels, to remove methane gas); and

– if carbon monoxide is detected in the tunnel, it shall be "negative-pressure" ventilated (more exhaust than supply in the tunnels, to remove carbon monoxide). The release of carbon monoxide may be an indication of self-heating.

Procedures for gas monitoring of coal cargoes

1 Observations

1.1 Carbon monoxide monitoring, when conducted in accordance with the following procedures, will provide a reliable early indication of self-heating within this cargo. This allows preventive action to be considered without delay.

A steady rise in the level of carbon monoxide detected within a cargo space is a conclusive indication that self-heating is taking place.

1.2 All vessels engaged in the carriage of this cargo shall carry on board an instrument for measuring methane, oxygen and carbon monoxide gas concentrations, to enable the monitoring of the atmosphere within the cargo space. This instrument shall be regularly serviced and calibrated in accordance with the manufacturer's instructions. Care shall be exercised in interpreting methane measurements carried out in the low oxygen concentrations often found in unventilated cargo holds. The catalytic sensors normally used for the detection of methane rely on the presence of sufficient oxygen for accurate measurement. This phenomenon does not affect the measurement of carbon monoxide, or measurement of methane by infrared sensor. Further guidance may be obtained from the instrument manufacturer.

COAL *(appendix, continued)*

2   Sampling and measurement procedure

2.1   Equipment

2.1.1   An instrument which is capable of measuring methane, oxygen and carbon monoxide concentrations shall be provided on board a ship carrying this cargo. The instrument shall be fitted with an aspirator, flexible connection and a length of spark-proof metal tubing to enable a representative sample to be obtained from within the square of the hatch.

2.1.2   When recommended by the manufacturer, a suitable filter shall be used to protect the instrument against the ingress of moisture. The presence of even a small amount of moisture will compromise the accuracy of the measurement.

2.2   Siting of sampling points

2.2.1   In order to obtain meaningful information about the behaviour of this cargo in a cargo space, gas measurements shall be made via one sample point per cargo space. To ensure flexibility of measurement in adverse weather, two sample points shall be provided per cargo space, one on the port side and one on the starboard side of the hatch cover or hatch coaming. (Refer to the diagram of gas sampling point.) Measurement from either of these locations is satisfactory.

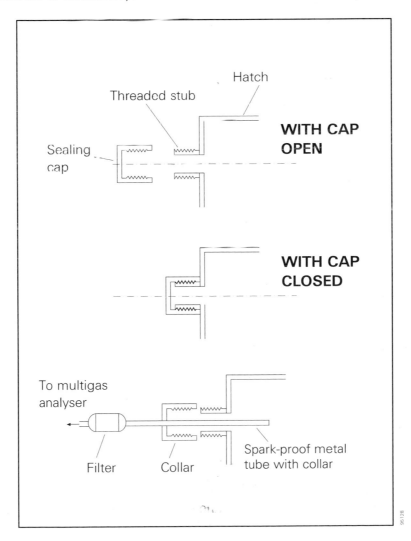

Diagram of gas sampling point

COAL (appendix, continued)

2.2.2 Each sample point shall comprise a hole of diameter approximately 12 mm positioned as near to the top of the hatch coaming as possible. It shall be sealed with a sealing cap to prevent ingress of water and air. It is essential that this cap is securely replaced after each measurement to maintain a tight seal.

2.2.3 The provisions of any sample point shall not compromise the seaworthiness of the vessel.

2.3 *Measurement*

2.3.1 The explanation on procedures for measurement is as follows:

.1 remove the sealing cap, insert the spark-proof metal tube into the sampling point and tighten the collar to ensure an adequate seal;

.2 connect the instrument to the sampling tube;

.3 draw a sample of the atmosphere through the tube, using the aspirator, until steady readings are obtained;

.4 log the results on a form which records cargo space, date and time for each measurement; and

.5 put back the sealing cap.

2.4 *Measurement strategy*

The identification of incipient self-heating from measurement of gas concentrations is more readily achieved under unventilated conditions. This is not always desirable because of the possibility of the accumulation of methane to dangerous concentrations. This is primarily, but not exclusively, a problem in the early stages of a voyage. Therefore it is recommended that cargo spaces are initially ventilated until measured methane concentrations are at an acceptably low level.

2.5 *Measurement in unventilated holds*

Under normal conditions one measurement per day is sufficient as a precautionary measure. However, if carbon monoxide levels are higher than 30 ppm then the frequency shall be increased to at least twice a day at suitably spaced intervals. Any additional results shall be logged.

2.6 *Measurement in ventilated holds*

2.6.1 If the presence of methane is such that the ventilators are required to remain open, then a different procedure shall be applied to enable the onset of any incipient self-heating to be detected.

2.6.2 To obtain meaningful data the ventilators shall be closed for a period before the measurements are taken. This period may be chosen to suit the operational requirements of the vessel, but it is recommended that it is not less than four hours. It is vital in the interests of data interpretation that the shutdown time is constant whichever time period is selected. These measurements shall be taken on a daily basis.

2.7 *Measurement in cargo and self-unloading spaces of gravity fed self-unloading bulk carrier*

2.7.1 Measurement in unventilated cargo and self-unloading spaces

2.7.1.1 When the shipper has declared that the coal cargo has or may have self-heating characteristics, the holds shall not be ventilated unless otherwise specified in this section.

COAL *(appendix, concluded)*

2.7.1.2 Under normal conditions, one measurement per day is sufficient as a precautionary measure. If carbon monoxide levels are higher than 30 ppm then the frequency of measurements shall be increased to at least twice daily, at suitable intervals. Any additional results shall be logged.

2.7.1.3 If the carbon monoxide level in any hold indicates a steady rise or reaches 50 ppm, a self-heating condition may be developing and the owners of the vessel shall be notified as outlined in the procedures. Above this level, the vessel shall operate on "negative-pressure" ventilation, in order to reduce the amount of carbon monoxide. Regular monitoring of carbon monoxide levels shall continue.

2.7.1.4 Persons entering cargo or unloading spaces with carbon monoxide levels higher than 30 ppm shall not do so without self-contained breathing apparatus.*

2.7.2 *Measurement in ventilated cargo and self-unloading spaces*

2.7.2.1 If the presence of methane is indicated by monitor, and such that ventilation is required, then a different procedure shall be applied to enable the onset of any possible self-heating to be detected. "Positive-pressure" or "through" ventilation shall be operated to remove the methane.

2.7.2.2 To obtain meaningful data, the ventilators and/or ventilation shall be closed for a period before measurements are taken. This period may be chosen to suit the operational requirements of the vessel, but it is recommended that it is not less than four hours. It is vital, in the interests of data interpretation, that the shutdown time is constant whichever time period is selected. These measurements shall be taken on a daily basis. If the carbon monoxide results exhibit a steady rise, or exceed 50 ppm on any day, the owner shall be notified.

2.7.2.3 In addition, the following points shall be considered:

at no time shall ventilation be shut down when crew members are in the self-unloading spaces;

– special fire-fighting equipment and/or procedures may be necessary for the vessel; and

– establish specific crew training for gravity-fed self-unloading bulk carriers.

---

* Refer to the Recommendations for entering enclosed spaces aboard ships, adopted by the Organization by resolution A.864(20), as may be amended (see the supplement of this publication).

COAL SLURRY

Description
Coal slurry is a mixture of fine particles of coal and water.

Characteristics

Angle of repose	Bulk density (kg/m³)	Stowage factor (m³/t)
Not applicable	870 to 1020	0.98 to 1.15
Size	**Class**	**Group**
Under 1 mm	Not applicable	A

Hazard
Coal slurry is liable to liquefy during sea transport. Spontaneous combustion is possible if the coal dries out but is unlikely under normal conditions.

This cargo is non-combustible or has a low fire-risk.

Stowage & segregation
No special requirements.

Hold cleanliness
Clean and dry as relevant to the hazards of the cargo.

Weather precautions
When a cargo is carried in a ship other than a specially constructed or fitted cargo ship complying with the requirements in subsection 7.3.2 of this Code, the following provisions shall be complied with:

.1 the moisture content of the cargo shall be kept less than its TML during voyage;

.2 unless expressly provided otherwise in this individual schedule, the cargo shall not be handled during precipitation;

.3 unless expressly provided otherwise in this individual schedule, during handling of the cargo, all non-working hatches of the cargo spaces into which the cargo is loaded or to be loaded shall be closed;

.4 the cargo may be handled during precipitation provided that the actual moisture content of the cargo is sufficiently less than its TML so that the actual moisture content is not liable to be increased beyond the TML by the precipitation; and

.5 the cargo in a cargo space may be discharged during precipitation provided that the total amount of the cargo in the cargo space is to be discharged in the port.

Loading
Trim in accordance with the relevant provisions required under sections 4 and 5 of the Code.

Precautions
Bilge wells shall be clean, dry and covered as appropriate, to prevent ingress of the cargo.

Ventilation
As this cargo, in general, may emit methane, the cargo spaces carrying this cargo shall be tested regularly, using a suitable gas detector, and natural surface ventilation shall be conducted, as necessary.

COAL SLURRY *(concluded)*

Carriage

The appearance of the surface of this cargo shall be checked regularly during voyage. If free water above the cargo or fluid state of the cargo is observed during voyage, the master shall take appropriate actions to prevent cargo shifting and potential capsize of the ship, and give consideration to seeking emergency entry into a place of refuge.

Discharge

No special requirements.

Clean-up

No special requirements.

COARSE CHOPPED TYRES

Description
Chopped or shredded fragments of used tyres in coarse size.

Characteristics

Angle of repose	Bulk density (kg/m^3)	Stowage factor (m^3/t)
Not applicable	555	1.8
Size	**Class**	**Group**
15 cm × 20 cm approximately	Not applicable	C

Hazard
May self-heat slowly if contaminated by oily residual, if not properly aged before shipment and if offered to the shipment in smaller size than indicated in "Characteristics".

This cargo is non-combustible or has a low fire-risk.

Stowage & segregation
No special requirements.

Hold cleanliness
Clean and dry as relevant to the hazards of the cargo.

Weather precautions
This cargo shall be kept as dry as practicable before loading, during loading and during voyage. This cargo shall not be loaded during precipitation. During loading of this cargo, all non-working hatches of the cargo spaces to which this cargo is loaded or to be loaded shall be closed.

Loading
Trim in accordance with the relevant provisions required under sections 4 and 5 of the Code.

Precautions
During handling and carriage, no hot work, burning and smoking shall be permitted in the vicinity of the cargo spaces containing this cargo. Prior to shipment, a certificate shall be given to the master by the shipper stating that this cargo is free of oily products or oily residual and has been stored under cover but in the open air for not less than 15 days prior to shipment.

When the planned interval between the commencement of loading and the completion of discharge of this cargo exceeds 5 days, the cargo shall not be accepted for loading unless the cargo is to be carried in cargo spaces fitted with a fixed gas fire-extinguishing system. The administration may, if it considers that the planned voyage does not exceed 5 days from the commencement of loading to the completion of discharge, grant exemption from the requirements of a fitted fixed gas fire-extinguishing system in the cargo spaces for the carriage of this cargo.

Ventilation
No special requirements.

Carriage
No special requirements.

COARSE CHOPPED TYRES *(concluded)*

Discharge

No special requirements.

Clean-up

No special requirements.

COKE

Description
Grey lumps may contain fines (Breeze).

Characteristics

Angle of repose	Bulk density (kg/m^3)	Stowage factor (m^3/t)
Not applicable	341 to 800	1.25 to 2.93
Size	**Class**	**Group**
Up to 200 mm	Not applicable	C

Hazard
No special hazards.

This cargo is non-combustible or has a low fire-risk.

Stowage & segregation
No special requirements.

Hold cleanliness
No special requirements.

Weather precautions
No special requirements.

Loading
Trim in accordance with the relevant provisions required under sections 4 and 5 of the Code.

Precautions
Bilge wells shall be clean, dry and covered as appropriate, to prevent ingress of the cargo.

Ventilation
No special requirements.

Carriage
No special requirements.

Discharge
No special requirements.

Clean-up
After discharge of this cargo, the bilge wells and the scuppers of the cargo spaces shall be checked and any blockage in the bilge wells and the scuppers shall be removed.

COKE BREEZE

Description
Greyish powder.

Characteristics

Angle of repose	Bulk density (kg/m³)	Stowage factor (m³/t)
Not applicable	556	1.8
Size	**Class**	**Group**
Less than 10 mm	Not applicable	A

Hazard
Coke breeze is liable to flow if it has sufficiently high moisture content.

This cargo is non-combustible or has a low fire-risk.

Stowage & segregation
No special requirements.

Hold cleanliness
No special requirements.

Weather precautions
When a cargo is carried in a ship other than a specially constructed or fitted cargo ship complying with the requirements in subsection 7.3.2 of this Code, the following provisions shall be complied with:

.1   the moisture content of the cargo shall be kept less than its TML during voyage;

.2   unless expressly provided otherwise in this individual schedule, the cargo shall not be handled during precipitation;

.3   unless expressly provided otherwise in this individual schedule, during handling of the cargo, all non-working hatches of the cargo spaces into which the cargo is loaded or to be loaded shall be closed;

.4   the cargo may be handled during precipitation provided that the actual moisture content of the cargo is sufficiently less than its TML so that the actual moisture content is not liable to be increased beyond the TML by the precipitation; and

.5   the cargo in a cargo space may be discharged during precipitation provided that the total amount of the cargo in the cargo space is to be discharged in the port.

Loading
Trim in accordance with the relevant provisions required under sections 4 and 5 of the Code.

Precautions
Bilge wells shall be clean, dry and covered as appropriate, to prevent ingress of the cargo.

Ventilation
The cargo spaces carrying this cargo shall not be ventilated during voyage.

COKE BREEZE *(concluded)*

Carriage

The appearance of the surface of this cargo shall be checked regularly during voyage. If free water above the cargo or fluid state of the cargo is observed during voyage, the master shall take appropriate actions to prevent cargo shifting and potential capsize of the ship, and give consideration to seeking emergency entry into a place of refuge.

Discharge

No special requirements.

Clean-up

After discharge of this cargo, the bilge wells and the scuppers of the cargo spaces shall be checked and any blockage in the bilge wells and the scuppers shall be removed.

COLEMANITE

Description

A natural hydrated calcium borate. Fine to lumps, light grey appearance similar to clay. Moisture approximately 7%.

Characteristics

Angle of repose	Bulk density (kg/m³)	Stowage factor (m³/t)
Not applicable	1639	0.61
Size	**Class**	**Group**
Up to 300 mm	Not applicable	C

Hazard

No special hazards.

This cargo is non-combustible or has a low fire-risk.

Stowage & segregation

No special requirements.

Hold cleanliness

No special requirements.

Weather precautions

No special requirements.

Loading

Trim in accordance with the relevant provisions required under sections 4 and 5 of the Code.

Precautions

No special requirements.

Ventilation

No special requirements.

Carriage

No special requirements.

Discharge

No special requirements.

Clean-up

No special requirements.

COPPER GRANULES

Description

Sphere-shaped pebbles. 75% Copper with lead, tin, zinc, traces of others. Moisture content 1.5% approximately. Light grey colour when dry, dark green when wet. Odourless.

Characteristics

Angle of repose	Bulk density (kg/m³)	Stowage factor (m³/t)
Not applicable	4000 to 4545	0.22 to 0.25
Size	**Class**	**Group**
Fines up to 10 mm Clinkers up to 50 mm	Not applicable	C

Hazard

No special hazards.

This cargo is non-combustible or has a low fire-risk.

Stowage & segregation

No special requirements.

Hold cleanliness

No special requirements.

Weather precautions

No special requirements.

Loading

Trim in accordance with the relevant provisions required under sections 4 and 5 of the Code.

As the density of the cargo is extremely high, the tanktop may be overstressed unless the cargo is evenly spread across the tanktop to equalize the weight distribution. Due consideration shall be paid to ensure that the tanktop is not overstressed during voyage and during loading by a pile of the cargo.

Precautions

No special requirements.

Ventilation

No special requirements.

Carriage

No special requirements.

Discharge

No special requirements.

Clean-up

No special requirements.

COPPER MATTE

Description

Crude black copper ore. Composed of 75% copper and 25% impurities. Small metallic round stones or pellets. Odourless.

Characteristics

Angle of repose	Bulk density (kg/m^3)	Stowage factor (m^3/t)
Not applicable	2857 to 4000	0.25 to 0.35
Size	**Class**	**Group**
3 mm to 25 mm	Not applicable	C

Hazard

No special hazards.

This cargo is non-combustible or has a low fire-risk.

Stowage & segregation

No special requirements.

Hold cleanliness

No special requirements.

Weather precautions

No special requirements.

Loading

Trim in accordance with the relevant provisions required under sections 4 and 5 of the Code.

As the density of the cargo is extremely high, the tanktop may be overstressed unless the cargo is evenly spread across the tanktop to equalize the weight distribution. Due consideration shall be paid to ensure that the tanktop is not overstressed during voyage and during loading by a pile of the cargo.

Precautions

No special requirements.

Ventilation

No special requirements.

Carriage

No special requirements.

Discharge

No special requirements.

Clean-up

No special requirements.

COPRA (dry) UN 1363

Description

Dried kernels of coconuts with a penetrating rancid odour which may taint other cargoes.

Characteristics

Angle of repose	Bulk density (kg/m^3)	Stowage factor (m^3/t)
Not applicable	500	2.0
Size	**Class**	**Group**
Not applicable	4.2	B

Hazard

Liable to heat and ignite spontaneously, especially when in contact with water. Liable to cause oxygen depletion in the cargo space.

Stowage & segregation

This cargo shall not be stowed on or adjacent to heated surfaces, including fuel oil tanks.

Hold cleanliness

Clean and dry as relevant to the hazards of the cargo.

Weather precautions

This cargo shall be kept as dry as practicable. This cargo shall not be handled during precipitation. During handling of this cargo, all non-working hatches of the cargo spaces into which this cargo is loaded or to be loaded shall be closed.

Loading

Trim in accordance with the relevant provisions required under sections 4 and 5 of the Code.

This cargo shall not be accepted for loading when wet.

Precautions

This cargo shall only be accepted for loading when the cargo has been weathered for at least one month before shipment or when the shipper provides the master with a certificate issued by a person recognized by the competent authority of the country of origin stating that the moisture content of the cargo is not more than 5%. Smoking and the use of naked lights in cargo spaces and adjacent areas shall be prohibited. Entry into the cargo space for this cargo shall not be permitted until the cargo space has been ventilated and the atmosphere tested for concentration of oxygen.

Ventilation

Surface ventilation only, either natural or mechanical, shall be conducted, as necessary, during the voyage for this cargo.

Carriage

The temperature of this cargo shall be measured and recorded regularly during voyage to monitor for possible self-heating.

Discharge

No special requirements.

Clean-up

No special requirements.

COPRA (dry) UN 1363 *(concluded)*

Emergency procedures

Special emergency equipment to be carried

Nil

Emergency procedures

Nil

Emergency action in the event of fire

Batten down; use ship's fixed fire-fighting installation, if fitted.
Exclusion of air may be sufficient to control fire.

Medical First Aid

Refer to the *Medical First Aid Guide (MFAG)*, as amended.

CRYOLITE

Description

A fluoride of sodium and aluminium used in the production of aluminium and for ceramic glazes. Grey pellets.

Characteristics

Angle of repose	Bulk density (kg/m³)	Stowage factor (m³/t)
Not applicable	1429	0.70
Size	**Class**	**Group**
6.4 mm to 12.7 mm	Not applicable	C

Hazard

Prolonged contact may cause serious damage to the skin and nervous system.

This cargo is non-combustible or has a low fire-risk.

Stowage & segregation

No special requirements.

Hold cleanliness

No special requirements.

Weather precautions

No special requirements.

Loading

Trim in accordance with the relevant provisions required under sections 4 and 5 of the Code.

Precautions

Appropriate precautions shall be taken to protect machinery and accommodation spaces from the dust of the cargo. Bilge wells of the cargo spaces shall be protected from ingress of the cargo. Due consideration shall be paid to protect equipment from the dust of the cargo. Persons who may be exposed to the dust of the cargo shall wear goggles or other equivalent dust eye-protection and dust filter masks. Those persons shall wear protective clothing, as necessary.

Ventilation

No special requirements.

Carriage

No special requirements.

Discharge

No special requirements.

Clean-up

No special requirements.

DIAMMONIUM PHOSPHATE (D.A.P.)

Description

Odourless white crystals or powder. Depending on source, it can be dusty. Hygroscopic.

Characteristics

Angle of repose	Bulk density (kg/m³)	Stowage factor (m³/t)
30° to 40°	833 to 999	1.10 to 1.20
Size	**Class**	**Group**
Diameter: 2.54 mm	Not applicable	C

Hazard

No special hazards.

This cargo is non-combustible or has a low fire-risk.

This cargo is hygroscopic and may harden in the cargo space under humid conditions.

Stowage & segregation

No special requirements.

Hold cleanliness

Clean and dry as relevant to the hazards of the cargo.

Weather precautions

This cargo shall be kept as dry as practicable. This cargo shall not be handled during precipitation. During handling of this cargo, all non-working hatches of the cargo spaces into which this cargo is loaded or to be loaded shall be closed.

Loading

Trim in accordance with the relevant provisions required under sections 4 and 5 of the Code.

Precautions

Appropriate precautions shall be taken to protect machinery and accommodation spaces from the dust of the cargo. Bilge wells of the cargo spaces shall be protected from ingress of the cargo. Due consideration shall be paid to protect equipment from the dust of the cargo. Persons who may be exposed to the dust of the cargo shall wear protective clothing, goggles or other equivalent dust eye-protection and dust filter masks, as necessary.

Ventilation

The cargo spaces carrying this cargo shall not be ventilated during voyage.

Carriage

Condensation in the cargo spaces carrying this cargo, sweating of this cargo and entering of water from hatch covers to the cargo spaces shall be checked regularly during the voyage. Due attention shall be paid to the sealing of hatches of the cargo spaces.

Discharge

If this cargo has hardened, it shall be trimmed to avoid the formation of overhangs, as necessary.

Clean-up

After discharge of this cargo, particular attention shall be paid to bilge wells of the cargo spaces.

DIRECT REDUCED IRON (A)
Briquettes, hot-moulded

Description

Direct reduced iron (DRI) (A) is a metallic grey material, moulded in a briquette form, emanating from a densification process whereby the direct reduced iron (DRI) feed material is moulded at a temperature greater than 650°C and has a density greater than 5000 kg/m³. Fines and small particles (under 6.35 mm) shall not exceed 5% by weight.

Characteristics

Angle of repose	Bulk density (kg/m³)	Stowage factor (m³/t)
Not applicable	2500 to 3300	0.3 to 0.4 To be verified by the shipper
Size	**Class**	**Group**
Approximate size: Length 50 mm to 140 mm Width 40 mm to 100 mm Thickness 20 mm to 50 mm Briquette weight 0.2 to 3.0 kg Fines and small particles under 6.35 mm	MHB	B

Hazard

Temporary increase in temperature of about 30°C due to self-heating may be expected after material handling in bulk. The material may slowly evolve hydrogen after contact with water (notably saline water). Hydrogen is a flammable gas that can form an explosive mixture when mixed with air in concentration above 4% by volume. It is liable to cause oxygen depletion in cargo spaces. This cargo is non-combustible or has a low fire-risk.

Stowage & segregation

"Separated from" goods of class 1 (division 1.4S), 2, 3, 4 and 5 and class 8 acids in packaged form (see IMDG Code).

"Separated from" solid bulk materials of classes 4 and 5.

"Separated longitudinally by an intervening complete compartment or hold from" goods of class 1 other than division 1.4S.

Boundaries of compartments where this cargo is carried shall be resistant to fire and passage of liquid.

Hold cleanliness

The cargo spaces shall be clean, dry and free from salt and residues of previous cargoes. Prior to loading, wooden fixtures such as battens, loose dunnage, debris and combustible materials shall be removed.

Weather precautions

This cargo shall be kept as dry as practicable during loading and the voyage. Open storage is acceptable prior to loading. This cargo shall not be loaded onto ships or transferred between ships or barges during precipitation. During loading of this cargo, all non-working hatches of the cargo spaces into which this cargo is loaded or to be loaded shall be kept closed. Only when weather permits may non-working hatch covers be left open for a minimum of 1 hour after completion of each pour, to allow cooling after cargo handling in bulk.

DIRECT REDUCED IRON (A)
Briquettes, hot-moulded *(continued)*

Loading

Prior to loading this cargo, the shipper shall provide the master with a certificate issued by a competent person recognized by the national administration of the port of loading stating that the cargo, at the time of loading, is suitable for shipment and that it conforms with the requirements of this Code; that the quantity of fines and small particles (up to 6.35 mm in size) is no more than 5% by weight; the moisture content is less than 1.0% and the temperature does not exceed 65°C.

This cargo shall not be loaded when the temperature is in excess of 65°C, if its moisture content is in excess of 1.0% or if the quantity of fines and small particles (up to 6.35 mm in size) exceeds 5% by weight.

Appropriate precautions shall be taken during loading in order to have a cargo composed of essentially whole briquettes. The cargo shall be loaded in such a way so as to minimize breakage of briquettes and the additional generation of fines and small particles and concentration of fines in any area of the cargo. The addition of fines and particles less than 6.35 mm or dust in homogenous cargoes of briquettes shall be prohibited.

Trim in accordance with the relevant provisions required under sections 4 and 5 of the Code. Due consideration shall be given to evenly spreading the cargo across the tanktop to minimize the concentration of fines.

The cargo temperature shall be monitored during loading and recorded in a log detailing the temperature for each lot of cargo loaded, a copy of which shall be provided to the master. After loading, a certificate, confirming that throughout the whole consignment the fines and small particles (under 6.35 mm in size) are less than 5% by weight, shall be issued by a competent person recognized by the national administration of the port of loading.

Precautions

The carrier's nominated technical persons or other representatives shall have reasonable access to stockpiles and loading installations for inspection.

Shippers shall provide comprehensive information on the cargo and safety procedures to be followed in the event of emergency. The shipper may also provide advice in amplification of this Code but the advice shall not be contrary thereto in respect of safety.

Where practicable, ballast tanks adjacent to the cargo spaces containing this cargo, other than double-bottom tanks, shall be kept empty. Weather-deck closures and hatch covers shall be inspected and tested to ensure integrity and weathertightness, which shall be maintained throughout the voyage.

Appropriate precautions shall be taken to protect machinery, equipment and accommodation spaces from the dust of the cargo. Radars and exposed radiocommunications equipment of the ship shall be protected from the dust of this cargo. Bilge wells of the cargo spaces shall be clean, dry and protected from ingress of the cargo, using non-combustible material. Persons who may be exposed to the dust of the cargo shall wear protective clothing, goggles or other equivalent dust eye-protection and dust filter masks, as necessary.

During handling of this cargo, "NO SMOKING" signs shall be posted on decks and in areas adjacent to cargo spaces, and no naked lights shall be permitted in these areas.

Cargo spaces containing this cargo and adjacent spaces may become oxygen-depleted. Flammable gas may also build up in these spaces. All precautions shall be taken upon entering the cargo and adjacent spaces.

DIRECT REDUCED IRON (A)
Briquettes, hot-moulded *(continued)*

Ventilation

Surface ventilation only, either natural or mechanical, shall be conducted, as necessary, during the voyage for this cargo. On no account shall air be directed into the body of the cargo. When mechanical ventilation is used, the fans shall be certified as explosion-proof and shall prevent any spark generation, thereby avoiding the possibility of ignition of hydrogen–air mixture. Suitable wire mesh guards shall be fitted over inlet and outlet ventilation openings. Ventilation shall be such that escaping gases cannot enter living quarters in hazardous concentrations.

Carriage

For quantitative measurements of hydrogen, a suitable detector shall be on board while this cargo is carried. The detector shall be suitable for use in an oxygen-depleted atmosphere and of a type certified safe for use in an explosive atmosphere. The concentrations of hydrogen in the cargo spaces carrying this cargo shall be measured regularly during the voyage, and the results of the measurements shall be recorded and kept on board for a minimum of two years. When the monitored hydrogen concentration is higher than 1% (>25% LEL) by volume, appropriate safety precautions shall be taken in accordance with those procedures provided by the shipper in case of emergency. If in doubt, expert advice shall be sought.

Bilge wells shall be checked regularly for the presence of water. If water is found, it shall be removed by pumping or draining the bilge wells.

The temperature of the cargo shall be taken regularly during the voyage and a record kept on board for a minimum of two years. If the temperature in the cargo space exceeds 65°C, appropriate safety precautions shall be taken in accordance with the procedures provided by the shipper in case of emergency. If in doubt, expert advice shall be sought.

Discharge

The hydrogen concentration in the cargo space shall be measured immediately before any opening action of the hatch covers. If the hydrogen concentration is greater than 1% (>25% LEL) by volume, all appropriate safety precautions in conformity with the procedures provided by the shipper or the recommendations of the competent authority shall be taken. If in doubt, expert advice shall be sought.

During discharge, a fine spray of fresh water may be applied to this cargo, for dust control, only when the cargo will be stored in an open area. It is not recommended to apply a fine spray of fresh water to this cargo when it will be stored in an enclosed space or is to be transhipped.

Clean-up

Accumulations of dust from this cargo on deck or in proximity to cargo spaces shall be removed as quickly as possible. Consideration shall be given to carefully cleaning exposed radio-communications equipment to which dust from the cargo might adhere, such as radar, radio aerials, VHF installations, AIS and GPS. Hosing with seawater should be avoided.

DIRECT REDUCED IRON (A)
Briquettes, hot-moulded *(concluded)*

Emergency procedures

<table>
<tr><td align="center">

Special emergency equipment to be carried

Nil

</td></tr>
<tr><td align="center">

Emergency procedures

Nil

Emergency action in the event of fire

Do not use water. Do not use steam. Do not use CO_2.

Batten down.

The specific procedures in the event of emergency provided by the shipper should be consulted and followed, as appropriate. If in doubt, expert advice should be sought as quickly as possible.

Preparations should be made for grab discharge if serious heating occurs.

Medical First Aid

Refer to the *Medical First Aid Guide (MFAG)*, as amended.

</td></tr>
</table>

DIRECT REDUCED IRON (B)
Lumps, pellets, cold-moulded briquettes

Description
Direct reduced iron (DRI) (B) is a highly porous, black/grey metallic material formed by the reduction (removal of oxygen) of iron oxide at temperatures below the fusion point of iron. Cold-moulded briquettes are defined as those which have been moulded at a temperature less than 650°C or which have a density of less than 5000 kg/m^3. Fines and small particles under 6.35 mm in size shall not exceed 5% by weight.

Characteristics

Angle of repose	Bulk density (kg/m^3)	Stowage factor (m^3/t)
Not applicable	1750 to 2000	0.5 to 0.57

Size	Class	Group
Lumps and pellets: Average particle size 6.35 mm to 25 mm. Cold-moulded briquettes: Approximate maximum dimensions 35 mm to 40 mm. Fines and small particles under 6.35 mm up to 5% by weight.	MHB	B

Hazard
Temporary increase in temperature of about 30°C due to self-heating may be expected after material handling in bulk.

There is a risk of overheating, fire and explosion during transport. This cargo reacts with air and with fresh water or seawater to produce heat and hydrogen. Hydrogen is a flammable gas that can form an explosive mixture when mixed with air in concentrations above 4% by volume. The reactivity of this cargo depends upon the origin of the ore, the process and temperature of reduction, and the subsequent ageing procedures. Cargo heating may generate very high temperatures that are sufficient to ignite the cargo. Build-up of fines may also lead to self-heating, auto-ignition and explosion. Oxygen in cargo spaces and enclosed spaces may be depleted.

Stowage & segregation
"Separated from" goods of classes 1 (division 1.4S), 2, 3, 4 and 5, and class 8 acids in packaged form (See IMDG Code).

"Separated from" solid bulk materials of classes 4 and 5.

Goods of class 1, other than division 1.4S, shall not be carried in the same ship.

Boundaries of compartments where this cargo is carried shall be resistant to fire and passage of liquid.

Hold cleanliness
The cargo spaces shall be clean, dry and free from salt and residues of previous cargoes. Prior to loading, wooden fixtures such as battens, loose dunnage, debris and combustible materials shall be removed.

Weather precautions
The cargo shall be kept dry at all times during storage, before and during loading, and during transportation. The cargo shall not be loaded onto ships, or transferred between ships or barges, during precipitation. During loading of this cargo, all non-working hatches of cargo spaces into which this cargo is loaded, or is to be loaded, shall be kept closed.

DIRECT REDUCED IRON (B)
Lumps, pellets, cold-moulded briquettes *(continued)*

Loading

Prior to loading, the terminal shall ensure that the conveyor belts used for loading this cargo contain no accumulation of water or other substances. Each time cargo operations are commenced or restarted, particularly after rain or washing down, any loading belt shall be operated empty and not over a ship's cargo space.

Prior to loading, an ultrasonic test or another equivalent method with a suitable instrument shall be conducted to ensure weathertightness of the hatch covers and closing arrangements and all readings shall confirm weathertightness.

Prior to loading this cargo, the shipper shall provide the master with a certificate issued by a competent person recognized by the national administration of the port of loading stating that the cargo, at the time of loading, is suitable for shipment, and that it conforms with the requirements of this Code; that the quantity of fines and small particles is no more than 5% by weight; that the moisture content is less than 0.3%; and that the temperature does not exceed 65°C. This certificate shall state the date of manufacture for each lot of cargo to be loaded in order to meet the loading criteria in regards to ageing and material temperature.

The cargo shall not be accepted for loading when its temperature is in excess of 65°C or if its moisture content is in excess of 0.3% or if the quantity of fines and small particles exceeds 5% by weight. Any cargo that has been wetted, or is known to have been wetted, shall not be loaded into any cargo space.

Prior to loading, provision shall be made to introduce a dry, inert gas at tanktop level so that the inert gas purges the air from the cargo and fills the free volume above. Nitrogen is preferred for this purpose. All vents, accesses and other openings, such as coaming drains, that could allow the inert atmosphere to be lost from cargo spaces carrying this cargo shall be closed and sealed.

The cargo shall be loaded in such a way as to minimize both the breakage of the cold-moulded briquettes, pellets, lumps and the additional generation of fines and the concentrating of fines in any area of the cargo. This cargo shall be homogenous, with no added waste. The addition of DRI particles, fines or dust in this cargo shall be prohibited.

Due consideration shall be given to evenly spreading the cargo across the tanktop to minimize the concentration of fines. Trim in accordance with the relevant provisions required under sections 4 and 5 of the Code.

The cargo temperature and moisture shall be monitored during loading and recorded in a log detailing the temperature and moisture for each lot of cargo loaded, a copy of which shall be provided to the master. After loading, a certificate shall be issued by a competent person recognized by the national administration of the port of loading, confirming that, throughout the whole consignment, fines and small particles (under 6.35 mm size) are less than 5% by weight, that the moisture content has not exceeded 0.3% and the temperature does not exceed 65°C.

On completion of loading of a cargo space, it shall be immediately closed and sealed. Sufficient inert gas shall then be introduced to achieve an oxygen concentration less than 5% throughout the cargo space.

Precautions

Due consideration shall be given to the possibility of moisture inside the cargo pile in order to avoid loading of wet cargo or a wet part of the cargo, recognizing that the bottom of the pile can be wet even though the surface of cargo pile looks dry. The carrier's nominated technical persons or other representatives shall have reasonable access to stockpiles and loading installations for inspection.

Prior to shipment, the cargo shall be aged for at least 3 days, or treated with an air-passivation technique, or another equivalent method, that reduces the reactivity to the same level as the aged product. Such ageing process shall be approved by the competent authority which shall also provide a certificate to that effect.

DIRECT REDUCED IRON (B)
Lumps, pellets, cold-moulded briquettes *(continued)*

Shippers shall provide comprehensive information on the cargo and safety procedures to be followed in the event of emergency. This advice may be an amplification of this Code, but shall not be contrary thereto in respect of safety.

Where practicable, ballast tanks adjacent to the cargo spaces containing this cargo, other than double-bottom tanks, shall be kept empty. Weathertightness shall be maintained throughout the voyage. Bilge wells of the cargo spaces shall be clean, dry and protected from ingress of the cargo, using non-combustible material.

Due consideration shall be given to protecting equipment, machinery and accommodation spaces from the dust of the cargo. Radars and exposed radiocommunications equipment of ships which carry this cargo shall be protected from the dust of this cargo. Persons who may be exposed to the dust of the cargo shall wear protective clothing, goggles or other equivalent dust eye-protection and dust filter masks, as necessary.

During any handling of this cargo, "NO SMOKING" signs shall be posted on decks and in areas adjacent to cargo spaces, and no naked lights shall be permitted in these areas. Smoking, burning, cutting, chipping, grinding or other sources of ignition shall not be allowed in the vicinity of cargo spaces containing this cargo at any time.

Cargo spaces containing this cargo and adjacent spaces may become oxygen-depleted. Flammable gas may also build up in these spaces. All precautions shall be taken when entering the cargo spaces.

The ship shall be provided with the means to ensure that the requirement of this Code to maintain the oxygen concentration below 5% can be achieved throughout the voyage. The ship's fixed CO_2 fire-fighting system shall not be used for this purpose. Consideration shall be given to providing the vessel with the means to top up the cargo spaces with additional supplies of inert gas, taking into account the duration of the voyage.

The ship shall be provided with the means for reliably measuring the temperatures at several points within the stow, and determining the concentrations of hydrogen and oxygen in the cargo space atmosphere on voyage whilst minimizing as far as practicable the loss of the inert atmosphere.

Any cargo that has already been loaded into a cargo space and which subsequently becomes wetted, or in which reactions have started, shall be discharged without delay.

The ship shall not sail until the master and a competent person recognized by the national administration of the port of loading are satisfied:

.1   that all loaded cargo spaces are correctly sealed and inerted;

.2   that the temperature of the cargo has stabilized at all measuring points and that the temperature does not exceed 65°C; and

.3   that, at the end of the inerting process, the concentration of hydrogen in the free space of the holds has stabilized and does not exceed 0.2% by volume.

Ventilation

The cargo spaces carrying this cargo shall remain tightly sealed and the inert condition maintained during the voyage.

Carriage

For quantitative measurements of hydrogen and oxygen, suitable detectors shall be on board while this cargo is carried. The detectors shall be suitable for use in an oxygen-depleted atmosphere and of a type certified safe for use in explosive atmospheres. The concentrations of hydrogen and oxygen in the cargo spaces carrying this cargo shall be measured at regular intervals during voyage, and the results of the measurements shall be recorded and kept on board for a minimum of two years.

DIRECT REDUCED IRON (B)
Lumps, pellets, cold-moulded briquettes *(continued)*

The oxygen concentration in the cargo spaces carrying this cargo shall be maintained at less than 5% throughout the duration of the voyage. When the monitored hydrogen concentration is higher than 1% (>25% LEL) by volume, appropriate safety precautions shall be taken in accordance with those procedures provided by the shipper in the event of emergency. If in doubt, expert advice shall be sought.

Cargo temperatures shall be taken at regular intervals during voyage and the results of the measurements shall be recorded and kept on board for a minimum of two years. If the temperature in the cargo space exceeds 65°C, appropriate safety precautions shall be taken in accordance with the procedures provided by the shipper in the event of emergency. If in doubt, expert advice shall be sought.

Bilge wells shall be checked regularly for the presence of water. If water is found, it shall be removed by pumping or draining the bilge wells. Consideration shall be given to increasing the frequency of cargo monitoring following periods of bad weather. All measurements shall be taken so as to minimize as far as practicable the loss of inert gas from the cargo spaces.

Discharge
The hydrogen concentration in the cargo space shall be measured immediately before any opening action of the hatch covers. If the hydrogen concentration is greater than 1% (>25% LEL) by volume, all appropriate safety precautions in conformity with the procedures provided by the shipper or the recommendations of the competent authority shall be taken. If in doubt, expert advice shall be sought.

During precipitation, all cargo operations shall be suspended and holds containing cargo shall be closed. Monitoring for hydrogen in those holds containing cargo shall be resumed.

Clean-up
Accumulations of dust from this cargo on deck or in proximity to cargo spaces shall be removed as quickly as possible. Hosing with seawater should be avoided. Consideration shall be given to carefully cleaning exposed radiocommunications equipment to which dust from the cargo might adhere, such as radar, radio aerials, VHF installations, AIS and GPS.

DIRECT REDUCED IRON (B)
Lumps, pellets, cold-moulded briquettes *(concluded)*

Emergency procedures

Special emergency equipment to be carried
Nil

Emergency procedures

Nil

Emergency action in the event of fire

In the event of emergency, the specific procedures provided by the shipper should be consulted and followed, as appropriate.

Do not use CO_2. Do not use water. Do not use steam.

Batten down and reinstate the inert atmosphere using supplies or equipment if available on board. Increase the frequency of monitoring. If temperature and/or hydrogen concentration steadily rise, seek expert advice as quickly as possible.

If the temperature in the cargo space exceeds 120°C, the ship should make for the nearest appropriate port to discharge the cargo affected. Preparations should be made for grab discharge.

If additional nitrogen gas is available, the use of this gas will assist in keeping the oxygen concentration down and may contain the fire and prevent an explosive atmosphere if hydrogen is produced.

Flooding with water of the affected cargo hold should only be contemplated as a last resort, always taking the stability and strength of the ship into account.

Medical First Aid

Refer to the *Medical First Aid Guide (MFAG)*, as amended.

DIRECT REDUCED IRON (C)
(By-product fines)

Description

Direct reduced iron (DRI) (C) is a porous, black/grey metallic material generated as a by-product of the manufacturing and handling processes of DRI (A) and/or DRI (B). The density of DRI (C) is less than 5000 kg/m^3.

Characteristics

Angle of repose	Bulk density (kg/m^3)	Stowage factor (m^3/t)
Not applicable	1850 to 3300	0.30 to 0.54

Size	Class	Group
Fines and small particles with an average size less than 6.35 mm, no particles to exceed 12 mm	MHB	B

Hazard

Temporary increase in temperature of about 30°C due to self-heating may be expected after material handling in bulk.

There is a risk of overheating, fire and explosion during transport. This cargo reacts with air and with fresh water or seawater, to produce hydrogen and heat. Hydrogen is a flammable gas that can form an explosive mixture when mixed with air in concentrations above 4% by volume. Cargo heating may generate very high temperatures that are sufficient to lead to self-heating, auto-ignition and explosion.

Oxygen in cargo spaces and in enclosed adjacent spaces may be depleted. Flammable gas may also build up in these spaces. All precautions shall be taken when entering cargo and enclosed adjacent spaces.

The reactivity of this cargo is extremely difficult to assess due to the nature of the material that can be included in the category. A worst case scenario should therefore be assumed at all times.

Stowage & segregation

"Separated from" goods of classes 1 (division 1.4S), 2, 3, 4 and 5, and class 8 acids in packaged form (see IMDG Code).

"Separated from" solid bulk materials of classes 4 and 5.

Goods of class 1, other than division 1.4S, shall not be carried in the same ship. Boundaries of compartments where this cargo is carried shall be resistant to fire and passage of liquid.

Hold cleanliness

Cargo spaces shall be clean, dry and free of salt and residues of previous cargoes. Prior to loading, wooden fixtures such as battens, loose dunnage, debris and combustible materials shall be removed.

Weather precautions

The cargo shall be kept within the permissible moisture content indicated in this schedule at all times during loading, and during transportation.

This cargo shall not be loaded onto ships, or transferred between ships or barges, during ANY precipitation. During loading of this cargo, all non-working hatches of cargo spaces into which this cargo is loaded, or is to be loaded, shall be kept closed.

DIRECT REDUCED IRON (C)
(By-product fines) *(continued)*

Loading

Prior to loading, the terminal shall ensure that the conveyor belts and all other equipment used for loading this cargo contain no accumulation of water or other substances. Each time cargo operations are commenced or restarted, particularly after rain or washing down, any loading belt shall be operated empty and not over a ship's cargo space.

Prior to loading, an ultrasonic test or another equivalent method with a suitable instrument shall be conducted to ensure weathertightness of the hatch covers and closing arrangements and all readings shall confirm weathertightness.

Prior to loading this cargo, the shipper shall provide the master with a certificate issued by a competent person recognized by the national administration of the port of loading stating that the cargo, at the time of loading, is suitable for shipment; that it conforms with the requirements of this Code; that the moisture content is less than 0.3%; and the temperature does not exceed 65°C. This certificate shall state that the cargo meets the loading criteria in regards to ageing and material temperature.

The cargo shall not be accepted for loading when its temperature is in excess of 65°C or if its moisture content is in excess of 0.3%. Any cargo that has been wetted, or is known to have been wetted, shall not be loaded into any cargo space.

Trim in accordance with the relevant provisions required under sections 4 and 5 of the Code.

The cargo temperature shall be monitored during loading and recorded in a log detailing the temperature for each lot of cargo loaded, a copy of which shall be provided to the master. After loading, a certificate shall be issued by a competent person recognized by the national administration of the port of loading confirming that throughout the whole consignment of fines and small particles the moisture content has not exceeded 0.3% and the temperature does not exceed 65°C.

On completion of loading of a cargo space it shall be immediately closed and sealed. Sufficient inert gas shall then be introduced to achieve an oxygen concentration less than 5% throughout the cargo space.

Precautions

Due consideration shall be given to the possibility of moisture inside the cargo pile in order to avoid loading of wet cargo or a wet part of the cargo, recognizing that the bottom of the pile can be wet even though the surface of cargo pile looks dry. The carrier's nominated technical persons or other representatives shall have reasonable access to stockpiles and loading installations for inspection.

Prior to shipment, the cargo shall be aged for at least 30 days and a certificate confirming this shall be issued by a competent person recognized by the National Administration of the port of loading.

Shippers shall provide to the master, prior to loading, comprehensive information on the cargo and safety procedures to be followed in the event of emergency. This advice may be an amplification of this Code, but shall not be contrary thereto in respect of safety.

Where practicable, ballast tanks adjacent to the cargo spaces containing this cargo, other than double-bottom tanks, shall be kept empty. Weathertightness shall be maintained throughout the voyage. Bilge wells of the cargo spaces shall be clean, dry and protected from ingress of the cargo, using non-combustible material. The introduction of moisture and accumulation of condensation in the cargo spaces shall be avoided.

Appropriate precautions shall be taken to protect equipment, machinery and accommodation spaces from the dust of the cargo. Radars and exposed radiocommunications equipment of ships which carry this cargo shall be protected from the dust of this cargo. Persons who may be exposed to the dust of the cargo shall wear protective clothing, goggles or other equivalent dust eye-protection and dust filter masks, as necessary.

DIRECT REDUCED IRON (C)
(By-product fines) *(continued)*

During any handling of this cargo, "NO SMOKING" signs shall be posted on decks and in areas adjacent to cargo spaces, and no naked light shall be permitted in these areas. Smoking, burning, cutting, chipping, grinding or other sources of ignition shall not be allowed in the vicinity of cargo spaces containing this cargo at any time.

Cargo spaces containing this cargo and adjacent spaces may become oxygen-depleted. No person shall enter a loaded cargo space or an enclosed adjacent space unless the space has been ventilated and the atmosphere tested and found to be gas-free and to have sufficient oxygen to support life. Notwithstanding, emergency entry may be permitted without ventilation, testing, or both provided that the entry into the space is undertaken only by trained personnel wearing self-contained breathing apparatus under the supervision of a responsible officer and no source of ignition is introduced into the space.

Prior to loading, provision shall be made to introduce a dry, inert gas at tanktop level so that the inert gas purges the air from the cargo and fills the free volume above. Nitrogen is preferred for this purpose. All vents, accesses and other openings, such as coaming drains, that could allow the inert atmosphere to be lost from cargo spaces carrying this cargo shall be closed and sealed.

The ship shall be provided with the means to ensure that a requirement of this Code to maintain the oxygen concentration below 5% can be achieved and maintained throughout the voyage. The ship's fixed CO_2 fire-fighting system shall not be used for this purpose. Consideration shall be given to providing the vessel with the means to top up the cargo spaces with additional supplies of inert gas, taking into account the duration of the voyage.

The ship shall be provided with the means for reliably measuring the temperatures at several points within the stow and determining the concentrations of hydrogen and oxygen in the cargo space atmosphere on voyage. Appropriate precautions shall be taken to minimize, as far as practicable, the loss of the inert atmosphere.

Any cargo that has already been loaded into a cargo space and which subsequently is exposed to additional fresh water or seawater over its natural moisture content and becomes wetted, or in which reactions have started and its temperature has exceeded 120°C, shall be discharged without delay.

On completion of loading of a cargo space it shall be immediately closed and sealed. Sufficient inert gas shall then be introduced to achieve an oxygen concentration less than 5% throughout the cargo space.

The ship shall not sail until the master and a competent person recognized by the national administration of the port of loading are satisfied:

.1 that all loaded cargo spaces are correctly sealed and inerted;

.2 that the temperature of the cargo has stabilized at all measuring points and that the temperature does not exceed 65°C; and

.3 that, at the end of the inerting process, the concentration of hydrogen in the free space of the holds has stabilized and does not exceed 0.2% by volume.

Ventilation

The cargo spaces carrying this cargo shall remain tightly sealed and the inert condition maintained during the voyage.

Carriage

For quantitative measurements of hydrogen and oxygen, suitable detectors shall be on board while this cargo is carried. The detectors shall be suitable for use in an oxygen-depleted atmosphere and of a type certified safe for use in explosive atmospheres. The concentrations of

DIRECT REDUCED IRON (C)
(By-product fines) *(continued)*

hydrogen and oxygen in the cargo spaces carrying this cargo shall be measured at regular intervals during voyage, and the results of the measurements shall be recorded and kept on board for a minimum of two years.

The oxygen concentration in the cargo spaces carrying this cargo shall be maintained at less than 5% throughout the duration of the voyage by topping up with inert gas.

Cargo temperatures shall be taken at regular intervals during the voyage and the results of the measurements shall be recorded and kept on board for a minimum of two years. If the temperature in the cargo space exceeds 65°C or the monitored hydrogen concentration exceeds 1% (>25% LEL) by volume, appropriate safety precautions shall be taken in accordance with the procedures provided by the shipper in the event of emergency. If in doubt, expert advice shall be sought.

Bilge wells shall be checked regularly for the presence of water. If water is found, it shall be removed by pumping or draining the bilge wells. Consideration shall be given to increasing the frequency of cargo monitoring following periods of bad weather. All measurements shall be taken so as to minimize, as far as practicable, the loss of inert gas from the cargo spaces.

Discharge

The hydrogen concentration in the cargo space shall be measured immediately before any opening action of the hatch covers. If the hydrogen concentration is greater than 1% (>25% LEL) by volume, all appropriate safety precautions in conformity with the procedures provided by the shipper or the recommendations of the competent authority shall be taken. If in doubt, expert advice shall be sought.

During precipitation, all cargo operations shall be suspended and holds containing cargo shall be closed. Monitoring for hydrogen of those holds containing cargo shall be resumed.

Clean-up

Accumulations of dust from this cargo on deck or in proximity to cargo spaces shall be removed as quickly as possible. Hosing with seawater shall be avoided. Consideration shall be given to carefully cleaning exposed radiocommunications equipment to which dust from the cargo might adhere, such as radar, radio aerials, VHF installations, AIS and GPS.

DIRECT REDUCED IRON (C)
(By-product fines) *(concluded)*

Emergency procedures

Special emergency equipment to be carried Nil
Emergency procedures Nil **Emergency action in the event of fire** In the event of emergency, the specific procedures provided by the shipper should be consulted and followed, as appropriate. **Do not use CO_2. Do not use water. Do not use steam.** Batten down and reinstate the inert atmosphere using supplies or equipment if available on board. Increase the frequency of monitoring. If temperature and/or hydrogen concentration steadily rise, seek expert advice as quickly as possible. If the temperature in the cargo space exceeds 120°C, the ship should make for the nearest appropriate port to discharge the cargo affected. Preparations should be made for grab discharge. If additional nitrogen gas is available, the use of this gas will assist in keeping the oxygen concentration down and may contain the fire and prevent an explosive atmosphere if hydrogen is produced. Flooding with water of the affected cargo hold should only be contemplated as a last resort, always taking the stability and strength of the ship into account. **Medical First Aid** Refer to the *Medical First Aid Guide (MFAG)*, as amended.

DOLOMITE

Description

Dolomite is a light yellow/brown coloured mineral stone which is very hard and compact.

Dolomite may sometimes, incorrectly, be used to describe a material consisting of the oxides of calcium and magnesium (dolomitic quicklime). In this case, see "LIME (UNSLAKED)".

Characteristics

Angle of repose	Bulk density (kg/m³)	Stowage factor (m³/t)
Not applicable	1429 to 1667	0.6 to 0.7
Size	**Class**	**Group**
Up to 32 mm	Not applicable	C

Hazard

No special hazards.

This cargo is non-combustible or has a low fire-risk.

Stowage & segregation

No special requirements.

Hold cleanliness

No special requirements.

Weather precautions

No special requirements.

Loading

Trim in accordance with the relevant provisions required under sections 4 and 5 of the Code.

Precautions

No special requirements.

Ventilation

No special requirements.

Carriage

No special requirements.

Discharge

No special requirements.

Clean-up

No special requirements.

FELSPAR LUMP

Description
Crystalline minerals consisting of silicates of aluminium with potassium sodium, calcium and barium. White or reddish in colour.

Characteristics

Angle of repose	Bulk density (kg/m³)	Stowage factor (m³/t)
Not applicable	1667	0.60
Size	**Class**	**Group**
0.1 mm to 300 mm	Not applicable	C

Hazard
No special hazards.

This cargo is non-combustible or has a low fire-risk.

Stowage & segregation
No special requirements.

Hold cleanliness
No special requirements.

Weather precautions
No special requirements.

Loading
Trim in accordance with the relevant provisions required under sections 4 and 5 of the Code.

Precautions
No special requirements.

Ventilation
No special requirements.

Carriage
No special requirements.

Discharge
No special requirements.

Clean-up
No special requirements.

FERROCHROME

Description
Raw material of iron mixed with chrome. Extremely heavy cargo.

Characteristics

Angle of repose	Bulk density (kg/m³)	Stowage factor (m³/t)
Not applicable	3571 to 5556	0.18 to 0.26
Size	**Class**	**Group**
Up to 300 mm	Not applicable	C

Hazard
No special hazards.

This cargo is non-combustible or has a low fire-risk.

Stowage & segregation
No special requirements.

Hold cleanliness
No special requirements.

Weather precautions
No special requirements.

Loading
Trim in accordance with the relevant provisions required under sections 4 and 5 of the Code.

As the density of the cargo is extremely high, the tanktop may be overstressed unless the cargo is evenly spread across the tanktop to equalize the weight distribution. Due consideration shall be paid to ensure that the tanktop is not overstressed during voyage and during loading by a pile of the cargo.

Precautions
No special requirements.

Ventilation
No special requirements.

Carriage
No special requirements.

Discharge
No special requirements.

Clean-up
No special requirements.

FERROCHROME, exothermic

Description
An alloy of iron and chromium. Extremely heavy cargo.

Characteristics

Angle of repose	Bulk density (kg/m³)	Stowage factor (m³/t)
Not applicable	3571 to 5556	0.18 to 0.28
Size	**Class**	**Group**
Up to 300 mm	Not applicable	C

Hazard
No special hazards.

This cargo is non-combustible or has a low fire-risk.

Stowage & segregation
No special requirements.

Hold cleanliness
No special requirements.

Weather precautions
No special requirements.

Loading
Trim in accordance with the relevant provisions required under sections 4 and 5 of the Code.

As the density of the cargo is extremely high, the tanktop may be overstressed unless the cargo is evenly spread across the tanktop to equalize the weight distribution. Due consideration shall be paid to ensure that the tanktop is not overstressed during voyage and during loading by a pile of the cargo.

Precautions
During loading, carriage and discharging, welding or other hot work shall not be carried out in the vicinity of the cargo spaces containing this cargo.

Ventilation
No special requirements.

Carriage
No special requirements.

Discharge
No special requirements.

Clean-up
No special requirements.

FERROMANGANESE

Description
Raw material or iron mixed with manganese.

Characteristics

Angle of repose	Bulk density (kg/m^3)	Stowage factor (m^3/t)
Not applicable	3571 to 5556	0.18 to 0.28
Size	**Class**	**Group**
Up to 300 mm	Not applicable	C

Hazard
No special hazards.

This cargo is non-combustible or has a low fire-risk.

Stowage & segregation
No special requirements.

Hold cleanliness
No special requirements.

Weather precautions
No special requirements.

Loading
Trim in accordance with the relevant provisions required under sections 4 and 5 of the Code.

As the density of the cargo is extremely high, the tanktop may be overstressed unless the cargo is evenly spread across the tanktop to equalize the weight distribution. Due consideration shall be paid to ensure that the tanktop is not overstressed during voyage and during loading by a pile of the cargo.

Precautions
No special requirements.

Ventilation
No special requirements.

Carriage
No special requirements.

Discharge
No special requirements.

Clean-up
No special requirements.

FERRONICKEL

Description
An alloy of iron and nickel.

Characteristics

Angle of repose	Bulk density (kg/m³)	Stowage factor (m³/t)
Not applicable	4167	0.24
Size	**Class**	**Group**
Up to 300 mm	Not applicable	C

Hazard
No special hazards.

This cargo is non-combustible or has a low fire-risk.

Stowage & segregation
No special requirements.

Hold cleanliness
No special requirements.

Weather precautions
No special requirements.

Loading
Trim in accordance with the relevant provisions required under sections 4 and 5 of the Code.

As the density of the cargo is extremely high, the tanktop may be overstressed unless the cargo is evenly spread across the tanktop to equalize the weight distribution. Due consideration shall be paid to ensure that the tanktop is not overstressed during voyage and during loading by a pile of the cargo.

Precautions
No special requirements.

Ventilation
No special requirements.

Carriage
No special requirements.

Discharge
No special requirements.

Clean-up
No special requirements.

FERROPHOSPHORUS
(including briquettes)

Description
An alloy of iron and phosphorus used in the steel industry.

Characteristics

Angle of repose	Bulk density (kg/m^3)	Stowage factor (m^3/t)
Not applicable	5000	(0.2 for briquettes)
Size	**Class**	**Group**
Diameter: 2.54 mm	MHB	B

Hazard
May evolve flammable and toxic gases (e.g., phosphine) in contact with water.

This cargo is non-combustible or has a low fire-risk.

Stowage & segregation
Segregation as for class 4.3 materials. "Separated from" foodstuffs and class 8 liquids.

Hold cleanliness
Clean and dry as relevant to the hazards of the cargo.

Weather precautions
This cargo shall be kept as dry as practicable. This cargo shall not be handled during precipitation. During handling of this cargo, all non-working hatches of the cargo spaces into which this cargo is loaded or to be loaded shall be closed.

Loading
Trim in accordance with the relevant provisions required under sections 4 and 5 of the Code.

As the density of the cargo is extremely high, the tanktop may be overstressed unless the cargo is evenly spread across the tanktop to equalize the weight distribution. Due consideration shall be paid to ensure that the tanktop is not overstressed during voyage and during loading by a pile of the cargo.

Precautions
This cargo shall be kept as dry as reasonably practicable.

Ventilation
Mechanical ventilation shall be conducted during the voyage for the cargo spaces carrying this cargo. Ventilation fans shall be of certified safe type for use in a flammable atmosphere. They shall normally be run continuously whenever this cargo is on board. Where this is impracticable, they shall be operated as weather permits and in any case for a reasonable period prior to discharge.

Carriage
No special requirements.

Discharge
No special requirements.

FERROPHOSPHORUS (including briquettes) *(concluded)*

Clean-up

After discharge of this cargo, the cargo spaces shall be swept clean.

Water shall not be used for cleaning of the cargo space which has contained this cargo, because of danger of gas.

Emergency procedures

Special emergency equipment to be carried Self-contained breathing apparatus.
Emergency procedures Wear self-contained breathing apparatus. **Emergency action in the event of fire** Batten down and use CO_2 if available. **Do not use water.** **Medical First Aid** Refer to the *Medical First Aid Guide (MFAG)*, as amended.

FERROSILICON UN 1408
with 30% or more but less than 90% silicon
(including briquettes) (see appendix to this schedule)

Description
Ferrosilicon is an extremely heavy cargo.

Characteristics

Angle of repose	Bulk density (kg/m^3)		Stowage factor (m^3/t)
Not applicable	1389 to 2083 (1111 to 1538 for briquettes)		0.48 to 0.72 (0.65 to 0.90 for briquettes)
Size	**Class**	**Subsidiary risk**	**Group**
Up to 300 mm Briquettes	4.3	6.1	B

Hazard
In contact with moisture or water it may evolve hydrogen, a flammable gas which may form explosive mixtures with air and may, under similar circumstances, produce phosphine and arsine, which are highly toxic gases.

This cargo is non-combustible or has a low fire-risk.

Stowage & segregation
"Separated from" foodstuffs and all class 8 liquids.

Hold cleanliness
Clean and dry as relevant to the hazards of the cargo.

Weather precautions
This cargo shall be kept as dry as practicable before loading, during loading and during voyage. This cargo shall not be loaded during precipitation. During loading of this cargo, all non-working hatches of the cargo spaces to which this cargo is loaded or to be loaded shall be closed.

Loading
Trim in accordance with the relevant provisions required under sections 4 and 5 of the Code. As the density of the cargo is extremely high, the tanktop may be overstressed unless the cargo is evenly spread across the tanktop to equalize the weight distribution. Due consideration shall be paid to ensure that the tanktop is not overstressed during voyage and during loading by a pile of the cargo. *Refer to the appendix to this schedule.*

Precautions
The manufacturer or the shipper shall provide the master with a certificate stating that, after manufacture, the cargo was stored under cover, but exposed to dry weather for not less than three days prior to shipment.

Ventilation
Continuous mechanical ventilation shall be conducted during the voyage for the cargo spaces carrying this cargo. If maintaining ventilation endangers the ship or the cargo, it may be interrupted unless there is a risk of explosion or other danger due to interruption of the ventilation. In any case, mechanical ventilation shall be maintained for a reasonable period prior to discharge. *Refer to the appendix to this schedule.*

FERROSILICON UN 1408 *(continued)*

Carriage

For quantitative measurements of hydrogen, phosphine and arsine, suitable detectors for each gas or combination of gases shall be on board while this cargo is carried. The detectors shall be of certified safe type for use in explosive atmosphere. The concentrations of these gases in the cargo spaces carrying this cargo shall be measured regularly, during voyage, and the results of the measurements shall be recorded and kept on board.

Discharge

Refer to the appendix to this schedule.

Clean-up

After discharge of this cargo, the cargo spaces shall be swept clean twice.

Water shall not be used for cleaning of the cargo space which has contained this cargo, because of danger of gas.

Emergency procedures

Special emergency equipment to be carried
Self-contained breathing apparatus.
Emergency procedures Wear self-contained breathing apparatus. **Emergency action in the event of fire** Batten down and use CO_2 if available. **Do not use water.** **Medical First Aid** Refer to the *Medical First Aid Guide (MFAG)*, as amended.

Appendix

FERROSILICON UN 1408

General requirements for carriage of ferrosilicon

1   Chapter II-2 of SOLAS requires fire-fighter's outfits, full chemical protective suits and self-contained breathing apparatus to be readily available on board.

2   Gas concentrations shall be measured, during the voyage, at least once during every eight hours at each outlet ventilator and in any other accessible space adjacent to the cargo space carrying this cargo and the results shall be recorded in the log-book. Facilities shall be provided to make accurate determinations of the gas concentrations at each outlet ventilator without danger to the operator.

3   Ventilation fans shall be in operation at all times from commencement of loading until the cargo space is free of ferrosilicon.

4   The bilge wells shall be in a clean, dry condition before loading. The bilge timbers shall be in good condition and covered with double burlap.

5   The bilge wells shall be opened up and the cargo space cleaned up after discharging. A gas check shall be made before commencement of cleaning up.

FERROSILICON UN 1408 *(appendix, continued)*

Detailed requirements

Prior to loading, the bulkheads to the engine-room shall be inspected and approved by the competent authority as gastight and the safety of the bilge pumping arrangements shall be approved by the competent authority. Inadvertent pumping through machinery spaces shall be avoided.

(i) Where the bilge suction valve of the cargo space is located in the machinery space, the valve shall be checked and the valve lid and seat lapped to a fine finish, as necessary. After re-assembly, the valve shall be locked shut and a notice shall be placed adjacent to the valve warning against opening without the master's permission.

(ii) All pipes passing through the cargo space shall be in good order and condition. Hold atmosphere sampling units shall be effectively blanked off.

(iii) Electrical circuits for equipment in cargo spaces which is unsuitable for use in an explosive atmosphere shall be isolated by removal of links in the system other than fuses.

(iv) The cargo spaces shall be ventilated by at least two separate fans which shall be explosion-proof and arranged so that the escaping gas flow is separated from electrical cables and components. The total ventilation shall be at least 6 air changes per hour, based on an empty cargo space.

(v) Ventilator trunkings shall be in sound condition and so arranged to preclude interconnection of the atmosphere in the cargo space with other cargo spaces, accommodation or work areas.

Operational requirements

(i) Smoking and naked flame shall be prohibited on deck in the vicinity of the cargo space or in the cargo space itself during loading or discharging.

(ii) Any portable lighting shall be safe for use in an explosive atmosphere.

(iii) The cargo shall be kept dry and, during wet weather conditions, cargo handling shall be suspended and the cargo space shall be closed.

(iv) Sets of self-contained breathing apparatus shall be located and stored for immediate use together with a lifeline and a gas detector.

(v) Prior to commencement of discharging, the atmosphere in the cargo space shall be tested for the presence of toxic and flammable gases.

(vi) Checks for contaminant gases shall be carried out at 30-minute intervals while persons are in the cargo space.

(vii) Entry into the cargo space shall be prohibited when gas concentrations exceed the Threshold Limit Values for phosphine (0.3 ppm) or for arsine (0.05 ppm) or where the oxygen level is below 18%.

Gases released from ferrosilicon impurities when water is added

(i) Arsine

Arsine is a toxic, colourless gas with a garlic-like odour.

Toxicity

Arsine is a nerve and blood poison. There is generally a delay before the onset of symptoms (sometimes a day or so). These are at first indefinite.

Symptoms

1 Feeling of malaise, difficulty in breathing, severe headache, giddiness, fainting fits, nausea, vomiting and gastric disturbances.

2 In severe cases, vomiting may be pronounced, the mucous membranes may have a bluish discoloration and urine is dark and bloodstained. After a day or so there is severe anaemia and jaundice.

FERROSILICON UN 1408 *(appendix, concluded)*

Concentration

A concentration of 500 ppm is lethal to humans after exposure of a few minutes, while concentrations of 250 ppm are dangerous to life after 30 minutes exposure. Concentrations of 6.25 to 15.5 ppm are dangerous after exposure of 30 to 60 minutes. A concentration of 0.05 ppm is the threshold long limit to which a person may be exposed.

(ii) Phosphine

Phosphine is colourless, flammable and highly toxic and has the odour of rotting fish.

Toxicity

Phosphine acts on the central nervous system and the blood.

Symptoms

The symptoms exhibited by phosphine poisoning are an oppressed feeling in the chest, headache, vertigo, general debility, loss of appetite and great thirst. Concentrations of 2000 ppm for a few minutes and 400 to 600 ppm are dangerous to life. 0.3 ppm is the maximum concentration tolerable for several hours without symptoms.

No long-term exposures to this gas shall be permitted.

FERROSILICON
with 25% to 30% silicon, or 90% or more silicon
(including briquettes) (see appendix to this schedule)

Description
Ferrosilicon is an extremely heavy cargo.

Characteristics

Angle of repose	Bulk density (kg/m³)	Stowage factor (m³/t)
Not applicable	1389 to 2083 (1111 to 1538 for briquettes)	0.48 to 0.72 (0.65 to 0.90 for briquettes)
Size	**Class**	**Group**
Diameter: 2.54 mm	MHB	B

Hazard
In contact with moisture or water it may evolve hydrogen, a flammable gas which may form explosive mixtures with air and may, under similar circumstances, produce phosphine and arsine, which are highly toxic gases.

This cargo is non-combustible or has a low fire-risk.

Stowage & segregation
Segregation as required for class 4.3 materials. "Separated from" foodstuffs and all class 8 liquids.

Hold cleanliness
Clean and dry as relevant to the hazards of the cargo.

Weather precautions
This cargo shall be kept as dry as practicable before loading, during loading and during voyage. This cargo shall not be loaded during precipitation. During loading of this cargo, all non-working hatches of the cargo spaces to which this cargo is loaded or to be loaded shall be closed.

Loading
Trim in accordance with the relevant provisions required under sections 4 and 5 of the Code. Stow evenly across tanktops. *Refer to the appendix to this schedule.*

Precautions
The manufacturer or the shipper shall provide the master with a certificate stating that, after manufacture, the cargo was stored under cover, but exposed to open air for not less than three days prior to shipment.

Ventilation
Continuous mechanical ventilation shall be conducted during the voyage for the cargo spaces carrying this cargo. If maintaining ventilation endangers the ship or the cargo, it may be interrupted unless there is a risk of explosion or other danger due to interruption of the ventilation. In any case, mechanical ventilation shall be maintained for a reasonable period prior to discharge. *Refer to the appendix to this schedule.*

FERROSILICON *(continued)*

Carriage

For quantitative measurements of hydrogen, phosphine and arsine, suitable detectors for each gas or combination of gases shall be on board while this cargo is carried. The detectors shall be of certified safe type for use in explosive atmosphere. The concentrations of these gases in the cargo spaces carrying this cargo shall be measured regularly, during voyage, and the results of the measurements shall be recorded and kept on board.

Discharge

Refer to the appendix to this schedule.

Clean-up

After discharge of this cargo, the cargo spaces shall be swept clean twice.

Water shall not be used for cleaning of the cargo space which has contained this cargo, because of danger of gas.

Emergency procedures

Special emergency equipment to be carried
Self-contained breathing apparatus.
Emergency procedures Wear self-contained breathing apparatus. **Emergency action in the event of fire** Batten down and use CO_2 if available. **Do not use water.** **Medical First Aid** Refer to the *Medical First Aid Guide (MFAG)*, as amended.

Appendix

FERROSILICON

General requirements for carriage of ferrosilicon

1   Two sets of self-contained breathing apparatus shall be carried in the ship in addition to normal fire-fighter's outfit.

2   Gas concentrations shall be measured, during the voyage, at least once during every eight hours at each outlet ventilator and in any other accessible space adjacent to the cargo space carrying this cargo and the results shall be recorded in the log-book. Facilities shall be provided to make accurate determinations of the gas concentrations at each outlet ventilator without danger to the operator.

3   Ventilation fans shall be in operation at all times from commencement of loading until the cargo space is free of ferrosilicon.

4   The bilge wells shall be in a clean, dry condition before loading. The bilge timbers shall be in good condition and covered with double burlap.

5   The bilge wells shall be opened up and the cargo space cleaned up after discharging. A gas check shall be made before commencement of cleaning up.

FERROSILICON *(appendix, continued)*

Detailed requirements

Prior to loading, the bulkheads to the engine-room shall be inspected and approved by the competent authority as gastight. Satisfaction with the safety of the bilge pumping arrangements shall be approved by the competent authority. Inadvertent pumping through machinery spaces shall be avoided.

(i)   Where the bilge suction valve of the cargo space is located in the machinery space, the valve shall be checked and the valve lid and seat lapped to a fine finish, as necessary. After re-assembly, the valve shall be locked shut and a notice shall be placed adjacent to the valve warning against opening without the master's permission.

(ii)   All pipes passing through the cargo space shall be in good order and condition. Hold atmosphere sampling units shall be effectively blanked off.

(iii)   Electrical circuits for equipment in cargo spaces which is unsuitable for use in an explosive atmosphere shall be isolated by removal of links in the system other than fuses.

(iv)   The cargo spaces shall be ventilated by at least two separate fans which shall be explosion-proof and arranged so that the escaping gas flow is separated from electrical cables and components. The total ventilation shall be at least 6 air changes per hour, based on an empty cargo space.

(v)   Ventilator trunkings shall be in sound condition and so arranged to preclude interconnection of the atmosphere in the cargo space with other cargo spaces, accommodation or work areas.

Operational requirements

(i)   Smoking and naked flame shall be prohibited on deck in the vicinity of the cargo space or in the cargo space itself during loading or discharging.

(ii)   Any portable lighting shall be safe for use in an explosive atmosphere.

(iii)   The cargo shall be kept dry and, during wet weather conditions, cargo handling shall be suspended and the cargo space shall be closed.

(iv)   Sets of self-contained breathing apparatus shall be located and stored for immediate use together with a lifeline and a gas detector.

(v)   Prior to commencement of discharging, the atmosphere in the cargo space shall be tested for the presence of toxic and flammable gases.

(vi)   Checks for contaminant gases shall be carried out at 30-minute intervals while persons are in the cargo space.

(vii)   Entry into the cargo space shall be prohibited when gas concentrations exceed the Threshold Limit Values for phosphine (0.3 ppm) or for arsine (0.05 ppm) or where the oxygen level is below 18%.

Gases released from ferrosilicon impurities when water is added

(i) Arsine

Arsine is a toxic, colourless gas with a garlic-like odour.

Toxicity

Arsine is a nerve and blood poison. There is generally a delay before the onset of symptoms (sometimes a day or so). These are at first indefinite.

Symptoms

1   Feeling of malaise, difficulty in breathing, severe headache, giddiness, fainting fits, nausea, vomiting and gastric disturbances.

FERROSILICON *(appendix, concluded)*

2   In severe cases, vomiting may be pronounced, the mucous membranes may have a bluish discoloration and urine is dark and bloodstained. After a day or so there is severe anaemia and jaundice.

Concentration

A concentration of 500 ppm is lethal to humans after exposure of a few minutes, while concentrations of 250 ppm are dangerous to life after 30 minutes exposure. Concentrations of 6.25 to 15.5 ppm are dangerous after exposure of 30 to 60 minutes. A concentration of 0.05 ppm is the threshold long limit to which a person may be exposed.

(ii) Phosphine

Phosphine is colourless, flammable and highly toxic and has the odour of rotting fish.

Toxicity

Phosphine acts on the central nervous system and the blood.

Symptoms

The symptoms exhibited by phosphine poisoning are an oppressed feeling in the chest, headache, vertigo, general debility, loss of appetite and great thirst. Concentrations of 2000 ppm for a few minutes and 400 to 600 ppm are dangerous to life. 0.3 ppm is the maximum concentration tolerable for several hours without symptoms.

No long-term exposures to this gas shall be permitted.

FERROUS METAL BORINGS, SHAVINGS, TURNINGS or CUTTINGS UN 2793
in a form liable to self-heating

Description
Metal drillings usually wet or contaminated with such materials as unsaturated cutting oil, oily rags and other combustible material.

This schedule should **not** apply to consignments of materials which are accompanied by a declaration submitted prior to loading by the shipper and stating that they have no self-heating properties when transported in bulk.

Characteristics

Angle of repose	Bulk density (kg/m³)	Stowage factor (m³/t)
Not applicable	Various	Various
Size	**Class**	**Group**
Not applicable	4.2	B

Hazard
These materials are liable to self-heat and ignite spontaneously, particularly when in a finely divided form, wet or contaminated with such materials as unsaturated cutting oil, oily rags and other combustible matter.

Excessive amounts of cast iron borings or organic materials may encourage heating. Self-heating or inadequate ventilation may cause dangerous depletion of oxygen in cargo spaces.

Stowage & segregation
"Separated from" foodstuffs.

Hold cleanliness
Clean and dry as relevant to the hazards of the cargo.

Weather precautions
This cargo shall be kept as dry as practicable. This cargo shall not be handled during precipitation. During handling of this cargo, all non-working hatches of the cargo spaces into which this cargo is loaded or to be loaded shall be closed.

Loading
During loading, the material shall be compacted in the cargo space as frequently as practicable with a bulldozer or other means. The bilge of each cargo space in which the cargo is loaded shall be kept as dry as practicable. After loading, the cargo shall be trimmed to eliminate peaks and compacted. Wooden wet battens and dunnage shall be removed from the cargo space before the cargo is loaded.

Precautions
The temperature of this cargo shall be measured prior to and during loading. The temperature of the cargo in the stockyard shall be measured at points between 200 mm and 350 mm from the surface of the cargo pile. This cargo shall only be accepted for loading when the temperature of the cargo prior to loading does not exceed 55°C. If the temperature of the cargo in any cargo space exceeds 90°C during loading, loading shall be suspended and shall not be recommenced until the temperature of the cargo in all cargo spaces has fallen below 85°C. The ship shall not depart unless the temperature of the cargo in all cargo spaces is below 65°C and has shown a steady or downward trend in temperature for at least eight hours.

FERROUS METAL BORINGS, SHAVINGS, TURNINGS or CUTTINGS UN 2793
(concluded)

Ventilation

The cargo spaces carrying this cargo shall not be ventilated during voyage.

Carriage

The surface temperature of the cargo shall be monitored and recorded daily during the voyage. Temperature readings shall be taken in such a way as not to require entry into the cargo space or, alternatively, if entry is required for this purpose, at least two sets of self-contained breathing apparatus, additional to those required by SOLAS regulation II-2/10.10 shall be provided.

Discharge

Entry into the cargo spaces containing this cargo shall only be permitted for trained personnel wearing self-contained breathing apparatus when the main hatches are open and after adequate ventilation is conducted or for personnel using appropriate breathing apparatus.

Clean-up

Prior to washing out the residues of this cargo, any oil spillages shall be cleaned from the tanktops and the bilge wells of the cargo spaces for this cargo.

Emergency procedures

Special emergency equipment to be carried
Self-contained breathing apparatus
Emergency procedures Nil **Emergency action in the event of fire** Whilst at sea, any rise in surface temperature of the material indicates a self-heating reaction problem. If the temperature should rise to 80°C, a potential fire situation is developing and the ship should make for the nearest suitable port. Batten down. **Water should not be used at sea.** Early application of an inert gas to a smouldering situation may be effective. **Medical First Aid** Refer to the *Medical First Aid Guide (MFAG)*, as amended.

Remarks

In port, copious quantities of water may be used, but due consideration should be given to factors affecting the stability of the ship.

FERTILIZERS WITHOUT NITRATES
(non-hazardous)

Description

Powder and granular. Greenish, brown or beige in colour. Odourless. Very low moisture content (0% to 1%). Hygroscopic.

Characteristics

Angle of repose	Bulk density (kg/m³)	Stowage factor (m³/t)
Not applicable	714 to 1111	0.90 to 1.40
Size	**Class**	**Group**
1 mm to 3 mm	Not applicable	C

Hazard

No special hazards.

This cargo is non-combustible or has a low fire-risk.

This cargo is hygroscopic and will cake if wet.

Stowage & segregation

No special requirements.

Hold cleanliness

No special requirements.

Weather precautions

This cargo shall be kept as dry as practicable. This cargo shall not be handled during precipitation. During handling of this cargo, all non-working hatches of the cargo spaces into which this cargo is loaded or to be loaded shall be closed.

Loading

Trim in accordance with the relevant provisions required under sections 4 and 5 of the Code.

Precautions

No special requirements.

Ventilation

The cargo spaces carrying this cargo shall not be ventilated during voyage.

Carriage

No special requirements.

Discharge

If this cargo has hardened, it shall be trimmed to avoid the formation of overhangs, as necessary.

Clean-up

No special requirements.

FISH (IN BULK)

Description
Fish carried in bulk after freezing.

Characteristics

Angle of repose	Bulk density (kg/m^3)	Stowage factor (m^3/t)
Not applicable	–	–
Size	**Class**	**Group**
Various	Not applicable	A

Hazard
Fish carried in bulk may liquefy.

This cargo is non-combustible or has a low fire-risk.

Stowage & segregation
No special requirements.

Hold cleanliness
No special requirements.

Weather precautions
No special requirements

Loading
Trim in accordance with the relevant provisions required under sections 4 and 5 of the Code.

Precautions
Prior to the carriage of this cargo, due consideration shall be paid to consult with the competent authority. The requirement in chapter 7 of this Code, requiring a determination of TML and moisture content declaration, may be dispensed with for this cargo.

Bilge wells shall be clean, dry and covered as appropriate, to prevent ingress of the cargo.

Ventilation
No special requirements.

Carriage
No special requirements.

Discharge
No special requirements.

Clean-up
After completion of discharge, attention shall be paid to residues of this cargo, which are liable to decompose, resulting in emission of toxic gases and depletion of oxygen.

FISHMEAL (FISHSCRAP), STABILIZED UN 2216
Anti-oxidant treated

*The provisions of this entry should **not** apply to consignments of fishmeal, Group C, which are accompanied by a certificate issued by the competent authority of the country of shipment, stating that the material has no self-heating properties when transported in bulk.*

Description

Brown to greenish-brown material obtained through heating and drying of oily fish. Moisture content: greater than 5% but not exceeding 12%, by mass. Strong odour may affect other cargo.

Fat content: not more than 15%, by mass.

Characteristics

Angle of repose	Bulk density (kg/m³)	Stowage factor (m³/t)
Not applicable	300 to 700	1.5 to 3.0
Size	**Class**	**Group**
Not applicable	9	B

Hazard

Liable to heat spontaneously unless has low fat content or is effectively anti-oxidant treated. Liable to cause oxygen depletion in cargo space.

Stowage & segregation

Segregation as required for class 4.2 materials.

Hold cleanliness

Clean and dry as relevant to the hazards of the cargo.

Weather precautions

This cargo shall be kept as dry as practicable. This cargo shall not be handled during precipitation. During handling of this cargo, all non-working hatches of the cargo spaces into which this cargo is loaded or to be loaded shall be closed.

Loading

Trim in accordance with the relevant provisions required under sections 4 and 5 of the Code.

The cargo shall not be accepted for loading when the temperature of the cargo exceeds 35°C or 5°C above the ambient temperature, whichever is higher. The cargo may be loaded without weathering/curing prior to loading.

Precautions

1 This cargo shall only be accepted for loading when the stabilization of the cargo is achieved to prevent spontaneous combustion by effective application:

   .1 of between 400 and 1000 mg/kg (ppm) ethoxyquin, or

   .2 of between 1000 and 4000 mg/kg (ppm) butylated hydroxytoluene

   at the time of production, within 12 months prior to shipment, and anti-oxidant remnant concentration shall be not less than 100 mg/kg (ppm) at the time of shipment.

FISHMEAL (FISHSCRAP), STABILIZED UN 2216 *(concluded)*

2   The shipper shall provide the master with a certificate issued by a person recognized by the competent authority of the country of shipment specifying:

- moisture content;
- fat content;
- details of anti-oxidant treatment for meals older than six months;
- anti-oxidant concentrations at the time of shipment, which must exceed 100 mg/kg (ppm);
- total weight of the consignment;
- temperature of fishmeal at the time of dispatch from the factory; and
- date of production.

A suitable equipment for quantitative measurement of the concentration of oxygen in the cargo space shall be provided on board the ship.

Ventilation

Surface ventilation, either natural or mechanical, shall be conducted during the voyage, as necessary, for the cargo spaces carrying this cargo. If the temperature of the cargo exceeds 55°C and continues to increase, ventilation to the cargo space shall be stopped. If self-heating continues, then carbon dioxide or inert gas shall be introduced to the cargo spaces.

Carriage

This cargo shall be kept as cool and dry as reasonably practicable. The temperature of this cargo shall be measured at eight-hour intervals during the voyage. The results of measurements shall be recorded and kept on board.

Discharge

No special requirements.

Clean-up

No special requirements.

Emergency procedures

Special emergency equipment to be carried
Self-contained breathing apparatus.
Emergency procedures
Wear self-contained breathing apparatus.
Emergency action in the event of fire
Batten down; use ship's fixed fire-fighting installation, if fitted.
Medical First Aid
Refer to the *Medical First Aid Guide (MFAG)*, as amended.

FLUORSPAR

Description
Yellow, green or purple crystals. Coarse dust.

Characteristics

Angle of repose	Bulk density (kg/m³)	Stowage factor (m³/t)
Not applicable	Dry: 1429 to 1786 Wet: 1786 to 2128	Dry: 0.56 to 0.70 Wet: 0.47 to 0.56
Size	**Class**	**Group**
Not applicable	MHB	A and B

Hazard
This material may liquefy if shipped at moisture content in excess of their transportable moisture limit. See section 7 of the Code. Harmful and irritating by dust inhalation.

Stowage & segregation
"Separated from" foodstuffs and all class 8 materials (goods in packaged form and solid bulk materials).

Hold cleanliness
No special requirements.

Weather precautions
When a cargo is carried in a ship other than a specially constructed or fitted cargo ship complying with the requirements in subsection 7.3.2 of this Code, the following provisions shall be complied with:

.1 the moisture content of the cargo shall be kept less than its TML during voyage;

.2 unless expressly provided otherwise in this individual schedule, the cargo shall not be handled during precipitation;

.3 unless expressly provided otherwise in this individual schedule, during handling of the cargo, all non-working hatches of the cargo spaces into which the cargo is loaded or to be loaded shall be closed;

.4 the cargo may be handled during precipitation provided that the actual moisture content of the cargo is sufficiently less than its TML so that the actual moisture content is not liable to be increased beyond the TML by the precipitation; and

.5 the cargo in a cargo space may be discharged during precipitation provided that the total amount of the cargo in the cargo space is to be discharged in the port.

Loading
Trim in accordance with the relevant provisions required under sections 4 and 5 of the Code.

Precautions
Appropriate precautions shall be taken to protect machinery and accommodation spaces from the dust of the cargo. Bilge wells of the cargo spaces shall be protected from ingress of the cargo. Due consideration shall be paid to protect equipment from the dust of the cargo. Persons who may be exposed to the dust of the cargo shall wear goggles or other equivalent dust eye-protection and dust filter masks. Those persons shall wear protective clothing, as necessary.

Protect machinery, accommodation and bilge wells from dust.

FLUORSPAR *(concluded)*

Ventilation

No special requirements.

Carriage

No special requirements.

Discharge

No special requirements.

Clean-up

No special requirements.

Emergency procedures

Special emergency equipment to be carried Nil
Emergency procedures Nil **Emergency action in the event of fire** Nil **Medical First Aid** Refer to the *Medical First Aid Guide (MFAG)*, as amended.

FLY ASH

Description
Fly ash is the light, finely divided dusty fine powder residue from coal- and oil-fired power stations. Do not confuse with calcined pyrites.

Characteristics

Angle of repose	Bulk density (kg/m^3)	Stowage factor (m^3/t)
Not applicable	794	1.26
Size	**Class**	**Group**
Not applicable	Not applicable	C

Hazard
May shift when aerated.

This cargo is non-combustible or has a low fire-risk.

Stowage & segregation
"Separated from" foodstuffs.

Hold cleanliness
Clean and dry as relevant to the hazards of the cargo.

Weather precautions
This cargo shall be kept as dry as practicable. This cargo shall not be handled during precipitation. During handling of this cargo, all non-working hatches of the cargo spaces into which this cargo is loaded or to be loaded shall be closed.

Loading
Trim in accordance with the relevant provisions required under sections 4 and 5 of the Code.

The ship carrying this cargo shall not depart until the cargo has settled.

Precautions
Bilge wells shall be clean, dry and covered as appropriate, to prevent ingress of the cargo. Appropriate precautions shall be taken to protect machinery and accommodation spaces from the dust of the cargo. Bilge wells of the cargo spaces shall be protected from ingress of the cargo. Due consideration shall be paid to protect equipment from the dust of the cargo. Persons who may be exposed to the dust of the cargo shall wear protective clothing, goggles or other equivalent dust eye-protection and dust filter masks, as necessary.

Ventilation
No special requirements.

Carriage
After the completion of loading of this cargo, the hatches of the cargo spaces shall be sealed. All vents and access ways to the cargo spaces shall be shut during the voyage. Bilges in the cargo spaces carrying this cargo shall not be pumped unless absolutely necessary.

Discharge
No special requirements.

FLY ASH *(concluded)*

Clean-up

In the case that the residues of this cargo are to be washed out, the cargo spaces and the other structures and equipment which may have been in contact with this cargo or its dust shall be thoroughly swept prior to washing out. Particular attention shall be paid to bilge wells and framework in the cargo spaces. After complying with the foregoing requirements, the cargo spaces shall be washed out and the water for washing out shall be pumped out in an appropriate manner, except in the case that the BCSN of the cargo to be loaded subsequent to discharge is FLY ASH.

GRANULATED SLAG

Description
Residue from steelworks blast furnaces with a dirty grey, lumpy appearance. Iron: 0.5%.

Characteristics

Angle of repose	Bulk density (kg/m³)	Stowage factor (m³/t)
Not applicable	1111	0.90
Size	**Class**	**Group**
Up to 5 mm	Not applicable	C

Hazard
No special hazards. Slag dust is fine and has abrasive characteristics.

This cargo is non-combustible or has a low fire-risk.

Stowage & segregation
No special requirements.

Hold cleanliness
No special requirements.

Weather precautions
No special requirements.

Loading
Trim in accordance with the relevant provisions required under sections 4 and 5 of the Code.

This cargo shall not be accepted for loading when the temperature of the cargo exceeds 50°C.

Precautions
Appropriate precautions shall be taken to protect machinery and accommodation spaces from the dust of the cargo. Bilge wells of the cargo spaces shall be protected from ingress of the cargo. Due consideration shall be paid to protect equipment from the dust of the cargo. Persons who may be exposed to the dust of the cargo shall wear protective clothing, goggles or other equivalent dust eye-protection and dust filter masks, as necessary.

Ventilation
No special requirements.

Carriage
No special requirements.

Discharge
No special requirements.

Clean-up
No special requirements.

GRANULATED TYRE RUBBER

Description
Fragmented rubber tyre material cleaned and free from other materials.

Characteristics

Angle of repose	Bulk density (kg/m^3)	Stowage factor (m^3/t)
Not applicable	555	1.8
Size	**Class**	**Group**
Granular, up to 10 mm	Not applicable	C

Hazard
No special hazards.

This cargo is non-combustible or has a low fire-risk.

Stowage & segregation
No special requirements.

Hold cleanliness
No special requirements.

Weather precautions
No special requirements.

Loading
Trim in accordance with the relevant provisions required under sections 4 and 5 of the Code.

Precautions
During handling and carriage, no hot work, burning and smoking shall be permitted in the vicinity of the cargo spaces containing this cargo. Prior to shipment, a certificate shall be given to the master by the shipper stating that this cargo consists of clean rubber material only. When the planned interval between the commencement of loading and the completion of discharge of this cargo exceeds 5 days, the cargo shall not be accepted for loading unless the cargo is to be carried in cargo spaces fitted with a fixed gas fire-extinguishing system. The administration may, if it considers that the planned voyage does not exceed 5 days from the commencement of loading to the completion of discharge, exempt from the requirements of a fitted fixed gas fire-extinguishing system in the cargo spaces for the carriage of this cargo.

Ventilation
No special requirements.

Carriage
No special requirements.

Discharge
No special requirements.

Clean-up
No special requirements.

GYPSUM

Description

A natural hydrated calcium sulphate. Insoluble in water. It is loaded as a fine powder that aggregates into lumps. Gypsum is not water soluble. Average moisture content is 1% to 2%.

Characteristics

Angle of repose	Bulk density (kg/m³)	Stowage factor (m³/t)
Not applicable	1282 to 1493	0.67 to 0.78
Size	**Class**	**Group**
Up to 100 mm	Not applicable	C

Hazard

No special hazards.

This cargo is non-combustible or has a low fire-risk.

Stowage & segregation

No special requirements.

Hold cleanliness

No special requirements.

Weather precautions

This cargo shall be kept as dry as practicable. This cargo shall not be handled during precipitation. During handling of this cargo, all non-working hatches of the cargo spaces into which this cargo is loaded or to be loaded shall be closed.

Loading

Trim in accordance with the relevant provisions required under sections 4 and 5 of the Code.

Precautions

No special requirements.

Ventilation

No special requirements.

Carriage

No special requirements.

Discharge

No special requirements.

Clean-up

Prior to washing out the residues of this cargo, the decks and the cargo spaces shall be shovelled and swept clean, because washing out of this cargo is difficult.

ILMENITE CLAY

Description

Very heavy black clay. Abrasive. May be dusty. Titanium, silicate and iron oxides are obtained from ilmenite clay. Moisture content: 10% to 20%.

Characteristics

Angle of repose	Bulk density (kg/m³)	Stowage factor (m³/t)
Not applicable	2000 to 2500	0.4 to 0.5
Size	**Class**	**Group**
Up to 0.15 mm	Not applicable	A

Hazard

The material may liquefy if shipped at a moisture content in excess of its Transportable Moisture Limit (TML).

This cargo is non-combustible or has a low fire-risk.

Stowage & segregation

No special requirements.

Hold cleanliness

No special requirements.

Weather precautions

When a cargo is carried in a ship other than a specially constructed or fitted cargo ship complying with the requirements in subsection 7.3.2 of this Code, the following provisions shall be complied with:

.1   the moisture content of the cargo shall be kept less than its TML during voyage;

.2   unless expressly provided otherwise in this individual schedule, the cargo shall not be handled during precipitation;

.3   unless expressly provided otherwise in this individual schedule, during handling of the cargo, all non-working hatches of the cargo spaces into which the cargo is loaded or to be loaded shall be closed;

.4   the cargo may be handled during precipitation provided that the actual moisture content of the cargo is sufficiently less than its TML so that the actual moisture content is not liable to be increased beyond the TML by the precipitation; and

.5   the cargo in a cargo space may be discharged during precipitation provided that the total amount of the cargo in the cargo space is to be discharged in the port.

Loading

Trim in accordance with the relevant provisions required under sections 4 and 5 of the Code.

As the density of the cargo is extremely high, the tanktop may be overstressed unless the cargo is evenly spread across the tanktop to equalize the weight distribution. Due consideration shall be paid to ensure that the tanktop is not overstressed during voyage and during loading by a pile of the cargo.

Precautions

Bilge wells shall be clean, dry and covered as appropriate, to prevent ingress of the cargo.

ILMENITE CLAY *(concluded)*

Ventilation

No special requirements.

Carriage

The appearance of the surface of this cargo shall be checked regularly during voyage. If free water above the cargo or fluid state of the cargo is observed during voyage, the master shall take appropriate actions to prevent cargo shifting and potential capsize of the ship, and give consideration to seeking emergency entry into a place of refuge.

Discharge

No special requirements.

Clean-up

No special requirements.

ILMENITE SAND

This cargo can be categorized as Group A or C.

Description

Very heavy black sand. Abrasive. May be dusty. Titanium, monazite and zinc ore are obtained from ilmenite sand. The moisture content of this cargo in Group C is 1% to 2%. When moisture content is above 2%, this cargo is to be categorized in Group A.

Characteristics

Angle of repose	Bulk density (kg/m³)	Stowage factor (m³/t)
Not applicable	2380 to 3225	0.31 to 0.42
Size	**Class**	**Group**
Up to 0.15 mm	Not applicable	A or C

Hazard

This cargo in Group C has no special hazards. This cargo in Group A may liquefy if shipped at a moisture content in excess of its IML. See section 7 of this Code.

This cargo is non combustible or has a low fire-risk.

Stowage & segregation

No special requirements.

Hold cleanliness

No special requirements.

Weather precautions

This cargo shall be kept as dry as practicable before loading, during loading and during voyage. This cargo shall not be loaded during precipitation. During loading of this cargo, all non-working hatches of the cargo spaces to which this cargo is loaded or to be loaded shall be closed.

Loading

Trim in accordance with the relevant provisions required under sections 4 and 5 of the Code.

As the density of the cargo is extremely high, the tanktop may be overstressed unless the cargo is evenly spread across the tanktop to equalize the weight distribution. Due consideration shall be paid to ensure that the tanktop is not overstressed during voyage and during loading by a pile of the cargo.

Precautions

Bilge wells shall be clean, dry and covered as appropriate, to prevent ingress of the cargo.

Ventilation

No special requirements.

Carriage

The appearance of the surface of this cargo shall be checked regularly during voyage. If free water above the cargo or fluid state of the cargo is observed during voyage, the master shall take appropriate actions to prevent cargo shifting and potential capsize of the ship, and give consideration to seeking emergency entry into a place of refuge.

ILMENITE SAND *(concluded)*

Discharge
No special requirements.

Clean-up
No special requirements.

IRON ORE

Description

Iron ore varies in colour from dark grey to rusty red. It varies in iron content from haematite, (high grade ore) to ironstone of the lower commercial ranges. Moisture content: 0% to 16%. Mineral Concentrates are different cargoes (see IRON CONCENTRATE).

Characteristics

Angle of repose	Bulk density (kg/m³)	Stowage factor (m³/t)
Not applicable	1250 to 3448	0.29 to 0.80
Size	**Class**	**Group**
Up to 250 mm	Not applicable	C

Hazard

No special hazards.

This cargo is non-combustible or has a low fire-risk.

Iron ore cargoes may affect magnetic compasses.

Stowage & segregation

No special requirements.

Hold cleanliness

No special requirements.

Weather precautions

No special requirements.

Loading

Trim in accordance with the relevant provisions required under sections 4 and 5 of the Code.

As the density of the cargo is extremely high, the tanktop may be overstressed unless the cargo is evenly spread across the tanktop to equalize the weight distribution. Due consideration shall be paid to ensure that the tanktop is not overstressed during voyage and during loading by a pile of the cargo.

Precautions

Loading rates of this cargo are normally very high. Due consideration shall be paid on the ballasting operation to develop the loading plan required by regulation VI/9.3 in the SOLAS Convention.

Ventilation

No special requirements.

Carriage

No special requirements.

Discharge

No special requirements.

Clean-up

No special requirements.

IRON ORE PELLETS

Description

Pellets are approximately spherical lumps formed by crushing iron ore into a powder. This iron oxide is formed into pellets by using clay as a binder and then hardening by firing in kilns at 1315°C. Moisture content: 0% to 2%.

Characteristics

Angle of repose	Bulk density (kg/m³)	Stowage factor (m³/t)
Not applicable	1900 to 2400	0.45 to 0.52
Size	**Class**	**Group**
Up to 20 mm	Not applicable	C

Hazard

No special hazards.

This cargo is non-combustible or has a low fire-risk.

Stowage & segregation

No special requirements.

Hold cleanliness

No special requirements.

Weather precautions

No special requirements.

Loading

Trim in accordance with the relevant provisions required under sections 4 and 5 of the Code.

As the density of the cargo is extremely high, the tanktop may be overstressed unless the cargo is evenly spread across the tanktop to equalize the weight distribution. Due consideration shall be paid to ensure that the tanktop is not overstressed during voyage and during loading by a pile of the cargo.

Precautions

No special requirements.

Bilge wells shall be clean, dry and covered as appropriate, to prevent ingress of the cargo.

Ventilation

No special requirements.

Carriage

No special requirements.

Discharge

No special requirements.

Clean-up

No special requirements.

IRON OXIDE, SPENT or
IRON SPONGE, SPENT UN 1376
obtained from coal gas purification

Description
Powdery material, black, brown, red or yellow. Strong odour may taint other cargo.

Characteristics

Angle of repose	Bulk density (kg/m³)	Stowage factor (m³/t)
Not applicable	2222	0.45
Size	**Class**	**Group**
Up to 20 mm	4.2	B

Hazard
Liable to heat and ignite spontaneously, especially if contaminated with oil or moisture. Toxic gases: hydrogen sulphide, sulphur dioxide, and hydrogen cyanide may be produced. Dust may cause an explosion hazard. Liable to reduce the oxygen in the cargo space.

Stowage & segregation
"Separated from" foodstuffs.

Hold cleanliness
Clean and dry as relevant to the hazards of the cargo.

Weather precautions
This cargo shall be kept as dry as practicable. This cargo shall not be handled during precipitation. During handling of this cargo, all non-working hatches of the cargo spaces into which this cargo is loaded or to be loaded shall be closed.

Loading
Trim in accordance with the relevant provisions required under sections 4 and 5 of the Code.

As the density of the cargo is extremely high, the tanktop may be overstressed unless the cargo is evenly spread across the tanktop to equalize the weight distribution. Due consideration shall be paid to ensure that the tanktop is not overstressed during voyage and during loading by a pile of the cargo.

Precautions
Prior to loading, the shipper or the manufacturer shall provide the master with a certificate stating that the cargo has been cooled and then weathered for not less than 8 weeks prior to shipment.

Ventilation
Surface ventilation only, either natural or mechanical, shall be conducted, as necessary, during the voyage for this cargo.

IRON OXIDE, SPENT or IRON SPONGE, SPENT UN 1376 *(concluded)*

Carriage

For quantitative measurements of oxygen and hydrogen cyanide, suitable detectors for each gas or combination of gases shall be on board while this cargo is carried. The detectors shall be suitable for use in an atmosphere without oxygen and of certified safe type for use in explosive atmosphere. The concentrations of these gases in the cargo spaces carrying this cargo shall be measured regularly, during voyage, and the results of the measurements shall be recorded and kept on board.

Discharge

No special requirements.

Clean-up

No special requirements.

Emergency procedures

Special emergency equipment to be carried Protective clothing (gloves, boots, coveralls, headgear). Self-contained breathing apparatus. Spray nozzles.
Emergency procedures Wear protective clothing and self-contained breathing apparatus. **Emergency action in the event of fire** Batten down; use ship's fixed fire-fighting installation, if available. Exclusion of air may be sufficient to control fire. **Medical First Aid** Refer to the *Medical First Aid Guide (MFAG)*, as amended.

IRONSTONE

Description

Ore. Moisture: 1% to 2%

Characteristics

Angle of repose	Bulk density (kg/m³)	Stowage factor (m³/t)
Not applicable	2564	0.39
Size	**Class**	**Group**
75 mm	Not applicable	C

Hazard

No special hazards.

This cargo is non-combustible or has a low fire-risk.

Stowage & segregation

No special requirements.

Hold cleanliness

No special requirements.

Weather precautions

No special requirements.

Loading

Trim in accordance with relevant provisions required under sections 4 and 5 of the Code. If doubt exists, trim reasonably level to the boundaries of the cargo space so as to minimize the risk of shifting and to ensure that adequate stability will be maintained during the voyage.

As the density of the cargo is extremely high, the tanktop may be overstressed unless the cargo is evenly spread across the tanktop to equalize the weight distribution. Due consideration shall be paid to ensure that the tanktop is not overstressed during voyage and during loading by a pile of the cargo.

Precautions

Appropriate precautions shall be taken to protect machinery and accommodation spaces from the dust of the cargo. Bilge wells of the cargo spaces shall be protected from ingress of the cargo. Due consideration shall be paid to protect equipment from the dust of the cargo. Persons who may be exposed to the dust of the cargo shall wear protective clothing, goggles or other equivalent dust eye-protection and dust filter masks, as necessary.

Ventilation

No special requirements.

Carriage

No special requirements.

Discharge

No special requirements.

Clean-up

No special requirements.

LABRADORITE

Description
A lime-soda rock form of felspar. May give off dust.

Characteristics

Angle of repose	Bulk density (kg/m^3)	Stowage factor (m^3/t)
Not applicable	1667	0.60
Size	**Class**	**Group**
Lumps: 50 mm to 300 mm	Not applicable	C

Hazard
No special hazards.

This cargo is non-combustible or has a low fire-risk.

Stowage & segregation
No special requirements.

Hold cleanliness
Clean and dry as relevant to the hazards of the cargo.

Weather precautions
This cargo shall be kept as dry as practicable before loading, during loading and during voyage. This cargo shall not be loaded during precipitation. During loading of this cargo, all non-working hatches of the cargo spaces to which this cargo is loaded or to be loaded shall be closed.

Loading
Trim in accordance with the relevant provisions required under sections 4 and 5 of the Code.

Precautions
Appropriate precautions shall be taken to protect machinery and accommodation spaces from the dust of the cargo. Bilge wells of the cargo spaces shall be protected from ingress of the cargo. Due consideration shall be paid to protect equipment from the dust of the cargo. Persons who may be exposed to the dust of the cargo shall wear protective clothing, goggles or other equivalent dust eye-protection and dust filter masks, as necessary.

Ventilation
No special requirements.

Carriage
No special requirements.

Discharge
No special requirements.

Clean-up
No special requirements.

LEAD NITRATE UN 1469

Description
White crystals. Soluble in water. Derived from the action of nitric acid on lead.

Characteristics

Angle of repose	Bulk density (kg/m^3)		Stowage factor (m^3/t)
Not applicable	–		–
Size	**Class**	**Subsidiary risk**	**Group**
Not applicable	5.1	6.1	B

Hazard
Toxic if swallowed or dust inhaled.

Not combustible by itself, but mixtures with combustible materials are easily ignited and burn fiercely.

Stowage & segregation
"Separated from" foodstuffs.

Hold cleanliness
Clean and dry as relevant to the hazards of the cargo.

Weather precautions
This cargo shall be kept as dry as practicable before loading, during loading and during voyage. This cargo shall not be loaded during precipitation. During loading of this cargo, all non-working hatches of the cargo spaces to which this cargo is loaded or to be loaded shall be closed.

Loading
Trim in accordance with the relevant provisions required under sections 4 and 5 of the Code.

Precautions
Bilge wells shall be clean, dry and covered as appropriate, to prevent ingress of the cargo. Appropriate precautions shall be taken to protect machinery and accommodation spaces from the dust of the cargo. Bilge wells of the cargo spaces shall be protected from ingress of the cargo. Due consideration shall be paid to protect equipment from the dust of the cargo. Persons who may be exposed to the dust of the cargo shall wear goggles or other equivalent dust eye-protection and dust filter masks. Those persons shall wear protective clothing, as necessary.

Ventilation
Natural surface ventilation shall be conducted during the voyage, as necessary, for the cargo spaces carrying this cargo.

Carriage
No special requirements.

Discharge
No special requirements.

Clean-up
No special requirements.

LEAD NITRATE UN 1469 *(concluded)*

Emergency procedures

Special emergency equipment to be carried
Protective clothing (gloves, coveralls, headgear).
Self-contained breathing apparatus.
Spray nozzles.

Emergency procedures
Wear protective clothing and self-contained breathing apparatus.

Emergency action in the event of fire
Use copious quantities of water, which is best applied in the form of a spray to avoid disturbing the surface of the material. The material may fuse or melt, in which condition application of water may result in extensive scattering of the molten materials. Exclusion of air or the use of CO_2 will not control the fire. Due consideration should be given to the effect on the stability of the ship due to accumulated water.

Medical First Aid
Refer to the *Medical First Aid Guide (MFAG)*, as amended.

LEAD ORE

Description
Heavy soft grey solid material.

Characteristics

Angle of repose	Bulk density (kg/m³)	Stowage factor (m³/t)
Not applicable	1493 to 4167	0.24 to 0.67
Size	**Class**	**Group**
Powder	Not applicable	C

Hazard
Toxic, with acids evolves highly toxic vapour.

This cargo is non-combustible or has a low fire-risk.

Stowage & segregation
"Separated from" all class 8 liquids.

Hold cleanliness
Clean and dry as relevant to the hazards of the cargo.

Weather precautions
This cargo shall be kept as dry as practicable before loading, during loading and during voyage. This cargo shall not be loaded during precipitation. During loading of this cargo, all non-working hatches of the cargo spaces to which this cargo is loaded or to be loaded shall be closed.

Loading
Trim in accordance with the relevant provisions required under sections 4 and 5 of the Code.

As the density of the cargo is extremely high, the tanktop may be overstressed unless the cargo is evenly spread across the tanktop to equalize the weight distribution. Due consideration shall be paid to ensure that the tanktop is not overstressed during voyage and during loading by a pile of the cargo.

Precautions
No special requirements.

Ventilation
No special requirements.

Carriage
No special requirements.

Discharge
No special requirements.

Clean-up
No special requirements.

LIME (UNSLAKED)

Description
White or greyish-white in colour.

Characteristics

Angle of repose	Bulk density (kg/m³)	Stowage factor (m³/t)
Not applicable	–	–
Size	**Class**	**Group**
Lump	MHB	B

Hazard
Unslaked lime combines with water to form calcium hydroxide (hydrated lime) or magnesium hydroxide. This reaction develops a great deal of heat which may be sufficient to cause ignition of nearby combustible materials. This is not combustible or has a low fire-risk. Corrosive to eyes and mucous membranes.

Stowage & segregation
"Separated from" all packaged dangerous goods and solid bulk cargoes in Group B.

Hold cleanliness
Clean and dry as relevant to the hazards of the cargo.

Weather precautions
This cargo shall be kept as dry as practicable. This cargo shall not be handled during precipitation. During handling of this cargo, all non-working hatches of the cargo spaces into which this cargo is loaded or to be loaded shall be closed.

Loading
Trim in accordance with the relevant provisions required under sections 4 and 5 of the Code.

Precautions
This cargo shall be kept as dry as practicable. Bilge wells shall be clean, dry and covered as appropriate, to prevent ingress of the cargo. Appropriate precautions shall be taken to protect machinery and accommodation spaces from the dust of the cargo. Bilge wells of the cargo spaces shall be protected from ingress of the cargo. Due consideration shall be paid to protect equipment from the dust of the cargo. Persons who may be exposed to the dust of the cargo shall wear goggles or other equivalent dust eye-protection and dust filter masks. Those persons shall wear protective clothing, as necessary.

Ventilation
No special requirements.

Carriage
No special requirements.

Discharge
Do not discharge during precipitation.

Clean-up
No special requirements.

LIME (UNSLAKED) *(concluded)*

Emergency procedures

Special emergency equipment to be carried Nil
Emergency procedures Nil **Emergency action in the event of fire** Nil (non-combustible). **Do not use water**, if involved in a fire. **Medical First Aid** Refer to the *Medical First Aid Guide (MFAG)*, as amended.

LIMESTONE

Description

Limestone varies in colour from cream through white to medium dark grey (when freshly broken).

Moisture: up to 4%.

Characteristics

Angle of repose	Bulk density (kg/m³)	Stowage factor (m³/t)
Not applicable	1190 to 1493	0.67 to 0.84
Size	**Class**	**Group**
Fines to 90 mm	Not applicable	C

Hazard

No special hazards.

This cargo is non-combustible or has a low fire-risk.

Stowage & segregation

No special requirements.

Hold cleanliness

No special requirements.

Weather precautions

No special requirements.

Loading

Trim in accordance with the relevant provisions required under sections 4 and 5 of the Code.

Precautions

Bilge wells shall be clean, dry and covered as appropriate, to prevent ingress of the cargo.

Ventilation

No special requirements.

Carriage

No special requirements.

Discharge

No special requirements.

Clean-up

No special requirements.

LINTED COTTON SEED
with not more than 9% moisture and not more than 20.5% oil

Description
Cottonseed with short cotton fibres adhering to the kernel after approximately 90–98% of the cotton has been removed by machine.

Characteristics

Angle of repose	Bulk density (kg/m^3)	Stowage factor (m^3/t)
Not applicable	490	2.02
Size	**Class**	**Group**
–	MHB	B

Hazard
May self-heat and deplete oxygen in cargo space.

Stowage & segregation
No special requirements.

Hold cleanliness
Clean and dry as relevant to the hazards of the cargo.

Weather precautions
This cargo shall be kept as dry as practicable. This cargo shall not be handled during precipitation. During handling of this cargo, all non-working hatches of the cargo spaces into which this cargo is loaded or to be loaded shall be closed.

Loading
Trim in accordance with the relevant provisions required under sections 4 and 5 of the Code.

Precautions
Entry into the cargo space for this cargo shall not be permitted until the cargo space has been ventilated and the atmosphere tested for concentration of oxygen.

Ventilation
No special requirements.

Carriage
Hatches should be weathertight to prevent the ingress of water.

Discharge
If this cargo has hardened, it shall be trimmed to avoid the formation of overhanging faces, as necessary.

Clean-up
No special requirements.

LINTED COTTON SEED *(concluded)*

Emergency procedures

Special emergency equipment to be carried
Self-contained breathing apparatus.

Emergency procedures
Wear self-contained breathing apparatus.

Emergency action in the event of fire
Batten down; use ship's fixed fire-fighting installation, if fitted.

Medical First Aid
Refer to the *Medical First Aid Guide (MFAG)*, as amended.

MAGNESIA (DEADBURNED)

Description

Manufactured in briquette form and is usually white, brown or grey. It is very similar in size, appearance and handling to gravel and is dry and dusty. Deadburned magnesia is natural magnesite calcined at very high temperatures, which results in a non-reactive magnesium oxide, which does not hydrate or produce spontaneous heat.

Characteristics

Angle of repose	Bulk density (kg/m³)	Stowage factor (m³/t)
Not applicable	2000	0.5
Size	**Class**	**Group**
Fines to approx. 30 mm	Not applicable	C

Hazard

No special hazards.

This cargo is non-combustible or has a low fire-risk.

Stowage & segregation

No special requirements.

Hold cleanliness

No special requirements.

Weather precautions

No special requirements.

Loading

Trim in accordance with the relevant provisions required under sections 4 and 5 of the Code.

Precautions

Prior to loading, the shipper or the manufacturer shall provide the master with a declaration stating that the cargo has been sufficiently heat-treated and is ready for loading.

Ventilation

No special requirements.

Carriage

No special requirements.

Discharge

No special requirements.

Clean-up

No special requirements.

MAGNESIA (UNSLAKED)

Description

Characteristics

Angle of repose	Bulk density (kg/m³)	Stowage factor (m³/t)
Not applicable	1250	0.80
Size	**Class**	**Group**
Fines to 90 mm	MHB	B

Hazard

Combines with water to form magnesium hydroxide with an expansion in volume and a release of heat. May ignite materials with low ignition temperatures. Similar to LIME (UNSLAKED) but is less reactive. Corrosive to eyes and mucous membranes.

This cargo is non-combustible or has a low fire-risk.

Stowage & segregation

"Separated from" all packaged dangerous goods and solid bulk cargoes in Group B.

Hold cleanliness

Clean and dry as relevant to the hazards of the cargo.

Weather precautions

This cargo shall be kept as dry as practicable. This cargo shall not be handled during precipitation. During handling of this cargo, all non-working hatches of the cargo spaces into which this cargo is loaded or to be loaded shall be closed.

Loading

Trim in accordance with the relevant provisions required under sections 4 and 5 of the Code.

Precautions

Appropriate precautions shall be taken to protect machinery and accommodation spaces from the dust of the cargo. Bilge wells of the cargo spaces shall be protected from ingress of the cargo. Due consideration shall be paid to protect equipment from the dust of the cargo. Persons who may be exposed to the dust of the cargo shall wear goggles or other equivalent dust eye-protection and dust filter masks. Those persons shall wear protective clothing, as necessary.

Ventilation

No special requirements.

Carriage

No special requirements.

Discharge

Do not discharge during precipitation.

Clean-up

No special requirements.

MAGNESIA (UNSLAKED) *(concluded)*

Emergency procedures

Special emergency equipment to be carried Nil
Emergency procedures Nil **Emergency action in the event of fire** Nil (non-combustible). **Do not use water** if cargo is involved in a fire. **Medical First Aid** Refer to the *Medical First Aid Guide (MFAG)*, as amended.

MAGNESITE, natural

Description

Magnesite is white to yellow in colour.

Characteristics

Angle of repose	Bulk density (kg/m^3)	Stowage factor (m^3/t)
Not applicable	1429	0.7
Size	**Class**	**Group**
3 mm to 30 mm	Not applicable	C

Hazard

No special hazards.

This cargo is non-combustible or has a low fire-risk.

Stowage & segregation

No special requirements.

Hold cleanliness

No special requirements.

Weather precautions

No special requirements.

Loading

Trim in accordance with the relevant provisions required under sections 4 and 5 of the Code.

Precautions

No special requirements.

Ventilation

No special requirements.

Carriage

No special requirements.

Discharge

No special requirements.

Clean-up

No special requirements.

MAGNESIUM NITRATE UN 1474

Description
White crystals, soluble in water. Hygroscopic.

Characteristics

Angle of repose	Bulk density (kg/m^3)	Stowage factor (m^3/t)
Not applicable	–	–
Size	**Class**	**Group**
Not applicable	5.1	B

Hazard
Although non-combustible by itself, mixtures with combustible material are easily ignited and may burn fiercely.

This cargo is hygroscopic and will cake if wet.

Stowage & segregation
"Separated from" foodstuffs.

Hold cleanliness
Clean and dry as relevant to the hazards of the cargo.

Weather precautions
No special requirements.

Loading
Trim in accordance with the relevant provisions required under sections 4 and 5 of the Code.

Precautions
No special requirements.

Ventilation
No special requirements.

Carriage
No special requirements.

Discharge
If this cargo has hardened, it shall be trimmed to avoid the formation of overhangs, as necessary.

Clean-up
No special requirements.

MAGNESIUM NITRATE UN 1474 *(concluded)*

Emergency procedures

Special emergency equipment to be carried

Protective clothing (gloves, boots, coveralls, headgear).

Self-contained breathing apparatus.

Spray nozzles.

Emergency procedures

Wear protective clothing and self-contained breathing apparatus.

Emergency action in the event of fire

Use copious quantities of water, which is best applied in the form of a spray to avoid disturbing the surface of the material. The material may fuse or melt, in which condition application of water may result in extensive scattering of the molten materials. Exclusion of air or the use of CO_2 will not control the fire. Due consideration should be given to the effect on the stability of the ship due to the accumulated water.

Medical First Aid

Refer to the *Medical First Aid Guide (MFAG)*, as amended.

Remarks

Material is non-combustible unless contaminated.

MANGANESE ORE

Description

Manganese ore is black to brownish black in colour. It is a very heavy cargo.

Moisture content: up to 15%.

Characteristics

Angle of repose	Bulk density (kg/m³)	Stowage factor (m³/t)
Not applicable	1429 to 3125	Fines to 0.32 Lumps to 0.70

Size	Class	Group
Fine dust to 250 mm	Not applicable	C

Hazard

No special hazards.

This cargo is non-combustible or has a low fire-risk.

Stowage & segregation

No special requirements.

Hold cleanliness

No special requirements.

Weather precautions

No special requirements.

Loading

Trim in accordance with the relevant provisions required under sections 4 and 5 of the Code.

As the density of the cargo is extremely high, the tanktop may be overstressed unless the cargo is evenly spread across the tanktop to equalize the weight distribution. Due consideration shall be paid to ensure that the tanktop is not overstressed during voyage and during loading by a pile of the cargo.

Precautions

Appropriate precautions shall be taken to protect machinery and accommodation spaces from the dust of the cargo. Bilge wells of the cargo spaces shall be protected from ingress of the cargo. Due consideration shall be paid to protect equipment from the dust of the cargo. Persons who may be exposed to the dust of the cargo shall wear protective clothing, goggles or other equivalent dust eye-protection and dust filter masks, as necessary.

Ventilation

No special requirements.

Carriage

No special requirements.

Discharge

No special requirements.

Clean-up

No special requirements.

MARBLE CHIPS

Description
Dry, dusty, white to grey lumps, particles and powder mixed with a small amount of gravel and pebbles.

Characteristics

Angle of repose	Bulk density (kg/m³)	Stowage factor (m³/t)
Not applicable	654	1.53
Size	**Class**	**Group**
Not applicable	Not applicable	C

Hazard
No special hazards.

This cargo is non-combustible or has a low fire-risk.

Stowage & segregation
No special requirements.

Hold cleanliness
No special requirements.

Weather precautions
No special requirements.

Loading
Trim in accordance with the relevant provisions required under sections 4 and 5 of the Code.

Precautions
Appropriate precautions shall be taken to protect machinery and accommodation spaces from the dust of the cargo. Bilge wells of the cargo spaces shall be protected from ingress of the cargo. Due consideration shall be paid to protect equipment from the dust of the cargo. Persons who may be exposed to the dust of the cargo shall wear protective clothing, goggles or other equivalent dust eye-protection and dust filter masks, as necessary.

Ventilation
No special requirements.

Carriage
No special requirements.

Discharge
No special requirements.

Clean-up
No special requirements.

METAL SULPHIDE CONCENTRATES
(See also Mineral Concentrates schedule)

Description

Mineral concentrates are refined ores in which the valuable components have been enriched by eliminating the bulk of waste materials. Generally the particle size is small although agglomerates sometimes exist in concentrates which have not been freshly produced.

The most common concentrates in this category are: zinc concentrates, lead concentrates, copper concentrates and low-grade middling concentrates.

Characteristics

Angle of repose	Bulk density (kg/m^3)	Stowage factor (m^3/t)
Not applicable	1790 to 3230	0.31 to 0.56
Size	**Class**	**Group**
Various	MHB	A and B

Hazard

Some sulphide concentrates are liable to oxidation and may have a tendency to self-heat, with associated oxygen depletion and emission of toxic fumes. Some materials may present corrosion problems.

When a Metal Sulphide Concentrate is considered as presenting a low fire-risk, the carriage of such cargo on a ship not fitted with a fixed gas fire-extinguishing system should be subject to the Administration's authorization as provided by SOLAS regulation II-2/10.7.1.4.

Stowage & segregation

Unless determined by the competent authority, segregation as required for class 4.2 materials.

"Separated from" foodstuffs and all class 8 acids.

Hold cleanliness

Clean and dry as relevant to the hazards of the cargo.

Weather precautions

When a cargo is carried in a ship other than a specially constructed or fitted cargo ship complying with the requirements in subsection 7.3.2 of this Code, the following provisions shall be complied with:

 .1 the moisture content of the cargo shall be kept less than its TML during voyage;

 .2 unless expressly provided otherwise in this individual schedule, the cargo shall not be handled during precipitation;

 .3 unless expressly provided otherwise in this individual schedule, during handling of the cargo, all non-working hatches of the cargo spaces into which the cargo is loaded or to be loaded shall be closed;

 .4 the cargo may be handled during precipitation provided that the actual moisture content of the cargo is sufficiently less than its TML so that the actual moisture content is not liable to be increased beyond the TML by the precipitation; and

 .5 the cargo in a cargo space may be discharged during precipitation provided that the total amount of the cargo in the cargo space is to be discharged in the port.

METAL SULPHIDE CONCENTRATES *(continued)*

Loading

This cargo shall be trimmed to ensure that the height difference between peaks and troughs does not exceed 5% of the ship's breadth and that the cargo slopes uniformly from the hatch boundaries to the bulkheads and no shearing faces remain to collapse during voyage, in particular on smaller ships, i.e., 100 m long or less.

As the density of the cargo is extremely high, the tanktop may be overstressed unless the cargo is evenly spread across the tanktop to equalize the weight distribution. Due consideration shall be paid to ensure that the tanktop is not overstressed during the voyage and during loading by a pile of the cargo.

Precautions

Entry into the cargo space for this cargo shall not be permitted until the cargo space has been ventilated and the atmosphere tested for concentration of oxygen. Appropriate precautions shall be taken to protect machinery and accommodation spaces from the dust of the cargo. Bilge wells of the cargo spaces shall be protected from ingress of the cargo. Due consideration shall be paid to protect equipment from the dust of the cargo. Persons who may be exposed to the dust of the cargo shall wear goggles or other equivalent dust eye-protection and dust filter masks. Those persons shall wear protective clothing, as necessary.

Ventilation

The cargo spaces carrying this cargo shall not be ventilated during voyage.

Carriage

The appearance of the surface of this cargo shall be checked regularly during voyage. If free water above the cargo or fluid state of the cargo is observed during voyage, the master shall take appropriate actions to prevent cargo shifting and potential capsize of the ship, and give consideration to seeking emergency entry into a place of refuge. For quantitative measurements of oxygen and toxic fumes liable to be evolved by the cargo, suitable detectors for each gas and fume or combination of these shall be on board while this cargo is carried. The detectors shall be suitable for use in an atmosphere without oxygen. The concentrations of these gases in the cargo spaces carrying this cargo shall be measured regularly, during voyage, and the results of the measurements shall be recorded and kept on board.

Discharge

No special requirements.

Clean-up

No special requirements.

METAL SULPHIDE CONCENTRATES *(concluded)*

Emergency procedures

Special emergency equipment to be carried .   Self-contained breathing apparatus.
Emergency procedures   Wear self-contained breathing apparatus.   **Emergency action in the event of fire**   Batten down; use ship's fixed fire-fighting installation.   Exclusion of air may be sufficient to control the fire. **Do not use water.**   **Medical First Aid**   Refer to the *Medical First Aid Guide (MFAG)*, as amended.

Remarks

Fire may be indicated by the smell of sulphur dioxide.

Mineral Concentrates

(See Bulk Cargo Shipping Names below)

CEMENT COPPER	NICKEL CONCENTRATE
COPPER CONCENTRATE	PENTAHYDRATE CRUDE
IRON CONCENTRATE	PYRITES
IRON CONCENTRATE (pellet feed)	PYRITIC ASHES (iron)
IRON CONCENTRATE (sinter feed)	PYRITIC CINDERS
LEAD AND ZINC CALCINES (mixed)	SILVER LEAD CONCENTRATE
LEAD AND ZINC MIDDLINGS	SLIG (iron ore)
LEAD CONCENTRATE	ZINC AND LEAD CALCINES (mixed)
LEAD ORE RESIDUE	ZINC AND LEAD MIDDLINGS
LEAD SILVER CONCENTRATE	ZINC CONCENTRATE
MANGANESE CONCENTRATE	ZINC SINTER
NEFELINE SYENITE (mineral)	ZINC SLUDGE

All known Bulk Cargo Shipping Names (BCSN) of mineral concentrates are listed above but the list is not exhaustive. See also the entries for METAL SULPHIDE CONCENTRATES.

Description

Mineral concentrates are refined ores in which valuable components have been enriched by eliminating the bulk of waste materials.

Characteristics

Angle of repose	Bulk density (kg/m^3)	Stowage factor (m^3/t)
Not applicable	1754 to 3030	0.33 to 0.57
Size	**Class**	**Group**
Various	Not applicable	A

Hazard

The above materials may liquefy if shipped at moisture content in excess of their transportable moisture limit (TML). See section 7 of the Code. These cargoes are non-combustible or have low fire-risks.

This cargo will decompose burlap or canvas cloth covering bilge wells. Continuous carriage of this cargo may have detrimental structural effects over a long period of time.

Stowage & segregation

No special requirements.

Hold cleanliness

No special requirements.

Weather precautions

When a cargo is carried in a ship other than a specially constructed or fitted cargo ship complying with the requirements in subsection 7.3.2 of this Code, the following provisions shall be complied with:

 .1 the moisture content of the cargo shall be kept less than its TML during voyage;

 .2 unless expressly provided otherwise in this individual schedule, the cargo shall not be handled during precipitation;

Mineral Concentrates *(concluded)*

.3   unless expressly provided otherwise in this individual schedule, during handling of the cargo, all non-working hatches of the cargo spaces into which the cargo is loaded or to be loaded shall be closed;

.4   the cargo may be handled during precipitation provided that the actual moisture content of the cargo is sufficiently less than its TML so that the actual moisture content is not liable to be increased beyond the TML by the precipitation; and

.5   the cargo in a cargo space may be discharged during precipitation provided that the total amount of the cargo in the cargo space is to be discharged in the port.

Loading

This cargo shall be trimmed to ensure that the height difference between peaks and troughs does not exceed 5% of the ship's breadth and that the cargo slopes uniformly from the hatch boundaries to the bulkheads and no shearing faces remain to collapse during voyage, in particular on smaller ships, i.e., 100 m long or less.

As the density of the cargo is extremely high, the tanktop may be overstressed unless the cargo is evenly spread across the tanktop to equalize the weight distribution. Due consideration shall be paid to ensure that the tanktop is not overstressed during the voyage and during loading by a pile of the cargo.

Precautions

Bilge wells shall be clean, dry and covered as appropriate, to prevent ingress of the cargo. The bilge system of a cargo space to which this cargo is to be loaded shall be tested to ensure it is working.

Ventilation

The cargo spaces carrying this cargo shall not be ventilated during voyage.

Carriage

The appearance of the surface of this cargo shall be checked regularly during voyage. If free water above the cargo or fluid state of the cargo is observed during voyage, the master shall take appropriate actions to prevent cargo shifting and potential capsize of the ship, and give consideration to seeking emergency entry into a place of refuge.

Discharge

No special requirements.

Clean-up

No special requirements.

MONOAMMONIUM PHOSPHATE (M.A.P.)

Description
M.A.P. is odourless and comes in the form of brownish-grey granules. It can be very dusty. Hygroscopic.

Characteristics

Angle of repose	Bulk density (kg/m³)	Stowage factor (m³/t)
35° to 40°	826 to 1000	1.0 to 1.21
Size	**Class**	**Group**
Not applicable	Not applicable	C

Hazard
Bulk M.A.P. has a pH of 4.5 and in the presence of moisture content can be highly corrosive.

This cargo is non-combustible or has a low fire-risk.

This cargo is hygroscopic and will cake if wet.

This cargo will decompose burlap or canvas cloth covering bilge wells. Continuous carriage of this cargo may have detrimental structural effects over a long period of time.

Stowage & segregation
No special requirements.

Hold cleanliness
Clean and dry as relevant to the hazards of the cargo.

Weather precautions
This cargo shall be kept as dry as practicable. This cargo shall not be handled during precipitation. During handling of this cargo, all non-working hatches of the cargo spaces into which this cargo is loaded or to be loaded shall be closed.

Loading
Trim in accordance with the relevant provisions required under sections 4 and 5 of the Code.

Precautions
Appropriate precautions shall be taken to protect machinery and accommodation spaces from the dust of the cargo. Bilge wells of the cargo spaces shall be protected from ingress of the cargo. Due consideration shall be paid to protect equipment from the dust of the cargo. Persons who may be exposed to the dust of the cargo shall wear goggles or other equivalent dust eye-protection and dust filter masks. Those persons shall wear protective clothing, as necessary.

Ventilation
The cargo spaces carrying this cargo shall not be ventilated during voyage.

Carriage
Condensation in the cargo spaces carrying this cargo, sweating of this cargo and entering of water from hatch covers to the cargo spaces shall be checked regularly during the voyage. Due attention shall be paid to the sealing of hatches of the cargo spaces.

Discharge
If this cargo has hardened, it shall be trimmed to avoid the formation of overhangs, as necessary.

Clean-up
After discharge of this cargo, particular attention shall be paid to bilge wells of the cargo spaces.

PEANUTS (in shell)

Description
An edible, tan-coloured nut. Variable moisture content. Extremely dusty.

Characteristics

Angle of repose	Bulk density (kg/m³)	Stowage factor (m³/t)
Not applicable	304	3.29
Size	**Class**	**Group**
Not applicable	Not applicable	C

Hazard
May heat spontaneously.

This cargo is non-combustible or has a low fire-risk.

Stowage & segregation
"Away from" sources of heat.

Hold cleanliness
Clean and dry as relevant to the hazards of the cargo.

Weather precautions
No special requirements.

Loading
Trim in accordance with the relevant provisions required under sections 4 and 5 of the Code.

Precautions
Appropriate precautions shall be taken to protect machinery and accommodation spaces from the dust of the cargo. Bilge wells of the cargo spaces shall be protected from ingress of the cargo. Due consideration shall be paid to protect equipment from the dust of the cargo. Persons who may be exposed to the dust of the cargo shall wear protective clothing, goggles or other equivalent dust eye-protection and dust filter masks, as necessary.

Ventilation
The cargo spaces carrying this cargo shall not be ventilated during voyage.

Carriage
No special requirements.

Discharge
No special requirements.

Clean-up
No special requirements.

PEAT MOSS

Description

Surface mined from mires, bogs, fens, muskeg and swamps. Types include moss peat, sedge peat and grass peat. Physical properties depend on organic matter, water and air content, botanical decomposition and degree of decomposition.

May range from a highly fibrous cohesive mass of plant remains which, when squeezed in its natural state, exudes clear to slightly coloured water, to a well decomposed, largely amorphous material with little or no separation of liquid from solids when squeezed.

Typically air-dried peat has low density, high compressibility and high water content; in its natural state it can hold 90 percent or more of water by weight of water when saturated.

Characteristics

Angle of repose	Bulk density (kg/m^3)	Stowage factor (m^3/t)
Not applicable	80 to 500	2 to 12.5
Size	**Class**	**Group**
Fine powder	MHB	A and B

Hazard

Oxygen depletion and an increase in carbon dioxide in cargo and adjacent spaces.

Risk of dust explosion when loading. Caution should be exercised when walking or landing heavy machinery on the surface of uncompressed peat moss.

Peat moss having a moisture content of more than 80% by weight should only be carried on specially fitted or constructed ships (see paragraphs 7.2.2 to 7.2.4 of this Code).

Dust may cause eye, nose and respiratory irritation.

Stowage & segregation

No special requirements.

Hold cleanliness

Clean and dry as relevant to the hazards of the cargo.

Weather precautions

Prior to loading, this cargo shall be stockpiled under cover to effect drainage for reduction of moisture content. This cargo shall be kept as dry as practicable. This cargo shall not be handled during precipitation. During handling of this cargo, all non-working hatches of the cargo spaces into which this cargo is loaded or to be loaded shall be closed.

Loading

Trim in accordance with the relevant provisions required under sections 4 and 5 of the Code.

Precautions

Bilge wells shall be clean, dry and covered as appropriate, to prevent ingress of the cargo.

Appropriate precautions shall be taken to protect machinery and accommodation spaces from the dust of the cargo. Bilge wells of the cargo spaces shall be protected from ingress of the cargo. Due consideration shall be paid to protect equipment from the dust of the cargo. Persons who may be exposed to the dust of the cargo shall wear goggles or other equivalent dust eye-protection and dust filter masks. Those persons shall wear protective clothing, as necessary.

PEAT MOSS *(concluded)*

All personnel of the ship carrying this cargo and all personnel involved in handling of this cargo shall be cautioned that washing hands before eating or smoking and prompt treatment of cuts and scrapes are necessary in case of contact with this cargo or its dust. Entry of personnel into cargo spaces shall not be permitted until tests have been carried out and it has been established that the oxygen content has been restored to a normal level.

Ventilation
Surface ventilation only, either natural or mechanical, shall be conducted, as necessary, during the voyage for this cargo.

Carriage
No special requirements.

Discharge
No special requirements.

Clean-up
No special precautions.

Emergency procedures

Special emergency equipment to be carried
Nil
Emergency procedures Nil **Emergency action in the event of fire** Batten down; use ship's fixed fire-fighting installation, if fitted. Exclusion of air may be sufficient to control fire **Medical First Aid** Refer to the *Medical First Aid Guide (MFAG)*, as amended.

PEBBLES (sea)

Description
Round pebbles. Rolls very easily.

Characteristics

Angle of repose	Bulk density (kg/m^3)	Stowage factor (m^3/t)
Not applicable	1695	0.59
Size	**Class**	**Group**
30 mm to 110 mm	Not applicable	C

Hazard
No special hazards.

This cargo is non-combustible or has a low fire-risk.

Stowage & segregation
No special requirements.

Hold cleanliness
No special requirements.

Weather precautions
No special requirements.

Loading
Trim in accordance with the relevant provisions required under sections 4 and 5 of the Code.

Precautions
This cargo shall be loaded carefully to prevent damage to the tanktop.

Ventilation
No special requirements.

Carriage
No special requirements.

Discharge
No special requirements.

Clean-up
No special requirements.

PELLETS (concentrates)

Description
Concentrate ore which has been pelletized. Moisture up to 6%.

Characteristics

Angle of repose	Bulk density (kg/m³)	Stowage factor (m³/t)
Not applicable	2128	0.47
Size	**Class**	**Group**
10 mm approximately	Not applicable	C

Hazard
No special hazards.

This cargo is non-combustible or has a low fire-risk.

Stowage & segregation
No special requirements.

Hold cleanliness
Clean and dry as relevant to the hazards of the cargo.

Weather precautions
No special requirements.

Loading
Trim in accordance with the relevant provisions required under sections 4 and 5 of the Code.

Precautions
No special requirements.

Ventilation
No special requirements.

Carriage
No special requirements.

Discharge
No special requirements.

Clean-up
No special requirements.

PERLITE ROCK

Description

Clay-like and dusty. Light grey. Odourless. Moisture: 0.5% to 1%.

Characteristics

Angle of repose	Bulk density (kg/m³)	Stowage factor (m³/t)
Not applicable	943 to 1020	0.98 to 1.06
Size	**Class**	**Group**
Not applicable	Not applicable	C

Hazard

No special hazards.

This cargo is non-combustible or has a low fire-risk.

Stowage & segregation

No special requirements.

Hold cleanliness

No special requirements.

Weather precautions

No special requirements.

Loading

Trim in accordance with the relevant provisions required under sections 4 and 5 of the Code.

Precautions

Appropriate precautions shall be taken to protect machinery and accommodation spaces from the dust of the cargo. Bilge wells of the cargo spaces shall be protected from ingress of the cargo. Due consideration shall be paid to protect equipment from the dust of the cargo. Persons who may be exposed to the dust of the cargo shall wear protective clothing, goggles or other equivalent dust eye-protection and dust filter masks, as necessary.

Ventilation

No special requirements.

Carriage

No special requirements.

Discharge

No special requirements.

Clean-up

No special requirements.

PETROLEUM COKE (calcined or uncalcined)

Description
Black, finely divided residue from petroleum refining in the form of powder and small pieces. The provisions of this schedule should not apply to materials having a temperature below 55°C when loaded.

Characteristics

Angle of repose	Bulk density (kg/m³)	Stowage factor (m³/t)
Not applicable	599 to 800	1.25 to 1.67
Size	**Class**	**Group**
Powder to small pieces	MHB	B

Hazard
Uncalcined petroleum coke is liable to heat and ignite spontaneously when not loaded and transported under the provisions of this entry.

This cargo is non-combustible or has a low fire-risk.

Stowage & segregation
"Separated from" foodstuffs.

"Separated longitudinally by an intervening complete compartment or hold from" all goods of class 1, divisions 1.1 and 1.5.

"Separated by a complete compartment or hold from" all other hazardous materials and dangerous goods (goods in packaged form and solid bulk materials).

Hold cleanliness
Clean and dry as relevant to the hazards of the cargo.

Weather precautions
No special requirements.

Loading
1   When the cargo is loaded in a cargo space over a tank containing fuel or other material having a flashpoint under 93°C, the cargo having a temperature of 55°C or higher shall not be loaded in the cargo space, unless part of the cargo having a temperature 44°C or lower is loaded in a layer of at least 0.6 m thickness throughout the cargo space prior to loading the cargo having a temperature of 55°C or higher.

2   When the cargo having a temperature of 55°C or higher is loaded in accordance with the above requirement and the thickness of the layer of the cargo to be loaded is bigger than 1.0 m, the cargo shall first be loaded within a layer, the thickness of which is between 0.6 m and 1.0 m.

3   After the completion of the loading operation specified in the above paragraphs, the loading operation may proceed.

The cargo shall be trimmed in accordance with the cargo information required by section 4 of this Code.

Precautions
This cargo shall not be loaded when the temperature of this cargo exceeds 107°C. The master shall post warnings about the high temperature of this cargo near the cargo spaces.

PETROLEUM COKE (calcined or uncalcined) *(concluded)*

Ventilation

No special requirements.

Carriage

No special requirements.

Discharge

No special requirements.

Clean-up

No special requirements.

Emergency procedures

Special emergency equipment to be carried Protective clothing (gloves, boots, coveralls, headgear). Self-contained breathing apparatus. Spray nozzles.
Emergency procedures Wear protective clothing and self-contained breathing apparatus. **Emergency action in the event of fire** Batten down; use ship's fixed fire-fighting installation, if available. Exclusion of air may be sufficient to control fire. **Medical First Aid** Refer to the *Medical First Aid Guide (MFAG)*, as amended.

PHOSPHATE (defluorinated)

Description
Granular, similar to fine sand. Shipped dry. Dark grey. No moisture content.

Characteristics

Angle of repose	Bulk density (kg/m^3)	Stowage factor (m^3/t)
Not applicable	893	1.12
Size	**Class**	**Group**
Not applicable	Not applicable	C

Hazard
No special hazards.

This cargo is non-combustible or has a low fire-risk.

Stowage & segregation
No special requirements.

Hold cleanliness
No special requirements.

Weather precautions
No special requirements.

Loading
Trim in accordance with the relevant provisions required under sections 4 and 5 of the Code.

Precautions
Appropriate precautions shall be taken to protect machinery and accommodation spaces from the dust of the cargo. Bilge wells of the cargo spaces shall be protected from ingress of the cargo. Due consideration shall be paid to protect equipment from the dust of the cargo. Persons who may be exposed to the dust of the cargo shall wear protective clothing, goggles or other equivalent dust eye-protection and dust filter masks, as necessary.

Ventilation
No special requirements.

Carriage
No special requirements.

Discharge
No special requirements.

Clean-up
No special requirements.

PHOSPHATE ROCK (calcined)

Description
Usually in the form of fine ground rock or prills. Extremely dusty. Hygroscopic.

Characteristics

Angle of repose	Bulk density (kg/m^3)	Stowage factor (m^3/t)
Not applicable	794 to 1563	0.64 to 1.26
Size	**Class**	**Group**
Not applicable	Not applicable	C

Hazard
No special hazards.

This cargo is non-combustible or has a low fire-risk.

This cargo is hygroscopic and will cake if wet.

Stowage & segregation
No special requirements.

Hold cleanliness
No special requirements.

Weather precautions
This cargo shall be kept as dry as practicable before loading, during loading and during voyage. This cargo shall not be loaded during precipitation. During loading of this cargo, all non-working hatches of the cargo spaces to which this cargo is loaded or to be loaded shall be closed.

Loading
Trim in accordance with the relevant provisions required under sections 4 and 5 of the Code.

Precautions
Appropriate precautions shall be taken to protect machinery and accommodation spaces from the dust of the cargo. Bilge wells of the cargo spaces shall be protected from ingress of the cargo. Due consideration shall be paid to protect equipment from the dust of the cargo. Persons who may be exposed to the dust of the cargo shall wear protective clothing, goggles or other equivalent dust eye-protection and dust filter masks, as necessary.

Ventilation
No special requirements.

Carriage
No special requirements.

Discharge
If this cargo has hardened, it shall be trimmed to avoid the formation of overhangs, as necessary.

Clean-up
No special requirements.

PHOSPHATE ROCK (uncalcined)

Description

Phosphate rock is an ore in which phosphorus and oxygen are chemically united. Depending on the source, it is tan to dark grey, dry and dusty. Moisture: 0% to 2%. Depending on its source this cargo may have flow characteristic, but once settled it is not liable to shift.

Characteristics

Angle of repose	Bulk density (kg/m^3)	Stowage factor (m^3/t)
Not applicable	1250 to 1429	0.70 to 0.80
Size	**Class**	**Group**
Powder to lumps	Not applicable	C

Hazard

No special hazards.

This cargo is non-combustible or has a low fire-risk.

Stowage & segregation

No special requirements.

Hold cleanliness

No special requirements.

Weather precautions

No special requirements.

Loading

Trim in accordance with the relevant provisions required under sections 4 and 5 of the Code.

Precautions

Appropriate precautions shall be taken to protect machinery and accommodation spaces from the dust of the cargo. Bilge wells of the cargo spaces shall be protected from ingress of the cargo. Due consideration shall be paid to protect equipment from the dust of the cargo. Persons who may be exposed to the dust of the cargo shall wear protective clothing, goggles or other equivalent dust eye-protection and dust filter masks, as necessary.

Ventilation

No special requirements.

Carriage

No special requirements.

Discharge

No special requirements.

Clean-up

No special requirements.

PIG IRON

Description

Foundry pig iron is cast in 28 grades into 20 kg pigs. In a random heap, pig iron occupies approximately 50% of the apparent volume.

Characteristics

Angle of repose	Bulk density (kg/m³)	Stowage factor (m³/t)
Not applicable	3333 to 3571	0.28 to 0.30
Size	**Class**	**Group**
550 mm × 90 mm × 80 mm	Not applicable	C

Hazard

No special hazards.

This cargo is non-combustible or has a low fire-risk.

Stowage & segregation

No special requirements.

Hold cleanliness

No special requirements.

Weather precautions

No special requirements.

Loading

This cargo is usually loaded using tubs. In such case, tubs are usually lowered by a crane into the hold and the contents are spilled out. When this cargo is loaded using tubs, the first few tubs shall be lowered onto the tanktop to avoid damage.

Trim in accordance with the relevant provisions required under sections 4 and 5 of the Code.

As the density of the cargo is extremely high, the tanktop may be overstressed unless the cargo is evenly spread across the tanktop to equalize the weight distribution. Due consideration shall be paid to ensure that the tanktop is not overstressed during voyage and during loading by a pile of the cargo.

Precautions

No special requirements.

Ventilation

No special requirements.

Carriage

No special requirements.

Discharge

No special requirements.

Clean-up

Prior to washing out the residues of this cargo, the bilge wells of the cargo spaces shall be cleaned.

PITCH PRILL

Description

Pitch prill is made from tar produced during the coking of coal. It is black with a distinctive odour. It is extruded into its characteristic pencil shape to make handling easier.

Cargo softens between 40°C to 50°C. Melting point: 105°C to 107°C.

Characteristics

Angle of repose	Bulk density (kg/m³)	Stowage factor (m³/t)
Not applicable	500 to 800	1.25 to 2.0
Size	**Class**	**Group**
9 mm diameter and up to 0.7 cm long	MHB	B

Hazard

Melts when heated. Combustible, burns with a dense black smoke. Dust may cause skin and eye irritation. Normally this cargo has a low fire-risk. However, powder of the cargo is easy to ignite and may cause fire and explosion. Special care should be taken for preventing fire during loading or discharging.

Stowage & segregation

Segregation as required for class 4.1 materials.

Hold cleanliness

No special requirements.

Weather precautions

Refer to the appendix to this schedule.

Loading

Trim in accordance with the relevant provisions required under sections 4 and 5 of the Code.

This cargo shall not be stowed in a cargo space adjacent to heated tanks to avoid softening and melting of the cargo.

Precautions

Refer to the appendix to this schedule.

Ventilation

Surface ventilation only, either natural or mechanical, shall be conducted, as necessary, during the voyage for this cargo.

Carriage

After the completion of loading of this cargo, the hatches of the cargo spaces shall be sealed. Condensation in the cargo spaces carrying this cargo shall be checked regularly during voyage.

Discharge

Adequate measures shall be taken to prevent dust generation.

Clean-up

No special requirements.

PITCH PRILL *(concluded)*

Emergency procedures

Special emergency equipment to be carried

Protective clothing, gloves, boots, overalls, and headgear.
Self-contained breathing apparatus, spray nozzles.

Emergency procedures

Wear protective clothing and self contained breathing apparatus.

Emergency action in the event of a fire

Batten down: use ship's fixed fire-fighting installation if available.
Exclusion of air may be sufficient to control fire.

Medical first aid

Refer to the *Medical First Aid Guide (MFAG)*, as amended.

Appendix

PITCH PRILL

General precautions

1   Personnel engaged in loading shall be supplied with gloves, dust masks, approved protective clothing and goggles.

2   Eyewashes and sunscreen creams shall be readily available.

3   Number of personnel in area of loading shall be kept to a minimum. Personnel in area of loading shall be aware of all the hazards involved.

4   Personnel engaged in the handling of this cargo shall wash well and keep out of the sun for a few days, after the cargo handling.

5   The hatch shall be closed after loading or discharge has ceased and the ship shall be washed out to remove all dust.

6   Due consideration shall be paid to suspending the cargo handling when wind is blowing dust.

7   After completion of discharging this cargo, the deck shall be cleaned up to remove all spillages.

8   Ventilation of the accommodation spaces shall be closed and the air-conditioning systems for the accommodation spaces shall be on re-cycle mode when this cargo is being handled – either loading or discharging.

9   The cargo dust is easily ignited and may cause fire and explosion. Special care shall be taken to prevent fire during loading and discharging the cargo.

POTASH

Description
Brown, pink or white in colour, potash is produced in granular crystals. It is odourless and hygroscopic.

Characteristics

Angle of repose	Bulk density (kg/m³)	Stowage factor (m³/t)
32° to 35°	971 to 1299	0.77 to 1.03
Size	**Class**	**Group**
Powder to 4 mm	Not applicable	C

Hazard
No special hazards.

This cargo is non-combustible or has a low fire-risk. This cargo is hygroscopic and will cake if wet.

Stowage & segregation
No special requirements.

Hold cleanliness
No special requirements.

Weather precautions
This cargo shall be kept as dry as practicable before loading, during loading and during voyage. This cargo shall not be loaded during precipitation. During loading of this cargo, all non-working hatches of the cargo spaces to which this cargo is loaded or to be loaded shall be closed.

Loading
Trim in accordance with the relevant provisions required under sections 4 and 5 of the Code.

Precautions
No special requirements.

Ventilation
The cargo spaces carrying this cargo shall not be ventilated during voyage.

Carriage
After the completion of loading of this cargo, the hatches of the cargo spaces shall be sealed to prevent water ingress, as necessary.

Discharge
If this cargo has hardened, it shall be trimmed to avoid the formation of overhangs, as necessary.

Clean-up
This cargo is mildly corrosive. After discharge of this cargo, the cargo spaces and the bilge wells shall be thoroughly swept clean and washed out to remove all traces of the cargo, except in the case that the BCSN of the cargo to be loaded subsequent to discharge is POTASH.

POTASSIUM CHLORIDE

Description

Brown, pink or white in colour, powder. Potassium chloride is produced in granular crystals. It is odourless and is soluble in water. Hygroscopic.

Characteristics

Angle of repose	Bulk density (kg/m^3)	Stowage factor (m^3/t)
30° to 47°	893 to 1235	0.81 to 1.12
Size	**Class**	**Group**
Up to 4 mm	Not applicable	C

Hazard

Even though this cargo is classified as non-hazardous, it may cause heavy corrosion when wet.

This cargo is non-combustible or has a low fire-risk.

This cargo is hygroscopic and will cake if wet.

Stowage & segregation

No special requirements.

Hold cleanliness

Clean and dry as relevant to the hazards of the cargo.

Weather precautions

This cargo shall be kept as dry as practicable. This cargo shall not be handled during precipitation. During handling of this cargo, all non-working hatches of the cargo spaces into which this cargo is loaded or to be loaded shall be closed.

Loading

Trim in accordance with the relevant provisions required under sections 4 and 5 of the Code.

Precautions

No special requirements.

Ventilation

The cargo spaces carrying this cargo shall not be ventilated during voyage.

Carriage

After the completion of loading of this cargo, the hatches of the cargo spaces shall be sealed to prevent water ingress.

Discharge

If this cargo has hardened, it shall be trimmed to avoid the formation of overhangs, as necessary.

Clean-up

After discharge of this cargo, the cargo spaces and the bilge wells shall be swept clean and thoroughly washed out.

POTASSIUM NITRATE UN 1486

Description
Transparent, colourless or white crystalline powder or crystals. Hygroscopic.

Characteristics

Angle of repose	Bulk density (kg/m^3)	Stowage factor (m^3/t)
30° to 31°	1136	0.88
Size	**Class**	**Group**
Crystals or powder	5.1	B

Hazard
Oxidizes when wet. Mixtures with combustible materials are readily ignited and may burn fiercely.

This cargo is hygroscopic and will cake if wet.

Stowage & segregation
"Separated from" foodstuffs.

Hold cleanliness
Clean and dry as relevant to the hazards of the cargo.

Weather precautions
This cargo shall be kept as dry as practicable. This cargo shall not be handled during precipitation. During handling of this cargo, all non-working hatches of the cargo spaces into which this cargo is loaded or to be loaded shall be closed.

Loading
Trim in accordance with the relevant provisions required under sections 4 and 5 of the Code.

Precautions
Due regard shall be paid to prevent contact of the cargo and combustible materials.

Ventilation
The cargo spaces carrying this cargo shall not be ventilated during voyage.

Carriage
No special requirements.

Discharge
If this cargo has hardened, it shall be trimmed to avoid the formation of overhangs, as necessary.

Clean-up
No special requirements.

POTASSIUM NITRATE UN 1486 *(concluded)*

Emergency procedures

Special emergency equipment to be carried

Protective clothing (gloves, boots, coveralls, headgear).

Self-contained breathing apparatus.

Spray nozzles.

Emergency procedures

Wear protective clothing and self-contained breathing apparatus.

Emergency action in the event of fire

Use copious quantities of water, which is best applied in the form of a spray to avoid disturbing the surface of the material. The material may fuse or melt, in which condition application of water may result in extensive scattering of the molten materials. Exclusion of air or the use of CO_2 will not control the fire. Due consideration should be given to the effect on the stability of the ship due to accumulated water.

Medical First Aid

Refer to the *Medical First Aid Guide (MFAG)*, as amended.

Remarks

This material is non-combustible unless contaminated.

POTASSIUM SULPHATE

Description
Hard crystals or powder. Colourless or white.

Characteristics

Angle of repose	Bulk density (kg/m³)	Stowage factor (m³/t)
31°	1111	0.90
Size	**Class**	**Group**
Not applicable	Not applicable	C

Hazard
No special hazards.

This cargo is non-combustible or has a low fire-risk.

Stowage & segregation
No special requirements.

Hold cleanliness
No special requirements.

Weather precautions
No special requirements.

Loading
Trim in accordance with the relevant provisions required under sections 4 and 5 of the Code.

Precautions
No special requirements.

Ventilation
No special requirements.

Carriage
No special requirements.

Discharge
No special requirements.

Clean-up
No special requirements.

PUMICE

Description
Highly porous rock of volcanic origin. Greyish-white.

Characteristics

Angle of repose	Bulk density (kg/m³)	Stowage factor (m³/t)
Not applicable	308 to 526	1.90 to 3.25
Size	**Class**	**Group**
Powder to lumps	Not applicable	C

Hazard
No special hazards.

This cargo is non-combustible or has a low fire-risk.

Stowage & segregation
No special requirements.

Hold cleanliness
No special requirements.

Weather precautions
No special requirements.

Loading
Trim in accordance with the relevant provisions required under sections 4 and 5 of the Code.

Precautions
No special requirements.

Ventilation
No special requirements.

Carriage
No special requirements.

Discharge
No special requirements.

Clean-up
No special requirements.

PYRITE (containing copper and iron)

This cargo can be categorized as Group A or C. This cargo entry is for cargo in Group C.

Description

Iron disulphide, containing copper and iron. Moisture 0% to 7%. Extremely dusty.

Characteristics

Angle of repose	Bulk density (kg/m³)	Stowage factor (m³/t)
Not applicable	2000 to 3030	0.33 to 0.50
Size	**Class**	**Group**
Fines to lumps of 300 mm	Not applicable	C

Hazard

No special hazards.

This cargo is non-combustible or has a low fire-risk.

Stowage & segregation

No special requirements.

Hold cleanliness

No special requirements.

Weather precautions

No special requirements.

Loading

Trim in accordance with the relevant provisions required under sections 4 and 5 of the Code.

As the density of the cargo is extremely high, the tanktop may be overstressed unless the cargo is evenly spread across the tanktop to equalize the weight distribution. Due consideration shall be paid to ensure that the tanktop is not overstressed during voyage and during loading by a pile of the cargo.

Precautions

Appropriate precautions shall be taken to protect machinery and accommodation spaces from the dust of the cargo. Bilge wells of the cargo spaces shall be protected from ingress of the cargo. Due consideration shall be paid to protect equipment from the dust of the cargo. Persons who may be exposed to the dust of the cargo shall wear protective clothing, goggles or other equivalent dust eye-protection and dust filter masks, as necessary.

Ventilation

No special requirements.

Carriage

No special requirements.

Discharge

No special requirements.

Clean-up

No special requirements.

PYRITES, CALCINED (Calcined Pyrites)

Description

Dust to fines, calcined pyrites is the residual product from the chemical industry where all types of metal sulphides are either used for the production of sulphuric acid or are processed to recover the elemental metals – copper, lead, zinc, etc. The acidity of the residue can be considerable, in particular, in the presence of water or moist air, where pH values between 1.3 and 2.1 are frequently noted.

Characteristics

Angle of repose	Bulk density (kg/m³)	Stowage factor (m³/t)
Not applicable	2326	0.43
Size	**Class**	**Group**
Not applicable	MHB	A and B

Hazard

Highly corrosive to steel when wet. Inhalation of dust is irritating and harmful. Cargo may liquefy.

This cargo is non-combustible or has a low fire-risk.

Stowage & segregation

"Separated from" foodstuffs.

Hold cleanliness

Due consideration shall be paid to cleaning and drying of the cargo spaces.

Weather precautions

This cargo shall be kept as dry as practicable before loading, during loading and during voyage. This cargo shall not be loaded during precipitation. During loading of this cargo, all non-working hatches of the cargo spaces to which this cargo is loaded or to be loaded shall be closed.

Loading

Trim in accordance with the relevant provisions required under sections 4 and 5 of the Code.

As the density of the cargo is extremely high, the tanktop may be overstressed unless the cargo is evenly spread across the tanktop to equalize the weight distribution. Due consideration shall be paid to ensure that the tanktop is not overstressed during voyage and during loading by a pile of the cargo.

Precautions

Bilge wells shall be clean, dry and covered as appropriate, to prevent ingress of the cargo. Ceiling boards shall be removed or sealed to prevent penetration by this cargo. The tanktop on which this cargo is to be loaded shall be covered with lime before loading.

Appropriate precautions shall be taken to protect machinery and accommodation spaces from the dust of the cargo. Bilge wells of the cargo spaces shall be protected from ingress of the cargo. Due consideration shall be paid to protect equipment from the dust of the cargo. Persons who may be exposed to the dust of the cargo shall wear goggles or other equivalent dust eye-protection and dust filter masks. Those persons shall wear protective clothing, as necessary.

Ventilation

No special requirements.

PYRITES, CALCINED (Calcined Pyrites) *(concluded)*

Carriage

After the completion of loading of this cargo, the hatches of the cargo spaces shall be sealed to prevent water ingress, as necessary.

Discharge

No special requirements.

Clean-up

No special requirements.

Emergency procedures

Special emergency equipment to be carried
Nil
Emergency procedures
Nil
Emergency action in the event of fire
Nil (non-combustible).
Medical First Aid
Refer to the *Medical First Aid Guide (MFAG)*, as amended.

PYROPHYLLITE

Description

A natural hydrous aluminium silicate. Chalk-white. May be dusty.

Lumps: 75%, Rubble: 20%, Fines: 5%.

Characteristics

Angle of repose	Bulk density (kg/m³)	Stowage factor (m³/t)
Not applicable	2000	0.50
Size	**Class**	**Group**
Lump to fines	Not applicable	C

Hazard

No special hazards.

This cargo is non-combustible or has a low fire-risk.

Stowage & segregation

No special requirements.

Hold cleanliness

No special requirements.

Weather precautions

No special requirements.

Loading

Trim in accordance with the relevant provisions required under sections 4 and 5 of the Code.

Precautions

Appropriate precautions shall be taken to protect machinery and accommodation spaces from the dust of the cargo. Bilge wells of the cargo spaces shall be protected from ingress of the cargo. Due consideration shall be paid to protect equipment from the dust of the cargo. Persons who may be exposed to the dust of the cargo shall wear protective clothing, goggles or other equivalent dust eye-protection and dust filter masks, as necessary.

Ventilation

No special requirements.

Carriage

No special requirements.

Discharge

No special requirements.

Clean-up

No special requirements.

QUARTZ

Description
Crystalline lumps.

Characteristics

Angle of repose	Bulk density (kg/m³)	Stowage factor (m³/t)
Not applicable	1667	0.60
Size	**Class**	**Group**
Lumps: 50 mm to 300 mm	Not applicable	C

Hazard
No special hazards.

This cargo is non-combustible or has a low fire-risk.

Stowage & segregation
No special requirements.

Hold cleanliness
No special requirements.

Weather precautions
No special requirements.

Loading
Trim in accordance with the relevant provisions required under sections 4 and 5 of the Code.

Precautions
No special requirements.

Ventilation
No special requirements.

Carriage
No special requirements.

Discharge
No special requirements.

Clean-up
No special requirements.

QUARTZITE

Description

Quartzite is a compact, granular, metamorphosed sandstone containing quartz. It is white, red, brown or grey in colour and its size varies from large rocks to pebbles. It may also be shipped in semi-crushed and graded sizes.

Characteristics

Angle of repose	Bulk density (kg/m^3)	Stowage factor (m^3/t)
Not applicable	1563	0.64
Size	**Class**	**Group**
10 mm to 200 mm	Not applicable	C

Hazard

No special hazards.

Dust of this cargo is very abrasive. This cargo is non-combustible or has a low fire-risk.

Stowage & segregation

No special requirements.

Hold cleanliness

No special requirements.

Weather precautions

No special requirements.

Loading

Trim in accordance with the relevant provisions required under sections 4 and 5 of the Code.

Precautions

Protect machinery and equipment from dust. Appropriate precautions shall be taken to protect machinery and accommodation spaces from the dust of the cargo. Bilge wells of the cargo spaces shall be protected from ingress of the cargo. Due consideration shall be paid to protect equipment from the dust of the cargo. Persons who may be exposed to the dust of the cargo shall wear goggles or other equivalent dust eye-protection and dust filter masks. Those persons shall wear protective clothing, as necessary.

Ventilation

No special requirements.

Carriage

No special requirements.

Discharge

No special requirements.

Clean-up

No special requirements.

RADIOACTIVE MATERIAL, LOW SPECIFIC ACTIVITY (LSA-I), non-fissile or fissile – excepted UN 2912

Description
This schedule includes ores containing naturally occurring radionuclides (e.g., uranium, thorium) and natural or depleted uranium and thorium concentrates of such ores, including metals, mixtures and compounds.

Characteristics

Angle of repose	Bulk density (kg/m³)	Stowage factor (m³/t)
Not applicable	–	–
Size	**Class**	**Group**
Not applicable	7	B

Hazard
Low radiotoxicity. Some materials may possess chemical hazards.

This cargo is non-combustible or has a low fire-risk.

Stowage & segregation
"Separated from" foodstuffs.

Hold cleanliness
Clean and dry as relevant to the hazards of the cargo.

Weather precautions
This cargo shall be kept as dry as practicable. This cargo shall not be handled during precipitation. During handling of this cargo, all non-working hatches of the cargo spaces into which this cargo is loaded or to be loaded shall be closed.

Loading
Trim in accordance with the relevant provisions required under sections 4 and 5 of the Code.

Precautions
Personnel shall not be unnecessarily exposed to dust of this cargo. Persons who may be exposed to the dust of the cargo shall wear protective clothing, goggles or other equivalent dust eye-protection and facemasks. There shall be no leakage outside the cargo space in which this cargo is stowed.

Ventilation
The cargo spaces carrying this cargo shall not be ventilated during voyage.

Carriage
All instructions provided by the shipper shall be followed for the carriage of this cargo.

Discharge
All instructions provided by the shipper shall be followed for the discharge of this cargo.

Clean-up
Cargo spaces used for this cargo shall not be used for other goods until decontaminated. Refer to subsection 9.3.2.3 of this Code.

RADIOACTIVE MATERIAL, LOW SPECIFIC ACTIVITY (LSA-I), non-fissile or fissile – excepted UN 2912 *(concluded)*

Emergency procedures

Special emergency equipment to be carried

Protective clothing (gloves, boots, coveralls, headgear).
Self-contained breathing apparatus.

Emergency procedures

Wear protective clothing and self-contained breathing apparatus.

Emergency action in the event of fire

Batten down; use ship's fixed fire-fighting installation, if fitted.
Use water spray to control spread of dust, if necessary.

Medical First Aid

Refer to the *Medical First Aid Guide (MFAG)*, as amended.
Radio for medical advice.

Remarks

Most materials are likely to be non-combustible. Speedily collect and isolate potentially contaminated equipment and cover. Seek expert advice.

RADIOACTIVE MATERIAL, SURFACE CONTAMINATED OBJECTS (SCO-I), non-fissile or fissile – excepted UN 2913

Description

The radioactivity of SCO-I is low. This schedule includes solid objects of non-radioactive material having a radioactive material distributed on its surfaces which:

1   the non-fixed contamination on the accessible surface, averaged over 300 cm^2 (or the area of the surface if less than 300 cm^2), does not exceed 4 Bq/cm^2 for beta and gamma emitters and low-toxicity alpha emitters, or 0.4 Bq/cm^2 for all other alpha emitters;

2   the fixed contamination on the accessible surface, averaged over 300 cm^2 (or the area of the surface if less than 300 cm^2), does not exceed 4×10^4 Bq/cm^2 for beta and gamma emitters and low-toxicity alpha emitters, or 4×10^3 Bq/cm^2 for all other alpha emitters; and

3   the non-fixed contamination plus the fixed contamination on the inaccessible surface, averaged over 300 cm^2 (or the area of the surface if less than 300 cm^2), does not exceed 4×10^4 Bq/cm^2 for beta and gamma emitters and low-toxicity alpha emitters, or 4×10^3 Bq/cm^2 for all other alpha emitters.

Characteristics

Angle of repose	Bulk density (kg/m^3)	Stowage factor (m^3/t)
Not applicable	–	–
Size	**Class**	**Group**
Not applicable	7	B

Hazard

Low radioactivity.

This cargo is non-combustible or has a low fire-risk.

Stowage & segregation

"Separated from" foodstuffs.

Hold cleanliness

Clean and dry as relevant to the hazards of the cargo.

Weather precautions

This cargo shall be kept as dry as practicable. This cargo shall not be handled during precipitation. During handling of this cargo, all non-working hatches of the cargo spaces into which this cargo is loaded or to be loaded shall be closed.

Loading

Trim in accordance with the relevant provisions required under sections 4 and 5 of the Code.

Precautions

Personnel shall not be exposed to dust of this cargo. Persons who may be exposed to the dust of the cargo shall wear protective clothing, goggles and facemasks. There shall be no leakage outside the cargo space in which this cargo is stowed.

Ventilation

The cargo spaces carrying this cargo shall not be ventilated during voyage.

RADIOACTIVE MATERIAL, SURFACE CONTAMINATED OBJECTS (SCO-I), non-fissile or fissile – excepted UN 2913 *(concluded)*

Carriage

All instructions provided by the shipper shall be followed for the carriage of this cargo.

Discharge

All instructions provided by the shipper shall be followed for the discharge of this cargo.

Clean-up

Cargo spaces used for this cargo shall not be used for other goods until decontaminated. Refer to subsection 9.3.2.3 of this Code.

Emergency procedures

Special emergency equipment to be carried
Protective clothing (gloves, boots, coveralls, headgear).
Self-contained breathing apparatus.

Emergency procedures
Wear protective clothing and self-contained breathing apparatus.
Emergency action in the event of fire
Batten down; use ship's fixed fire-fighting installation, if fitted.
Use water spray to control spread of dust, if necessary.
Medical First Aid
Refer to the *Medical First Aid Guide (MFAG)*, as amended.
Radio for medical advice.

Remarks

Most materials are likely to be non-combustible. Speedily collect and isolate potentially contaminated equipment and cover. Seek expert advice.

RASORITE (ANHYDROUS)

Description
A granular, yellow-white crystalline material with little or no dust. Abrasive. Hygroscopic.

Characteristics

Angle of repose	Bulk density (kg/m³)	Stowage factor (m³/t)
Not applicable	1282 to 1493	0.67 to 0.78
Size	**Class**	**Group**
Less than 2.36 mm	Not applicable	C

Hazard
No special hazards.

This cargo is non-combustible or has a low fire-risk.

This cargo is hygroscopic and will cake if wet.

Stowage & segregation
No special requirements.

Hold cleanliness
No special requirements.

Weather precautions
No special requirements.

Loading
Trim in accordance with the relevant provisions required under sections 4 and 5 of the Code.

Precautions
No special requirements.

Ventilation
No special requirements.

Carriage
No special requirements.

Discharge
If this cargo has hardened, it shall be trimmed to avoid the formation of overhangs, as necessary.

Clean-up
No special requirements.

RUTILE SAND

Description

Fine-particled brown to black sand. Abrasive. Shipped dry. May be dusty.

Characteristics

Angle of repose	Bulk density (kg/m³)	Stowage factor (m³/t)
Not applicable	2500 to 2700	0.37 to 0.40
Size	**Class**	**Group**
0.15 mm or less	Not applicable	C

Hazard

No special hazards.

This cargo is non-combustible or has a low fire-risk.

Stowage & segregation

No special requirements.

Hold cleanliness

No special requirements.

Weather precautions

This cargo shall be kept as dry as practicable before loading, during loading and during voyage. This cargo shall not be loaded during precipitation. During loading of this cargo, all non-working hatches of the cargo spaces to which this cargo is loaded or to be loaded shall be closed.

Loading

Trim in accordance with the relevant provisions required under sections 4 and 5 of the Code.

As the density of the cargo is extremely high, the tanktop may be overstressed unless the cargo is evenly spread across the tanktop to equalize the weight distribution. Due consideration shall be paid to ensure that the tanktop is not overstressed during voyage and during loading by a pile of the cargo.

Precautions

Bilge wells shall be clean, dry and covered as appropriate, to prevent ingress of the cargo.

Appropriate precautions shall be taken to protect machinery and accommodation spaces from the dust of the cargo. Bilge wells of the cargo spaces shall be protected from ingress of the cargo. Due consideration shall be paid to protect equipment from the dust of the cargo. Persons who may be exposed to the dust of the cargo shall wear goggles or other equivalent dust eye-protection and dust filter masks. Those persons shall wear protective clothing, as necessary.

Ventilation

No special requirements.

Carriage

No special requirements.

Discharge

No special requirements.

Clean-up

No special requirements.

SALT

Description

Fine white grains. Moisture variable to 5.5%. This cargo is highly soluble. In the case of ingress of water into the holds, there is a risk of the loss of the stability of the ship through dissolution of this cargo (formation of a wet base and shifting of cargo).

Characteristics

Angle of repose	Bulk density (kg/m³)	Stowage factor (m³/t)
Not applicable	893 to 1235	0.81 to 1.12
Size	**Class**	**Group**
Grains up to 12 mm	Not applicable	C

Hazard

No special hazards.

This cargo is non-combustible or has a low fire-risk.

Stowage & segregation

No special requirements.

Hold cleanliness

Clean and dry as relevant to the hazards of the cargo.

Weather precautions

This cargo shall be kept as dry as practicable. This cargo shall not be handled during precipitation. During handling of this cargo, all non-working hatches of the cargo spaces into which this cargo is loaded or to be loaded shall be closed.

Loading

Trim in accordance with the relevant provisions required under sections 4 and 5 of the Code.

Precautions

The parts of the cargo space in contact with the cargo such as tanktops, hoppers, side plating and bulkheads shall be lime-washed or coated with paint to prevent corrosion.

Ventilation

The cargo spaces carrying this cargo shall not be ventilated during voyage.

Carriage

After the completion of loading of this cargo, the hatches of the cargo spaces shall be sealed.

Discharge

No special requirements.

Clean-up

No special requirements.

SALT CAKE

Description
Impure sodium sulphate. White in colour. Granular, shipped dry.

Characteristics

Angle of repose	Bulk density (kg/m^3)	Stowage factor (m^3/t)
Not applicable	1052 to 1124	0.89 to 0.95
Size	**Class**	**Group**
10 mm to 200 mm	Not applicable	C

Hazard
No special hazards.

This cargo is non-combustible or has a low fire-risk.

Stowage & segregation
No special requirements.

Hold cleanliness
No special requirements.

Weather precautions
No special requirements.

Loading
Trim in accordance with the relevant provisions required under sections 4 and 5 of the Code.

Precautions
No special requirements.

Ventilation
No special requirements.

Carriage
No special requirements.

Discharge
No special requirements.

Clean-up
No special requirements.

SALT ROCK

Description
White. Moisture content 0.02%.

Characteristics

Angle of repose	Bulk density (kg/m³)	Stowage factor (m³/t)
Not applicable	943 to 1020	0.98 to 1.06
Size	**Class**	**Group**
Small granules	Not applicable	C

Hazard
No special hazards.

This cargo is non-combustible or has a low fire-risk.

Stowage & segregation
No special requirements.

Hold cleanliness
No special requirements.

Weather precautions
No special requirements.

Loading
Trim in accordance with the relevant provisions required under sections 4 and 5 of the Code.

Precautions
No special requirements.

Ventilation
No special requirements.

Carriage
No special requirements.

Discharge
No special requirements.

Clean-up
No special requirements.

SAND

Description

Usually fine particles. Abrasive and dusty.

Sands included in this schedule are:

FOUNDRY SAND
POTASSIUM FELSPAR SAND
QUARTZ SAND

SILICA SAND
SODA FELSPAR SAND

Characteristics

Angle of repose	Bulk density (kg/m³)	Stowage factor (m³/t)
Not applicable	1020 to 2000	0.50 to 0.98
Size	**Class**	**Group**
0.1 mm to 5 mm	Not applicable	C

Hazard

Inhalation of silica dust can result in respiratory disease. Silica particulates are easily transported by air and inhaled.

Industrial sand may be coated with resin and will cake if exposed to heat (55°C to 60°C).

This cargo is non-combustible or has a low fire-risk.

Stowage & segregation

Industrial sand coated with resin shall be "separated from" sources of heat.

Hold cleanliness

Clean and dry as relevant to the hazards of the cargo.

Weather precautions

This cargo shall be kept as dry as practicable before loading, during loading and during voyage. This cargo shall not be loaded during precipitation. During loading of this cargo, all non-working hatches of the cargo spaces to which this cargo is loaded or to be loaded shall be closed.

Loading

Trim in accordance with the relevant provisions required under sections 4 and 5 of the Code.

Precautions

Appropriate precautions shall be taken to protect machinery and accommodation spaces from the dust of the cargo. Bilge wells of the cargo spaces shall be protected from ingress of the cargo. Due consideration shall be paid to protect equipment from the dust of the cargo. Persons who may be exposed to the dust of the cargo shall wear goggles or other equivalent dust eye-protection and dust filter masks. Those persons shall wear protective clothing, as necessary.

Ventilation

No special requirements.

Carriage

The bilge wells of the cargo spaces carrying this cargo shall be kept dry.

Discharge

No special requirements.

Clean-up

After discharge of this cargo, particular attention shall be paid to bilge wells of the cargo spaces.

SAWDUST

Description
Fine particles of wood.

Characteristics

Angle of repose	Bulk density (kg/m³)	Stowage factor (m³/t)
Not applicable	–	–
Size	**Class**	**Group**
Not applicable	MHB	B

Hazard
Liable to spontaneous combustion if not clean, dry and free from oil. Liable to cause oxygen depletion within the cargo space.

Stowage & segregation
Segregation as required for class 4.1 materials.

"Separated from" all class 5.1 liquids and all class 8 liquids.

Hold cleanliness
Clean and dry as relevant to the hazards of the cargo.

Weather precautions
This cargo shall be kept as dry as practicable. This cargo shall not be handled during precipitation. During handling of this cargo, all non-working hatches of the cargo spaces into which this cargo is loaded or to be loaded shall be closed.

Loading
Trim in accordance with the relevant provisions required under sections 4 and 5 of the Code.

Precautions
Bilge wells shall be clean, dry and covered as appropriate, to prevent ingress of the cargo. Prior to loading this cargo, the shipper shall provide the master with a certificate stating that the cargo is clean, dry and free from oil.

Ventilation
Surface ventilation only, either natural or mechanical, shall be conducted, as necessary, during the voyage for this cargo.

Carriage
No special requirements.

Discharge
No special requirements.

Clean-up
No special requirements.

SAWDUST *(concluded)*

Emergency procedures

Special emergency equipment to be carried
Nil

Emergency procedures
Nil
Emergency action in the event of fire
Batten down; use ship's fixed fire-fighting installation, if fitted. Exclusion of air may be sufficient to control fire.
Medical First Aid
Refer to the *Medical First Aid Guide (MFAG)*, as amended.

SCRAP METAL

Description
"Scrap" iron or steel covers an enormous range of ferrous metals, principally intended for recycling.

Characteristics

Angle of repose	Bulk density (kg/m^3)	Stowage factor (m^3/t)
Not applicable	Varies	Varies
Size	**Class**	**Group**
Varies	Not applicable	C

Hazard
No special hazards.

This cargo is non-combustible or has a low fire risk except when cargo contains swarf (fine metal turnings liable to spontaneous combustion); refer to the entry for FERROUS METAL BORINGS, SHAVINGS, TURNINGS OR CUTTINGS in this Code.

Stowage & segregation
No special requirements.

Hold cleanliness
No special requirements.

Weather precautions
This cargo shall be kept as dry as practicable before loading, during loading and during voyage. This cargo shall not be loaded during precipitation. During loading of this cargo, all non-working hatches of the cargo spaces to which this cargo is loaded or to be loaded shall be closed.

Loading
Refer to the appendix to this schedule.

Precautions
Refer to the appendix to this schedule.

Ventilation
Surface ventilation only, either natural or mechanical, shall be conducted, as necessary, during the voyage for this cargo.

Carriage
Bilges in the cargo spaces carrying this cargo shall not be pumped unless absolutely necessary. Bilgewater of this cargo may contain a certain amount of dirt and oil from old machinery. *Refer to the appendix to this individual schedule.*

Discharge
When this cargo is discharged by magnet or spider grab:
- .1   the deck and deck machineries shall be protected from falling cargo; and
- .2   damages to the ship shall be checked, after the completion of discharge.

Clean-up
Prior to cleaning up the cargo spaces for this cargo, the crew shall be informed of danger due to broken glass and sharp edges. Prior to washing out the residues of this cargo, any oil spillages shall be cleaned from the tanktops and the bilge wells of the cargo spaces for this cargo.

SCRAP METAL *(concluded)*

Appendix

SCRAP METAL

Handling of this cargo varies from magnets to spider grabs, depending usually on the size of material. This cargo may include articles from the size of car bodies to fine metal turnings (swarf). The weight of individual pieces will also vary greatly, ranging from heavy machinery to tin cans.

Loading

Before loading, the cargo spaces shall be prepared as per general loading practice and any areas liable to be damaged by falling cargo shall be protected with dunnage. This includes decks and coamings in way of the material's path to the cargo spaces. Removing the ship's side rails may be advisable.

A layer of this cargo shall be carefully placed over the tanktop in the square to cushion any fallout. Magnet and grab drivers shall be instructed not to release their loads too high above the pile.

The usual method of loading is to form a pile along the ship's centreline and use the slope to roll material into the ends and sides. Every effort must be made to work the wings and ends to evenly distribute the weight. If this is not done, the light high-volume pieces will roll to the wings and the small heavy pieces will concentrate in the square.

When pumping the bilge wells, the master shall be aware that a certain amount of dirt and oil can be expected from old machinery. Broken glass and sharp jagged edges may be present and care shall be taken by personnel working near scrap.

Before hatches are closed, the cargo spaces shall be checked that no sharp projections could pierce the ship's side.

SEED CAKE, containing vegetable oil UN 1386

(a) mechanically expelled seeds, containing more than 10% of oil or more than 20% of oil and moisture combined.

The range of oil and moisture content is indicated in the figure.

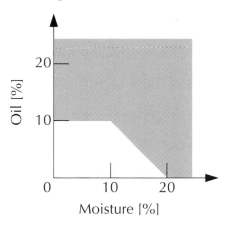

To be carried in bulk only with special permission from the competent authority.

Description

Residue remaining after oil has been expelled mechanically from oil-bearing seeds. The cereals and cereal products included in this schedule are those derived from:

Bakery materials
Barley malt pellets
Beet
Bran pellets
Brewer's grain pellets
Citrus pulp pellets
Coconut
Copra
Corn gluten
Cotton seed
Expellers
Gluten pellets
Ground nuts, meal
Hominy chop
Linseed
Maize
Meal, oily

Mill feed pellets
Niger seed, expellers
Oil cake
Palm kernel
Peanuts
Pellets, cereal
Pollard pellets
Rape seed
Rice bran
Rice broken
Safflower seed
Seed expellers, oily
Soya bean
Strussa pellets
Sunflower seed
Toasted meals

The above may be shipped in the form of pulp, meals, cake, pellets and expellers.

Characteristics

Angle of repose	Bulk density (kg/m³)	Stowage factor (m³/t)
Not applicable	478 to 719	1.39 to 2.09
Size	**Class**	**Group**
Not applicable	4.2	B

SEED CAKE, containing vegetable oil UN 1386 (a) *(continued)*

Hazard

May self-heat slowly and, if wet or containing an excessive proportion of unoxidized oil, ignite spontaneously. Liable to oxidize, causing subsequent reduction of oxygen in the cargo space. Carbon dioxide may be produced.

Stowage & segregation

No special requirements other than prescribed in section 9.3 of this Code.

Hold cleanliness

Clean and dry as relevant to the hazards of the cargo.

Weather precautions

This cargo shall be kept as dry as practicable. This cargo shall not be handled during precipitation. During handling of this cargo, all non-working hatches of the cargo spaces into which this cargo is loaded or to be loaded shall be closed.

Loading

Trim in accordance with the relevant provisions required under sections 4 and 5 of the Code.

Precautions

This cargo shall only be accepted for loading when the temperature of the cargo is not higher than ambient temperature plus 10°C or 55°C, whichever is lower. Before shipment, this cargo shall be properly aged; the duration of ageing required varies with the oil content. The competent authority may permit seed cakes described in this schedule to be carried under conditions governing SEED CAKE (b), when satisfied, as a result of tests, that such relaxation is justified (see following schedule). Certificates from the competent authority giving such permission shall state the oil content and moisture content. The temperature of this cargo shall be measured regularly at a number of depths in the cargo spaces and recorded during the voyage. If the temperature of the cargo reaches 55°C and continues to increase, ventilation to the cargo shall be stopped. If self-heating continues, then carbon dioxide or inert gas shall be introduced to the cargo space. Entry of personnel into cargo spaces for this cargo shall not be permitted until tests have been carried out and it has been established that the oxygen content has been restored to a normal level.

Ventilation

The cargo spaces carrying this cargo shall not be mechanically ventilated during voyage to prevent self-heating of the cargo, except in case of emergency.

Carriage

Hatches of the cargo spaces carrying this cargo shall be weathertight to prevent the ingress of water.

Discharge

No special requirements.

Clean-up

No special requirements.

SEED CAKE, containing vegetable oil UN 1386 (a) *(concluded)*

Emergency procedures

Special emergency equipment to be carried
Self-contained breathing apparatus.

Emergency procedures
Wear self-contained breathing apparatus.
Emergency action in the event of fire
Batten down; use ship's fixed fire-fighting installation, if fitted.
Medical First Aid
Refer to the *Medical First Aid Guide (MFAG)*, as amended.

SEED CAKE, containing vegetable oil UN 1386

*(b) solvent extractions and expelled seeds, containing not more
than 10% of oil and when the amount of moisture is higher than 10%,
not more than 20% of oil and moisture combined.*

Note: This entry covers the following:

.1 all solvent-extracted and expelled seed cakes containing not more than 10% oil, and not more than 10% moisture; and

.2 all solvent-extracted and expelled seed cakes containing not more than 10% oil and moisture content higher than 10%, in which case the oil and moisture combined must not exceed 20%.

The range of oil and moisture content is indicated in the figure.

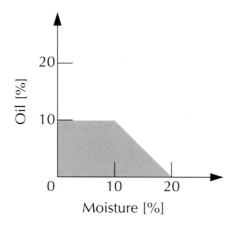

When, in solvent-extracted seed cake, the oil or oil and moisture content exceeds the percentages stated above, guidance should be sought from the competent authorities.

Description

Residue remaining after oil has been extracted by a solvent process or expelled mechanically from oil-bearing seeds. The cereals and cereal products included in this schedule are those derived from:

Bakery materials	**Mill feed pellets**
Barley malt pellets	**Niger seed, expellers**
Beet	**Oil cake**
Bran pellets	**Palm kernel**
Brewer's grain pellets	**Peanuts**
Citrus pulp pellets	**Pellets, cereal**
Coconut	**Pollard pellets**
Copra	**Rape seed**
Corn gluten	**Rice bran**
Cotton seed	**Rice broken**
Expellers	**Safflower seed**
Gluten pellets	**Seed expellers, oily**
Ground nuts, meal	**Soya bean**
Hominy chop	**Strussa pellets**
Linseed	**Sunflower seed**
Maize	**Toasted meals**
Meal, oily	

The above may be shipped in the form of pulp, meals, cake, pellets and expellers.

SEED CAKE, containing vegetable oil UN 1386 (b) *(continued)*

The provisions of this schedule should not apply to solvent-extracted rape seed meal, pellets, soya bean meal, cotton seed meal and sunflower seed meal containing not more than 4% oil and 15% oil and moisture combined. A certificate from a person recognized by the competent authority of the country of shipment should be provided by the shipper, prior to loading, stating that the provisions for the exemption are met.

Characteristics

Angle of repose	Bulk density (kg/m³)	Stowage factor (m³/t)
Not applicable	478 to 719	1.39 to 2.09
Size	**Class**	**Group**
Not applicable	4.2	B

Hazard

May self-heat slowly and, if wet or containing an excessive proportion of unoxidized oil, ignite spontaneously. Liable to oxidize, causing subsequent reduction of oxygen in the cargo space. Carbon dioxide may also be produced.

Stowage & segregation

No special requirements other than prescribed in section 9.3 of this Code.

If the bulkhead between the cargo space and the engine-room is not insulated to class A-60 standard, solvent extraction seed shall be stowed "away from" the bulkhead.

Hold cleanliness

Clean and dry as relevant to the hazards of the cargo.

Weather precautions

This cargo shall be kept as dry as practicable. This cargo shall not be handled during precipitation. During handling of this cargo, all non-working hatches of the cargo spaces into which this cargo is loaded or to be loaded shall be closed.

Loading

This cargo shall only be accepted for loading when the cargo is substantially free from flammable solvent and a certificate from a person recognized by the competent authority of the country of shipment specifying the oil content and moisture content is issued.

Trim in accordance with the relevant provisions required under sections 4 and 5 of the Code.

Precautions

Before shipment, this cargo shall be properly aged; the duration of ageing required varies with the oil content. The temperature of this cargo shall be measured regularly at a number of depths in the cargo spaces and recorded during the voyage. If the temperature of the cargo reaches 55°C and continues to increase, ventilation to the cargo shall be stopped. If self-heating continues, then carbon dioxide or inert gas shall be introduced to the cargo space. In the case of solvent-extracted seed cakes the use of carbon dioxide or inert gas shall be withheld until it becomes apparent that fire is not liable to take place in the cargo space, to avoid the possibility of ignition of solvent vapours. Entry of personnel into cargo spaces for this cargo shall not be permitted until tests have been carried out and it has been established that the oxygen content has been restored to a normal level. When the planned interval between the commencement of loading and the completion of discharge of this cargo exceeds 5 days, the cargo shall not be accepted for loading unless the cargo is to be carried in a cargo space equipped with facilities for

SEED CAKE, containing vegetable oil UN 1386 (b) *(concluded)*

introducing carbon dioxide or inert gas into the space. Smoking and the use of naked lights shall be prohibited in the vicinity of the cargo space during loading and unloading and on entry into the cargo spaces at any other time. Electrical circuits for equipment in cargo spaces which is unsuitable for use in an explosive atmosphere shall be isolated by removal of links in the system other than fuses. Spark-arresting screens shall be fitted to ventilators to the cargo spaces containing this cargo.

Ventilation

Surface ventilation, either natural or mechanical, should be conducted, as necessary, for removing any residual solvent vapour. To prevent self-heating of the cargo, caution is required when using mechanical ventilation.

Carriage

Hatches of the cargo spaces carrying this cargo shall be weathertight to prevent the ingress of water.

Discharge

No special requirements.

Clean-up

No special requirements.

Emergency procedures

Special emergency equipment to be carried
Self-contained breathing apparatus.

Emergency procedures
Wear self-contained breathing apparatus.
Emergency action in the event of fire
Batten down; use ship's fixed fire-fighting installation, if fitted.
Medical First Aid
Refer to the *Medical First Aid Guide (MFAG)*, as amended.

Remarks

In the case of solvent-extracted seed cake, the use of CO_2 should be withheld until fire is apparent.

The use of CO_2 is limited to controlling the fire and further amounts may need to be injected from time to time during the sea passage to reduce the oxygen content in the hold. On arrival in port, the cargo will need to be dug out to reach the seat of the fire.

SEED CAKE UN 2217
with not more than 1.5% oil and not more than 11% moisture

The range of oil and moisture content is indicated in the figure.

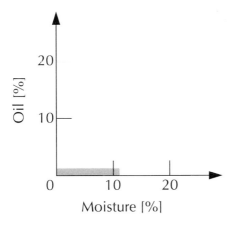

Description

Residue remaining after oil has been extracted by a solvent process from oil-bearing seeds. The cereals and cereal products included in this schedule are those derived from:

Bakery materials	**Meal, oily**
Barley malt pellets	**Mill feed pellets**
Beet	**Niger seed, expellers**
Bran pellets	**Oil cake**
Brewer's grain pellets	**Palm kernel**
Citrus pulp pellets	**Peanuts**
Coconut	**Pellets, cereal**
Copra	**Pollard pellets**
Corn gluten	**Rape seed**
Cotton seed	**Rice bran**
Expellers	**Rice broken**
Gluten pellets	**Safflower seed**
Ground nuts, meal	**Seed expellers, oily**
Hominy chop	**Soyabean**
Linseed	**Strussa pellets**
Maize	**Sunflower seed**

The above may be shipped in the form of pulp, meals, cake, pellets, expellers.

The provisions of this entry should not apply to solvent-extracted rape seed meal pellets, soya bean meal, cotton seed meal and sunflower seed meal containing not more than 1.5% oil and not more than 11% moisture and being substantially free from flammable solvent. A certificate from a person recognized by the competent authority of the country of shipment should be provided by the shipper, prior to loading, stating that the provisions for the exemption are met.

Characteristics

Angle of repose	Bulk density (kg/m³)	Stowage factor (m³/t)
Not applicable	478 to 719	1.39 to 2.09
Size	**Class**	**Group**
0.1 mm to 5 mm	4.2	B

SEED CAKE UN 2217 with not more than 1.5% oil and not more than 11% moisture (*continued*)

Hazard

May self-heat slowly and, if wet or containing an excessive proportion of unoxidized oil, ignite spontaneously. Liable to oxidize, causing subsequent reduction of oxygen in the cargo space. Carbon dioxide may also be produced.

Stowage & segregation

No special requirements other than prescribed in section 9.3 of this Code.

If the bulkhead between the cargo space and the engine-room is not insulated to class A-60 standard, this cargo shall be stowed "away from" the bulkhead.

Hold cleanliness

Clean and dry as relevant to the hazards of the cargo.

Weather precautions

This cargo shall be kept as dry as practicable. This cargo shall not be handled during precipitation. During handling of this cargo, all non-working hatches of the cargo spaces into which this cargo is loaded or to be loaded shall be closed.

Loading

This cargo shall only be accepted for loading when the cargo is substantially free from flammable solvent and a certificate from a person recognized by the competent authority of the country of shipment specifying the oil content and moisture content is issued.

Trim in accordance with the relevant provisions required under sections 4 and 5 of the Code.

Precautions

The temperature of this cargo shall be measured regularly at a number of depths in the cargo spaces and recorded during the voyage. If the temperature of the cargo reaches 55°C and continues to increase, ventilation to the cargo shall be stopped. If self-heating continues, then carbon dioxide or inert gas shall be introduced to the cargo space. The use of carbon dioxide or inert gas shall be withheld until it becomes apparent that fire is not liable to take place in the cargo space, to avoid the possibility of ignition of solvent vapours. Entry of personnel into cargo spaces for this cargo shall not be permitted until tests have been carried out and it has been established that the oxygen content has been restored to a normal level. When the planned interval between the commencement of loading and the completion of discharge of this cargo exceeds 5 days, the cargo shall not be accepted for loading unless the cargo is to be carried in a cargo space equipped with facilities for introducing carbon dioxide or inert gas into the space. Smoking and the use of naked lights shall be prohibited in the vicinity of the cargo space during loading and unloading and on entry into the cargo spaces at any other time. Electrical circuits for equipment in cargo spaces which is unsuitable for use in an explosive atmosphere shall be isolated by removal of links in the system other than fuses. Spark-arresting screens shall be fitted to ventilators to the cargo spaces containing this cargo.

Ventilation

Surface ventilation, either natural or mechanical, should be conducted, as necessary, for removing any residual solvent vapour. To prevent self-heating of the cargo, caution is required when using mechanical ventilation.

Carriage

Hatches of the cargo spaces carrying this cargo shall be weathertight to prevent the ingress of water.

SEED CAKE UN 2217 with not more than 1.5% oil and not more than 11% moisture
(concluded)

Discharge

No special requirements.

Clean-up

No special requirements.

Emergency procedures

Special emergency equipment to be carried
Self-contained breathing apparatus.

Emergency procedures
Wear self-contained breathing apparatus.
Emergency action in the event of fire
Batten down; use ship's fixed fire-fighting installation, if fitted.
Medical First Aid
Refer to the *Medical First Aid Guide (MFAG)*, as amended.

Remarks

For solvent-extracted seed cake, the use of CO_2 should be withheld until fire is apparent.

The use of CO_2 is limited to controlling the fire, and further amounts may need to be injected from time to time during passage to reduce the oxygen content in the hold. On arrival in port, the cargo will need to be dug out to reach the seat of the fire.

SEED CAKE
(non-hazardous)

Description

The provisions of this schedule apply to solvent-extracted rape seed meal, pellets, soya bean meal, cotton seed meal and sunflower seed meal, containing not more than 4% oil and 15% oil and moisture combined and being substantially free from flammable solvents.

A certificate from a person recognized by the competent authority of the country of shipment shall be provided by the shipper, prior to loading, stating that the requirements for exemption as set out either in the schedule for SEED CAKE UN 1386 (b) or UN 2217, whichever is applicable, are met.

Characteristics

Angle of repose	Bulk density (kg/m^3)	Stowage factor (m^3/t)
Not applicable	478 to 719	1.39 to 2.09
Size	**Class**	**Group**
Not applicable	Not applicable	C

Hazard

No special hazards.

This cargo is non-combustible or has a low fire-risk.

Stowage & segregation

No special requirements.

Hold cleanliness

Clean and dry as relevant to the hazards of the cargo.

Weather precautions

This cargo shall be kept as dry as practicable. This cargo shall not be handled during precipitation. During handling of this cargo, all non-working hatches of the cargo spaces into which this cargo is loaded or to be loaded shall be closed.

Loading

Trim in accordance with the relevant provisions required under sections 4 and 5 of the Code.

Precautions

No special requirements.

Ventilation

No special requirements.

Carriage

Hatches of the cargo spaces carrying this cargo shall be weathertight to prevent the ingress of water.

Discharge

No special requirements.

Clean-up

No special requirements.

SILICOMANGANESE (low carbon)
(with known hazard profile or known to evolve gases)
(with silicon content of 25% or more)

Description
Silicomanganese is an extremely heavy cargo, silvery metallic material with a grey oxide coating.

Characteristics

Angle of repose	Bulk density (kg/m^3)	Stowage factor (m^3/t)
Not applicable	Approx. 3000	0.18 to 0.26
Size	**Class**	**Group**
Approx. 10 mm to 100 mm	MHB	B

Hazard
In contact with water may evolve hydrogen, a flammable gas that may form explosive mixtures with air and may, under similar conditions produce phosphine and arsine, which are highly toxic gases.

Cargo is liable to reduce oxygen content in a cargo space.

This cargo is non-combustible or has a low fire-risk.

Stowage & segregation
Segregation as required for class 4.3 materials.

"Separated from" foodstuffs and all class 8 liquids.

Hold cleanliness
Clean and dry as relevant to the hazards of the cargo.

Weather precautions
This cargo shall be kept as dry as practicable before loading, during loading and during voyage. This cargo shall not be loaded during precipitation. During loading of this cargo, all non-working hatches of the cargo spaces to which this cargo is loaded or to be loaded shall be closed.

Loading
Trim in accordance with the relevant provisions required under sections 4 and 5 of the Code.

As the density of the cargo is extremely high, the tanktop may be overstressed unless the cargo is evenly spread across the tanktop to equalize the weight distribution. Due consideration shall be paid to ensure that the tanktop is not overstressed during voyage and during loading by a pile of the cargo.

Precautions
The manufacturer or the shipper shall provide the master with a certificate stating that, after manufacture, the cargo was stored under cover, but exposed to open air for not less than three days prior to shipment. Smoking shall not be allowed on deck and in the cargo spaces and "NO SMOKING" signs shall be displayed on deck whenever this cargo is on board. Electrical fittings and cables shall be in good condition and properly safeguarded against short circuits and sparking. Where a bulkhead is required to be suitable for segregation purposes, cable and conduit penetrations of the decks and bulkheads shall be sealed against the passage of gas and vapour. Whenever practicable, ventilation systems for the living quarters shall be shut down or screened and air condition systems shall be placed on recirculation during loading and discharge of this cargo, in order to minimize the entry of dust into living quarters or other interior spaces of

SILICOMANGANESE (low carbon) *(continued)*

the ship. Precautions shall be taken to minimize the extent to which dust of this cargo may come in contact with moving parts of deck machinery and external navigation aids such as navigation lights.

Entry of personnel into enclosed spaces shall not be permitted until tests have been carried out and it has been established that the oxygen content has been restored to a normal level throughout the space and that no toxic gas is present, unless adequate ventilation and air circulation throughout the free space above the material has been effected.

Prohibition of smoking in dangerous areas shall be enforced, and clearly legible "NO SMOKING" signs shall be displayed.

Electrical fittings and cables shall be in good condition and properly safeguarded against short circuits and sparking. Where a bulkhead is required to be suitable for segregation purposes, cable and conduit penetrations of the decks and bulkheads shall be sealed against the passage of gas and vapour.

Ventilation systems shall be shut down or screened and air condition systems, if any, placed on recirculation during loading or discharge, in order to minimize the entry of dust into living quarters or other interior spaces of the ship.

Precautions shall be taken to minimize the extent to which dust may come in contact with moving parts of deck machinery and external navigation aids (e.g., navigation lights).

Ventilation

Mechanical surface ventilation shall be conducted during the voyage, as necessary, for the cargo spaces carrying this cargo.

Carriage

For quantitative measurements of oxygen and flammable gases liable to be evolved by the cargo, a suitable detector for each gas or combination of gases shall be on board while this cargo is carried. The detector shall be suitable for use in an atmosphere without oxygen and of certified safe type for use in explosive atmosphere. The concentrations of these gases in the cargo spaces carrying this cargo shall be measured regularly, during voyage, and the results of the measurements shall be recorded and kept on board.

Discharge

No special requirements.

Clean-up

No special requirements.

SILICOMANGANESE (low carbon) *(concluded)*

Emergency procedures

Special emergency equipment to be carried Self-contained breathing apparatus.
Emergency procedures Wear self-contained breathing apparatus. **Emergency action in the event of fire** Batten down and use CO_2 if available. **Do not use water.** **Medical First Aid** Refer to the *Medical First Aid Guide (MFAG)*, as amended.

Remarks

Material is virtually non-combustible when dry.

SODA ASH
(Dense and light)

Description

Powdery; composed of white, odourless grains and dust. It is made by the combustion of salt and limestone. Soluble in water. Soda ash is ruined on contact with oil.

Characteristics

Angle of repose	Bulk density (kg/m³)	Stowage factor (m³/t)
Not applicable	599 to 1053	0.95 to 1.67
Size	**Class**	**Group**
Powdery	Not applicable	C

Hazard

No special hazards.

This cargo is non-combustible or has a low fire-risk.

Stowage & segregation

No special requirements.

Hold cleanliness

No special requirements.

Weather precautions

This cargo shall be kept as dry as practicable. This cargo shall not be handled during precipitation. During handling of this cargo, all non-working hatches of the cargo spaces into which this cargo is loaded or to be loaded shall be closed.

Loading

Trim in accordance with the relevant provisions required under sections 4 and 5 of the Code.

Precautions

Appropriate precautions shall be taken to protect machinery and accommodation spaces from the dust of the cargo. Bilge wells of the cargo spaces shall be protected from ingress of the cargo. Due consideration shall be paid to protect equipment from the dust of the cargo. Persons who may be exposed to the dust of the cargo shall wear protective clothing, goggles or other equivalent dust eye-protection and dust filter masks, as necessary.

Ventilation

No special requirements.

Carriage

No special requirements.

Discharge

No special requirements.

Clean-up

After discharge of this cargo, the cargo spaces shall be swept clean except in cases where the BCSN of the cargo to be loaded subsequent to discharge is SODA ASH. The residues of this cargo may be pumped as slurry during washing out.

SODIUM NITRATE UN 1498

Description
Colourless, transparent, odourless crystals. Hygroscopic and soluble in water.

Characteristics

Angle of repose	Bulk density (kg/m³)	Stowage factor (m³/t)
Not applicable	508 to 719	1.39 to 1.97
Size	**Class**	**Group**
Not applicable	5.1	B

Hazard
Although non-combustible, mixtures with combustible material are readily ignited and may burn fiercely.

This cargo is hygroscopic and will cake if wet.

Stowage & segregation
"Separated from" foodstuffs.

Hold cleanliness
Clean and dry as relevant to the hazards of the cargo.

Weather precautions
This cargo shall be kept as dry as practicable. This cargo shall not be handled during precipitation. During handling of this cargo, all non-working hatches of the cargo spaces into which this cargo is loaded or to be loaded shall be closed.

Loading
Trim in accordance with the relevant provisions required under sections 4 and 5 of the Code.

Precautions
Bilge wells shall be clean, dry and covered as appropriate, to prevent ingress of the cargo.

Ventilation
The cargo spaces carrying this cargo shall not be ventilated during voyage.

Carriage
No special requirements.

Discharge
If this cargo has hardened, it shall be trimmed to avoid the formation of overhangs, as necessary.

Clean-up
No special requirements.

SODIUM NITRATE UN 1498 *(concluded)*

Emergency procedures

Special emergency equipment to be carried Protective clothing (gloves, boots, coveralls, headgear). Self-contained breathing apparatus. Spray nozzles.
Emergency procedures Wear protective clothing and self-contained breathing apparatus. **Emergency action in the event of fire** Use copious quantities of water, which is best applied in the form of a spray to avoid disturbing the surface of the material. The material may fuse or melt, in which condition application may result in extensive scattering of the molten material. Exclusion of air or the use of CO_2 will not control the fire. Due consideration should be given to the effect on the stability of the ship due to accumulated water. **Medical First Aid** Refer to the *Medical First Aid Guide (MFAG)*, as amended.

Remarks

This material is non-combustible unless contaminated.

SODIUM NITRATE AND POTASSIUM NITRATE MIXTURE UN 1499

Description

A hygroscopic mixture, soluble in water.

Characteristics

Angle of repose	Bulk density (kg/m³)	Stowage factor (m³/t)
30°	1136	0.88
Size	**Class**	**Group**
Not applicable	5.1	B

Hazard

Although non-combustible, mixtures with combustible material may readily ignite and burn fiercely.

This cargo is hygroscopic and will cake if wet.

Stowage & segregation

"Separated from" foodstuffs.

Hold cleanliness

Clean and dry as relevant to the hazards of the cargo.

Weather precautions

This cargo shall be kept as dry as practicable. This cargo shall not be handled during precipitation. During handling of this cargo, all non-working hatches of the cargo spaces into which this cargo is loaded or to be loaded shall be closed.

Loading

Trim in accordance with the relevant provisions required under sections 4 and 5 of the Code.

Precautions

Due regard shall be paid to prevent contact of the cargo and combustible materials.

Bilge wells shall be clean, dry and covered as appropriate, to prevent ingress of the cargo.

Ventilation

The cargo spaces carrying this cargo shall not be ventilated during voyage.

Carriage

No special requirements.

Discharge

If this cargo has hardened, it shall be trimmed to avoid the formation of overhangs, as necessary.

Clean-up

No special requirements.

SODIUM NITRATE AND POTASSIUM NITRATE MIXTURE UN 1499 *(concluded)*

Emergency procedures

Special emergency equipment to be carried
Protective clothing (gloves, boots, coveralls, headgear).
Self-contained breathing apparatus.
Spray nozzles.

Emergency procedures
Wear protective clothing and self-contained breathing apparatus.

Emergency action in the event of fire
Use copious quantities of water, which is best applied in the form of a spray to avoid disturbing the surface of the material. The material may fuse or melt, in which condition application of water may result in extensive scattering of the molten materials. Exclusion of air or the use of CO_2 will not control the fire. Due consideration should be given to the effect on the stability of the ship due to the accumulated water.

Medical First Aid
Refer to the *Medical First Aid Guide (MFAG)*, as amended.

Remarks
Material is non-combustible unless contaminated.

STAINLESS STEEL GRINDING DUST

Description

Brown lumps: Moisture content 1% to 3%. May give off dust.

Characteristics

Angle of repose	Bulk density (kg/m³)	Stowage factor (m³/t)
Not applicable	2381	0.42
Size	**Class**	**Group**
Lumps: 75 mm to 380 mm	Not applicable	C

Hazard

No special hazards.

This cargo is non-combustible or has a low fire-risk.

Stowage & segregation

No special requirements.

Hold cleanliness

No special requirements.

Weather precautions

No special requirements.

Loading

Trim in accordance with the relevant provisions required under sections 4 and 5 of the Code.

As the density of the cargo is extremely high, the tanktop may be overstressed unless the cargo is evenly spread across the tanktop to equalize the weight distribution. Due consideration shall be paid to ensure that the tanktop is not overstressed during voyage and during loading by a pile of the cargo.

Precautions

Appropriate precautions shall be taken to protect machinery and accommodation spaces from the dust of the cargo. Bilge wells of the cargo spaces shall be protected from ingress of the cargo. Due consideration shall be paid to protect equipment from the dust of the cargo. Persons who may be exposed to the dust of the cargo shall wear protective clothing, goggles or other equivalent dust eye-protection and dust filter masks, as necessary.

Ventilation

No special requirements.

Carriage

No special requirements.

Discharge

No special requirements.

Clean-up

No special requirements.

STONE CHIPPINGS

Description

Characteristics

Angle of repose	Bulk density (kg/m³)	Stowage factor (m³/t)
Not applicable	1408	0.71
Size	**Class**	**Group**
Fines to 25 mm	Not applicable	C

Hazard
No special hazards.

This cargo is non-combustible or has a low fire-risk.

Stowage & segregation
No special requirements.

Hold cleanliness
No special requirements.

Weather precautions
No special requirements.

Loading
Trim in accordance with the relevant provisions required under sections 4 and 5 of the Code.

Precautions
No special requirements.

Ventilation
No special requirements.

Carriage
No special requirements.

Discharge
No special requirements.

Clean-up
No special requirements.

SUGAR

Description
Depending on type, sugar may be either brown or white granules, with a very low moisture content to the order of 0% to 0.05%.

Characteristics

Angle of repose	Bulk density (kg/m^3)	Stowage factor (m^3/t)
Not applicable	625 to 1000	1.00 to 1.60
Size	**Class**	**Group**
Granules, up to 3 mm	Not applicable	C

Hazard
As sugar dissolves in water, ingress of water may result in the creation of air pockets in the body of the cargo with the ship's motion. The hazards are then similar to the hazards presented by cargoes which may liquefy. In case of ingress of water into the holds, the risk to the stability of the ship through dissolution of sugar (formation of a liquid base and shifting of cargo) should be recognized. This cargo is highly soluble.

Stowage & segregation
No special requirements.

Hold cleanliness
No special requirements.

Weather precautions
This cargo shall be kept as dry as practicable. This cargo shall not be handled during precipitation. During handling of this cargo, all non-working hatches of the cargo spaces into which this cargo is loaded or to be loaded shall be closed.

Loading
Trim in accordance with the relevant provisions required under sections 4 and 5 of the Code.

Precautions
No special requirements.

Ventilation
No special requirements.

Carriage
After the completion of loading of this cargo, the hatches of the cargo spaces shall be sealed to prevent water ingress, as necessary.

Discharge
No special requirements.

Clean-up
No special requirements.

SULPHATE OF POTASH AND MAGNESIUM

Description

Granular light brown material. Solution in water is almost neutral. May have a slight odour, depending on the process of manufacturer. Melting point: 72°C. Moisture: 0.02%.

Characteristics

Angle of repose	Bulk density (kg/m^3)	Stowage factor (m^3/t)
Not applicable	1000 to 1124	0.89 to 1.00
Size	**Class**	**Group**
Not applicable	Not applicable	C

Hazard

No special hazards.

This cargo is highly soluble. This cargo is non-combustible or has a low fire-risk.

Stowage & segregation

No special requirements.

Hold cleanliness

Clean and dry as relevant to the hazards of the cargo.

Weather precautions

This cargo shall be kept as dry as practicable. This cargo shall not be handled during precipitation. During handling of this cargo, all non-working hatches of the cargo spaces into which this cargo is loaded or to be loaded shall be closed.

Loading

The cargo shall be trimmed in accordance with the cargo information required by section 4 of this Code. If doubt exists, trim reasonably level to the boundaries of the cargo space so as to minimize the risk of shifting and to ensure that adequate stability will be maintained during the voyage.

Precautions

No special requirements.

Ventilation

No special requirements.

Carriage

No special requirements.

Discharge

No special requirements.

Clean-up

No special requirements.

SULPHUR (formed, solid)

Description

A co-product recovered from sour gas processing or oil refinery operations that has been subjected to a forming process that converts sulphur from a molten state into specific solid shapes (e.g., prills, granules, pellets, pastilles or flakes); bright yellow in colour; odourless. This schedule is not applicable to crushed, lump and coarse-grained sulphur (see SULPHUR UN 1350), or to co-products from sour gas processing or oil refinery operations NOT subjected to the above-described forming process.

Characteristics

Angle of repose	Bulk density (kg/m^3)	Stowage factor (m^3/t)
Not applicable	900 to 1350	0.74 to 1.11
Size	**Class**	**Group**
Approx. 1 mm to 10 mm	Not applicable	C

Hazard

This cargo is non-combustible or has a low fire risk. If involved in a fire, cargo may generate harmful gases.

When handled and shipped in accordance with the provisions of the schedule, this cargo poses no corrosion or dust hazards for human tissue or vessel.

Stowage & segregation

"Separated from" strong oxidizers, such as fluorine, chlorine, chlorates, nitrates (nitric acid), peroxides, liquid oxygen, permanganates, dichromates or the like.

Hold cleanliness

Clean and dry as relevant to the hazards of the cargo. Holds shall not be washed with seawater.

Weather precautions

No special requirements.

Loading

Trim in accordance with the relevant provisions required under sections 4 and 5 of the Code. Appropriate precautions shall be taken to minimize impact, abrasion and crushing when handling to prevent dust from forming. Standard application of surfactants* inhibits airborne dust from forming.

Precautions

Protect machinery, accommodations and equipment from small particles or any dust, if formed. Persons involved in cargo handling shall wear protective clothing, goggles and dust filter masks. Holds including trimming plates and tanktops shall be treated with effective, commercially available protective coating or lime-washed to avoid any potential corrosive reaction between sulphur, water and steel. Upper sections shall have a sound coating of paint. Hatches shall be sealed tightly.

---

* A fine water-based spray that promotes the binding of smaller particles to larger particles.

SULPHUR (formed, solid) *(concluded)*

Ventilation

Surface ventilation only, either natural or mechanical, shall be conducted, as necessary, during the voyage for this cargo.

Carriage

As a fine spray of fresh water or surfactant is added during loading, bilges shall be sounded and pumped out as necessary throughout the voyage.

Discharge

Appropriate safety precautions shall be taken when entering the cargo spaces, particularly in the area of the bottom layers of sulphur in ship's hold, taking into account the recommendations developed by the Organization.*

Appropriate precautions shall be taken to minimize impact, abrasion and crushing when handling to prevent dust from forming.

Clean-up

Persons involved in clean-up shall wear hard hats, protective goggles, long-sleeve shirts, long pants, and impervious gloves. Use of approved respirators shall be considered. Holds shall be thoroughly washed using only fresh water following discharge.

Appropriate safety precautions shall be taken when entering the cargo spaces, taking into account the recommendations developed by the Organization.*

---

* Refer to Recommendations for entering enclosed spaces aboard ships, adopted by the Organization by resolution A.864(20) (see the supplement of this publication).

SULPHUR UN 1350
(crushed lump and coarse grained)
Note: Fine grained sulphur (flowers of sulphur) shall not be transported in bulk.

Description

A mineral substance found free in volcanic countries. Yellow in colour, brittle, insoluble in water, but readily fusible by heat. Sulphur is loaded in a damp or wet condition.

Characteristics

Angle of repose	Bulk density (kg/m³)	Stowage factor (m³/t)
Not applicable	1053 to 1176	0.85 to 0.95
Size	**Class**	**Group**
Particles or lumps of any size	4.1	B

Hazard

Flammability and dust explosion especially during loading and unloading and after discharge and cleaning.

This cargo may ignite readily.

This cargo is non-combustible or has a low fire-risk.

Stowage & segregation

"Separated from" foodstuffs.

Hold cleanliness

Clean and dry as relevant to the hazards of the cargo.

Must be thoroughly clean and washed with fresh water.

Weather precautions

No special requirements.

Loading

Trim in accordance with the relevant provisions required under sections 4 and 5 of the Code.

Precautions

When this cargo is involved in a fire, a toxic, very irritating and suffocating gas is evolved. This cargo forms explosive and sensitive mixtures with most oxidizing material. This cargo has a liability to dust explosion, which may occur especially after discharge and during cleaning. The hold trimming plates and tanktops of the cargo spaces for this cargo shall be lime-washed or coated with paint to prevent corrosion. Upper sections shall have a sound coating of paint. Electrical circuits for the equipment in cargo spaces for this cargo which is unsuitable for use in an explosive atmosphere shall be isolated by removal of links in the system other than fuses. Due consideration shall be paid to the isolation of electrical circuits for the equipment in the adjacent spaces of the cargo spaces which is unsuitable for use in an explosive atmosphere. Any ventilators of the cargo spaces for this cargo shall be fitted with spark-arresting screens.

Fine grained sulphur (flowers of sulphur) shall not be transported in bulk.

SULPHUR UN 1350 (crushed lump and coarse grained) *(concluded)*

Ventilation

Surface ventilation only, either natural or mechanical, shall be conducted, as necessary, during the voyage for this cargo.

Carriage

Bilges in the cargo spaces carrying this cargo shall be pumped regularly to prevent accumulation of water/acid solution.

Discharge

No special requirements.

Clean-up

The cargo spaces and other structures which may have been in contact with this cargo or the dust shall not be swept. After discharge of this cargo, the cargo spaces, and other structures as necessary, shall be washed out with fresh water to remove all residues of this cargo. Then the cargo spaces shall be thoroughly dried. Wet dust or residues may form highly corrosive sulphurous acid, which is extremely dangerous to personnel and corrosive to steel. Persons involved in cleaning up shall be provided with protective clothing, goggles and facemasks to wear.

Emergency procedures

Special emergency equipment to be carried
Self-contained breathing apparatus.
Emergency procedures   Wear self-contained breathing apparatus.   **Emergency action in the event of fire**   Batten down; use ship's fixed fire-fighting installation, if available.   Exclusion of air may be sufficient to control the fire. **Do not use water.**   **Medical First Aid**   Refer to the *Medical First Aid Guide (MFAG)*, as amended.

SUPERPHOSPHATE

Description

Greyish-white. Moisture: 0% to 7%. Hygroscopic.

Characteristics

Angle of repose	Bulk density (kg/m^3)	Stowage factor (m^3/t)
30° to 40°	1000 to 1190	0.81 to 1.00
Size	**Class**	**Group**
Granular, fines and powder to 0.15 mm diameter	Not applicable	C

Hazard

No special hazards.

This cargo is non-combustible or has a low fire-risk. This cargo is hygroscopic and will cake if wet.

Stowage & segregation

No special requirements.

Hold cleanliness

Clean and dry as relevant to the hazards of the cargo.

Weather precautions

This cargo shall be kept as dry as practicable. This cargo shall not be handled during precipitation. During handling of this cargo, all non-working hatches of the cargo spaces into which this cargo is loaded or to be loaded shall be closed.

Loading

Trim in accordance with the relevant provisions required under sections 4 and 5 of the Code.

Precautions

The hold trimming plates and tanktops of the cargo spaces for this cargo shall be lime-washed or coated with paint to prevent corrosion.

Ventilation

The cargo spaces carrying this cargo shall not be ventilated during voyage.

Carriage

Moisture from condensation, cargo heating or leaking hatchcovers may cause formation of phosphoric or phosphorous acid, which may cause corrosion to steelwork. After the completion of loading of this cargo, the hatches of the cargo spaces shall be sealed, as necessary. This cargo will decompose burlap or canvas cloth covering bilge wells.

Discharge

If this cargo has hardened, it shall be trimmed to avoid the formation of overhangs, as necessary.

Clean-up

After discharge of this cargo, particular attention shall be paid to bilge wells of the cargo spaces.

SUPERPHOSPHATE (triple, granular)

Description
Granular in form, dark grey colour and, depending on its source, can be dusty. Hygroscopic.

Characteristics

Angle of repose	Bulk density (kg/m^3)	Stowage factor (m^3/t)
Not applicable	813 to 909	1.10 to 1.23
Size	**Class**	**Group**
2 mm to 4 mm	Not applicable	C

Hazard
No special hazards.

This cargo is non-combustible or has a low fire-risk. This cargo is hygroscopic and will cake if wet.

Stowage & segregation
No special requirements.

Hold cleanliness
Clean and dry as relevant to the hazards of the cargo.

Weather precautions
This cargo shall be kept as dry as practicable. This cargo shall not be handled during precipitation. During handling of this cargo, all non-working hatches of the cargo spaces into which this cargo is loaded or to be loaded shall be closed.

Loading
Trim in accordance with the relevant provisions required under sections 4 and 5 of the Code.

Precautions
Hold trimming plates and tanktops should be lime-washed to prevent corrosion.

Ventilation
The cargo spaces carrying this cargo shall not be ventilated during voyage.

Carriage
Moisture from condensation, cargo heating or leaking hatchcovers may cause formation of phosphoric or phosphorous acid, which may cause corrosion to steelwork. After the completion of loading of this cargo, the hatches of the cargo spaces shall be sealed, as necessary. This cargo will decompose burlap or canvas cloth covering bilge wells.

Discharge
If this cargo has hardened, it shall be trimmed to avoid the formation of overhangs, as necessary.

Clean-up
After discharge of this cargo, particular attention should be paid to bilge wells of the cargo spaces.

TACONITE PELLETS

Description
Ore. Grey, round steel pellets. Moisture: 2%.

Characteristics

Angle of repose	Bulk density (kg/m^3)	Stowage factor (m^3/t)
Not applicable	599 to 654	1.53 to 1.67
Size	**Class**	**Group**
Pellets to 15 mm diameter	Not applicable	C

Hazard
No special hazards.

This cargo is non-combustible or has a low fire-risk.

Stowage & segregation
No special requirements.

Hold cleanliness
No special requirements.

Weather precautions
No special requirements.

Loading
Trim in accordance with the relevant provisions required under sections 4 and 5 of the Code.

Precautions
No special requirements.

Ventilation
No special requirements.

Carriage
No special requirements.

Discharge
No special requirements.

Clean-up
No special requirements.

TALC

Description

Talc is an extremely soft, whitish, green or greyish natural hydrated magnesium silicate. It has a characteristic soapy or greasy feel.

Characteristics

Angle of repose	Bulk density (kg/m³)	Stowage factor (m³/t)
Not applicable	1370 to 1563	0.64 to 0.73
Size	**Class**	**Group**
Powdery to 100 mm lumps	Not applicable	C

Hazard

No special hazards.

This cargo is non-combustible or has a low fire-risk.

Stowage & segregation

No special requirements.

Hold cleanliness

No special requirements.

Weather precautions

No special requirements.

Loading

Trim in accordance with the relevant provisions required under sections 4 and 5 of the Code.

Precautions

No special requirements.

Ventilation

No special requirements.

Carriage

No special requirements.

Discharge

No special requirements.

Clean-up

No special requirements.

TANKAGE

Description
The dried sweeping of animal matter from slaughterhouse floors. Very dusty.

Characteristics

Angle of repose	Bulk density (kg/m^3)	Stowage factor (m^3/t)
Not applicable	–	–
Size	**Class**	**Group**
Not applicable	MHB	B

Hazard
Subject to spontaneous heating and possible ignition. Possibly infectious.

Stowage & segregation
Segregation as required for class 4.2 materials.

"Separated by a complete cargo space or hold from" foodstuffs.

Hold cleanliness
Clean and dry as relevant to the hazards of the cargo.

Weather precautions
No special requirements.

Loading
Trim in accordance with the relevant provisions required under sections 4 and 5 of the Code.

Precautions
Bilge wells shall be clean, dry and covered as appropriate, to prevent ingress of the cargo.

Do not load if the temperature is above 38°C.

Appropriate precautions shall be taken to protect machinery and accommodation spaces from the dust of the cargo. Bilge wells of the cargo spaces shall be protected from ingress of the cargo. Due consideration shall be paid to protect equipment from the dust of the cargo. Persons who may be exposed to the dust of the cargo shall wear goggles or other equivalent dust eye-protection and dust filter masks. Those persons shall wear protective clothing, as necessary.

Ventilation
No special requirements.

Carriage
The temperature of this cargo shall be measured daily during voyage. The results of measurements shall be recorded to check possible self-heating.

Discharge
No special requirements.

Clean-up
No special requirements.

TANKAGE *(concluded)*

Emergency procedures

<table>
<tr><td align="center">

Special emergency equipment to be carried

Self-contained breathing apparatus.

</td></tr>
<tr><td align="center">

Emergency procedures

Wear self-contained breathing apparatus.

Emergency action in the event of fire

Batten down; use ship's fixed fire-fighting installation.
Use full protective clothing in case of fire situation.

Medical First Aid

Refer to the *Medical First Aid Guide (MFAG)*, as amended.

</td></tr>
</table>

TAPIOCA

Description

Dry, dusty mixture of powder and granules.

Characteristics

Angle of repose	Bulk density (kg/m³)	Stowage factor (m³/t)
32°	735	1.36
Size	**Class**	**Group**
Powder and granules	Not applicable	C

Hazard

May heat spontaneously with oxygen depletion in the cargo space.

This cargo is non-combustible or has a low fire-risk.

Stowage & segregation

No special requirements.

Hold cleanliness

No special requirements.

Weather precautions

No special requirements.

Loading

Trim in accordance with the relevant provisions required under sections 4 and 5 of the Code.

Precautions

Appropriate precautions shall be taken to protect machinery and accommodation spaces from the dust of the cargo. Bilge wells of the cargo spaces shall be protected from ingress of the cargo. Due consideration shall be paid to protect equipment from the dust of the cargo. Persons who may be exposed to the dust of the cargo shall wear protective clothing, goggles or other equivalent dust eye-protection and dust filter masks, as necessary.

Ventilation

The cargo spaces carrying this cargo shall not be ventilated during voyage.

Carriage

No special requirements.

Discharge

No special requirements.

Clean-up

No special requirements.

UREA

Description
White, granular, and odourless commodity. Moisture content is less than 1%. Hygroscopic.

Characteristics

Angle of repose	Bulk density (kg/m³)	Stowage factor (m³/t)
28° to 45°	645 to 855	1.17 to 1.56
Size	**Class**	**Group**
1 mm to 4 mm	Not applicable	C

Hazard
No special hazards.

This cargo is non-combustible or has a low fire-risk.

This cargo is hygroscopic and will cake if wet.

Urea (either pure or impure) may, in the presence of moisture, damage paintwork or corrode steel.

Stowage & segregation
No special requirements.

Hold cleanliness
No special requirements.

Weather precautions
This cargo shall be kept as dry as practicable. This cargo shall not be handled during precipitation. During handling of this cargo, all non-working hatches of the cargo spaces into which this cargo is loaded or to be loaded shall be closed.

Loading
Trim in accordance with the relevant provisions required under sections 4 and 5 of the Code.

Precautions
No special requirements.

Ventilation
The cargo spaces carrying this cargo shall not be ventilated during voyage.

Carriage
No special requirements.

Discharge
If this cargo has hardened, it shall be trimmed to avoid the formation of overhangs, as necessary.

Clean-up
After discharge of this cargo, the cargo spaces shall be swept, washed out and dried.

VANADIUM ORE

Description

Characteristics

Angle of repose	Bulk density (kg/m^3)	Stowage factor (m^3/t)
Not applicable	1786	0.560
Size	**Class**	**Group**
Not applicable	MHB	B

Hazard

Dust may be toxic.

This cargo is non-combustible or has a low fire-risk.

Stowage & segregation

Segregation as required for class 6.1 materials.

"Separated from" foodstuffs.

Hold cleanliness

No special requirements.

Weather precautions

No special requirements.

Loading

Trim in accordance with the relevant provisions required under sections 4 and 5 of the Code.

Precautions

Exposure of persons to dust should be minimized.

Appropriate precautions shall be taken to protect machinery and accommodation spaces from the dust of the cargo. Bilge wells of the cargo spaces shall be protected from ingress of the cargo. Due consideration shall be paid to protect equipment from the dust of the cargo. Persons who may be exposed to the dust of the cargo shall wear goggles or other equivalent dust eye-protection and dust filter masks. Those persons shall wear protective clothing, as necessary.

Ventilation

No special requirements.

Carriage

No special requirements.

Discharge

No special requirements.

Clean-up

No special requirements.

IMSBC Code

283

VANADIUM ORE *(concluded)*

Emergency procedures

Special emergency equipment to be carried
Self-contained breathing apparatus.

Emergency procedures
Wear self-contained breathing apparatus.

Emergency action in the event of fire
Batten down; use ship's fixed fire-fighting installation, if fitted.
Exclusion of air may be sufficient to control fire.

Medical First Aid
Refer to the *Medical First Aid Guide (MFAG)*, as amended.

VERMICULITE

Description

A mineral of the mica group. Grey. Average moisture: 6% to 10%. May give off dust.

Characteristics

Angle of repose	Bulk density (kg/m³)	Stowage factor (m³/t)
Not applicable	730	1.37
Size	**Class**	**Group**
3 mm	Not applicable	C

Hazard

No special hazards.

This cargo is non-combustible or has a low fire-risk.

Stowage & segregation

No special requirements.

Hold cleanliness

No special requirements.

Weather precautions

No special requirements.

Loading

Trim in accordance with the relevant provisions required under sections 4 and 5 of the Code.

Precautions

Appropriate precautions shall be taken to protect machinery and accommodation spaces from the dust of the cargo. Bilge wells of the cargo spaces shall be protected from ingress of the cargo. Due consideration shall be paid to protect equipment from the dust of the cargo. Persons who may be exposed to the dust of the cargo shall wear protective clothing, goggles or other equivalent dust eye-protection and dust filter masks, as necessary.

Prior to loading, a certificate based on test shall be provided by the manufacturer or shipper stating that the asbestos content is less than 1%.

Ventilation

No special requirements.

Carriage

No special requirements.

Discharge

No special requirements.

Clean-up

No special requirements.

WHITE QUARTZ

Description
99.6% silica content.

Characteristics

Angle of repose	Bulk density (kg/m^3)	Stowage factor (m^3/t)
Not applicable	1639	0.61
Size	**Class**	**Group**
Lumps to 150 mm	Not applicable	C

Hazard
No special hazards.

This cargo is non-combustible or has a low fire-risk.

Stowage & segregation
No special requirements.

Hold cleanliness
No special requirements.

Weather precautions
No special requirements.

Loading
Trim in accordance with the relevant provisions required under sections 4 and 5 of the Code.

Precautions
No special requirements.

Ventilation
No special requirements.

Carriage
No special requirements.

Discharge
No special requirements.

Clean-up
No special requirements.

WOODCHIPS

Description
Natural timber mechanically chipped into the approximate size of a business card.

Characteristics

Angle of repose	Bulk density (kg/m³)	Stowage factor (m³/t)
Not applicable	326	3.07
Size	**Class**	**Group**
As above	MHB	B

Hazard
This material possesses a chemical hazard. Some shipments may be subject to oxidation leading to depletion of oxygen and increase of carbon dioxide in cargo and adjacent spaces.

With moisture content of 15% or more this cargo has a low fire-risk. As the moisture content decreases the fire risk increases. When dry, woodchips can be easily ignited by external sources; are readily combustible and can ignite by friction. A condition with complete depletion of oxygen may be present in less than 48 hours.

Stowage & segregation
Segregation as for class 4.1 materials.

Hold cleanliness
No special requirements.

Weather precautions
No special requirements.

Loading
Trim in accordance with the relevant provisions required under sections 4 and 5 of the Code.

Precautions
Entry of personnel into cargo and adjacent confined spaces should not be permitted until tests have been carried out and it has been established that the oxygen level is 20.7%. If this condition is not met, additional ventilation should be applied to the cargo hold or adjacent enclosed spaces and re-measuring shall be conducted after a suitable interval.

An oxygen meter shall be worn and activated by all crew when entering cargo and adjacent enclosed spaces.

In dry weather, dust which settles on deck will dry out quickly and is easily ignited. Appropriate precautions shall be taken to prevent fire.

Ventilation
Ventilation of enclosed spaces adjacent to a cargo hold before entry may be necessary even if these spaces are apparently sealed from the cargo hold.

Carriage
No special requirements.

WOODCHIPS *(concluded)*

Discharge

No special requirements.

Clean-up

No special requirements.

Emergency procedures

Special emergency equipment to be carried

Self-contained breathing apparatus and oxygen meters should be available.

Emergency procedures

Nil

Emergency action in the event of fire

Batten down; use ship's fixed fire-fighting installation, if fitted.
Exclusion of air may be sufficient to control fire.

Medical First Aid

Refer to the *Medical First Aid Guide (MFAG)*, as amended.

WOOD PELLETS

Description

The wood pellets are light blond to chocolate brown in colour; very hard and cannot be easily squashed. Wood pellets have a typical specific density between 1100 to 1700 kg/m^3 and a bulk density of 600 to 750 kg/m^3. Wood pellets are made of sawdust, planer shavings and other wood waste such as bark coming out of the lumber manufacturing processes. Normally there are no additives or binders blended into the pellet, unless specified. The raw material is fragmented, dried and extruded into pellet form. The raw material is compressed approximately 3.5 times and the finished wood pellets typically have a moisture content of 4 to 8%. Wood pellets are used as a fuel in district heating and electrical power generation as well as a fuel for small space heaters such as stoves and fireplaces.

Wood pellets are also used as animal bedding due to the absorption characteristics. Such wood pellets typically have a moisture content of 8 to 10%.

Characteristics

Angle of repose	Bulk density (kg/m^3)	Stowage factor (m^3/t)
Approximately 30°	600 to 750	1.4 to 1.6
Size	**Class**	**Group**
Cylindrical with 3 mm to 12 mm Diameter: 10 to 20 mm	MHB	B

Hazard

Shipments may be subject to oxidation leading to depletion of oxygen and increase of carbon monoxide and carbon dioxide in cargo and communicating spaces.

Swelling if exposed to moisture. Wood pellets may ferment over time if moisture content is over 15%, leading to generation of asphyxiating and flammable gases which may cause spontaneous combustion.

Handling of wood pellets may cause dust to develop. Risk of explosion at high dust concentration.

Stowage & segregation

Segregate as for class 4.1 materials.

Hold cleanliness

Clean and dry as relevant to the hazards of the cargo.

Weather precautions

This cargo shall be kept as dry as practicable. This cargo shall not be handled during precipitation. During handling of this cargo, all non-working hatches of the cargo spaces into which this cargo is loaded or to be loaded shall be closed. There is a high risk of renewed oxygen depletion and carbon monoxide formation in previously ventilated adjacent spaces after such closure.

Loading

Trim in accordance with the relevant provisions required under sections 4 and 5 of the Code.

WOOD PELLETS *(concluded)*

Precautions

Entry of personnel into cargo and adjacent confined spaces shall not be permitted until tests have been carried out and it has been established that the oxygen content and carbon monoxide levels have been restored to the following levels: oxygen 20.7% and carbon monoxide <100 ppm. If these conditions are not met, additional ventilation shall be applied to the cargo hold or adjacent confined spaces and re-measuring shall be conducted after a suitable interval.

An oxygen and carbon monoxide meter shall be worn and activated by all crew when entering cargo and adjacent enclosed spaces.

Ventilation

Ventilation of enclosed spaces adjacent to a cargo hold before entry may be necessary even if these spaces are apparently sealed from the cargo hold.

Carriage

Hatches of the cargo spaces carrying this cargo shall be weathertight to prevent the ingress of water.

Discharge

No special requirements.

Clean-up

No special requirements.

Emergency procedures

Special emergency equipment to be carried

Self-contained breathing apparatus and combined or individual oxygen and carbon monoxide meters should be available.

Emergency procedures

Nil

Emergency action in the event of fire

Batten down; use ship's fixed fire-fighting installation, if fitted
Exclusion of air may be sufficient to control fire.
Extinguish fire with carbon dioxide, foam or water.

Medical First Aid

Refer to the *Medical First Aid Guide (MFAG)*, as amended.

WOOD PULP PELLETS

Description

The pellets are brown in colour; very hard and cannot be easily squashed. They are light and are about half the size of a bottle cork. The pellets are made of compacted woodchips.

Characteristics

Angle of repose	Bulk density (kg/m^3)	Stowage factor (m^3/t)
Not applicable	326	3.07
Size	**Class**	**Group**
Approx. 15 mm × 20 mm	MHB	B

Hazard

This cargo possesses a chemical hazard. Some shipments may be subject to oxidation leading to depletion of oxygen and increase of carbon dioxide in cargo and adjacent spaces.

With moisture content of 15% or more this cargo has a low fire-risk. As the moisture content decreases, the fire risk increases.

Stowage & segregation

Segregate as for class 4.1 materials.

Hold cleanliness

Clean and dry as relevant to the hazards of the cargo.

Weather precautions

No special requirements.

Loading

Trim in accordance with the relevant provisions required under sections 4 and 5 of the Code.

Precautions

Entry of personnel into the cargo spaces containing this cargo shall not be permitted until tests have been carried out and it has been established that the oxygen content has been restored to a normal level. In dry weather, dust, which settles on deck, will dry out quickly and becomes readily ignitable. Appropriate precautions shall be taken to prevent fire.

Ventilation

No special requirements.

Carriage

No special requirements.

Discharge

No special requirements.

Clean-up

No special requirements.

WOOD PULP PELLETS *(concluded)*

Emergency procedures

Special emergency equipment to be carried Nil
Emergency procedures Nil **Emergency action in the event of fire** Batten down; use ship's fixed fire-fighting installation, if fitted. Exclusion of air may be sufficient to control fire. **Medical First Aid** Refer to the *Medical First Aid Guide (MFAG)*, as amended.

ZINC ASHES UN 1435

Shipments require the approval of the competent authority of the countries of shipment and the flag State of the ship.

Description

Characteristics

Angle of repose	Bulk density (kg/m³)	Stowage factor (m³/t)
Not applicable	900	1.11
Size	**Class**	**Group**
Not applicable	4.3	B

Hazard

In contact with moisture or water liable to give off hydrogen, a flammable gas, and toxic gases.

This cargo is non-combustible or has a low fire-risk.

Stowage & segregation

"Separated from" foodstuffs and all class 8 liquids.

Hold cleanliness

Clean and dry as relevant to the hazards of the cargo.

Weather precautions

This cargo shall be kept as dry as practicable before loading, during loading and during voyage. This cargo shall not be loaded during precipitation. During loading of this cargo, all non-working hatches of the cargo spaces to which this cargo is loaded or to be loaded shall be closed.

Loading

Trim in accordance with the relevant provisions required under sections 4 and 5 of the Code.

This cargo shall not be accepted for loading when the cargo is damp or known to have been wetted.

Precautions

Reject any damp material or any material which is known to have been wetted. Possible ignition sources, including hot work, burning, smoking, electrical sparking, shall be eliminated in the vicinity of the cargo spaces containing this cargo during handling and carriage of this cargo.

Ventilation

Continuous mechanical ventilation shall be conducted during the voyage for the cargo spaces carrying this cargo. If maintaining ventilation endangers the ship or the cargo, it may be interrupted unless there is a risk of explosion or other danger due to interruption of the ventilation. In any case, mechanical ventilation shall be maintained for a reasonable period prior to discharge.

ZINC ASHES UN 1435 *(concluded)*

Carriage

For quantitative measurements of hydrogen, a suitable detector shall be on board while this cargo is carried. The detector shall be of certified safe type for use in explosive atmosphere. The concentration of hydrogen in the cargo spaces carrying this cargo shall be measured regularly, during voyage, and the results of the measurements shall be recorded and kept on board.

Discharge

No special requirements.

Clean-up

After discharge of this cargo, the cargo spaces shall be swept clean twice.

Water shall not be used for cleaning of the cargo space which has contained this cargo, because of danger of gas.

Emergency procedures

Special emergency equipment to be carried

Protective clothing (gloves, boots, coveralls, headgear).
Self-contained breathing apparatus.

Emergency procedures

Wear protective clothing and self-contained breathing apparatus.

Emergency action in the event of fire

Batten down; use ship's fixed fire-fighting installation, if available.
Do not use water.

Medical First Aid

Refer to the *Medical First Aid Guide (MFAG)*, as amended.

ZIRCONSAND

Description
Usually fine white to yellow, very abrasive extracted from ilmenite sand. May be dusty. Shipped dry.

Characteristics

Angle of repose	Bulk density (kg/m³)	Stowage factor (m³/t)
Not applicable	2600 to 3000	0.33 to 0.36
Size	**Class**	**Group**
0.15 mm or less	Not applicable	C

Hazard
No special hazards.

This cargo is non-combustible or has a low fire-risk.

Stowage & segregation
No special requirements.

Hold cleanliness
No special requirements.

Weather precautions
This cargo shall be kept as dry as practicable before loading, during loading and during voyage. This cargo shall not be loaded during precipitation. During loading of this cargo, all non-working hatches of the cargo spaces to which this cargo is loaded or to be loaded shall be closed.

Loading
Trim in accordance with the relevant provisions required under sections 4 and 5 of the Code.

As the density of the cargo is extremely high, the tanktop may be overstressed unless the cargo is evenly spread across the tanktop to equalize the weight distribution. Due consideration shall be paid to ensure that the tanktop is not overstressed during voyage and during loading by a pile of the cargo.

Precautions
Bilge wells shall be clean, dry and covered as appropriate, to prevent ingress of the cargo.

Appropriate precautions shall be taken to protect machinery and accommodation spaces from the dust of the cargo. Bilge wells of the cargo spaces shall be protected from ingress of the cargo. Due consideration shall be paid to protect equipment from the dust of the cargo. Persons who may be exposed to the dust of the cargo shall wear goggles or other equivalent dust eye-protection and dust filter masks. Those persons shall wear protective clothing, as necessary.

Ventilation
No special requirements.

Carriage
No special requirements.

Discharge
No special requirements.

Clean-up
No special requirements.

Appendix 2

Laboratory test procedures, associated apparatus and standards

1   Test procedures for materials which may liquefy and associated apparatus

Three methods of testing for the transportable moisture limit are currently in general use:

.1   flow table test;

.2   penetration test;

.3   Proctor/Fagerberg test.

As each method has its advantages, the selection of the test method should be determined by local practices or by the appropriate authorities.

1.1   Flow table test procedure

1.1.1   *Scope*

The flow table is generally suitable for mineral concentrates or other fine material with a maximum grain size of 1 mm. It may also be applicable to materials with a maximum grain size up to 7 mm. It will not be suitable for materials coarser than this and may also not give satisfactory results for some materials with high clay content. If the flow table test is not suitable for the material in question, the procedures to be adopted should be those approved by the authority of the port State.

The test described below provides for determination of:

.1   the moisture content of a sample of cargo, hereinafter referred to as the test material;

.2   the flow moisture point (FMP) of the test material under impact or cyclic forces of the flow table apparatus; and

.3   the transportable moisture limit of the test material.

1.1.2   *Apparatus* (see figure 1.1.2)

.1   Standard flow table and frame (ASTM Designation (C230-68) – see 3).

.2   Flow table mounting (ASTM Designation (C230-68) – see 3).

.3   Mould (ASTM Designation (C230-68) – see 3).

.4   Tamper (see figure 1.1.2.4): the required tamping pressure may be achieved by using calibrated, spring-loaded tampers (examples are included in figure 1.1.2.4) or some other suitable design of tamper that allows a controlled pressure to be applied via a 30 mm diameter tamper head.

.5   Scales and weights (ASTM Designation (C109-73) – see 3) and suitable sample containers.

.6   Glass graduated measuring cylinder and burette having capacities of 100–200 ml and 10 ml, respectively.

.7   A hemispherical mixing bowl approximately 30 cm diameter, rubber gloves and drying dishes or pans. Alternatively, an automatic mixer of similar capacity can be used for the mixing operations. In this case, care should be exercised to ensure that the use of such a mechanical mixer does not reduce the particle size or consistency of the test material.

.8   A drying oven with controlled temperature up to approximately 110°C. This oven should be without air circulation.

Figure 1.1.2 – *Flow table and accessory apparatus*

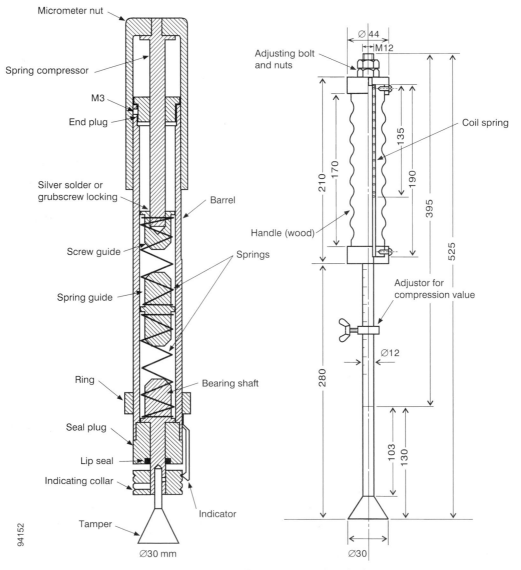

Figure 1.1.2.4 – *Examples of spring-loaded tampers*

1.1.3 *Temperature and humidity*

It is preferable to work in a room where the samples will be protected from excessive temperatures, air currents and humidity variations. All phases of the material preparation and testing procedure should be accomplished in a reasonable space of time to minimize moisture losses and, in any event, within the day of commencement. Where possible, sample containers should be covered with plastic film or other suitable cover.

1.1.4 *Procedure*

The quantity of material required for a flow moisture test will vary according to the specific gravity of the material to be tested. It will range from approximately 2 kg for coal to 3 kg for mineral concentrates. It should be collected as a representative sample of the cargo being shipped. Experience has shown that more accurate test results will be obtained by ensuring that the moisture content of the test sample is increased rather than decreased towards the FMP.

Consequently, it is recommended that a preliminary flow moisture test should be conducted, generally in accordance with the following, to indicate the condition of the test sample, i.e., the quantity of water and the rate at which it is to be added or whether the sample should be air-dried to reduce its moisture content before commencing the main flow moisture test.

1.1.4.1 *Preparation of the test sample*

The representative sample of test material is placed in the mixing bowl and thoroughly mixed. Three subsamples (A), (B) and (C) are removed from the mixing bowl as follows: about one fifth of the sample (A) should be immediately weighed and placed in the drying oven to determine the moisture content of the sample "as received". Two further subsamples, each of about two fifths of the gross weight, should then be taken, one (B) for the preliminary FMP test and the other (C) for the main FMP determination:

.1 *Filling the mould.* The mould is placed on the centre of the flow table and filled in three stages with the material from the mixing bowl. The first charge, after tamping, should aim to fill the mould to approximately one third of its depth. The quantity of sample required to achieve this will vary from one material to another, but can readily be established after some experience has been gained of the packing characteristics of the material being tested.

The second charge, after tamping, should fill the mould to about two thirds of its depth and the third and final charge, after tamping, should reach to just below the top of the mould (see figure 1.1.4 2).

.2 *Tamping procedure.* The aim of tamping is to attain a degree of compaction similar to that prevailing at the bottom of a shipboard cargo of the material being tested. The correct pressure to be applied is calculated from:

$$\text{Tamping pressure (Pa)} = \text{Bulk density of cargo (kg/m}^3) \times \text{Maximum depth of cargo (m)} \times \text{Gravity acceleration (m/s}^2)$$

Bulk density can be measured by a single test, using the Proctor C apparatus described in ASTM Standard D-698 or JIS-A-1210, on a sample of the cargo at the proposed moisture content of loading.

When calculating the tamping pressure, if no information concerning cargo depth is available the maximum likely depth should be used.

Alternatively, the pressure may be estimated from table 1.1.4.1.

The number of tamping actions (applying the correct, steady pressure each time) should be about 35 for the bottom layer, 25 for the middle and 20 for the top layer, tamping successively over the area completely to the edges of the sample to achieve a uniformly flat surface for each layer.

.3 *Removal of the mould.* The mould is tapped on its side until it becomes loose, leaving the sample in the shape of a truncated cone on the table.

Table 1.1.4.1

Typical cargo	Bulk density (kg/m³)	Maximum cargo depth			
		2 m	5 m	10 m	20 m
		Tamper pressure (kPa)			
Coal	1000	20 (1.4)	50 (3.5)	100 (7.1)	200 (14.1)
	2000	40 (2.8)	100 (7.1)	200 (14.1)	400 (28.3)
Metal ore	3000	60 (4.2)	150 (10.6)	300 (21.2)	600 (42.4)
Iron ore concentrate	4000	80 (5.7)	200 (14.1)	400 (28.3)	800 (56.5)
Lead ore concentrate	5000	100 (7.1)	250 (17.7)	500 (35.3)	1000 (70.7)
(values in parenthesis are equivalent kgf when applied via a 30 mm diameter tamper head)					

1.1.4.2   *The preliminary flow moisture test*

.1   Immediately after removing the mould, the flow table is raised and dropped up to 50 times through a height of 12.5 mm at a rate of 25 times per minute. If the material is below the FMP, it usually crumbles and bumps off in fragments with successive drops of the table (see figure 1.1.4-3).

.2   At this stage, the flow table is stopped and the material returned to the mixing bowl, where 5–10 mℓ of water, or possibly more, is sprinkled over the surface and thoroughly mixed into the material, either with rubber-gloved fingers or an automatic mixer.

The mould is again filled and the flow table is operated as described in 1.1.4.2.1 for up to 50 drops. If a flow state is not developed, the process is repeated with further additions of water until a flow state has been reached.

.3   *Identification of a flow state.* The impacting action of the flow table causes the grains to rearrange themselves to produce compaction of the mass. As a result, the fixed volume of moisture contained in the material at any given level increases as a percentage of the total volume. A flow state is considered to have been reached when the moisture content and compaction of the sample produce a level of saturation such that plastic deformation occurs.* At this stage, the moulded sides of the sample may deform, giving a convex or concave profile (see figure 1.1.4-4).

With repeated action of the flow table, the sample continues to slump and to flow outwards. In certain materials, cracks may also develop on the top surface. Cracking, with the appearance of free moisture, is not, however, an indication of development of a flow state. In most cases, measurement of the deformation is helpful in deciding whether or not plastic flow has occurred. A template which, for example, will indicate an increase in diameter of up to 3 mm in any part of the cone is a useful guide for this purpose. Some additional observations may be useful. For example: when the (increasing) moisture content is approaching the FMP, the sample cone begins to show a tendency to stick to the mould. Further, when the sample is pushed off the table, the sample may leave tracks (stripes) of moisture on the table. If such stripes are seen, the moisture content may be above the FMP: the absence of tracks (stripes) is not necessarily an indication of being below the FMP.

Measuring the diameter of the cone, at the base or at half height, will always be useful. By addition of water in increments of 0.4% to 0.5% and applying 25 drops of the flow table, the first diameter increase will generally be between 1 and 5 mm and after a further increment of water the base diameter will have expanded by between 5 and 10 mm.

---

* In certain conditions, the diameter of the cone may increase before the flow moisture point is reached, due to low friction between the grains rather than to plastic flow. This must not be mistaken for a flow state.

.4 As an alternative to the procedure described above, for many concentrates a fast way of finding the approximate FMP is as follows:

When the moisture content is definitely beyond the FMP, measure the diameter after 25 drops, repeat the test after adding a further increment of water, measure the diameter and draw a diagram as illustrated in figure 1.1.4-1, showing increase in diameter plotted against moisture content. A straight line drawn through the two points will cross the moisture content axis close to the FMP.

Having completed the preliminary FMP test, the sample for the main test is adjusted to the required level of moisture content (about 1% to 2%) below the flow point.

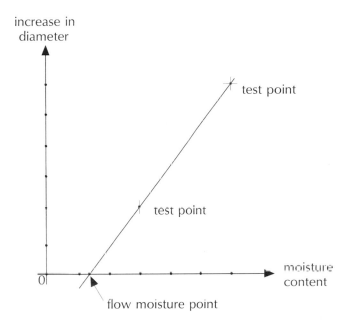

Figure 1.1.4-1

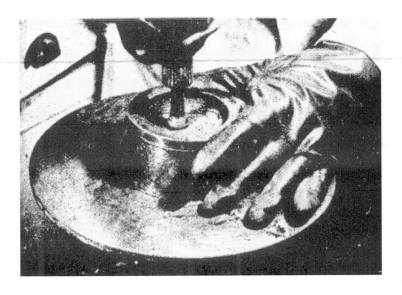

Figure 1.1.4-2

Figure 1.1.4-3

Figure 1.1.4-4

1.1.4.3 *Main flow moisture test*

When a flow state has been reached in the preliminary test, the moisture content of sub-sample (C) is adjusted to about 1% to 2% less than the last value which did not cause flow in the preliminary test (this is suggested simply to avoid starting the main test too close to the FMP and then having to waste time air-drying it and starting again). The final test is then carried out on this adjusted sample in the same manner as for the preliminary test, but in this case with the addition of water in increments of no more than 0.5% of the mass of the test material (the lower the "preliminary" FMP, the smaller the increments should be). After each stage, the whole moulded sample should be placed in a container, weighed immediately and retained for moisture determination if required. This will be necessary if the sample flowed or if the next, slightly wetter, sample flows. If not required, it may be returned to the mixing bowl.

When a flow state has been reached, the moisture content should be determined on two samples, one with moisture content just above the FMP and the other with moisture content just below the FMP. The difference between the two values should then be 0.5% or less, and the FMP is taken as the mean of these two values.

1.1.4.4 *Determination of moisture content*

Introduction

It should be noted that, for many materials, there are recognized international and national methods for determining moisture content. These methods, or ones that have been established to give equivalent results, should be followed.

Concentrates and similar materials

It is clearly important that the samples should be dried to a constant mass. In practice, this is ascertained after a suitable drying period at 105°C by weighing the sample successively with an interval of several hours elapsing. If the mass remains constant, drying has been completed, whereas if the mass is still decreasing, drying should be continued.

The length of the drying period depends upon many variables, such as the disposition of the material in the oven, the type of container used, the particle size, the rate of heat transfer, etc. It may be that a period of five hours is ample for one concentrate sample, whereas it is not sufficient for another. Sulphide concentrates tend to oxidize, and therefore the use of drying ovens with air circulation systems is not recommended for these materials, nor should the test sample be left in the drying oven for more than four hours.

Coal

The recommended methods for determination of the moisture content are those described in ISO 589-1974, "Hard Coal – Determination of Total Moisture". This method, or ones that have been established to give equivalent results, should be followed.

Calculation of moisture content, FMP and transportable moisture limit:

Taking m_1 as the exact mass of the subsample "as received" (see 1.1.4.1),

Taking m_2 as the exact mass of the "as received" subsample, after drying,

Taking m_3 as the exact mass of the sample just above the flow state (see 1.1.4.3),

Taking m_4 as the exact mass of the sample just above the flow state, after drying,

Taking m_5 as the exact mass of the sample just below the flow state (see 1.1.4.3),

Taking m_6 as the exact mass of the sample just below the flow state, after drying,

Then:

.1 The moisture content of the concentrate "as received" is

$$\frac{(m_1 - m_2)}{m_1} \times 100, \text{ in per cent} \qquad (1.1.4.4.1)$$

.2 The FMP of the material is

$$\frac{\frac{(m_3 - m_4)}{m_3} + \frac{(m_5 - m_6)}{m_5}}{2} \times 100, \text{ in per cent} \qquad (1.1.4.4.2)$$

.3 The transportable moisture limit of the material is 90% of the FMP.

Peat moss

For all peat moss, determine the bulk density, using either the ASTM or CEN (20 litres) method.

Peat should be above or below 90 kg/cubic metre on a dry weight basis in order to obtain the correct TML.

As indicated in 1.1.1, the following should be determined:

.1   The moisture content of a sample of cargo (MC).

.2   The flow moisture point (FMP).

.3   The transportable moisture limit (TML). The TML will be determined as follows:

    .3.1   for peat with a bulk density of greater than 90 kg/cubic metre on a dry weight, the TML is 85% of the FMP.

    .3.2   for peat with a bulk density of 90 kg/cubic metre or less on a dry weight, the TML is 90% of the FMP.

1.2   Penetration test procedure

The penetration test constitutes a procedure whereby a material in a cylindrical vessel is vibrated. The flow moisture point is determined on the basis of the penetration depth of an indicator.

1.2.1   *Scope*

.1   The penetration test is generally suitable for mineral concentrates, similar materials, and coals up to a top size of 25 mm.

.2   In this procedure, the sample, in a cylindrical vessel, is subjected to vertical vibration of 2g rms $\pm$ 10% (g = gravity acceleration) for 6 minutes. When the penetration depth of a bit put on the surface exceeds 50 mm, it is judged that the sample contains a moisture content greater than the flow moisture point.

.3   This procedure consists of a preliminary test to get an approximate value of the flow moisture point and a main test to determine the accurate flow moisture point. When the approximate value of the flow moisture point is known, the preliminary test can be omitted.

.4   The room where the samples are tested should be prepared as mentioned in 1.1.3.

1.2.2   *Apparatus* (see figure 1.2.2)

.1   The test apparatus consists of:

    .1   a vibrating table;

    .2   cylindrical vessels;

    .3   indicators (penetration bits and a holder);

    .4   a tamper (see 1.1.2.4); and

    .5   ancillary equipment (see 1.1.2.5 to .8).

.2   The vibrator (see figure 1.2.2.2), with a table on which a cylindrical vessel can be clamped, should be capable of exciting a mass of 30 kg at a frequency of either 50 Hz or 60 Hz with an acceleration of 3g rms or more, and it can be controlled to adjust the acceleration level.

.3   Dimensions of cylindrical vessels (see figures 1.2.2.3-1 and 1.2.2.3-2) are as follows:

Cylinder size	Inner diameter	Depth	Wall thickness
small	146 mm	202 mm	9.6 mm or more
large	194 mm	252 mm	10.3 mm or more

The vessels should be made of reasonably rigid, non-magnetic, impermeable and lightweight material such as acrylics or vinyl chloride.

The small cylindrical vessel is selected for the materials having a maximum particle size of 10 mm or less. The large cylindrical vessel is for those having a maximum particle size of 25 mm or less.

① Vibration table

② Cylindrical vessel (150 mm diameter)

③ Penetration bit (10 kPa)

④ Bit holder

⑤ Tamper

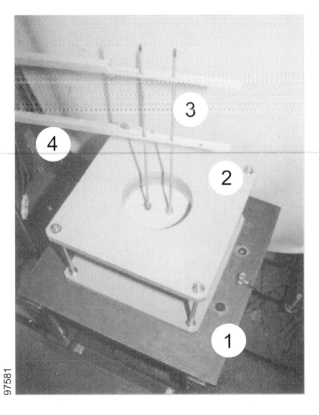

① Vibration table

② Cylindrical vessel (150 mm diameter)

③ Penetration bit (5 kPa)

④ Bit holder

Figure 1.2.2 – *Test apparatus*

FRONT VIEW

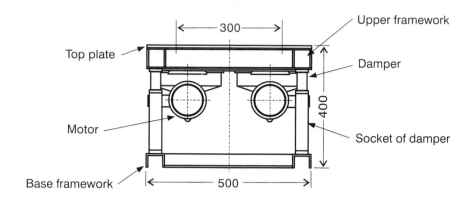

SIDE VIEW

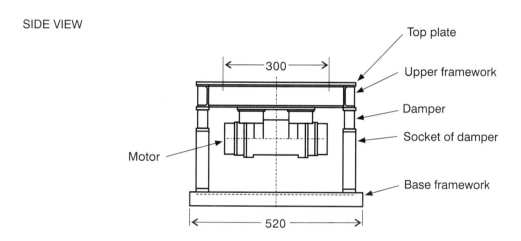

VIEW FROM BASE

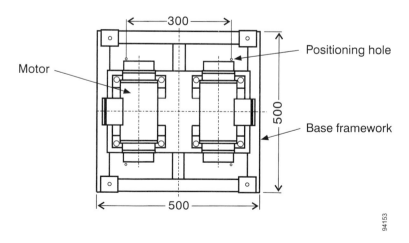

94153

Figure 1.2.2.2 – *Vibration table*

SIDE VIEW

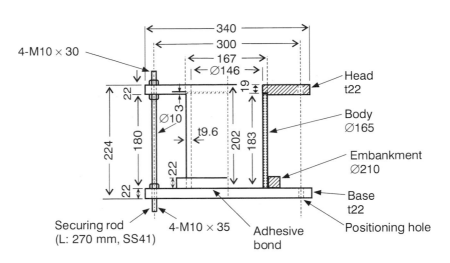

PLAN VIEW
after dismounting head and body

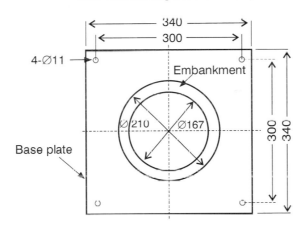

Figure 1.2.2.3-1 – *Cylindrical vessel, 150 mm diameter*

SIDE VIEW

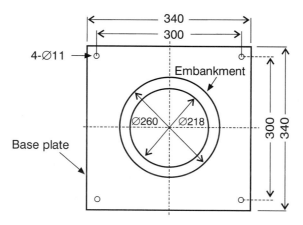

PLAN VIEW
after dismounting head and body

Figure 1.2.2.3-2 – *Cylindrical vessel, 200 mm diameter*

.4   Penetration bits (see figure 1.2.2.4) are made of brass. The mass of the bit for coal should be adjusted to 88 g (5 kPa), and that for concentrates to 177 g (10 kPa). When the sample contains coarse particles, it is recommended that two bits of the same pressure are put on the surface to avoid misjudgement.

.5   A holder (see figure 1.2.2.5) should be made to guide the rod of a bit with minimum friction to the centre of a cylindrical vessel. When two bits are used, they should be positioned in accordance with figure 1.2.2.

.6   A cylindrical vessel and penetration indicators should be selected in accordance with the nature and condition of the test sample, *viz.* size of particles and bulk density.

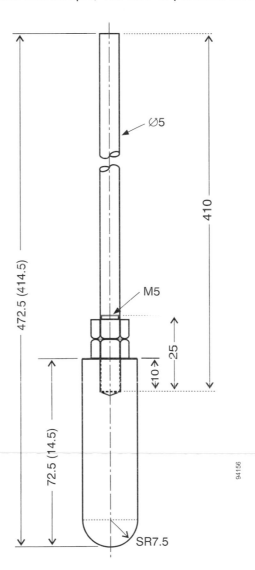

(Dimensions indicated in brackets are of the 5 kPa bit)
(unit: mm)

Figure 1.2.2.4 – *Penetration bit*

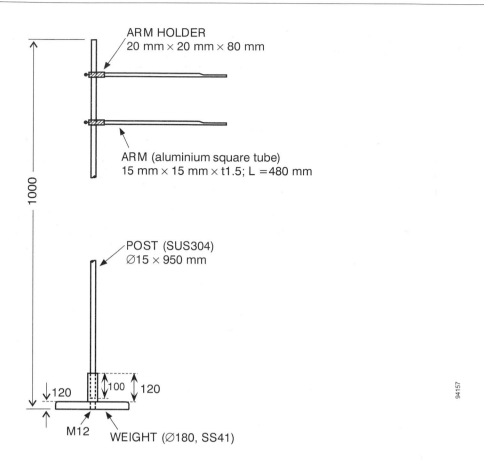

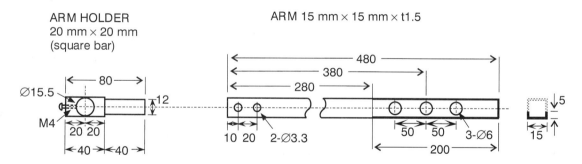

Figure 1.2.2.5 – *Bit holder*

1.2.3 *Procedure*

1.2.3.1 *Preparation of the test sample and the vibrating table*

.1 The quantity of the sample required is approximately six times or more the capacity of the selected cylindrical vessel. The amount of representative test sample with which each container is filled should be as follows: approximately 1700 cm³ for the small container, and 4700 cm³ for the large container.

.2 Mix the sample well and divide into three approximately equal subsamples, namely (A), (B) and (C). The subsample (A) should be immediately weighed and placed in the drying oven to determine the moisture content of the sample "as received".

The subsamples (B) and (C) are used for the preliminary test and the main test, respectively.

.3 The vibration level of the vibrating table should be calibrated, using an acceleration meter, prior to carrying out testing. The acceleration of the table should be adjusted to 2g rms $\pm$ 10% with a container filled with a sample mounted on the table.

1.2.3.2 *Preliminary flow moisture test*

This test is intended to measure quickly the approximate flow moisture point, using subsample (B). Water is added in increments after every penetration test. When a flow state has been reached, the moisture content of the sample just above the flow state is measured. The moisture content of the sample just below the flow state can be calculated by deducting the increment of water last added from the gross mass of the sample.

.1 Fill the appropriate cylindrical vessel with subsample (B) in four distinct stages and tamp after the addition of each layer, using a specified tamper. Tamp to a pressure denoted in 1.1.4.1 for mineral concentrates or to 40 kPa for coals, and apply the pressure evenly over the whole surface area of the material until a uniformly flat surface is obtained.

.2 Place the penetration bit on the surface of the material through the holder.

.3 Operate the vibrator at a frequency of 50 Hz or 60 Hz with an acceleration of 2g rms $\pm$ 10% for 6 minutes. If necessary, the acceleration level should be checked by referring to the output of the acceleration meter attached to the vibrating table.

.4 After 6 minutes of vibration, read the depth of penetration.

.5 When the depth of penetration is less than 50 mm, it is judged that liquefaction did not take place. Then:
   .1 Remove the material from the cylindrical vessel and replace in the mixing bowl with the remainder of the sample.
   .2 Mix well and weigh the contents of the mixing bowl.
   .3 Sprinkle an increment of water of not more than 1% of the mass of the material in the bowl and mix well.
   .4 Repeat the procedure described in 1.2.3.2.1 to 1.2.3.2.4.

.6 When the depth of penetration is greater than 50 mm, it is judged that liquefaction took place. Then:
   .1 Remove the material from the cylindrical vessel and replace in the mixing bowl.
   .2 Measure the moisture content in accordance with the procedure described in 1.1.4.4.
   .3 Calculate the moisture content of the sample just below the flow moisture point on the basis of the amount of water added.

.7 If the penetration depth in the first attempt exceeds 50 mm, i.e., the sample as received liquefied, mix subsamples (B) and (C) and dry at room temperature to reduce the moisture. Then, divide the material into two subsamples (B) and (C), and repeat the preliminary test.

1.2.3.3 *The main flow moisture test*

.1 On the basis of the preliminary test, the main test should be carried out to determine the flow moisture point more accurately.

.2 Adjust the moisture content of the subsample (C) to the last value which did not cause flow in the preliminary flow moisture test.

.3 The first test of the main flow moisture test is carried out on this adjusted sample in the same manner as described in 1.2.3.2. In this case, however, the addition of water in increments should not be more than 0.5% of the mass of the test material.

.4 When the approximate value of the flow moisture point is known in advance, the moisture content of the subsample (C) is adjusted to approximately 90% of this value.

.5 When a flow state has been reached, the flow moisture point is determined as described in 1.1.4.3.

1.3 Proctor/Fagerberg test procedure

1.3.1 *Scope*

.1 Test method for both fine and relatively coarse-grained ore concentrates or similar materials up to a top size of 5 mm. This method should not be used for coal or other porous materials.

.2 Before the Proctor/Fagerberg test is applied to coarser materials with a top size greater than 5 mm, an extensive investigation for adoption and improvement is required.

.3 The transportable moisture limit (TML) of a cargo is taken as equal to the critical moisture content at 70% degree of saturation according to the Proctor/Fagerberg method test.

1.3.2 *Proctor/Fagerberg test equipment*

.1 The Proctor apparatus (see figure 1.3.2) consists of a cylindrical iron mould with a removable extension piece (the compaction cylinder) and a compaction tool guided by a pipe open at its lower end (the compaction hammer).

.2 Scales and weights (see 3.2) and suitable sample containers.

.3 A drying oven with a controlled temperature interval from 100°C to maximum 105°C. This oven should be without air circulation.

.4 A suitable mixer. Care should be taken to ensure that the use of the mixer does not reduce the particle size or consistency of the test material.

.5 Equipment to determine the density of the solid material, for example a pycnometer.

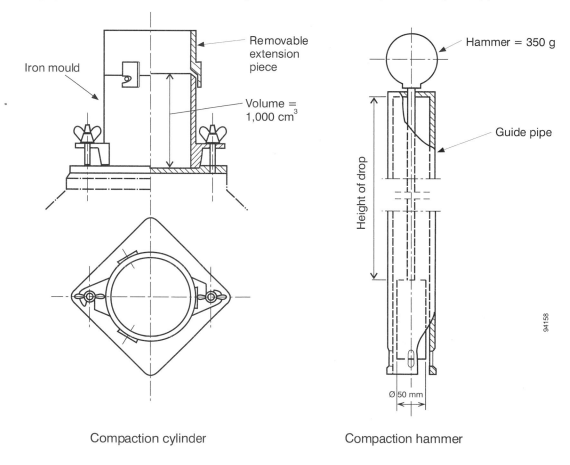

Compaction cylinder   Compaction hammer

Figure 1.3.2 – *Proctor apparatus*

1.3.3   Temperature and humidity
(see 1.1.3)

1.3.4   Procedure

.1   *Establishment of a complete compaction curve.* A representative sample according to a relevant standard (see section 4.7, page 27) of the test material is dried at a temperature of approximately 100°C. The total quantity of the test material should be at least three times as big as required for the complete test sequence. Compaction tests are executed for five to ten different moisture contents (five to ten separate tests). The samples are adjusted in order that dry to almost saturated (plastic) samples are obtained. The required quantity per compaction test is about 2000 cm^3.

At each compaction test, a suitable amount of water is added to the sample of the dried test material and mixed thoroughly for 5 minutes. Approximately one fifth of the mixed sample is filled into the mould and levelled and then the increment is tamped uniformly over the surface of the increment. Tamping is executed by dropping the hammer 25 times through the guide pipe, 0.2 m each time. The performance is repeated for all five layers. When the last layer has been tamped, the extension piece is removed and the sample is levelled off along the brim of the mould. When the weight of the cylinder with the tamped sample has been determined, the cylinder is emptied, the sample is dried and the weight is determined.

The test then is repeated for the other samples with different moisture contents.

.2   *Definitions and data for calculations (see figure 1.3.4.2)*

–   empty cylinder, mass in grams: A

–   cylinder with tamped sample, mass in grams: B

–   wet sample, mass in grams: C
      $$C = B - A$$

–   dry sample, mass in grams: D

–   water, mass in grams (equivalent to volume in cm^3): E
      $$E = C - D$$
      Volume of cylinder: 1000 cm^3

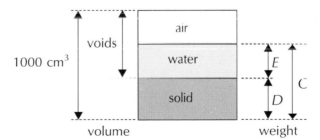

Figure 1.3.4.2

.3   *Calculation of main characteristics*

–   density of solid material, g/cm^3 (t/m^3): d

–   dry bulk density, g/cm^3 (t/m^3): γ
      $$\gamma = \frac{D}{1000}$$

–   net water content, volume %: e_v
      $$e_v = \frac{E}{D} \times 100 \times d$$

–   void ratio: e (volume of voids divided by volume of solids)
      $$e = \frac{1000d - D}{D} = \frac{d}{\gamma} - 1$$

– degree of saturation, percentage by volume: S

$$S = \frac{e_v}{e}$$

– gross water content, percentage by mass: W^1

$$W^1 = \frac{E}{C} \times 100$$

– net water content, percentage by mass: W

$$W = \frac{E}{D} \times 100$$

.4 *Presentation of the compaction tests*

For each compaction test, the calculated void ratio (e) value is plotted as the ordinate in a diagram with net water content (e_v) and degree of saturation (S) as the respective abscissa parameters.

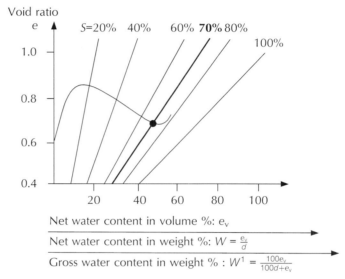

Figure 1.3.4.5

.5 *Compaction curve*

The test sequence results in a specific compaction curve (see figure 1.3.4.5).

The critical moisture content is indicated by the intersection of the compaction curve and the line S = 70% degree of saturation. The transportable moisture limit (TML) is the critical moisture content.

2 Test procedures to determine the angle of repose and associated apparatus

2.1 Determination of angle of repose of fine-grained materials (size less than 10 mm): "tilting box test". For use in laboratory or port of loading

2.1.1 *Scope*

The test provides for the determination of the angle of repose of fine-grained non-cohesive materials (size less than 10 mm). The results so obtained may be used when interpreting sections 5 and 6 of this Code for the materials in question.

2.1.2 *Definition*

The angle of repose obtained by this test is the angle formed between the horizontal and the top of the testbox when the material in the box just begins to slide in bulk.

2.1.3 **Principle of test**

When measuring the angle of repose by this method, the material surface should initially be level and parallel to the testbox base. The box is tilted without vibration and tilted without vibration and tilting is stopped when the product just begins to slide in bulk.

2.1.4 **Apparatus** *(see figure 2.1.4)*

Apparatus is as follows:

.1 A framework, on top of which is attached an open box. Attachment of the box to the frame is by means of a shaft passing through bearings affixed to both the frame and the end of the box, enabling the box to be subjected to a controlled tilt.

.2 The dimensions of the box are 600 mm long, 400 mm wide and 200 mm high.

.3 To prevent sliding of the material along the bottom of the box during tilting, a tightly fitting grating (openings 30 mm × 30 mm × 25 mm) is placed on the bottom of the box before filling.

.4 Tilting of the box is effected by a hydraulic cylinder fitted between the frame and the bottom of the box. Other means may be used to obtain the required tilting but in all cases vibration must be eliminated.

.5 To pressurize the hydraulic cylinder, a hydro-pneumatic accumulator may be used, pressurized by air or gas at a pressure of about 5 kp/cm^2.

.6 The rate of tilting should be approximately 0.3°/s.

.7 Range of tilt should be at least 50°.

.8 A protractor is fitted to the end of the shaft. One lever of the protractor is fitted so that it may be screw-adjusted to the horizontal.

.9 The protractor should measure the angle of the top of the box to the horizontal to within an accuracy of 0.5°.

.10 A spirit level or some other levelling device should be available to zero the protractor.

2.1.5 **Procedure**

The box is filled with the material to be tested by pouring it slowly and carefully from the lowest practical height into the box in order to obtain uniformity of loading.

The excess material is scraped off with the aid of a straight edge, inclined at about 45° towards the direction of scraping.

The tilting system is then activated and stopped when the material just begins to slide in bulk.

The angle of the top of the box to the horizontal is measured by the protractor and recorded.

2.1.6 **Evaluation**

The angle of repose is calculated as the mean of three measurements and is reported to within half a degree.

Notes: Preferably the test should be carried out with three independent samples.
Care should be taken to ensure that the shaft is adjusted to be horizontal before testing.

2.2 **Alternative or shipboard test method to be used for the determination of the angle of repose when the tilting box is not available**

2.2.1 **Definition**

According to this method, the angle of repose is the angle between the cone slope and the horizontal measured at half height.

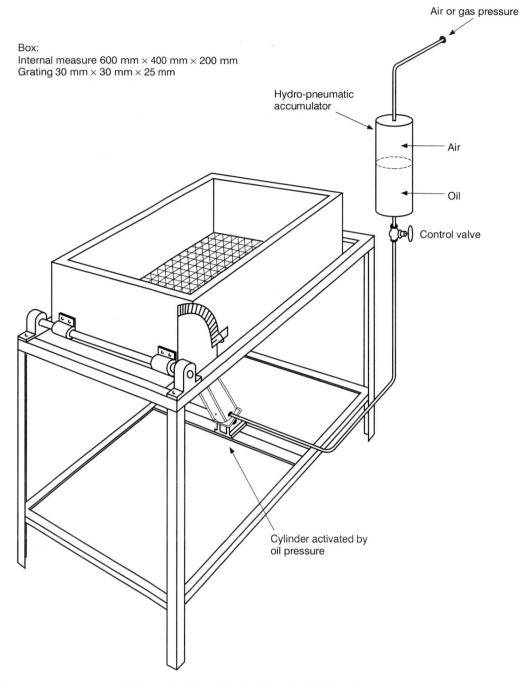

Box:
Internal measure 600 mm × 400 mm × 200 mm
Grating 30 mm × 30 mm × 25 mm

Air or gas pressure

Hydro-pneumatic accumulator

Air

Oil

Control valve

Cylinder activated by oil pressure

94159

Figure 2.1.4 – *Basic sketch of tilting box*

2.2.2 *Principle of test*

To determine the angle of repose, a quantity of the material to be tested is poured very carefully out of a flask onto a sheet of rough-textured paper, in such a way that a symmetrical cone is formed.

2.2.3 *Equipment*

The necessary equipment to carry out this test is as follows:

- a horizontal table free from vibrations;
- a sheet of rough-textured paper onto which the material should be poured;
- a protractor; and
- a 3-litre conical flask.

2.2.4   *Procedure*

Put the sheet of paper on the table. Split 10 ℓ of the material to be tested into three sub-samples and test each in the following way:

Pour two thirds of the sub-sample (i.e., 2 ℓ) onto the sheet, producing a starting cone. The remainder of this sub-sample is then poured very carefully from a height of a few millimetres on top of the cone. Care should be taken that the cone will be built up symmetrically. This may be achieved by revolving the flask slowly close around the top of the cone when pouring.

When measuring, care should be taken that the protractor does not touch the cone; otherwise this may result in sliding of the material and spoil the test.

The angle has to be measured at four places around the cone, about 90 degrees apart.

This test should be repeated on the other two sub-samples.

2.2.5   *Calculations*

The angle of repose is taken as the mean of the 12 measurements and is reported to half a degree. This figure can be converted to the tilting box value as follows:

$$a_t = a_s + 3^\circ \qquad\qquad (2.2.5)$$

where a_t = angle of repose according to the tilting box text

a_s = angle of repose according to the survey test

3   Standards used in test procedures

3.1   Standard flow table and frame*

3.1.1   *Flow table and frame*

3.1.1.1 The flow table apparatus shall be constructed in accordance with figure 3. The apparatus shall consist of an integrally cast rigid iron frame and a circular rigid table top, 10 inches $\pm$ 0.1 inch (254 mm $\pm$ 2.5 mm) in diameter, with a shaft attached perpendicular to the table top by means of a screw thread. The table top, to which the shaft with its integral contact shoulder is attached, shall be mounted on a frame in such a manner that it can be raised and dropped vertically through the specified height, with a tolerance in height of $\pm$ 0.005 inches (0.13 mm) for new tables and $\pm$ 0.015 inches (0.39 mm) for tables in use, by means of a rotated cam. The table top shall have a fine-machined plane surface, free of blowholes and surface defects, and shall be scribed as shown in figure 3. The table top shall be of cast brass or bronze having a Rockwell hardness number not less than HRB 25 with an edge thickness of 0.3 inches (8 mm), and shall have six integral radial stiffening ribs. The table top and attached shaft shall weigh 9 lb $\pm$ 0.1 lb (4 kg $\pm$ 0.05 kg) and the weight shall be symmetrical around the centre of the shaft.

3.1.1.2 The cam and vertical shaft shall be of medium-carbon machinery steel, hardened where indicated in figure 3. The shaft shall be straight and the difference between the diameter of the shaft and the diameter of the bore of the frame shall be not less than 0.002 inches (0.05 mm) and not more than 0.003 inches (0.08 mm) for new tables and shall be maintained at from 0.002 inches to 0.010 inches (0.26 mm) for tables in use. The end of the shaft shall not fall upon the cam at the end of the drop, but shall make contact with the cam not less than 120° from the point of drop. The face of the cam shall be a smooth spiralled curve of uniformly increasing radius from $\frac{1}{2}$ inch to $1\frac{1}{4}$ inches (13 mm to 32 mm) in 360° and there shall be no appreciable jar as the shaft comes into contact with the cam. The cam shall be so located and the contact faces of the cam and shaft shall be such that the table does not rotate more than one revolution in

* Source: "Standard Specification for Flow Table for Use in Tests of Hydraulic Cement", Designation C230-68. Reprinted by permission of American Society for Testing and Materials (ASTM), 1916 Race Street, Philadelphia, Penn., USA, © ASTM 1977.

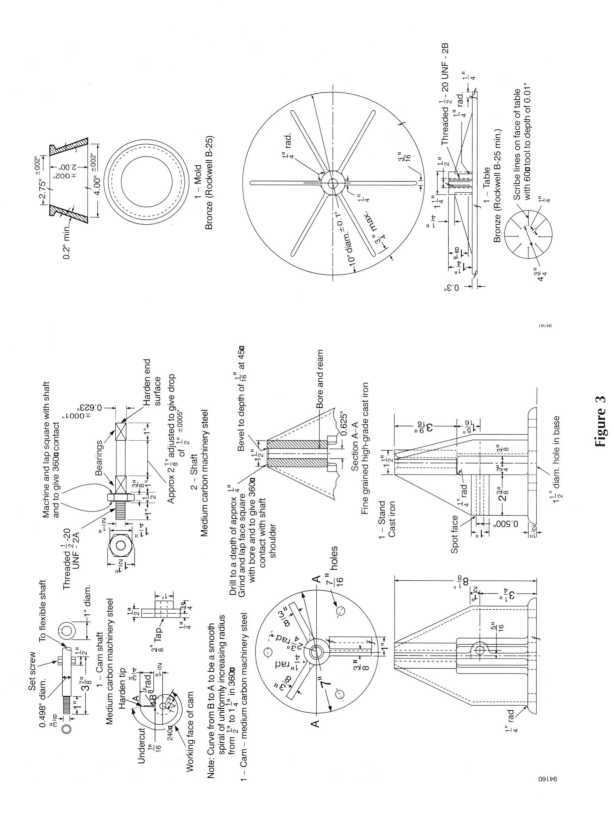

Figure 3

25 drops. The surfaces of the frame and of the table which come into contact at the end of the drop shall be maintained smooth, plane, and horizontal and parallel with the upper surface of the table and shall make continuous contact over a full 360°.

3.1.1.3 The supporting frame of the flow table shall be integrally cast of fine-grained, high-grade cast iron. The frame casting shall have three integral stiffening ribs extending the full height of the frame and located 120° apart. The top of the frame shall be drilled to a depth of approximately $\frac{1}{4}$ inch (6.4 mm) and the face shall be ground and lapped square with the bore to give 360° contact with the shaft shoulder. The underside of the base of the frame shall be ground to secure a complete contact with the steel plate beneath.

3.1.1.4 The flow table may be driven by a motor,* connected to the camshaft through an enclosed worm gear speed reducer and flexible coupling. The speed of the camshaft shall be approximately 100 rpm. The motor drive mechanism shall not be fastened or mounted on the table base plate or frame.

The performance of a flow table shall be considered satisfactory if, in calibration tests, the table gives a flow value that does not differ by more than 5 percentage points from flow values obtained with a suitable calibration material.†

3.1.2 *Flow table mounting*

3.1.2.1 The flow table frame shall be tightly bolted to a cast iron or steel plate at least 1 inch (25 mm) thick and 10 inches (250 mm) square. The top surface of this plate shall be machined to a smooth plane surface. The plate shall be anchored to the top of a concrete pedestal by four $\frac{1}{2}$ inch (13 mm) bolts that pass through the plate and are embedded at least 6 inches (150 mm) in the pedestal. The pedestal shall be cast inverted on the base plate. A positive contact between the base plate and the pedestal shall be obtained at all points. No nuts or other such levelling devices shall be used between the plate and the pedestal. Levelling shall be effected by suitable means under the base of the pedestal.

3.1.2.2 The pedestal shall be 10 inches to 11 inches (250 mm to 275 mm) square at the top, and 15 inches to 16 inches (375 mm to 400 mm) square at the bottom, 25 inches to 30 inches (625 mm to 750 mm) in height, and shall be of monolithic construction, cast from concrete weighing at least 140 lb/ft³ (2240 kg/m³). A stable gasket cork pad, $\frac{1}{2}$ inch (13 mm) thick and approximately 4 inches (102 mm) square, shall be inserted under each corner of the pedestal. The flow table shall be checked frequently for levelness of the table top, stability of the pedestal, and tightness of the bolts and nuts in the table base and the pedestal plate. (A torque of 20 lb ft (27 N m) is recommended when tightening those fastenings.)

3.1.2.3 The table top, after the frame has been mounted on the pedestal, shall be level along two diameters at right angles to each other, in both the raised and lowered positions.

3.1.3 *Flow table lubrication*

3.1.3.1 The vertical shaft of the table shall be kept clean and shall be lightly lubricated with a light oil (SAE-10). Oil shall not be present between the contact faces of the table top and the supporting frame. Oil on the cam face will lessen wear and promote smoothness of operation. The table should be raised and permitted to drop a dozen or more times just prior to use if it has not been operated for some time.

3.1.4 *Mould*

3.1.4.1 The mould for casting the flow specimen shall be of cast bronze or brass, constructed as shown in figure 3. The Rockwell hardness number of the metal shall be not less than HRB 25. The

---

* A 1/20 hp (40 W) motor has been found adequate. The flow table may be driven by a hand-operated camshaft as shown in the illustration.

† Such a material may be obtained from the Cement and Concrete Reference Laboratory at the National Bureau of Standards, Washington, D.C. 20234, USA.

diameter of the top opening shall be 2.75 inches ± 0.02 inches (69.8 mm ± 0.5 mm) for new moulds and 2.75 inches + 0.05 inches (+ 1.3 mm) and – 0.02 inches for moulds in use. The surfaces of the base and top shall be parallel and at right angles to the vertical axis of the cone. The mould shall have a minimum wall thickness of 0.2 inches (5 mm). The outside of the top edge of the mould shall be shaped so as to provide an integral collar for convenient lifting of the mould. All surfaces shall be machined to a smooth finish. A circular shield approximately 10 inches (254 mm) in diameter, with a centre opening approximately 4 inches (102 mm) in diameter, made of non-absorbing material not attacked by the cement, shall be used with the flow mould to prevent mortar from spilling on the table top.

3.2 Scales and weights*

3.2.1 Scales

3.2.1.1 The scales used shall conform to the following requirements. On scales in use, the permissible variation at a load of 2000 g shall be ± 2.0 g. The permissible variation on new scales shall be one half of this value. The sensibility reciprocal[†] shall be not greater than twice the permissible variation.

3.2.2 Weights

3.2.2.1 The permissible variations on weights shall be as prescribed in the table below. The permissible variations on new weights shall be one half of the values in the table below.

PERMISSIBLE VARIATIONS ON WEIGHTS

Weight (g)	Permissible variations on weights in use, plus or minus (g)
1000	0.50
900	0.45
750	0.40
500	0.35
300	0.30
250	0.25
200	0.20
100	0.15
50	0.10
20	0.05
10	0.04
5	0.03
2	0.02
1	0.01

---

* Source: "Standard Method of Test for Compressive Strength of Hydraulic Cement Mortars", Designation C109-3. Reprinted by permission of American Society for Testing and Materials (ASTM), 1916 Race Street, Philadelphia, Penn., USA, © ASTM 1977.

† Generally defined, the sensibility reciprocal is the change in load required to change the position of rest of the indicating element or elements of a non-automatic indicating scale a definite amount at any load. For a more complete definition, see "Specifications, Tolerances, and Regulations for Commercial Weighing and Measuring Devices", *Handbook H44*, National Bureau of Standards, Washington, D.C., USA, September 1949, pp. 92 and 93.

4 Trough test for determination of the self-sustaining exothermic decomposition of fertilizers containing nitrates*

4.1 Definition

A fertilizer capable of self-sustaining decomposition is defined as one in which decomposition initiated in a localized area will spread throughout the mass. The tendency of a fertilizer offered for transport to undergo this type of decomposition can be determined by means of the trough test. In this test localized decomposition is initiated in a bed of the fertilizer to be contained in a horizontally mounted trough. The amount of propagation, after removal of the initiating heat source, of decomposition through the mass is measured.

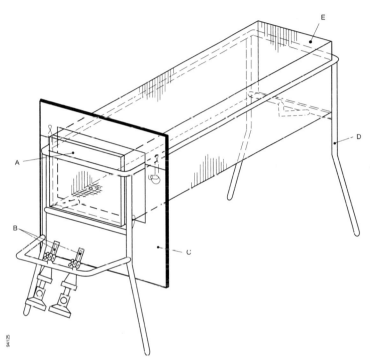

A Steel plate (150 x 150 mm and 1 to 3 mm thick)
B Gas burners (e.g. Teclu or Bunsen)
C Heat shield (2 mm thick)
D Stand (e.g. made from 15 mm wide, 2 mm thick steel bar)
E Gauze trough (150 x 150 x 500 mm)

Figure 4-1 – *Gauze trough with support and burners*

4.2 Apparatus and materials

The apparatus (figure 4-1) consists of a trough of internal dimensions 150 mm × 150 mm × 500 mm, open at the top. The trough is constructed of square-meshed gauze (preferably stainless steel) with a mesh width of about 1.5 mm and a wire thickness of 1.0 mm supported on a frame made from, for example, 15 mm wide, 2 mm thick steel bars. The gauze at each end of the trough may be replaced by 1.5 mm thick, 150 mm × 150 mm stainless steel plates. The trough should be rested on a suitable support. Fertilizers with a particle size distribution such that a significant amount falls through the mesh of the trough should be tested in a trough of smaller mesh gauze, or alternatively in a trough lined with gauze of a smaller mesh. During initiation, sufficient heat should be provided and maintained to establish a uniform decomposition front. Two alternative heating methods are recommended, viz:

---

* Source: Section 38 of the United Nations *Recommendation on the Transport of Dangerous Goods, Manual of Tests and Criteria.*

4.2.1 *Electrical heating*

An electrical heating element (capacity 250 W) enclosed in a stainless steel box is placed inside and at one end of the trough (figure 4-2). The dimensions of the stainless steel box are 145 mm × 145 mm × 10 mm, and the wall thickness is 3 mm. The side of the box which is not in contact with the fertilizer should be protected with a heat shield (insulation plate 5 mm thick). The heating side of the box may be protected with aluminium foil or a stainless steel plate.

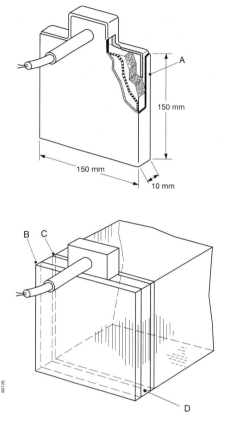

A Aluminium or stainless steel sheathing (thickness 3 mm)
B Insulating plate (thickness 5 mm)
C Aluminium foil or stainless steel plate (thickness 3 mm)
D Position of heating device in trough

Figure 4-2 – *Electrical heating device (capacity 250 W)*

4.2.2 *Gas burners*

A steel plate (thickness 1 mm to 3 mm) is placed inside one end of the trough and in contact with the wire gauze (figure 4-1). The plate is heated by means of two burners which are fixed to the trough support and are capable of maintaining the plate at temperatures between 400°C and 600°C, i.e., dull red heat.

4.2.3 To prevent heat transport along the outside of the trough, a heat shield consisting of a steel plate (2 mm thick) should be installed at about 50 mm from the end of the trough where the heating takes place.

4.2.4 The life of the apparatus may be prolonged if it is constructed of stainless steel throughout. This is particularly important in the case of the gauze trough.

4.2.5 Propagation may be measured using thermocouples in the substance and recording the time at which a sudden temperature rise occurs as the reaction front reaches the thermocouple.

4.3 Procedure

4.3.1 The apparatus should be set up under a fume hood to remove toxic decomposition gases or in an open area where the fumes can be readily dispersed. Although there is no explosion risk, when performing the test it is advisable to have a protective shield, e.g., of suitable transparent plastics, between the observer and the apparatus.

4.3.2 The trough is filled with the fertilizer in the form to be offered for shipment and decomposition is initiated at one end, either electrically or by means of gas burners as described above. Heating should be continued until decomposition of the fertilizer is well established and propagation of the front (over approximately 30 mm to 50 mm) has been observed. In the case of products with high thermal stability, it may be necessary to continue heating for two hours. If fertilizers show a tendency to melt, the heating should be done with care, i.e., using a small flame.

4.3.3 About 20 minutes after the heating has been discontinued, the position of the decomposition front is noted. The position of the reaction front can be determined by difference in colour, e.g., brown (undecomposed fertilizer) to white (decomposed fertilizer), or by the temperature indicated by adjacent pairs of thermocouples which bracket the reaction front. The rate of propagation may be determined by observation and timing or from thermocouple records. It should be noted whether there is no propagation after heating is discontinued or whether propagation occurs throughout the substance.

4.4 Test criteria and method of assessing results

4.4.1 If propagation of the decomposition continues throughout the substance, the fertilizer is considered capable of showing self-sustaining decomposition.

4.4.2 If propagation does not continue throughout the substance, the fertilizer is considered to be free from the hazard of self-sustaining decomposition.

5 Description of the test of resistance to detonation

5.1 Principle

5.1.1 The test sample is confined in a steel tube and subjected to detonation shock from an explosive booster charge. Propagation of the detonation is determined from the degree of compression of lead cylinders on which the tube rests horizontally during the test.

5.2 Sample preparation

5.2.1 The test must be carried out on a representative sample of material. Before being tested for resistance to detonation, the whole mass of the sample is to be thermally cycled five times between 25°C and 50°C (± 1°C) in sealed tubes. The sample shall be maintained at the extreme temperatures, measured at the centre of the sample, for at least 1 hour during each thermal cycle and at 20°C (± 3°C) after complete cycling until tested.

5.3 Materials

Seamless steel tube to ISO 65-1981-Heavy or equivalent

Tube length	1000 mm
Nominal external diameter	114 mm
Nominal wall thickness	5 to 6.5 mm

Bottom plate (160 × 160 mm) of good weldable quality steel, thickness 5 to 6 mm to be butt-welded to one end of the tube around the entire circumference.

Initiation system and booster

Electrical blasting cap or detonating cord with non-metallic sleeve (10 to 13 g/m).

Compressed pellet of secondary explosive, such as hexogen/wax 95/5 or tetryl, with a central recess to take the detonator.

500 ± 1 gram plastic explosive containing 83 to 86% penthrite, formed into a cylinder in a cardboard or plastic tube. Detonation velocity 7300–7700 m/s.

Six witness cylinders of refined, cast lead for detecting detonation

50 mm diameter × 100 mm high, refined lead of at least 99.5% purity.

5.4 Procedure

Test temperature: 15 to 20°C. Figures 1 and 2 show the test arrangement.

Fill the tube about one-third of its height with the test sample and drop it 10 cm vertically five times on the floor. Improve the compression by striking the side wall with a hammer between drops. A further addition shall be made such that, after compaction or by raising and dropping the tube 20 times and a total of 20 intermittent hammer blows, the charge fills the tube to a distance of 70 mm from its orifice.

Insert the plastic explosive into the tube and press it down with a wooden die. Place the compressed pellet centrally in the recess within the plastic explosive. Close it with a wooden disc so that it remains in contact with the test sample. Lay the test tube horizontally on the 6 lead cylinders placed at 150 mm intervals (centric), with the centre of the last cylinder 75 mm from the bottom plate, on a firm, level, solid surface that is resistant to deformation or displacement. Insert the electrical blasting cap or the detonating cord.

Ensure that all necessary safety precautions are taken, connect and detonate the explosive.

Record, for each of the lead cylinders, the degree of compression expressed as a percentage of the original height of 100 mm. For oblique compression, the deformation is taken as the average of the maximum and minimum deformation.

5.5 Results

The test is to be carried out twice. If in each test one or more of the supporting lead cylinders are crushed by less than 5%, the sample is deemed to satisfy the resistance to detonation requirements.

6 Self-heating test for charcoal

6.1 Apparatus

6.1.1 *Oven.* A laboratory oven fitted with internal air circulation and capable of being controlled at 140°C ± 2°C.

6.1.2 *Wire mesh cube.* Construct an open-top cube, 100 mm side, from phosphor bronze gauze 18,000 mesh per square centimetre (350 × 350 mesh). Insert it inside a slightly larger, well-fitting cube, made of phosphor bronze gauze 11 mesh per square centimetre (8 × 8 mesh). Fit the outer cube with a handle or hooks so that it can be suspended from above.

6.1.3 *Temperature measurement.* A suitable system to measure and record the temperature of the oven and in the centre of the cube. "Chromel–alumel" thermocouples, made from 0.27 mm diameter wire, are suitable for measuring the temperature range expected.

6.2 Procedure

6.2.1 Fill the cube with carbon and tap down gently, adding carbon until the cube is full. Suspend the sample in the centre of the oven which has been preheated to 140°C ± 2°C. Insert one of the thermocouples in the centre of the sample and the other between the cube and the oven wall. Maintain the temperature of the oven at 140°C ± 2°C for 12 hours and record the oven temperature and the sample temperature.

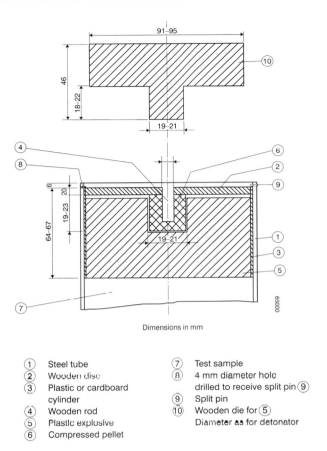

Dimensions in mm

①	Steel tube	⑦	Test sample
②	Wooden disc	⑧	4 mm diameter hole
③	Plastic or cardboard		drilled to receive split pin ⑨
	cylinder	⑨	Split pin
④	Wooden rod	⑩	Wooden die for ⑤
⑤	Plastic explosive		Diameter as for detonator
⑥	Compressed pellet		

Figure 1 – *Booster charge*

①	Steel tube	
②	Lead cylinders	
③	Steel block	
④	Bottom plate	
⑤	Booster charge	
[1] to [6]	Numbers of lead cylinders	

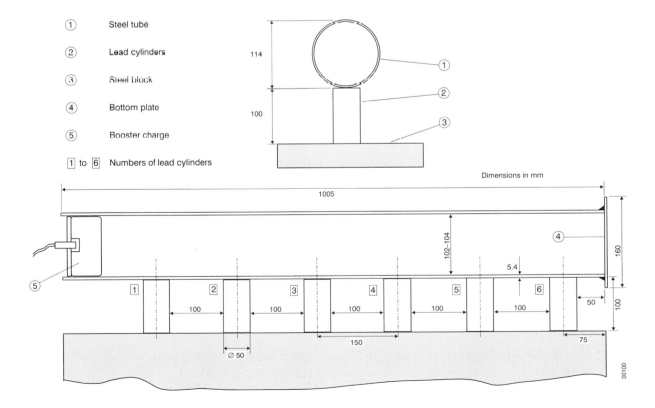

Figure 2 – *Positioning of the steel tube on the firing site*

6.3 Results

6.3.1 Non-activated carbon, non-activated charcoal, carbon black and lamp black fail the test if the temperature at any time during the 12 hours exceeded 200°C.

6.3.2 Activated carbon and activated charcoal fail the test if the temperature at any time during the 12 hours exceeded 400°C.

Appendix 3

Properties of solid bulk cargoes

1 Non-cohesive cargoes

1.1 The following cargoes are non-cohesive when dry:

AMMONIUM NITRATE
AMMONIUM NITRATE BASED FERTILIZERS
AMMONIUM SULPHATE
BORAX, ANHYDROUS
CALCIUM NITRATE FERTILIZER
CASTOR BEANS
DIAMMONIUM PHOSPHATE
MONOAMMONIUM PHOSPHATE
POTASH
POTASSIUM CHLORIDE
POTASSIUM NITRATE
POTASSIUM SULPHATE
SODIUM NITRATE
SODIUM NITRATE AND POTASSIUM NITRATE MIXTURE
SUPERPHOSPHATE
UREA

1.2 Prior to completion of loading, the angle of repose of the materials to be loaded should be determined (see section 6) so as to determine which provisions of this Code relating to trimming apply (see section 5).

1.3 All cargoes other than those listed in this appendix are cohesive, and the use of the angle of repose is, therefore, not appropriate. Cargoes not listed should be treated as cohesive until otherwise shown.

2 Cargoes which may liquefy

2.1 Many fine-particled cargoes, if possessing a sufficiently high moisture content, are liable to flow. Thus any damp or wet cargo containing a proportion of fine particles should be tested for flow characteristics prior to loading.

3 Precautions for the cargoes which may possess a chemical hazard

3.1 In circumstances where consultation with the competent authority is required prior to shipment of dry bulk cargoes, it is equally important to consult authorities at the port of loading and discharge concerning requirements which may be in force.

3.2 Where required, the *Medical First Guide for Use in Accidents Involving Dangerous Goods (MFAG)* should be consulted prior to loading.

Appendix 4

Index

Material	Group	References
ALFALFA	C	
ALUMINA	C	
ALUMINA, CALCINED	C	
ALUMINA SILICA	C	
ALUMINA SILICA, pellets	C	
ALUMINIUM DROSS	B	*see* ALUMINIUM SMELTING BY-PRODUCTS *or* ALUMINIUM REMELTING BY-PRODUCTS UN 3170
ALUMINIUM FERROSILICON POWDER UN 1395	B	
ALUMINIUM NITRATE UN 1438	B	
ALUMINIUM REMELTING BY-PRODUCTS UN 3170	B	
ALUMINIUM SALT SLAGS	B	*see* ALUMINIUM SMELTING BY-PRODUCTS *or* ALUMINIUM REMELTING BY-PRODUCTS UN 3170
ALUMINIUM SILICON POWDER, UNCOATED UN 1398	B	
ALUMINIUM SKIMMINGS	B	*see* ALUMINIUM SMELTING BY-PRODUCTS *or* ALUMINIUM REMELTING BY-PRODUCTS UN 3170
ALUMINIUM SMELTING BY-PRODUCTS UN 3170	B	
AMMONIUM NITRATE UN 1942	B	
AMMONIUM NITRATE BASED FERTILIZER UN 2067	B	
AMMONIUM NITRATE BASED FERTILIZER UN 2071	B	
AMMONIUM NITRATE, BASED FERTILIZER (non-hazardous)	C	
AMMONIUM SULPHATE	C	
ANTIMONY ORE AND RESIDUE	C	
Antimony ore residue	C	*see* ANTIMONY ORE AND RESIDUE
Bakery materials	B or C	*see* SEED CAKE
BARIUM NITRATE UN 1446	B	

Material	Group	References
Barley malt pellets	B or C	*see* SEED CAKE
BARYTES	C	
BAUXITE	C	
Beet, expelled	B or C	*see* SEED CAKE
Beet, extracted	B or C	*see* SEED CAKE
BIOSLUDGE	C	
Blende (zinc sulphide)	A	*see* ZINC CONCENTRATE
BORAX (PENTAHYDRATE CRUDE)	C	
BORAX, ANHYDROUS, crude	C	
BORAX, ANHYDROUS, refined	C	
Bran pellets	B or C	*see* SEED CAKE
Brewer's grain pellets	B or C	*see* SEED CAKE
BROWN COAL BRIQUETTES	B	
Calcined clay	C	*see* ALUMINA, CALCINED
Calcined pyrites	A and B	*see* PYRITES, CALCINED
Calcium fluoride	B	*see* FLUORSPAR
CALCIUM NITRATE UN 1454	B	
CALCIUM NITRATE FERTILIZER	C	
Calcium oxide	B	*see* LIME (UNSLAKED)
Canola pellets	B or C	*see* SEED CAKE
CARBORUNDUM	C	
CASTOR BEANS UN 2969	B	
CASTOR FLAKE UN 2969	B	
CASTOR MEAL UN 2969	B	
CASTOR POMACE UN 2969	B	
CEMENT	C	
CEMENT CLINKERS	C	
CEMENT COPPER	A	*see* Mineral Concentrates schedule
Chalcopyrite	A	*see* COPPER CONCENTRATE
CHAMOTTE	C	
CHARCOAL	B	
CHOPPED RUBBER AND PLASTIC INSULATION	C	
Chile saltpetre	B	*see* SODIUM NITRATE
Chilean natural nitrate	B	*see* SODIUM NITRATE
Chilean natural potassic nitrate	B	*see* SODIUM NITRATE AND POTASSIUM NITRATE MIXTURE
Chrome ore	C	*see* CHROMITE ORE

Material	Group	References
CHROME PELLETS	C	
CHROMITE ORE	C	
Chromium ore	C	*see* CHROMITE ORE
Citrus pulp pellets	B or C	*see* SEED CAKE
CLAY	C	
COAL	B (and A)	
COAL SLURRY	A	
COARSE CHOPPED TYRES	C	
Coconut	B or C	*see* SEED CAKE
COKE	C	
COKE BREEZE	A	
COLEMANITE	C	
COPPER CONCENTRATE	A	
COPPER GRANULES	C	
COPPER MATTE	C	
Copper nickel	A	*see* NICKEL CONCENTRATE
Copper ore concentrate	A	*see* COPPER CONCENTRATE
Copper precipitate	A	*see* CEMENT COPPER
COPRA (dry) UN 1363	B	
Copra, expelled	B or C	*see* SEED CAKE
Copra, extracted	B or C	*see* SEED CAKE
Corn gluten	B or C	*see* SEED CAKE
Cotton seed	B or C	*see* SEED CAKE
CRYOLITE	C	
Deadburned magnesite	C	*see* MAGNESIA (DEADBURNED)
DIAMMONIUM PHOSPHATE	C	
DIRECT REDUCED IRON (A) Briquettes, hot-moulded	B	
DIRECT REDUCED IRON (B) Lumps, pellets, cold-moulded briquettes	B	
DIRECT REDUCED IRON (C) By-product fines	B	
DOLOMITE	C	
Dolomitic quicklime	B	*see* LIME (UNSLAKED)
D.R.I.	B	*see* DIRECT REDUCED IRON (A) or (B) or (C)
Expellers	B	*see* SEED CAKE
FELSPAR LUMP	C	
FERROCHROME	C	

Material	Group	References
FERROCHROME, exothermic	C	
FERROMANGANESE	C	
Ferromanganese, exothermic	C	*see* FERROMANGANESE
FERRONICKEL	C	
FERROPHOSPHORUS	B	
Ferrophosphorus briquettes	B	*see* FERROPHOSPHORUS
FERROSILICON UN 1408	B	
FERROSILICON	B	
FERROUS METAL BORINGS UN 2793	B	
FERROUS METAL CUTTINGS UN 2793	B	
FERROUS METAL SHAVINGS UN 2793	B	
FERROUS METAL TURNINGS UN 2793	B	
FERTILIZERS WITHOUT NITRATES	C	
FISH (IN BULK)	A	
FISHMEAL, STABILIZED UN 2216	B	
FISHSCRAP, STABILIZED UN 2216	B	
FLUORSPAR	A and B	
FLY ASH	C	
Galena (lead sulphide)	A	*see* LEAD CONCENTRATE
Garbage tankage	B	*see* TANKAGE
Gluten pellets	B or C	*see* SEED CAKE
GRANULATED SLAG	C	
GRANULATED TYRE RUBBER	C	
Ground nuts, meal	B or C	*see* SEED CAKE
GYPSUM	C	
Hominy chop	B or C	*see* SEED CAKE
ILMENITE CLAY	A	
ILMENITE SAND	A or C	
IRON CONCENTRATE	A	*see* Mineral Concentrates schedule
IRON CONCENTRATE (pellet feed)	A	*see* Mineral Concentrates schedule
IRON CONCENTRATE (sinter feed)	A	*see* Mineral Concentrates schedule
Iron disulphide	C	*see* PYRITE
IRON ORE	C	
Iron ore (concentrate, pellet feed, sinter feed)	A	*see* IRON CONCENTRATE (pellet feed or sinter feed)
IRON ORE PELLETS	C	
IRON OXIDE, SPENT UN 1376	B	

Material	Group	References
Iron swarf	B	*see* FERROUS METAL BORINGS, SHAVINGS, TURNINGS or CUTTINGS UN 2793
IRON SPONGE, SPENT UN 1376	B	
IRONSTONE	C	
LABRADORITE	C	
LEAD AND ZINC CALCINES (mixed)	A	*see* Mineral Concentrates schedule
LEAD AND ZINC MIDDLINGS	A	*see* Mineral Concentrates schedule
LEAD CONCENTRATE	A	*see* Mineral Concentrates schedule
LEAD NITRATE UN 1469	B	
LEAD ORE	C	
Lead ore concentrate	A	*see* LEAD CONCENTRATE
LEAD ORE RESIDUE	A	*see* Mineral Concentrates schedule
LEAD SILVER CONCENTRATE	A	*see* Mineral Concentrates schedule
Lead silver ore	A	*see* LEAD SILVER CONCENTRATE
Lead sulphide	A	*see* LEAD CONCENTRATE
Lead sulphide (galena)	A	*see* LEAD CONCENTRATE
Lignite	B	*see* BROWN COAL BRIQUETTES
LIME (UNSLAKED)	B	
LIMESTONE	C	
LINTED COTTON SEED	B	
Linseed, expelled	B or C	*see* SEED CAKE
Linseed, extracted	B or C	*see* SEED CAKE
MAGNESIA (DEADBURNED)	C	
MAGNESIA (UNSLAKED)	B	
Magnesia, clinker	C	*see* MAGNESIA (DEADBURNED)
Magnesia, electro-fused	C	*see* MAGNESIA (DEADBURNED)
Magnesia lightburned	B	*see* MAGNESIA (UNSLAKED)
Magnesia calcined	B	*see* MAGNESIA (UNSLAKED)
Magnesia caustic calcined	B	*see* MAGNESIA (UNSLAKED)
Magnesite clinker	C	*see* MAGNESIA (DEADBURNED)
MAGNESITE, natural	C	
Magnesium carbonate	C	*see* MAGNESITE, natural
MAGNESIUM NITRATE UN 1474	B	
Maize, expelled	B or C	*see* SEED CAKE
Maize, extracted	B or C	*see* SEED CAKE
MANGANESE CONCENTRATE	A	*see* Mineral Concentrates schedule
MANGANESE ORE	C	

Material	Group	References
M.A.P.	C	*see* MONOAMMONIUM PHOSPHATE
MARBLE CHIPS	C	
Meal, oily	B or C	*see* SEED CAKE
METAL SULPHIDE CONCENTRATES	A and B	
Mill feed pellets	B or C	*see* SEED CAKE
Milorganite	C	*see* BIOSLUDGE
Mineral Concentrates	A	
MONOAMMONIUM PHOSPHATE	C	
Muriate of potash	C	*see* POTASSIUM CHLORIDE
NEFELINE SYENITE (mineral)	A	*see* Mineral Concentrates schedule
NICKEL CONCENTRATE	A	*see* Mineral Concentrates schedule
Nickel ore concentrate	A	*see* NICKEL CONCENTRATE
Niger seed, expelled	B or C	*see* SEED CAKE
Niger seed, extracted	B or C	*see* SEED CAKE
Oil cake	B or C	*see* SEED CAKE
Palm kernel, expelled	B or C	*see* SEED CAKE
Palm kernel, extracted	B or C	*see* SEED CAKE
Peanuts, expelled	B or C	*see* SEED CAKE
Peanuts, extracted	B or C	*see* SEED CAKE
PEANUTS (in shell)	C	
PEAT MOSS	A and B	
PEBBLES (sea)	C	
PELLETS (concentrates)	C	
Pellets (cereal)	B or C	*see* SEED CAKE
Pellets, wood pulp	B	*see* WOOD PULP PELLETS
Pencil pitch	B	*see* PITCH PRILL
PENTAHYDRATE CRUDE	A	*see* Mineral Concentrates schedule
PERLITE ROCK	C	
PETROLEUM COKE (calcined)	B	
PETROLEUM COKE (uncalcined)	B	
PHOSPHATE ROCK (calcined)	C	
PHOSPHATE ROCK (uncalcined)	C	
PHOSPHATE (defluorinated)	C	
PIG IRON	C	
PITCH PRILL	B	
Pollard pellets	B or C	*see* SEED CAKE
POTASH	C	

Material	Group	References
Potash muriate	C	*see* POTASSIUM CHLORIDE
POTASSIUM CHLORIDE	C	
POTASSIUM NITRATE UN 1486	B	
Potassium nitrate/sodium nitrate (mixture)	B	*see* SODIUM NITRATE AND POTASSIUM NITRATE MIXTURE UN 1499
POTASSIUM SULPHATE	C	
Prilled coal tar	B	*see* PITCH PRILL
PUMICE	C	
PYRITE (containing copper and iron)	C	
PYRITES, CALCINED	A and B	
PYRITES	A	*see* Mineral Concentrates schedule
Pyrites (cupreous, fine, flotation, or sulphur)	A	*see* PYRITES
Pyritic ash	A and B	*see* PYRITES, CALCINED
PYRITIC ASHES (iron)	A	*see* Mineral Concentrates schedule
PYRITIC CINDERS	A	*see* Mineral Concentrates schedule
PYROPHYLLITE	C	
QUARTZ	C	
QUARTZITE	C	
Quicklime	B	*see* LIME (UNSLAKED)
RADIOACTIVE MATERIAL, LOW SPECIFIC ACTIVITY (LSA-I) UN 2912	B	
RADIOACTIVE MATERIAL, SURFACE CONTAMINATED OBJECTS (SCO-I) UN 2913	B	
Rape seed, expelled	B or C	*see* SEED CAKE
Rape seed, extracted	B or C	*see* SEED CAKE
RASORITE (ANHYDROUS)	C	
Rice bran	B or C	*see* SEED CAKE
Rice broken	B or C	*see* SEED CAKE
Rough ammonia tankage	B	*see* TANKAGE
RUTILE SAND	C	
Safflower seed, expelled	B or C	*see* SEED CAKE
Safflower seed, extracted	B or C	*see* SEED CAKE
SALT	C	
SALT CAKE	C	
SALT ROCK	C	
Saltpetre	B	*see* POTASSIUM NITRATE
SAND	C	
Sand, ilmenite	C	*see* ILMENITE SAND

Material	Group	References
Sand, zircon	C	*see* ZIRCON SAND
SAWDUST	B	
SCRAP METAL	C	
SEED CAKE, containing vegetable oil UN 1386 (a) mechanically expelled seeds, containing more than 10% of oil or more than 20% of oil and moisture content	B	
SEED CAKE, containing vegetable oil UN 1386 (b) solvent extraction and expelled seeds, containing not more than 10% of oil and when the amount of moisture is higher than 10%, not more than 20% of oil and moisture combined	B	
SEED CAKE UN 2217	B	
SEED CAKE (non-hazardous)	C	
Seed expellers, oily	B or C	*see* SEED CAKE
SILICOMANGANESE	B	
SILVER LEAD CONCENTRATE	A	*see* Mineral Concentrates schedule
Silver lead ore concentrate	A	*see* SILVER LEAD CONCENTRATE
Sinter	A	*see* ZINC AND LEAD CALCINES (mixed)
Slag, granulated	C	*see* GRANULATED SLAG
SLIG, iron ore	A	*see* Mineral Concentrates schedule
SODA ASH	C	
SODIUM NITRATE UN 1498	B	
SODIUM NITRATE AND POTASSIUM NITRATE MIXTURE UN 1499	B	
Soyabean, expelled	B or C	*see* SEED CAKE
Soyabean, extracted	B or C	*see* SEED CAKE
SPENT CATHODES	B	*see* ALUMINIUM SMELTING BY-PRODUCTS or ALUMINIUM REMELTING BY-PRODUCTS UN 3170
SPENT POTLINER	B	*see* ALUMINIUM SMELTING BY-PRODUCTS or ALUMINIUM REMELTING BY-PRODUCTS UN 3170
STAINLESS STEEL GRINDING DUST	C	
Steel swarf	B	*see* FERROUS METAL BORINGS, SHAVINGS, TURNINGS or CUTTINGS
Stibnite	C	*see* ANTIMONY ORE AND RESIDUE
STONE CHIPPINGS	C	
Strussa pellets	B or C	*see* SEED CAKE
SUGAR	C	
SULPHATE OF POTASH AND MAGNESIUM	C	
Sulphide concentrates	B	*see* METAL SULPHIDE CONCENTRATES

Material	Group	References
SULPHUR UN 1350 (crushed lump and coarse grained)	B	
SULPHUR (formed, solid)	C	
Sunflower seed, expelled	B or C	*see* SEED CAKE
Sunflower seed, extracted	B or C	*see* SEED CAKE
SUPERPHOSPHATE	C	
SUPERPHOSPHATE (triple, granular)	C	
Swarf	B	*see* FERROUS METAL BORINGS, SHAVINGS, TURNINGS or CUTTINGS
TACONITE PELLETS	C	
TALC	C	
TANKAGE	B	
Tankage fertilizer	B	*see* TANKAGE
TAPIOCA	C	
Toasted meals	B or C	*see* SEED CAKE
Triple superphosphate	C	*see* SUPERPHOSPHATE (triple, granular)
UREA	C	
VANADIUM ORE	B	
VERMICULITE	C	
WHITE QUARTZ	C	
WOODCHIPS	B	
WOOD PELLETS	B	
WOOD PULP PELLETS	B	
ZINC AND LEAD CALCINES (mixed)	A	*see* Mineral Concentrates schedule
ZINC AND LEAD MIDDLINGS	A	*see* Mineral Concentrates schedule
ZINC ASHES UN 1435	B	
ZINC CONCENTRATE	A	
Zinc, dross, residue or skimmings	B	*see* ZINC ASHES
Zinc ore, burnt	A	*see* ZINC CONCENTRATE
Zinc ore, calamine	A	*see* ZINC CONCENTRATE
Zinc ore, concentrates	A	*see* ZINC CONCENTRATE
Zinc ore, crude	A	*see* ZINC CONCENTRATE
ZINC SINTER	A	*see* Mineral Concentrates schedule
ZINC SLUDGE	A	*see* Mineral Concentrates schedule
Zinc sulphide	A	*see* ZINC CONCENTRATE
Zinc sulphide (blende)	A	*see* ZINC CONCENTRATE
ZIRCONSAND	C	

Supplement

Contents

Please note that some of these IMO documents are currently under review with a view to harmonize the provisions with the IMSBC Code and other IMO instruments.

BLU Code

Code of Practice for the Safe Loading and Unloading of Bulk Carriers

Contents

Foreword

The safety of bulk carriers is one of the most important issues that IMO has addressed in recent years and, as a result, a number of safety measures, covering both structural and operational aspects of such ships, have been recently introduced by the Organization. The Code of Practice for the Safe Loading and Unloading of Bulk Carriers (BLU Code) is one such measure.

Being concerned about the continued loss of ships carrying solid bulk cargoes, sometimes without a trace, and the heavy loss of life incurred, and recognizing that a number of accidents have occurred as a result of improper loading and unloading of bulk carriers, the Sub-Committee on Dangerous Goods, Solid Cargoes and Containers (DSC) at its first session (February 1996) developed a draft code of practice for the safe loading and unloading of bulk carriers, with the aim of preventing such accidents.

The Code was reviewed by the Maritime Safety Committee (MSC) at its sixty-sixth session (June 1996) and by the DSC at its second session (February 1997), and was subsequently approved by the MSC at its sixty-eighth session (June 1997); finally, it was adopted by the Assembly at its twentieth session (November 1997) by resolution A.862(20). It has since been amended by resolution MSC.238(82).

In adopting the resolution, the Assembly urged Governments to implement the BLU Code at the earliest possible opportunity, and to inform IMO of any non-compliance. It further urged Governments in whose territories solid bulk cargo loading and unloading terminals are situated to introduce port by-laws as follows:

- terminal operators are required to comply with the relevant IMO codes and recommendations on ship/port co-operation.

- terminal operators are required to appoint a "terminal representative" as stipulated in section 1.6 of the annex to resolution A.797(19);

- the master is responsible at all times for the safe loading and unloading of the ship, the details of which should be confirmed with the terminal operator in the form of an agreed loading or unloading plan;

- in case of non-compliance with the agreed loading or unloading plans or any other situation which endangers the safety of the ship, the master has the right to stop the loading or unloading; and

- port authorities have the right to stop the loading or unloading of solid bulk cargoes when the safety of the ship carrying such cargoes is endangered.

The BLU Code, which provides guidance to ship masters of bulk carriers, terminal operators and other parties concerned for the safe handling, loading and unloading of solid bulk cargoes, is also linked to regulation VI/7 (Loading, unloading and stowage of bulk cargoes) of the 1974 SOLAS Convention, as amended.

Resolution A.862(20)
adopted on 27 November 1997

Code of Practice for the Safe Loading
and Unloading of Bulk Carriers

THE ASSEMBLY,

RECALLING Article 15(j) of the Convention on the International Maritime Organization concerning the functions of the Assembly in relation to regulations and guidelines concerning maritime safety,

RECALLING FURTHER that, by resolutions A.713(17) and A.797(19), it adopted measures to improve the safety of ships carrying solid bulk cargoes,

RECALLING ALSO that, in adopting resolution A.797(19), it requested the Maritime Safety Committee (MSC) to carry out, with high priority, its work on the safety of ships carrying solid bulk cargoes and to develop, as soon as possible, requirements and recommendations covering survivability standards, design and construction standards, management and training, operational standards, survey requirements and ship/shore interface aspects,

NOTING that, by resolution MSC.47(66), the MSC, at its sixty-sixth session, adopted amendments to the International Convention for the Safety of Life at Sea (SOLAS), 1974, to include a revised regulation 7 of chapter VI dealing with loading and unloading of bulk cargo,

NOTING FURTHER the approval by the MSC, at its sixty-sixth session, of MSC/Circ.743 on communications between maritime administrations and port authorities, whereby Governments in whose territories solid bulk cargo loading and unloading terminals are situated are invited to introduce port by-laws complying with operative paragraph 5 of that circular,

BEING CONCERNED at the continued loss of ships carrying solid bulk cargoes, sometimes without a trace, and the heavy loss of life incurred,

BEARING IN MIND that a number of accidents have occurred as a result of improper loading and unloading of bulk carriers and that the development of safe loading and unloading practices can prevent such accidents occurring in the future,

RECOGNIZING the need to improve the safe loading and unloading of bulk carriers,

RECOGNIZING FURTHER that such improvement could be achieved by the establishment of a composite code of practice for the safe loading and unloading of bulk carriers,

BELIEVING that the application of such a code of safe practice would enhance maritime safety,

HAVING CONSIDERED the recommendation made by the MSC at its sixty-sixth and sixty-eighth sessions,

1.   ADOPTS the Code of Practice for the Safe Loading and Unloading of Bulk Carriers, set out in the annex to the present resolution;

2.   URGES Governments to implement this Code at the earliest possible opportunity and to inform IMO of any non-compliance;

3.   FURTHER URGES Governments in whose territories solid bulk cargo loading and unloading terminals are situated, to introduce port by-laws to the effect that:

    .1   terminal operators are required to comply with the relevant IMO codes and recommendations on ship/port co-operation;

    .2   terminal operators are required to appoint a "terminal representative" as stipulated in section 1.6 of the annex to resolution A.797(19);

   .3   the master is responsible at all times for the safe loading and unloading of the ship, the details of which should be confirmed with the terminal operator in the form of an agreed loading or unloading plan;

   .4   in case of non-compliance with the agreed loading or unloading plans or any other situation which endangers the safety of the ship, the master has the right to stop the loading or unloading; and

   .5   port authorities have the right to stop the loading or unloading of solid bulk cargoes when the safety of the ship carrying such cargoes is endangered.

4.   REQUESTS the Maritime Safety Committee to keep this Code under review and to amend it, as necessary;

5.   REVOKES MSC/Circ.690 and DSC/Circ.3.

Code of Practice for the Safe Loading and Unloading of Bulk Carriers

Introduction

1   This Code of Practice for the Safe Loading and Unloading of Bulk Carriers has been developed by the International Maritime Organization to minimize losses of bulk carriers.

2   The purpose of the Code is to assist persons responsible for the safe loading or unloading of bulk carriers to carry out their functions and to promote the safety of bulk carriers.

3   The Code primarily covers the safety of ships loading and unloading solid bulk cargoes, and reflects current issues, best practices and legislative requirements. Broader safety and pollution issues such as those covered by the SOLAS, MARPOL and Load Line Conventions are not specifically included in the Code.

4   The recommendations in this Code provide guidance to shipowners, masters, shippers, operators of bulk carriers, charterers and terminal operators for the safe handling, loading, and unloading of solid bulk cargoes. The recommendations are subject to terminal and port requirements, or national regulations. Persons responsible for the loading or unloading of bulk carriers should also be aware of such regulations and requirements.

5   Masters and terminals loading and unloading solid bulk cargoes possessing chemical hazards should also refer to SOLAS chapters II-2 and VII and to MSC/Circ.675 (Recommendations on the safe transport of dangerous cargoes and related activities in port areas).

6   The requirements of individual terminals and port authorities should be published in terminal and port information books. The type of information usually given in these books is listed in appendix 1. The books should be given to the masters of ships where possible before or on arrival at a port or terminal.

7   It is recommended that a copy of this Code be made available to every ship, charterer and bulk loading or unloading terminal so that advice on operational procedures is readily available and respective responsibilities are identified.

8   In the event of a conflict between this Code and the International Code for the Safe Carriage of Grain in Bulk (International Grain Code), the provisions of the International Grain Code should prevail.

Section 1
Definitions

For the purpose of the Code the following definitions apply:

1.1   *Air draught* means the vertical distance from the surface of the water to the highest point of mast or aerial.

1.2   *Combination carriers (OBO or O/O)* means a ship whose design is similar to a conventional bulk carrier but is equipped with pipelines, pumps and inert gas plant so as to enable the carriage of oil cargoes in designated spaces.

1.3   *Conveyor system* means the entire system for delivering cargo from the shore stockpile or receiving point to the ship.

1.4   *Hot work* means the use of open fires and flames, power tools or hot rivets, grinding, soldering, burning, cutting, welding or any other repair work involving heat or creating sparks which may lead to a hazard because of the presence or proximity of flammable atmosphere.

1.5   *List indication lights* means lights, visible from the deck, which light up to show that a ship is listing.

1.6   *Master* means the master of the ship or a ship's officer designated by the master.

1.7   *Pour* means the quantity of cargo poured through one hatch opening as one step in the loading plan, i.e. from the time the spout is positioned over a hatch opening until it is moved to another hatch opening.

1.8   *Terminal representative* means a person appointed by the terminal or other facility where the ship is loading or unloading, who has responsibility for operations conducted by that terminal or facility with regard to the particular ship.

1.9   *Trimming* (loading cargo) is the partial or total levelling of the cargo within the holds, by means of loading spouts or chutes, portable machinery, equipment or manual labour.

1.10   *Trimming* (unloading cargo) is the shovelling or sweeping up of smaller quantities of the cargo in the holds by mechanical means (such as bulldozers) or other means to place them in a convenient position for discharge.

1.11   *Trimming* (ship) is the adding, removal or shifting of weight in a ship to achieve the required forward and aft draughts.

Section 2
Suitability of ships and terminals

2.1   General

2.1.1   All ships nominated for loading should hold the appropriate valid statutory certification including, if required, the document of compliance* for ships carrying solid dangerous goods in bulk. It is recommended that the period of validity of the ship's certificates be sufficient to remain valid during loading, voyage and unloading times, plus a reserve to allow for delays in berthing, inclement weather or both.

2.1.2   The shipowner, manager or operator, when offering a ship for a particular cargo or service, should ensure that the ship:

   .1   is maintained in a sound, seaworthy condition;

   .2   has on board a competent crew;

   .3   has on board at least one officer proficient in the languages used at both the loading and unloading ports, or has an officer available who is proficient in the English language; and

   .4   is free of defects that may prejudice the ship's safe navigation, loading or unloading.

2.1.3   It is essential that a ship selected to transport a solid bulk cargo be suitable for its intended purpose, taking into account the terminals at which it will load or unload.

2.1.4   The charterer and shipper, when accepting a ship for a particular cargo or service, should ensure that the ship:

   .1   is suitable for access to the planned loading or unloading facilities; and

   .2   does not have cargo handling equipment which would inhibit the safety of the loading and unloading operations.

---

* Applicable to ships constructed on or after 1 September 1984.

2.2 Ships

2.2.1 Ships nominated for bulk loading should be suitable for the intended cargo. Suitable ships should be:

    .1 weathertight, and efficient in all respects for the normal perils of the sea and the intended voyage;

    .2 provided with an approved stability and loading booklet written in a language understood by the ship's officers concerned and using standard expressions and abbreviations. If the language is neither English, nor French, nor Spanish, a translation into one of these languages should be included;

    .3 provided with hatch openings of sufficient size to enable the cargo to be loaded, stowed and unloaded satisfactorily; and

    .4 provided with the hatch identification numbers used in the loading manual and loading or unloading plan. The location, size and colour of these numbers should be chosen so that they are clearly visible to the operator of the loading or unloading equipment.

2.2.2 It is recommended that all ships which are required to carry out stress calculations should have on board an approved loading instrument for the rapid calculation of such stresses.

2.2.3 All propulsion and auxiliary machinery should be in good functional order. Deck equipment related to mooring and berthing operations, including anchors, cables, mooring lines, hawsers and winches, should be operable and in good order and condition.

2.2.4 All hatches, hatch operating systems and safety devices should be in good functional order, and used only for their intended purpose.

2.2.5 List indication lights, if fitted, should be tested prior to loading or unloading and proved operational.

2.2.6 Ship's own cargo handling equipment should be properly certificated and maintained, and used only under the general supervision of suitably qualified ship's personnel.

2.3 Terminals

2.3.1 Terminal operators should ensure that they only accept ships that can safely berth alongside their installation, taking into consideration issues such as:

    .1 water depth at the berth;

    .2 maximum size of the ship;

    .3 mooring arrangements;

    .4 fendering;

    .5 safe access; and

    .6 obstructions to loading/unloading operations.

2.3.2 Terminal equipment should be properly certificated and maintained in accordance with the relevant national regulations and/or standards, and only operated by duly qualified and, if appropriate, certificated personnel.

2.3.2.1 Where automatic weighing equipment is provided, this should be calibrated at regular intervals.

2.3.3 Terminal personnel should be trained in all aspects of safe loading and unloading of bulk carriers, commensurate with their responsibilities.

2.3.3.1 The training should be designed to provide familiarity with the general hazards of loading, unloading and carriage of bulk cargoes and the adverse effect improper cargo handling operations may have on the safety of the ship.

2.3.4 Terminal operators should ensure that personnel involved in the loading and unloading operations are duly rested to avoid fatigue.

Section 3

Procedures between ship and shore prior to the ship's arrival

3.1 Information exchange: general

3.1.1 It is important that the ship be provided with information about a terminal so the loading or unloading can be planned. Similarly, the terminal will need information about the ship to enable preparations to be made to load or unload the ship. It is important that the information be exchanged in sufficient time to allow preparations to be made.

3.1.2 Before loading commences there should be an agreement between the master and the terminal representative as to the rate of loading and order in which the cargo is to be distributed so as to achieve the final loading plan. In general, this agreement should be based on one or more of the following options:

.1 the limitations or restrictions on loading procedures, if such are specified in the ship's loading manual or trim and stability booklet, or both;

.2 if the restrictions mentioned in .1 do not exist, and the ship has a loading instrument which has been approved, the loading plan should be prepared on the instrument and there should be a protocol in place so that the loading remains, at all times, within the approved stress limits of the ship; and/or

.3 if neither .1 nor .2 can be satisfied, then a conservative procedure should be followed.

3.1.3 Details should be provided of any necessary repairs which may delay berthing, the commencement of loading or unloading, or may delay the ship sailing on completion of loading or unloading.

3.1.4 The master should ensure he receives from the shipper of the intended cargo details of the nature of the cargo required by chapter VI of SOLAS 1974, as amended.* Where additional details, such as trimming or continuous measurement of the water in the cargo, etc., are required, the master should inform the terminal accordingly.

3.2 Information given by the ship to the terminal

3.2.1 In order to plan the proper disposition and availability of the cargo so as to meet the ship's loading plan, the loading terminal should be given the following information:

.1 The ship's estimated time of arrival (ETA) off the port as early as possible. This advice should be updated as appropriate.

.2 At the time of initial ETA advice, the ship should also provide details of the following:

.2.1 name, call sign, IMO Number of the ship, its flag State and port of registry;

.2.2 a loading plan stating the quantity of cargo required, stowage by hatches, loading order and the quantity to be loaded in each pour, provided the ship has sufficient information to be able to prepare such a plan;

.2.3 arrival and proposed departure draughts;

.2.4 time required for deballasting;

.2.5 the ship's length overall, beam, and length of the cargo area from the forward coaming of the forwardmost hatch to the after coaming of the aftmost hatch into which cargo is to be loaded or from which cargo is to be removed;

.2.6 distance from the waterline to the first hatch to be loaded or unloaded and the distance from the ship's side to the hatch opening;

.2.7 the location of the ship's accommodation ladder;

.2.8 air draught;

.2.9 details and capacities of ship's cargo handling gear;

---

* Refer to MSC/Circ.663 and to the form for cargo information, which is set out in appendix 5.

.2.10   number and type of mooring lines; and

.2.11   any other item related to the ship requested by the terminal.

.3   Similar information in respect of ETA, unloading plan and details of the ship are required by unloading terminals.

3.2.2   Ships arriving at loading or unloading terminals in a part-loaded condition should also advise:

.1   berthing displacement and draughts;

.2   previous loading or unloading port;

.3   nature and stowage of cargo already on board and, when dangerous goods in bulk are on board, the name of the material, IMO Class and UN Number or BC Number.

.4   distribution of cargo on board, indicating that to be unloaded and that to remain on board.

3.2.3   Combination carriers (OBO or O/O) should advise of the following additional information:

.1   nature of the preceding three cargoes;

.2   date and place at which the last oil cargo was discharged;

.3   advice as to content of slop tanks and whether fully inerted and sealed; and

.4   date, place and name of authority that issued the last gas free certificate which includes pipelines and pumps.*

3.2.4   As soon as possible the ship should confirm that all holds into which cargo is to be loaded are clean, and free from previous cargo residues which in combination with the cargo to be loaded could create a hazard.

3.2.5   Information on the loading or unloading plan and on intended arrival and departure draughts should be progressively updated, and passed to the terminal as circumstances change.

3.3   Information given by the terminal to the ship

3.3.1   On receipt of the ship's initial notification of its ETA, the terminal should give the ship the following information as soon as possible:

.1   the name of the berth at which loading or unloading will take place and the estimated times for berthing and completion of loading or unloading;

.2   characteristics of the loading or unloading equipment, including the terminal's nominal loading or unloading rate and the number of loading or unloading heads to be used;

.3   features of the berth or jetty the master may need to be aware of, including the position of fixed and mobile obstructions, fenders, bollards and mooring arrangements;

.4   minimum depth of water alongside the berth and in approach or departure channels;

.5   water density at the berth;

.6   the maximum distance between the waterline and the top of cargo hatch covers or coamings, whichever is relevant to the loading operation, and the maximum air draught;

.7   arrangements for gangways and access;

.8   which side of the ship is to be alongside the berth;

.9   maximum allowable speed of approach to the jetty and availability of tugs, their type and bollard pull;

.10   the loading sequence for different parcels of cargo, and any other restrictions if it is not possible to take the cargo in any order or any hold to suit the ship;

.11   any properties of the cargo to be loaded which may present a hazard when placed in contact with cargo or residues on board;

---

* Refer to the chapter for combination carriers in the *International Safety Guide for Oil Tankers and Terminals (ISGOTT)* and in particular to the section on cargo change-over checklists and the section on discharge of bulk cargo.

.12 advance information on the proposed cargo handling operations or changes to existing plans for cargo handling;

.13 if the terminal's loading or unloading equipment is fixed, or has any limits to its movement;

.14 mooring lines required;

.15 warning of unusual mooring arrangements;

.16 any restrictions on deballasting;

.17 maximum sailing draught permitted by the port authority; and

.18 any other items related to the terminal requested by the master.

3.3.2 Information on estimated times for berthing and departure and on minimum water depth at the berth should be progressively updated and passed to the master on receipt of successive ETA advices.

3.3.3 The terminal representative should be satisfied that the ship has been advised as early as possible of the information contained in the cargo declaration as required by chapter VI of SOLAS 1974, as amended.

Section 4
Procedures between the ship and terminal prior to cargo handling

4.1 Principles

4.1.1 The master is responsible at all times for the safe loading and unloading of the ship, the details of which should be confirmed to the terminal representative in the form of a loading or unloading plan. In addition, the master should:

.1 ensure that the checklist in appendix 3 is completed in consultation with the terminal before loading or unloading is commenced;

.2 ensure that the loading or unloading of cargo and the discharge or intake of ballast water is under the control of the ship's officer in charge;

.3 ensure that the disposition of cargo and ballast water is monitored throughout the loading or unloading process to ensure that the ship's structure is not overstressed;

.4 ensure that the terminal representative is made aware of the requirements for harmonization between deballasting and cargo loading rates for his ship;

.5 ensure that ballast water is discharged at rates which conform to the agreed loading plan and do not result in flooding of the quay or of adjacent craft;

.6 retain on board sufficient officers and crew to attend to the adjustment of mooring lines or for any normal or emergency situation, having regard to the need of the crew to have sufficient rest periods to avoid fatigue;

.7 ensure the loading or unloading plans have been passed to and agreed with the terminal representative;

.8 ensure that the terminal representative is made aware of the cargo trimming requirements;

.9 ensure that appropriate information about the cargo to be loaded (appendix 5) has been received to enable safe stowage and carriage to be achieved;

.10 ensure that there is agreement between ship and shore as to the action to be taken in the event of rain, or other change in the weather, when the nature of the cargo would pose a hazard in the event of such a change; and

.11 ensure that no hot work is carried out on board the ship while the ship is alongside the berth except with the permission of the terminal representative and in accordance with any requirements of the port administration.

4.1.2 The terminal representative is responsible for loading or unloading cargo in accordance with the hatch sequence and tonnages stated on the ship's loading or unloading plan. In addition, the terminal representative should:

.1 complete the checklist in appendix 3 in consultation with the master before loading or unloading is commenced;

.2 not deviate from the loading or unloading plan unless by prior consultation and agreement with the master;

.3 trim the cargo, when loading or unloading, to the master's requirements;

.4 maintain a record of the weight and disposition of the cargo loaded or unloaded and ensure that the weights in the hold do not deviate from the plan;

.5 provide the master with the names and procedures for contacting the terminal personnel or shipper's agent who will have responsibility for the loading or unloading operation and with whom the master will have contact;

.6 avoid damage to the ship by the loading or unloading equipment and inform the master, if damage occurs;

.7 ensure that no hot work is carried out on board or in the vicinity of the ship while the ship is alongside the berth except with the permission of the master and in accordance with any requirements of the port administration; and

.8 ensure that there is agreement between the master and the terminal representative at all stages and in relation to all aspects of the loading or unloading operation.

4.2 Procedures

4.2.1 The following are considered important procedures in respect of cargo loading:

.1 the master and terminal representative should indicate agreement to the loading plan before commencement of loading by signing the plan in the spaces provided;

.2 the master should state, on the agreed loading plan, the order in which the holds are to be loaded, the weight of each pour, the total weight in each hold and the amount of cargo for vessel trimming purposes, if required;

.3 the terminal representative, on receipt of the ship's initial loading plan (see 3.2.1), should advise the master of the nominal loading rate at which the ship may expect to receive the cargo and the estimated time required to complete each pour;

.4 where it is not practical for the ship to completely discharge its ballast water prior to reaching the trimming stage in the loading process, the master and the terminal representative should agree on the times at which loading may need to be suspended and the duration of such suspensions;

.5 the loading plan should be prepared so as to ensure that all ballast pumping rates and loading rates are considered carefully to avoid overstressing the hull;

.6 the quantities of cargo required to achieve the departure draught and trim should allow for all cargo on the terminal's conveyor systems to be run off and empty on completion of a loading. The terminal representative should advise the master of the nominal tonnage contained on its conveyor system and any requirements for clearing the conveyor system on completion of loading; and

.7 communication arrangements between the ship and terminal should be capable of responding to requests for information on the loading process and of prompt compliance in the event that the master or terminal representative orders loading to be suspended. Consideration should be given to the disposition of cargo on the conveyor systems and to the response time in the event of an emergency stop.

4.2.2 The following are considered important procedures in respect of cargo unloading:

.1 the terminal representative, when proposing or accepting the initial unloading plan, should advise the master of the nominal unloading rate and the estimated time required for each stage of the discharge;

.2   the master should advise the hold order and the weight to be unloaded in each stage of the discharge;

.3   the terminal representative should give the ship the maximum warning when it is intended to increase, or to reduce, the number of unloading heads used; and

.4   communication arrangements between ship and terminal should be capable of responding to requests for information on the unloading process, and of prompt compliance in the event that the master orders unloading to be suspended.

4.3   Implementation

4.3.1   The loading or unloading plan should be prepared in a form such as that shown in appendix 2. Worked examples of this form are also shown in appendix 2. A different form may be used, provided it contains the essential information to meet the requirements of this Code. The minimum information for this purpose is that enclosed in the heavy line box on the sample form.

4.3.2   The loading or unloading plan should only be changed when a revised plan has been prepared, accepted and signed by both parties. Loading plans should be kept by the ship and terminal for a period of six months.

4.3.3   A copy of the agreed loading or unloading plan and any subsequent amendments to it should be lodged with the appropriate authority of the port State.

Section 5
Cargo loading and handling of ballast

5.1   General

5.1.1   When the cargo loading plan is agreed, the master and terminal representative should confirm the method of cargo operations so as to ensure no excessive stresses on the hull, tanktop and associated structures, and exchange information to avoid any structural damage to the ship by cargo handling equipment.

5.1.2   The terminal representative should alert the master, when the cargo is heavy, or when the individual grab loads are large, that there may be high, localized impact loads on the ship's structure until the tanktop is completely covered by cargo, especially when high free-fall drops are permitted. As such impacts have the potential for causing structural damage, special care should be taken at the start of the loading operation in each cargo hold.

5.1.3   Monitoring of the cargo handling operation, and effective communication between the terminal and ship, must be maintained at all times, and especially during final trimming of the ship.

5.1.4   Any requirement for cargo trimming should be in accordance with the procedures of the IMO Code of Safe Practice for Solid Bulk Cargoes (BC Code), or the International Grain Code, as appropriate.

5.1.5   In order to effectively monitor the progress of the cargo loading operation it is essential for both the master and terminal representative to have readily accessible information on the total quantity loaded, as well as the quantities per pour.

5.1.6   On completion of loading, the master and the terminal representative should agree in writing that the ship has been loaded in accordance with the loading plan, including any agreed variations.

5.2   Ship duties

5.2.1   The master should advise the terminal representative of any deviation from the deballasting plan or any other matter which may affect cargo loading.

5.2.2   The ship should be kept upright or, if a list is required for operational reasons, it should be kept as small as possible.

5.2.3   The master should ensure close supervision of the loading operation and of the ship during final stages of loading. The master should advise the terminal representative when final trimming of the ship has to commence in order to allow for the conveyor system run-off.

5.3   Terminal duties

5.3.1   The terminal representative should advise the master on any change to the agreed loading rate and, at the completion of each pour, the terminal representative should advise the master of the weight loaded and that cargo loading continues in accordance with the agreed cargo plan.

5.3.2   The ship should be kept upright with the cargo distributed so as to eliminate any twisting of the ship's structure.

5.3.3   The terminal should use weight meters which are well maintained and provide an accuracy to within 1% of the rated quantity required over the normal range of loading rates. The terminal should frequently monitor the weight of cargo that is being loaded and inform the ship so that it can be compared with the cargo loading plan and the ship's calculation by draught marks.

Section 6
Unloading cargo and handling of ballast

6.1   General

6.1.1   When the cargo unloading plan is agreed, the master and terminal representative must confirm the method of cargo operations so as to ensure no excessive stresses on the hull, tanktop and associated structures, including any measures to reduce and eliminate any structural damage to the ship by cargo handling equipment.

6.1.2   Monitoring and effective communication between the terminal and ship must be maintained at all times.

6.1.3   On completion of unloading, the master and the terminal representative should agree in writing that the ship has been unloaded in accordance with the agreed unloading plan, with the holds emptied and cleaned to the master's requirements, and should record any detected damage suffered by the ship.

6.1.4   In order to maintain an effective monitoring of the progress of the cargo unloading plan, it is essential for both the master and the terminal representative to have readily accessible information on the total unloaded quantity as well as on the quantities unloaded per hatch.

6.1.5   When ballasting one or more holds, master and terminal operator should take account of the possibility of the discharge of flammable vapours from the holds. Suitable precautions* should be taken before any hot work is permitted adjacent to or above that space.

6.2   Ship duties

6.2.1   The master will advise the terminal representative of any deviation from the ballasting plan or any other matter which may affect cargo unloading.

6.2.2   At the start and during all stages of unloading cargo, the master should ensure that frequent checks are made so that:

---

* Refer to the section on the operation of combination carriers in the *International Safety Guide for Oil Tankers and Terminals (ISGOTT)*.

.1   cargo spaces and other enclosed spaces are well ventilated, and persons are allowed to enter them only after they have been declared safe for entry in accordance with the guidelines* developed by the Organization;

.2   the cargo is being unloaded from each hold in accordance with the agreed unloading plan;

.3   the ballasting operation is proceeding in accordance with the agreed unloading plan;

.4   the ship is securely moored, and that weather conditions are being monitored and local weather forecasts obtained;

.5   the ship's draught is read regularly to monitor the progress of the unloading;

.6   the terminal representative is warned immediately if the unloading process has caused damage, has created a hazardous situation, or is likely to do so;

.7   the ship is kept upright, or, if a list is required for operational reasons, it is kept as small as possible; and

.8   the unloading of the port side closely matches that of the starboard side in the same hold, to avoid twisting the ship.

6.2.3   The master should ensure close supervision of the final stages of the unloading, to ensure that all cargo is unloaded.

6.3   Terminal duties

6.3.1   The terminal representative should follow the agreed unloading plan and should consult with the master if there is a need to amend the plan.

6.3.2   The ship is to be kept upright, or, if a list is required for operational reasons, it is to be kept as small as possible.

6.3.3   The unloading of the port side should closely match that of the starboard side in the same hold, to avoid twisting the ship.

6.3.4   Unloading rates and sequences should not be altered by the terminal unless by prior consultation and agreement between the master and the terminal representative.

6.3.5   The terminal representative should advise the master when unloading is considered to be completed from each hold.

6.3.6   The terminal should make every effort to avoid damage to the ship when using unloading or hold cleaning equipment. If damage does occur, it should be reported to the master and, if necessary, repaired. If the damage could impair the structural capability or watertight integrity of the hull, or the ship's essential engineering systems, the Administration or an organization recognized by it and the appropriate authority of the port State should be informed, so that they can decide whether immediate repair is necessary or whether it can be deferred. In either case, the action taken, whether to carry out the repair or defer it, should be to the satisfaction of the Administration or an organization recognized by it and the appropriate authority of the port State. Where immediate repair is considered necessary, it should be carried out to the satisfaction of the master before the ship leaves the port.

6.3.7   The terminal representative should monitor the weather conditions and provide the master with the forecast of any local adverse weather condition.

---

* Refer to Assembly resolution A.864(20), Recommendations for entering enclosed spaces aboard ships (see page 425 of this publication).

Appendix 1

*Recommended contents of port
and terminal information books*

1   It is recommended that information books prepared by terminal operators, port authorities or both should contain the following information relating to their site-specific requirements:

1.1   Port information books:

.1   location of the port and the terminal

.2   details of port administration

.3   radiocommunication procedures and frequencies

.4   arrival information requirements

.5   port health, immigration, quarantine and customs regulations and procedures

.6   relevant charts and nautical publications

.7   pilotage requirements

.8   towage and tug assistance

.9   berthing and anchorage facilities

.10   port emergency procedures

.11   significant weather features

.12   availability of fresh water, provisions, bunkers and lubricants

.13   the maximum size of ship the port can accept

.14   maximum permissible draught and minimum depth of water in navigation channels

.15   water density at the port

.16   maximum permissible air draught

.17   requirements for ship's draught and trim for navigation in the waterways

.18   tidal and current information, as it affects ship movements

.19   restrictions or conditions on the discharge of ballast water

.20   statutory requirements regarding loading and cargo declaration

.21   information on waste reception facilities in the port

1.2   Terminal information books:

.1   details of terminal contact personnel

.2   technical data on the berths and loading or unloading equipment

.3   depth of water at the berth

.4   water density at the berth

.5   the minimum and maximum size of ship which the terminal's facilities are designed to accept, including the minimum clearance between deck obstructions

.6   mooring arrangements and attendance of mooring lines

.7   loading or unloading rates and equipment clearances

.8   loading or unloading procedures and communications

.9   cargo weight determinations by weightmeter and draught survey

.10   conditions for acceptance of combination carriers

.11   access to and from ships and berths or jetties

.12   terminal emergency procedures

.13   damage and indemnity arrangements

.14   landing location of accommodation ladder

.15   information on waste reception facilities at the terminal

1.3   Extreme cold weather information

Ports and terminals situated in regions subject to extreme cold weather should advise masters where to obtain information on operation of ships under such conditions.

Appendix 2

Loading or unloading plan

97525

Example Loading/Unloading Plan

The loading or unloading plan should be prepared in a form such as shown below. Worked examples of this form are shown overleaf. A different form may be used provided it contains the essential information enclosed in the heavy line box.

LOADING OR UNLOADING PLAN Version No.	Date	Vessel				Voyage No.
Load/Unload Port	Cargo(es)	Assumed stowage factor of cargo(es)	Ballast pumping rate	Dock water density	Max draught available (HW)	Max air draught in berth
To/from Port	Last cargo	No. of loaders/ dischargers	Load/ discharge rate		Min draught available (LW)	Max sailing/ arrival draught

Tonnes	11	10	9	8	7	6	5	4	3	2	1	
Grade												
Totals	Grade:	Tonnes	Grade:		Tonnes	Grade:		Tonnes	Total:		Tonnes	

Pour No.	Cargo		Ballast operations	Time required (hours)	Comments	Calculated values							Observed Values			
	Hold No.	Tonnes				Draught			Maximum		Air draught	Draught mid	Trim	Draught		
						Fwd	Aft	BM*	SF*					Fwd	Aft	Mid
TOTAL																

Signed Terminal

Signed Ship

NO DEVIATION FROM ABOVE PLAN WITHOUT PRIOR APPROVAL OF CHIEF MATE

Pours to be numbered 1A, 1B, 2A, 2B, etc. when using two loaders.

Abbreviations: PI = Pump In G = Gravitate In F = Full PO = Pump Out GO = Gravitate Out MT = Empty

All entries within the box must be completed as far as possible. The entries outside the box are optional.

*Bending moments (BM) & shear forces (SF) are to be expressed as a percentage of maximum permitted import values for intermediate stages, and of maximum permitted arrival values for the final stage. Every step in the loading/unloading plan must remain within the allowable limits for hull girder shear forces, bending moments and tonnage per hold, where applicable. Loading/unloading operations may have to be paused to allow for ballasting/ deballasting in order to keep actual values within limits.

Worked examples

Example Loading/Unloading Plan

The loading or unloading plan should be prepared in a form such as shown below. A different form may be used provided it contains the essential information enclosed in the heavy line box.

LOADING OR/Unload PLAN Version No. 1	Date 96-03-24	Vessel BARBICAN		Voyage No. 064
Load/Unload Port BOCA GRANDE	Cargo(es) IRON ORE	Assumed stowage factor of cargo(es) FINES 0.45 / LUMP 0.48	Ballast pumping rate 4000 t/hr	Dock water density 1.025	Max draught available (HW) 17.88 m	Max air draught in berth N/A
To/from Port JAPAN F.O.	Last cargo IRON ORE & COAL	No. of loaders/dischargers 1	Load/discharge rate 4500 t/hr	Min draught available (LW) 9.42 m	Max sailing/arrival draught 17.88 m

Tonnes / Grade / Totals (cumulative):

Tonnes	914-756	817000	717382	616382	516382	416900	315382	215766	113050
Grade	FINES/LUMP	LUMP	LUMP	LUMP	LUMP	FINES	LUMP	LUMP	FINES

Totals: FINES = 44706 Tonnes, LUMP = 98294 — Total: 143000 Tonnes

Pour No.	Hold No.	Cargo Tonnes	Ballast operations	Time required (hours)	Comments	Draught Fwd	Draught Aft	BM*	SF*	Air draught	Draught mid	Trim	Obs Fwd	Obs Aft	Obs Mid
1	4	10000	GO 1&3 UWT's	2.22	FINES	9.99	10.77	73	49		10.38	0.78			
2	1	7000	GO Upper Fore Peak PO 2 hold	1.56	FINES changeover 2 Hold	10.14	10.48	66	53		10.31	0.34			
3	9	8000	GO 5 UWT's PO Aft peak	1.78	FINES	9.42	12.15	63	59		10.79	2.73			
4	4	6900	PO 1 DB's	1.53	FINES	10.12	12.50	80	43		11.31	2.38			
5	9	6756	PO 5 DB's	1.50	FINES	9.56	13.74	80	45		11.65	4.18			
6	1	6050	PO Lower FP GO 2 UWT's	1.36	FINES	9.61	13.57	75	49		11.59	3.96			
					Change grade to LUMP										
7	7	10000	GO 6 Hold to 50%	2.22	LUMP	8.94	14.38	-58	55		11.66	5.43			
8	5	10000	PO 6 Hold	2.22	LUMP	9.63	13.63	-67	49		11.63	4.00			
9	7	7382	Educt 6 Hold	1.64	LUMP changeover 6 Hold	9.57	15.24	-64	47		12.41	5.67			
10	3	10000	PO 2&3 DB's	2.22	LUMP	10.41	14.65	-49	38		12.53	4.24			
11	8	10000	GO 4 UWT's	2.22	LUMP	9.58	16.66	-50	43		13.12	7.08			
12	5	6382	PO 4 DB's	1.42	LUMP	10.28	16.24	58	37		13.26	5.96			
13	2	6000	Educt as required	1.33	LUMP	9.90	17.88	53	38		13.89	7.98			
14	8	8000	Educt as required	1.78	LUMP	12.51	16.68	-65	46		14.60	4.17			
15	6	9000	Educt as required	2.00	LUMP	13.64	17.80	42	-21		15.47	4.66			
16	2	6000	Educt as required	1.33	LUMP	15.06	16.98	33	-16		16.02	1.92			
17	6	7382	Educt ballast lines	1.64	LUMP	15.59	17.88	48	-30		16.74	2.29			
18	3	5382	Shut down ballast	1.20	LUMP	16.95	17.56	44	-27		17.02	0.59			
					Trim check										
19	8	1000		0.22	LUMP	16.94	17.72	49	-30		17.33	0.79			
20	2	1766		0.39	LUMP	17.51	17.51	46	-27		17.51	0.00			
			DRAUGHT SURVEY		SEAGOING CONDITION	17.51	17.51	62	-36		17.51	0.00			
TOTAL		143000													

Signed Terminal: *Goldstein*

Signed Ship: *A. Smith*

NO DEVIATION FROM ABOVE PLAN WITHOUT PRIOR APPROVAL OF CHIEF MATE
Pours to be numbered 1A, 1B, 2A, 2B, etc when using two loaders
Abbreviations: PI – Pump In F – Full PO – Pump Out GO – Gravitate Out MT – Empty
All entries within the box must be completed as far as possible. The entries outside the box are optional.

*Bending moments (BM) & shear forces (SF) are to be expressed as a percentage of maximum permitted inport values for intermediate stages, and of maximum permitted at-sea values for the final stage. Every step in the loading/unloading plan must remain within the allowable limits for hull girder shear forces, bending moments and tonnage per hold, where applicable. Loading/unloading operations may have to be paused to allow for ballasting/deballasting in order to keep actual values within limits.

Example Loading/Unloading Plan

The loading or unloading plan should be prepared in a form such as shown below.
A different form may be used provided it contains the essential information enclosed in the heavy line box.

LOADING/UNLOADING PLAN Version No.	1	Date 96-05-15	Vessel BARBICAN
Loading/Unload Port CHIBA		Cargo(es) IRON ORE	Assumed stowage factor of cargo(es) FINES / LUMP
To/From Port BOCA GRANDE		Last cargo IRON ORE & COAL	No. of loaders/dischargers 2

Max draught available (HW) 17.35m	Voyage No. 044
Min draught available (LW) 7.59m	Max air draught in berth 60m
	Max sailing/arrival draught 17m

| Ballast pumping rate 6000 t/hr | Dock water density 1.025 |
| Load/discharge rate 1250 t/hr per grab | |

Tonnes / Grade / Totals:

	914756 FINES	816910 LUMP	717382 LUMP	616382 LUMP	516382 LUMP	416900 FINES	315382 LUMP	215470 LUMP	113050 FINES
11	10								Total 142614 Tonnes

Grade: FINES = 44706 Tonnes   Grade: LUMP = 97908 Tonnes   Grade: LUMP = ___

Pour No.	Hold No.	Cargo Tonnes	Ballast operations	Time required (hours)	Comments	Draught Fwd	Draught Aft	Maximum BM*	Maximum SF*	Air draught	Draught mid	Trim	Observed Values Fwd	Observed Values Aft	Observed Values Mid
1A	2	15470	G1 1&2 DB's P1 2UWTS	13.2	LUMP 2 & 6 Holds MT	13.82	16.29	-72	48			2.47			
1B	6	16382													
2A	5	10000	G1 4 DB's P1 4 UWT's	8.0	LUMP	13.64	14.54	71	56			1.10			
2B	8	10000													
3A	3	9000	G1 3 DB's	7.2	LUMP	12.19	13.68	77	78			1.69			
3B	7	9000													
4A	5	6382	G1 5 DB's	5.5	LUMP 5 & 8 Holds MT	12.67	15.22	68	38			2.55			
4B	6	6910	P1 6 Hold to 0.5m ullage												
5A	3	6382		6.7	LUMP 3 & 7 Holds MT	11.05	13.94	-91	59			2.89			
5B	7	8382													
			Draught survey and change grade to FINES		Draught survey and change grade to FINES										
6A	1	6000	P1 1&5 UWT's	4.8	FINES	8.75	16.01	83	42			4.26			
6B	9	6000													
7A	4	8756		7.0	FINES	9.38	10.64	80	52			1.26			
7B	9	8756													
8A	1	7050	G1 & P1 lower forepeak	6.5	FINES	7.59	11.30	84	-82			3.71			
8B	4	8166	P1 upper forepeak & 3 UWTS												
			SEAGOING CONDITION		SEAGOING CONDITION	7.59	11.30	84	-82			3.31			

Instructions ① Please empty No.6 Hold and leave as clean as possible. This will then be used for bulldozer, stage 6.
② Grab and bulldozer blades must not be allowed to strike the ship's structure. Please instruct drivers to take special care.
③ Please note tank top ceiling and bilge and echo plate in the after corner of each hold required in this area.
④ All damage to be reported. Hold to be surveyed on cargo completion.

TOTAL 142614

Signed terminal *[signature]*

Signed Ship A. Smith

*Bending moments (BM) & shear forces (SF) are to be expressed as a percentage of maximum permitted in-port values for intermediate stages, and of maximum permitted at-sea values for the final stage. Every step in the loading/unloading plan must remain within the allowable limits for hull girder shear forces, bending moments and tonnage per hold, where applicable. Loading/unloading operations may have to be paused to allow for ballasting/deballasting in order to keep actual values within limits.

NO DEVIATION FROM ABOVE PLAN WITHOUT PRIOR APPROVAL OF CHIEF MATE
Pours to be numbered 1A, 1B, 2A, 2B, etc when using two loaders
Abbreviations: PI = Pump In GI = Gravitate In F = Full PO = Pump Out GO = Gravitate Out MT = Empty
All entries within the box must be completed as far as possible. The entries outside the box are optional.

Appendix 3

Ship/shore safety checklist
for loading or unloading dry bulk cargo carriers

Date: ....

Port: .... Terminal/Quay: ....

Available depth of water in berth .... Minimum air draught* ....

Ship's name: ....

Arrival draught (read/calculated) .... Air draught ....

Calculated departure draught .... Air draught ....

The master and terminal manager, or their representatives, should complete the checklist jointly. Advice on points to be considered is given in the accompanying guidelines. The safety of operations requires that all questions should be answered affirmatively and the boxes ticked. If this is not possible, the reason should be given, and agreement reached upon precautions to be taken between ship and terminal. If a question is considered to be not applicable, write "N/A", explaining why if appropriate.

	SHIP	TERMINAL
1. Is the depth of water at the berth, and the air draught, adequate for the cargo operations to be completed?	☐	☐
2. Are mooring arrangements adequate for all local effects of tide, current, weather, traffic and craft alongside?	☐	☐
3. In emergency, is the ship able to leave the berth at any time?	☐	☐
4. Is there safe access between the ship and the wharf? *Tended by ship/terminal* .... (cross out as appropriate)	☐	☐
5. Is the agreed ship/terminal communications system operative? *Communication method* .... *Language* .... *Radio channels/phone numbers*	☐	☐
6. Are the liaison contact persons during operations positively identified? *Ship contact persons* .... *Shore contact person(s)* .... *Location*	☐	☐
7. Are adequate crew on board, and adequate staff in the terminal, for emergency?	☐	☐
8. Have any bunkering operations been advised and agreed?	☐	☐

---

* The term *air draught* should be construed carefully: if the ship is in a river or an estuary, it usually refers to maximum mast height for passing under bridges, while on the berth it usually refers to the height available or required under the loader or unloader.

	SHIP	TERMINAL
9. Have any intended repairs to wharf or ship whilst alongside been advised and agreed?	☐	☐
10. Has a procedure for reporting and recording damage from cargo operations been agreed?	☐	☐
11. Has the ship been provided with copies of port and terminal regulations, including safety and pollution requirements and details of emergency services?	☐	☐
12. Has the shipper provided the master with the properties of the cargo in accordance with the requirements of chapter VI of SOLAS?	☐	☐
13. Is the atmosphere safe in holds and enclosed spaces to which access may be required, have fumigated cargoes been identified, and has the need for monitoring of atmosphere been agreed by ship and terminal?	☐	☐
14. Have the cargo handling capacity and any limits of travel for each loader/unloader been passed to the ship/terminal? *Loader* .... *Loader* .... *Loader*	☐	☐
15. Has a cargo loading or unloading plan been calculated for all stages of loading/deballasting or unloading/ballasting? *Copy lodged with*	☐	☐
16. Have the holds to be worked been clearly identified in the loading or unloading plan, showing the sequence of work, and the grade and tonnage of cargo to be transferred each time the hold is worked?	☐	☐
17. Has the need for trimming of cargo in the holds been discussed, and have the method and extent been agreed?	☐	☐
18. Do both ship and terminal understand and accept that, if the ballast programme becomes out of step with the cargo operation, it will be necessary to suspend cargo operation until the ballast operation has caught up?	☐	☐
19. Have the intended procedures for removing cargo residues lodged in the holds while unloading been explained to the ship and accepted?	☐	☐
20. Have the procedures to adjust the final trim of the loading ship been decided and agreed? *Tonnage held by the terminal conveyor system*	☐	☐
21. Has the terminal been advised of the time required for the ship to prepare for sea, on completion of cargo work?	☐	☐

THE ABOVE HAS BEEN AGREED:

Time .... Date ....

For ship .... For terminal ....

Rank .... Position/Title ....

Appendix 4

*Guidelines for completing
the ship/shore safety checklist*

The purpose of the ship/shore safety checklist is to improve working relationships between ship and terminal, and thereby to improve the safety of operations. Misunderstandings occur and mistakes can be made when ships' officers do not understand the intentions of the terminal personnel, and the same applies when terminal personnel do not understand what the ship can and cannot safely do.

Completing the checklist together is intended to help ship and terminal personnel to recognize potential problems, and to be better prepared for them.

1   **Is the depth of water at the berth, and the air draught,* adequate for the cargo operations to be completed?**

The depth of water should be determined over the entire area the ship will occupy, and the terminal should be aware of the ship's maximum air draught and water draught requirements during operations. Where the loaded draught means a small underkeel clearance at departure, the master should consult and confirm that the proposed departure draught is safe and suitable.

The ship should be provided with all available information about density and contaminates of the water at the berth.

2   **Are mooring arrangements adequate for all local effects of tide, current, weather, traffic and craft alongside?**

Due regard should be given to the need for adequate fendering arrangements. Ships should remain well secured in their moorings. Alongside piers or quays, ranging of the ship should be prevented by keeping mooring lines taut; attention should be given to the movement of the ship caused by tides, currents or passing ships and by the operation in progress.

Wire ropes and fibre ropes should not be used together in the same direction because of differences in their elastic properties.

3   **In emergency, is the ship able to leave the berth at any time?**

The ship should normally be able to move under its own power at short notice, unless agreement to immobilize the ship has been reached with the terminal representative, and the port authority where applicable.

In an emergency a ship may be prevented from leaving the berth at short notice by a number of factors. These include low tide, excessive trim or draught, lack of tugs, no navigation possible at night, main engine immobilized, etc. Both the ship and the terminal should be aware if any of these factors apply, so that extra precautions can be taken if need be.

The method to be used for any emergency unberthing operation should be agreed, taking into account the possible risks involved. If emergency towing-off wires are required, agreement should be reached on their position and method of securing.

---

* The term *air draught* should be construed carefully: if the ship is in a river or an estuary it usually refers to maximum mast height for passing under bridges, while on the berth it usually refers to the height available or required under the loader or unloaders.

4   **Is there safe access between the ship and the wharf?**

The means of access between the ship and the wharf must be safe and legal, and may be provided by either ship or terminal. It should consist of an appropriate gangway or accommodation ladder with a properly fastened safety net underneath it. Access equipment must be tended, since it can be damaged as a result of changing heights and draughts; *persons responsible for tending it must be agreed between the ship and terminal, and recorded in the checklist.*

The gangway should be positioned so that it is not underneath the path of cargo being loaded or unloaded. It should be well illuminated during darkness. A lifebuoy with a heaving line should be available on board the ship near the gangway or accommodation ladder.

5   **Is the agreed ship/terminal communications system operative?**

Communication should be maintained in the most efficient way between the responsible officer on duty on the ship and the responsible person ashore. *The selected system of communication and the language to be used, together with the necessary telephone numbers and/or radio channels, should be recorded in the checklist.*

6   **Are the liaison contact persons during operations positively identified?**

The controlling personnel on ship and terminal must maintain an effective communication with each other and their respective supervisors. *Their names, and if appropriate where they can be contacted, should be recorded in the checklist.*

The aim should be to prevent development of hazardous situations, but if such a situation does arise, good communication and knowing who has proper authority can be instrumental in dealing with it.

7   **Are adequate crew on board, and adequate staff in the terminal, for emergency?**

It is not possible or desirable to specify all conditions, but it is important that a sufficient number of personnel should be on board the ship, and in the terminal throughout the ship's stay, to deal with an emergency.

The signals to be used in the event of an emergency arising ashore or on board should be clearly understood by all personnel involved in cargo operations.

8   **Have any bunkering operations been advised and agreed?**

The person on board in charge of bunkering must be identified, together with the time, method of delivery (hose from shore, bunker barge, etc.) and the location of the bunker point on board. Loading of bunkers should be co-ordinated with the cargo operation. The terminal should confirm agreement to the procedure.

9   **Have any intended repairs to wharf or ship whilst alongside been advised and agreed?**

Hot work, involving welding, burning or use of naked flame, whether on the ship or the wharf, may require a hot work permit. Work on deck which could interfere with cargo work will need to be co-ordinated.

In the case of combination carrier a gas free certificate (including for pipelines and pumps) will be necessary, issued by a shore chemist approved by the terminal or port authority.

10   **Has a procedure for reporting and recording damage from cargo operations been agreed?**

Operational damage can be expected in a harsh trade. To avoid conflict, a procedure must be agreed, before cargo operations commence, to record such damage. An accumulation of small items of damage to steelwork can cause significant loss of strength for the ship, so it is essential that damage is noted, to allow prompt repair.

11   **Has the ship been provided with copies of port and terminal regulations, including safety and pollution requirements and details of emergency services?**

Although much information will normally be provided by a ship's agent, a fact sheet containing this information should be passed to the ship on arrival, and should include any local regulations controlling the discharge of ballast water and hold washings.

12   **Has the shipper provided the master with the properties of the cargo in accordance with the requirements of chapter VI of SOLAS?**

The shipper should pass to the master, for example, the grade of cargo, particle size, quantity to be loaded, stowage factor, and cargo moisture content. The IMO BC Code gives guidance on this.

The ship should be advised of any material which may contaminate or react with the planned cargo, and the ship should ensure that the holds are free of such material.

13   **Is the atmosphere safe in holds and enclosed spaces to which access may be required, have fumigated cargoes been identified, and has the need for monitoring of atmosphere been agreed by ship and terminal?**

Rusting of steelwork or the characteristics of a cargo may cause a hazardous atmosphere to develop. Consideration should be given to: oxygen depletion in holds; the effect of fumigation either of cargo to be discharged or of cargo in a silo before loading from where gas can be swept on board along with the cargo with no warning to the ship; and leakage of gases, whether poisonous or explosive, from adjacent holds or other spaces.

14   **Have the cargo handling capacity and any limits of travel for each loader/unloader been passed to the ship/terminal?**

The number of loaders or unloaders to be used should be agreed, and their capabilities understood by both parties. *The agreed maximum transfer rate for each loader/unloader should be recorded in the checklist.*

Limits of travel of loading or unloading equipment should be indicated. This is essential information when planning cargo operations in berths where a ship must be shifted from one position to another due to loading. Gear should always be checked for faults and that it is clear of contaminates from previous cargoes. The accuracy of weighing devices should be ascertained frequently.

15   **Has a cargo loading and unloading plan been calculated for *all* stages of loading/deballasting or unloading/ballasting?**

Where possible the ship should prepare the plan before arrival. To permit her to do so the terminal should provide whatever information the ship requests for planning purposes. On ships which require longitudinal strength calculations, the plan should take account of any permissible maxima for bending moments and shear forces.

The plan should be agreed with the terminal and a copy passed over for use by terminal staff. All watch officers on board and terminal supervisors should have access to a copy. No deviation from the plan should be allowed without agreement of the master.

According to SOLAS regulation VI/7, it is required to lodge a copy of the plan with the appropriate authority of the port State. The person receiving the plan should be recorded in the checklist.

16   **Have the holds to be worked been clearly identified in the loading or unloading plan, showing the sequence of work, and the grade and tonnage of cargo to be transferred each time the hold is worked?**

The necessary information should be provided in the form as set out in appendix 2 of this Code.

17   **Has the need for trimming of cargo in the holds been discussed, and have the method and extent been agreed?**

A well-known method is spout trimming, and this can usually achieve a satisfactory result. Other methods use bulldozers, front-end loaders, deflector blades, trimming machines or even manual trimming. The extent of trimming will depend upon the nature of the cargo, and must be in accordance with the BC Code, or the International Grain Code, as appropriate.

18   **Do both ship and terminal understand and accept that, if the ballast programme becomes out of step with the cargo operations, it will be necessary to suspend cargo operations until the ballast operation has caught up?**

All parties will prefer to load or discharge the cargo without stops if possible. However, if the cargo or ballast programmes are out of step a stop to cargo handling must be ordered by the master and accepted by the terminal to avoid the possibility of inadvertently overstressing the ship's structure.

A cargo operations plan will often indicate cargo check points, when conditions will also allow confirmation that the cargo and ballast handling operations are in alignment.

If the maximum rate at which the ship can safely accept the cargo is less than the cargo handling capacity of the terminal, it may be necessary to negotiate pauses in the cargo transfer programme or for the terminal to operate equipment at less than the maximum capacity.

In areas where extremely cold weather is likely, the potential for frozen ballast or ballast lines should be recognized.

19   **Have the intended procedures for removing cargo residues lodged in the holds while unloading been explained to the ship and accepted?**

The use of bulldozers, front-end loaders or pneumatic/hydraulic hammers to shake material loose should be undertaken with care, as wrong procedures can damage or distort ships' steelwork. Prior agreement to the need and method intended, together with adequate supervision of operators, will avoid subsequent claims or weakening of the ship's structure.

20   **Have the procedures to adjust the final trim of the loading ship been decided and agreed?**

Any tonnages proposed at the commencement of loading for adjusting the trim of the ship can only be provisional, and too much importance should not be attached to them. The significance lies in ensuring that the requirement is not overlooked or ignored. The actual quantities and positions to be used to achieve final ship's trim will depend upon the draught readings taken immediately beforehand. *The ship should be informed of the tonnage on the conveyor system since that quantity may be large and must still be loaded when the order "stop loading" is given. This figure should be recorded in the checklist.*

21   **Has the terminal been advised of the time required for the ship to prepare for sea, on completion of cargo work?**

The procedure of securing for sea remains as important as it ever was, and should not be skimped. Hatches should be progressively secured on completion so that only one or two remain to be closed after cargo work is finished.

Modern deep-water terminals for large ships may have very short passages before the open sea is encountered. The time needed to secure, therefore, may vary between day or night, summer or winter, fine weather or foul weather.

Early advice must be given to the terminal if any extension of time is necessary.

Appendix 5

Form for cargo information
(recommended layout)

Note: This form is not applicable if the cargo to be loaded requires a declaration under the requirements of SOLAS 1974, chapter VII, regulation 5; MARPOL 73/78, Annex III, regulation 4; and the IMDG Code, General Introduction section 9.

Shipper		Reference number(s)
Consignee		Carrier
Name/means of transport	Port/place of departure	Instructions or other matters
Port/place of destination		
General description of the cargo (Type of material/particle size)* * For solid bulk cargo		Gross mass (kg/tonnes) ☐ General cargo ☐ Cargo unit(s) ☐ Bulk cargo
Specification of bulk cargo* Stowage factor Angle of repose Trimming procedures Chemical properties† if potential hazard * If applicable † E.g., IMO class, UN No. or BC No. and EmS No.		
Relevant special properties of the cargo		Additional certificate(s)* ☐ Certificate of moisture content and transportable moisture limit ☐ Weathering certificate ☐ Exemption certificate ☐ Other (specify) * If required
DECLARATION I hereby declare that the consignment is fully and accurately described and that the given test results and other specifications are correct to the best of my knowledge and belief and can be considered as representative for the cargo to be loaded.		Name/status, company/organization of signatory Place and date Signature on behalf of shipper

As an aid to paper documentation, Electronic Data Processing (EDP) or Electronic Data Interchange (EDI) techniques may be used.

This form meets the requirements of SOLAS 1974, chapter VI, regulation 2; the BC Code and the CSS Code.

BLU Manual

**Manual on loading and unloading
of solid bulk cargoes for
terminal representatives**

Contents

Foreword

1   In response to the continuing loss of ships carrying solid bulk cargoes – sometimes without trace and with heavy loss of life – the Code of Safe Practice for the Safe Loading and Unloading of Bulk Carriers (BLU Code) was developed by IMO as one of a number of measures to enhance the operational and structural safety of bulk carriers. It was adopted as a recommendatory instrument by the International Maritime Organization's Assembly at its twentieth session in November 1997.

2   Possible stress and damage imposed by cargo handling throughout the life of a ship was considered to be a possible contributory cause of structural failure of bulk carriers leading to casualties and losses. The purpose of the BLU Code, therefore, is to provide guidance to ship masters of bulk carriers, terminal operators and other parties for the safe handling, loading and unloading of solid bulk cargoes.

3   To augment the BLU Code, the Manual on loading and unloading of solid bulk cargoes for terminal representatives (BLU Manual) is intended to provide more detailed guidance to terminal representatives (as defined in the BLU Code) and others involved in the handling of solid bulk cargoes; including those responsible for the training of personnel.

4   It should be noted that in this Manual, a reference to an appendix is a reference to an appendix in the BLU Code and a reference to an annex is to an annex in this Manual.

5   Further guidance on the safe loading and unloading of solid bulk cargoes is contained in the following publications:

Bulk Carriers, Handle with Care, IACS Ltd. 1998, 36 Broadway, London SW1H 0BH, United Kingdom,
Tel: +44 (0)207 976 0660, Fax: +44 (0)207 808 1100
E-mail: permsec@iacs.org.uk
Website: http://www.iacs.org.uk

The Loading and Unloading of Solid Bulk Cargoes, ICHCA International Ltd., Suite 2, 85 Western Road, Romford, Essex, RM1 3LS, United Kingdom
Tel: +44 (0)1708 735 295, Fax: +44 (0)1708 735 225
E-mail: info@ichcainternational.co.uk

MSC/Circ.1160

Manual on loading and unloading of solid bulk cargoes for terminal representatives

1   The Maritime Safety Committee (MSC), at its seventy-sixth session, in considering the Report of the Working Group on Bulk Carrier Safety concerning the issue of the risk control options for the improvement of the ship/terminal interface for bulk carriers noted the need to harmonize training programmes for terminal personnel world-wide.

2   The Maritime Safety Committee, at its seventy-sixth session, further noted that the above concern could be addressed by the application of the Code of Practice for the Safe Loading and Unloading of Bulk Carriers (BLU Code) and that the risk control options in the Manual on loading and unloading of solid bulk cargoes for terminal representatives under development would address the concerns referred to above.

3   The Maritime Safety Committee, at its seventy-eighth session (12 to 21 May 2004), agreed that the application of the BLU Code would address the concerns on risk control options above and urged Member Governments, shipowners, ship operators and terminals to apply the guidance contained therein.

4   The Maritime Safety Committee, at its seventy-eighth session (12 to 21 May 2004), agreed to continue the development of the Manual on loading and unloading of solid bulk cargoes for terminal representatives, taking into account the guidance in the IBTA guidelines for terminal representatives at ship/shore interface, when finalizing the Manual.

5   The Maritime Safety Committee, at its eightieth session (11 to 20 May 2005), approved the Manual on loading and unloading of solid bulk cargoes for terminal representatives set out in the annex and agreed that the application of the guidance contained therein would address the concerns on risk control options and urged Member Governments, shipowners, ship operators and terminals to apply the guidance contained therein.

6   Member Governments are invited to implement the BLU Code and to bring the annexed Manual on loading and unloading of solid bulk cargoes for terminal representatives, to the attention of terminals, shipowners, ship operators, shipmasters, shippers, receivers and other parties concerned.

Manual on loading and unloading of solid bulk cargoes for terminal representatives

Introduction

1   The BLU Code applies to the loading and unloading of solid bulk cargoes, to or from bulk carriers of more than 500 gross tonnage. The BLU Code does not apply to ships which are not bulk carriers, by definition, and ships which are being loaded or unloaded using shipboard equipment only.

2   The guidance in this Manual is intended to complement the BLU Code by providing guidance on good practice, regardless of ship size, terminal capacity or cargo quantity. This should assist terminal representatives to implement the Code.

3   Although this Manual is written primarily in the context of the operation of major bulk terminals operating ship loaders and unloaders, smaller bulk facilities and non-specialist terminals may also load and/or unload solid bulk cargoes by grabs, conveyors, chutes or even directly from vehicles etc. Not all the guidance in the Manual may be appropriate to such smaller terminals and facilities and the ships they serve, but the general principles should still apply and be followed.

4   The guidance in this Manual is intended primarily to assist terminal representatives to understand the key issues to be dealt with at the interface between the ship and the terminal. It should also assist relevant ships' personnel to understand the issues involved from the terminal's perspective.

5   It should be noted that, in this Manual, a reference to an appendix is a reference to an appendix in the BLU Code and a reference to an annex is to an annex in this Manual.

6   In the event of a conflict between the Code of Safe Practice for Solid Bulk Cargoes (BC Code) and the International Code for the Safe Carriage of Grain in Bulk (International Grain Code), the provisions of the International Grain Code should prevail.

Layout of guidelines

The text with the grey bar contains the specific language of the BLU Code and that without the grey bar contains the guidelines for the terminal representative.

Definitions

Definitions contained in the BLU Code are on page 383. In addition, the following definitions refer to a number of other expressions used in these guidelines.

BLU Code means the Code of Practice for the Safe Loading and Unloading of Bulk Carriers, as contained in the annex to IMO Assembly resolution A.862(20) of 27 November 1997.

Bulk carrier means a ship which is constructed generally with single deck, top-side tanks and hopper side tanks in cargo spaces, and is intended primarily to carry dry cargo in bulk, and includes such types as ore carriers and combination carriers.*

Cargo air draught means the distance from the surface of the water to the lowest point of the loader or unloader when in a fully raised position.

---

* Refer to resolution MSC.79(70) relating to interpretation of provisions of SOLAS chapter XII on additional safety measures for bulk carriers.

Dry or solid bulk cargo means any material, other than liquid or gas, consisting of a combination of particles, granules, or any larger pieces of material, generally uniform in composition, which is loaded directly into the cargo spaces of a ship without any intermediate form of containment.

Terminal means any fixed, floating or mobile facility equipped and used for the loading and/or unloading of bulk cargo. The term includes that part of a dock, pier, berth, jetty, quay, wharf or similar structure at which a ship may tie up.

Shipper/receiver means any person in whose name or on whose behalf a contract of carriage of goods by sea has been concluded, or on whose behalf the goods are delivered to or received from the ship in relation to the contract of carriage by sea.

Stowage factor is the number of cubic metres which one tonne of the material will occupy.

Section 1
Definitions

BLU Code

1.1 *Air draught* means the vertical distance from the surface of the water to the highest point of mast or aerial.

1.2 *Combination carriers (OBO or O/O)* means a ship whose design is similar to a conventional bulk carrier but is equipped with pipelines, pumps and inert gas plant so as to enable the carriage of oil cargoes in designated spaces.

1.3 *Conveyor system* means the entire system for delivering cargo from the shore stockpile or receiving point to the ship.

1.4 *Hot work* means the use of open fires and flames, power tools or hot rivets, grinding, soldering, burning, cutting, welding or any other repair work involving heat or creating sparks which may lead to a hazard because of the presence or proximity of flammable atmosphere.

1.5 *List indication lights* means lights, visible from the deck, which light up to show that a ship is listing.

1.6 *Master* means the master of the ship or a ship's officer designated by the master.

1.6 Standard shipping industry practice is that the Chief Officer (First Mate) is the designated officer in charge of cargo operations, and is the person with whom the terminal representative will normally liaise.

1.7 *Pour* means the quantity of cargo poured through one hatch opening as one step in the loading plan, i.e. from the time the spout is positioned over a hatch opening until it is moved to another hatch opening.

1.8 *Terminal representative* means a person appointed by the terminal or other facility where the ship is loading or unloading, who has responsibility for operations conducted by that terminal or facility with regard to the particular ship.

1.8 For reasons of practicality it is accepted that the role of terminal representative cannot be limited to one person throughout the entire loading or unloading period, and that provision must be made for shift patterns and compliance with hours of work agreements and regulations.

1.9 *Trimming* (loading cargo) is the partial or total levelling of the cargo within the holds, by means of loading spouts or chutes, portable machinery, equipment or manual labour.

1.10 *Trimming* (unloading cargo) is the shovelling or sweeping up of smaller quantities of the cargo in the holds by mechanical means (such as bulldozers) or other means to place them in a convenient position for discharge.

1.11 *Trimming* (ship) is the adding, removal or shifting of weight in a ship to achieve the required forward and aft draughts.

Section 2
Suitability of ships and terminals

2.1 General

2.1.1 All ships nominated for loading should hold the appropriate valid statutory certification including, if required, the document of compliance* for ships carrying solid dangerous goods in bulk. It is recommended that the period of validity of the ship's certificates be sufficient to remain valid during loading, voyage and unloading times, plus a reserve to allow for delays in berthing, inclement weather or both.

---

* Applicable to ships constructed on or after 1 September 1984.

2.1.2 The shipowner, manager or operator, when offering a ship for a particular cargo or service, should ensure that the ship:

- is maintained in a sound, seaworthy condition;
- has on board a competent crew;
- has on board at least one officer proficient in the languages used at both the loading and unloading ports, or has an officer available who is proficient in the English language; and
- is free of defects that may prejudice the ship's safe navigation, loading or unloading.

2.1.2 Terminals should determine the suitability of a ship for compatibility with both loading and/or unloading terminal infrastructure as appropriate.

2.1.3 It is essential that a ship selected to transport a solid bulk cargo be suitable for its intended purpose, taking into account the terminals at which it will load or unload.

2.1.3 It is important that the terminal operator keeps its relevant customers informed of current terminal standards, limitations and operating conditions in terms of any changes to relevant navigational conditions, water depths, loading/unloading equipment and rates.

2.1.4 The charterer and shipper, when accepting a ship for a particular cargo or service, should ensure that the ship:

- is suitable for access to the planned loading or unloading facilities; and
- does not have cargo handling equipment which would inhibit the safety of the loading and unloading operations.

2.1.4 In addition to the checks carried out by the charterer and/or shipper and/or receiver, the terminal operator should take reasonable steps to ensure that all bulk carriers nominated for loading/unloading at the terminal are operationally suitable in all respects for the purpose.

The following checks are examples of the type of checks that may be carried out:

.1 Check appropriate sources of information to confirm that ship meets berth maximum and minimum size limits.

- Length overall/beam/draught.

- Number of holds.

- Hatch lengths and widths. Compare dimensions with the most suitable hatch openings on the basis of the terminal's own experience. If hatches are less than the preferred size, loader/unloader operators should be informed and appropriate precautions taken.

- Gearless/geared/gear type. Location of gear.

- Working length from forward end of No. 1 hold to aft end of aft hold.

- Any equipment, design details or performance limitations that could affect the safety or efficiency of the operation.

.2 The ship's owner, master or agent and the terminal representative should exchange pre-arrival ship/shore information, as per the examples in annex 1.

2.2 Ships

2.2.1 Ships nominated for bulk loading should be suitable for the intended cargo. Suitable ships should be:

.1 weathertight, and efficient in all respects for the normal perils of the sea and the intended voyage;

.2 provided with an approved stability and loading booklet written in a language understood by the ship's officers concerned and using standard expressions and abbreviations. If the language is neither English, nor French, nor Spanish, a translation into one of these languages should be included;

.3 provided with hatch openings of sufficient size to enable the cargo to be loaded, stowed and unloaded satisfactorily; and

.4 provided with the hatch identification numbers used in the loading manual and loading or unloading plan. The location, size and colour of these numbers should be chosen so that they are clearly visible to the operator of the loading or unloading equipment.

2.2.1 The ship should ensure the hatches are adequately identified.

2.2.2 It is recommended that all ships which are required to carry out stress calculations should have on board an approved loading instrument for the rapid calculation of such stresses.

2.2.3 All propulsion and auxiliary machinery should be in good functional order. Deck equipment related to mooring and berthing operations, including anchors, cables, mooring lines, hawsers and winches, should be operable and in good order and condition.

2.2.4 All hatches, hatch operating systems and safety devices should be in good functional order, and used only for their intended purpose.

2.2.5 List indication lights, if fitted, should be tested prior to loading or unloading and proved operational.

2.2.6 Ship's own cargo handling equipment should be properly certificated and maintained, and used only under the general supervision of suitably qualified ship's personnel.

2.3 Terminals

2.3.1 Terminal operators should ensure that they only accept ships that can safely berth alongside their installation, taking into consideration issues such as:

.1 water depth at the berth;

.2 maximum size of the ship;

.3 mooring arrangements;

.4 fendering;

.5 safe access; and

.6 obstructions to loading/unloading operations.

2.3.1.1 Terminal representatives should ensure that the following matters are considered:

.1 Tidal situation for the period concerned.

.2 Weather forecasts.

.3 Whether ship will berth port or starboard side-to.

.4 Tug and line boat requirements.

.5 Mooring requirements, taking into account:

.1 The size and type of ship;

.2 Local tidal conditions and foreseeable weather conditions;

.3 The nature of the cargo and ballasting operations;

.6 Any obstructions to berthing/unberthing operations.

.7 The terminal operator should ensure an unobstructed and safe passage between the ship's gangway and the entrance (gate) of the terminal.

2.3.1.2 Pre-arrival ship/shore exchange of information should clarify:

.1 Whether ship or terminal will provide the gangway. Responsibility for providing safety net, lighting and care of gangway. Generally, the master is responsible for ensuring that there is safe access to and from the ship. Normally, the ship provides the gangway and master and terminal representative jointly confirm that it is safe and suitable. Where the ship's own gangway is not suitable the terminal may provide one. However, the master is still obliged to ensure that it is maintained in a safe condition at all times.

.2 If ship is geared, the ship/charterer should provide a plan of the ship giving the positions of the derricks or cranes, and the distances between them. The terminal representative should check the validity of test reports and certificates for cranes.

.3 Loader/unloader booms should be raised clear of berth in good time when a ship is berthing/unberthing.

.4 Loaders/unloaders should be parked clear of the normal angle of approach of a berthing ship, in case the bow overshoots the jetty.

> 2.3.2 Terminal equipment should be properly certificated and maintained in accordance with the relevant national regulations and/or standards, and only operated by duly qualified and, if appropriate, certificated personnel.

2.3.2 "Maintenance" refers not just to running repairs and upkeep of equipment, but to the planned and systematic inspection and maintenance of equipment at periodic intervals. This is normally carried out in accordance with manufacturer's recommendations, national requirements, and industry codes of practice.

> 2.3.2.1 Where automatic weighing equipment is provided, this should be calibrated at regular intervals.

2.3.2.1 "Examination and testing" means the thorough examination of the crane or equipment at regular intervals, in accordance with relevant legislation and insurance requirements. Items needing particular attention include:

.1 Lifting equipment.

.2 Rotating equipment.

.3 Access equipment.

.4 Safety devices – alarms, anemometers, limit switches and controls, emergency stops, emergency escape and fire control equipment.

.5 Structural steelwork for corrosion, fatigue or cracking.

.6 Travel drive motors and braking systems, including storm anchoring arrangements.

.7 Lubrication – adequate and regular application of correct lubricants.

2.3.2.2 "Good housekeeping" means that the entire terminal area and all the equipment on it should be:

.1 Kept in a clean and tidy manner, with everything in its place and a place for everything.

.2 Maintained to a high standard of safety and safety awareness.

.3 Kept to a high standard of mechanical, electrical and structural maintenance.

> 2.3.3 Terminal personnel should be trained in all aspects of safe loading and unloading of bulk carriers, commensurate with their responsibilities.

2.3.3 Commensurate with their responsibilities, terminal personnel should be able to:

.1 Understand the basic principles of bulk carrier construction.

.2 Understand how loading/unloading operations can overstress and damage a ship and know why and how this must be avoided.

.3 Understand the roles and responsibilities, as required under the BLU Code, of:

   .1 The terminal representative.

   .2 The ship loader/unloader operator, as applicable.

   .3 Ship's master, chief officer and crew.

.4 Know the standard procedures and plans by which bulk carriers are loaded and unloaded.

.5 Know the ship/shore communications and emergency procedures applicable.

.6 Know how to access and work safely on board a bulk carrier.

.7   Understand and know how to safely start up, operate and shut down the ship loading/unloading equipment on the terminal for which they are responsible. (See annex 4).

.8   Terminal personnel should be knowledgeable of their responsibilities under other relevant codes, for example the ISPS Code (International Ship and Port Facility Security Code), IMO/ILO Code of Practice on Security in Ports and the ILO Code of Practice on Safety and Health in Ports.

2.3.4 Terminal operators should ensure that personnel involved in the loading and unloading operations are duly rested to avoid fatigue.

2.3.4   In addition to ensuring that terminal personnel are duly rested, terminal personnel involved in cargo handling work should be provided with personal protective equipment such as safety helmets, safety footwear, high visibility jackets, gloves, hearing and respiratory protection, as required.

Section 3
Procedures between ship and shore prior to ship's arrival

3.1   Information exchange: general

3.1.1 It is important that the ship be provided with information about a terminal so the loading or unloading can be planned. Similarly, the terminal will need information about the ship to enable preparations to be made to load or unload the ship. It is important that the information be exchanged in sufficient time to allow preparations to be made.

3.1.1   (See annex 1).

3.1.2 Before loading commences there should be an agreement between the master and the terminal representative as to the rate of loading and order in which the cargo is to be distributed so as to achieve the final loading plan. In general, this agreement should be based on one or more of the following options:

.1   the limitations or restrictions on loading procedures, if such are specified in the ship's loading manual or trim and stability booklet, or both;

.2   if the restrictions mentioned in .1 do not exist, and the ship has a loading instrument which has been approved, the loading plan should be prepared on the instrument and there should be a protocol in place so that the loading remains, at all times, within the approved stress limits of the ship; and/or

.3   if neither .1 nor .2 can be satisfied, then a conservative procedure should be followed.

3.1.2   The master should forward the proposed loading/unloading plan to the terminal before the ship arrives:

.1   The terminal representative should check the plan and ensure it corresponds to its expectations. If it does not, the terminal may revert to the ship, requesting a review of the proposed plan.

.2   By giving the ship adequate time to prepare an alternative plan, in compliance with the ship's stability booklet and loading manual or instrument, it should be possible to identify a mutually acceptable loading sequence.

.3   However, even where the load plan is not the terminal's preferred option, the terminal representative should co-ordinate and agree to a plan before starting operations. Operations should not start until agreement has been obtained.

3.1.3 Details should be provided of any necessary repairs which may delay berthing, the commencement of loading or unloading, or may delay the ship sailing on completion of loading or unloading.

3.1.3   The terminal should be informed if any proposed visits by ship repair contractors or service personnel, or if cranes or other equipment are required on the jetty.

> 3.1.4 The master should ensure he receives from the shipper of the intended cargo, details of the nature of the cargo required by chapter VI of SOLAS 1974, as amended.* Where additional details, such as trimming or continuous measurement of the water in the cargo, etc., are required, the master should inform the terminal accordingly.

3.1.4 Before commencement of loading of a solid bulk cargo, the shipper must provide the master with the characteristics and properties of the cargo, including:

.1 Stowage factor, angle of repose, trimming procedures, and likelihood of shifting.

.2 The transportable moisture limit and average moisture content where appendix A of the BC Code (Code of Safe Practice for Solid Bulk Cargoes) applies.

.3 Flammability, toxicity, corrosiveness, chemical, oxygen depletion and any other hazards of the cargo, as applicable.

3.1.5 The terminal representative should verify that the master has received the relevant cargo declaration form information, as applicable, in good time. (See BLU Code – appendix 5)

3.1.6 The master should inform the terminal representative of any particular precautions to be taken with the loading or unloading of the cargo.

3.2 Information given by the ship to the terminal

3.2.1 In order to plan the proper disposition and availability of the cargo so as to meet the ship's loading plan, the loading terminal should be given the following information:

.1 The ship's estimated time of arrival (ETA) off the port as early as possible. This advice should be updated as appropriate.

.2 At the time of initial ETA advice, the ship should also provide details of the following:

.2.1 name, call sign, IMO Number of the ship, its flag State and port of registry;

.2.2 a loading plan stating the quantity of cargo required, stowage by hatches, loading order and the quantity to be loaded in each pour, provided the ship has sufficient information to be able to prepare such a plan;

.2.3 arrival and proposed departure draughts

.2.4 time required for deballasting;

.2.5 the ship's length overall, beam, and length of the cargo area from the forward coaming of the forwardmost hatch to the after coaming of the aftmost hatch into which cargo is to be loaded or from which cargo is to be removed;

.2.6 distance from the waterline to the first hatch to be loaded or unloaded and the distance from the ship's side to the hatch opening;

.2.7 the location of the ship's accommodation ladder;

.2.8 air draught;

.2.9 details and capacities of ship's cargo handling gear;

.2.10 number and type of mooring lines; and

.2.11 any other item related to the ship requested by the terminal.

.3 Similar information in respect of ETA, unloading plan and details of the ship are required by unloading terminals.

3.2.1 See example of pre-arrival exchange of information checklist (annex 1).

.1 It is important that the terminal receives updated ETAs.

.2 Notifying the terminal of the proposed loading or unloading plan well in advance of arrival gives the terminal the opportunity to check that the information on which it is based is correct. For example, a plan may be based on a terminal having two loaders/unloaders

---

* Refer to MSC/Circ.663 and to the form for cargo information, which is set out in appendix 5 to the BLU Code.

where there is actually only one available. It also allows the terminal to check the plan against its preferred rotation, and to request a modification.

.3 The master then has the opportunity to recalculate the plan and clarify any questions so that a safe, correct and mutually acceptable plan is agreed preferably before the ship berths.

.4 If the terminal's suggested plan is unsuitable for the ship, and does not meet its stability and hull stress criteria, then the terminal representative and master should co-ordinate and agree on a plan before operations begin.

.5 Other items of information requested by the terminal may include:

.5.1 Confirmation that ballast water is clean seawater ballast.

.5.2 Any ship defects which could affect operations.

.5.3 Ship's operational and navigational equipment safety status.

.5.4 Details of any planned bunkering and storing operations, or repairs to be carried out.

.5.5 Ballast handling rates.

.6 Terminals should require both a cargo stowage plan and a plan indicating the order of loading/unloading and the quantity to be loaded/unloaded into/from each hold.

3.2.2 Ships arriving at loading or unloading terminals in a part-loaded condition should also advise:

.1 berthing displacement and draughts.

.2 previous loading or unloading port.

.3 nature and stowage of cargo already on board and, when dangerous goods in bulk are on board, the name of the material, IMO Class and UN Number or BC Number.*

.4 distribution of cargo on board, indicating that to be unloaded and that to remain on board.

3.2.2 Ships should provide the terminal with a loading or unloading plan stating the cargo distribution plan for the cargo to be loaded/unloaded, the hold rotation and quantities to be loaded/unloaded per run.

3.2.3 Combination carriers (OBO or O/O) should advise of the following additional information:

.1 nature of the preceding three cargoes;

.2 date and place at which the last oil cargo was discharged;

.3 advice as to content of slop tanks and whether fully inerted and sealed; and

.4 date, place and name of authority that issued the last gas-free certificate which includes pipelines and pumps.†

3.2.3 During the unloading of dry bulk cargo it may be necessary to ballast one or more holds to reduce the cargo air draught of the ship. This is unlikely to introduce hazards if the pipeline system has been well washed. However, if a pump or pipeline has not been adequately washed, the ballasting operation may discharge residual oil into the hold. Atmospheric tests in the hold should therefore be made before any hot work is carried out in, adjacent to, or above a ballasted hold.

3.2.4 As soon as possible, the ship should confirm that all holds into which cargo is to be loaded are clean, and free from previous cargo residues which in combination with the cargo to be loaded could create a hazard.

3.2.5 Information on the loading or unloading plan and on intended arrival and departure draughts should be progressively updated, and passed to the terminal as circumstances change.

---

* The BC Numbers have been deleted in the revised Code of Safe Practice for Solid Bulk Cargoes (BC Code), 2004, as adopted by resolution MSC.193(79).

† Refer to the chapter for combination carriers in the *International Safety Guide for Oil Tankers and Terminals* (ISGOTT) and in particular to the section on cargo changeover checklists and the section on discharge of bulk cargoes.

3.3 Information given by the terminal to the ship

3.3.1 On receipt of the ship's initial notification of its ETA, the terminal should give the ship the following information as soon as possible:

.1 the name of the berth at which loading or unloading will take place and the estimated times for berthing and completion of loading or unloading;

.2 characteristics of the loading or unloading equipment, including the terminal's nominal loading or unloading rate and the number of loading or unloading heads to be used;

.3 features of the berth or jetty the master may need to be aware of, including the position of fixed and mobile obstructions, fenders, bollards and mooring arrangements;

.4 minimum depth of water alongside the berth and in approach or departure channels;

.5 water density at the berth;

.6 the maximum distance between the waterline and the top of cargo hatch covers or coamings, whichever is relevant to the loading operation, and the maximum air draught;

.7 arrangements for gangways and access;

.8 which side of the ship is to be alongside the berth;

.9 maximum allowable speed of approach to the jetty and availability of tugs, their type and bollard pull;

.10 the loading sequence for different parcels of cargo, and any other restrictions if it is not possible to take the cargo in any order or any hold to suit the ship;

.11 any properties of the cargo to be loaded which may present a hazard when placed in contact with cargo or residues on board;

.12 advance information on the proposed cargo handling operations or changes to existing plans for cargo handling;

.13 if the terminal's loading or unloading equipment is fixed, or has any limits to its movement;

.14 mooring lines required;

.15 warning of unusual mooring arrangements;

.16 any restrictions on deballasting;

.17 maximum sailing draught permitted by the port authority; and

.18 any other items related to the terminal requested by the master.

3.3.1 The terminal should furnish, as applicable:
(See example of pre-arrival ship/shore exchange of information (annex 1)).

.1 The expected maximum and average loading/unloading rates may be discussed and clarified during completion of the ship/shore checklist at the arrival meeting between the terminal representative and the master.

.2 Information regarding draught survey requirements where applicable.

.3 Information regarding any draught surveys to be carried out, usually requesting ballast tanks to be either full or empty, containing clean seawater ballast where possible.

.4 Usual anchorage and pilot embarkation area.

.5 Whether ships may berth/depart at any time, or if it is necessary to wait for certain tidal conditions.

.6 If ship or shore gangway is to be used, clarification of responsibility for ensuring that it is maintained in a safe manner throughout the ship's stay in port.

.7 Information on precautions regarding strong tides or currents, swell, "stand-off" effect at piled jetties, passing traffic, or high winds.

.8 Arrangements for immobilization of ship's engines alongside.

.9 Information on the characteristics and properties of the cargo to be loaded.

3.3.2 Information on estimated times for berthing and departure and on minimum water depth at the berth should be progressively updated and passed to the master on receipt of successive ETA advices.

3.3.3 The terminal representative should be satisfied that the ship has been advised as early as possible of the information contained in the cargo declaration as required by chapter VI of SOLAS 1974, as amended.

3.3.3   The shipper of the cargo is responsible for ensuring that this information is provided to the master in good time.

Section 4
Procedures between the ship and the terminal, prior to cargo loading/unloading

4.1   Principles

4.1.1 The master is responsible at all times for the safe loading and unloading of the ship, the details of which should be confirmed to the terminal representative in the form of a loading or unloading plan. In addition, the master should:

.1   ensure that the checklist in appendix 3 is completed in consultation with the terminal before loading or unloading is commenced;

.2   ensure that the loading or unloading of cargo and the discharge or intake of ballast water is under the control of the ship's officer in charge;

.3   ensure that the disposition of cargo and ballast water is monitored throughout the loading or unloading process to ensure that the ship's structure is not overstressed;

.4   ensure that the terminal representative is made aware of the requirements for harmonization between deballasting and cargo loading rates for his ship;

.5   ensure that ballast water is discharged at rates which conform to the agreed loading plan and do not result in flooding of the quay or of adjacent craft;

.6   retain on board sufficient officers and crew to attend to the adjustment of mooring lines or for any normal or emergency situation, having regard to the need of the crew to have sufficient rest periods to avoid fatigue;

.7   ensure the loading or unloading plans have been passed to and agreed with the terminal representative;

.8   ensure that the terminal representative is made aware of the cargo trimming requirements;

.9   ensure that appropriate information about the cargo to be loaded (appendix 5) has been received to enable safe stowage and carriage to be achieved;

.10   ensure that there is agreement between ship and shore as to the action to be taken in the event of rain, or other change in the weather, when the nature of the cargo would pose a hazard in the event of such a change; and

.11   ensure that no hot work is carried out on board the ship while the ship is alongside the berth except with the permission of the terminal representative and in accordance with any requirements of the port administration.

4.1.1   The loading/unloading plan should preferably be agreed in principle prior to the arrival of the ship.

.1   The terminal representative should ensure the loader/unloader operators and/or terminal control room personnel receive a copy of the agreed load/unload plan. They should also be immediately notified of any subsequently agreed changes. Copies should be retained in the terminal's file for that ship.

.2   The total quantity to be kept for trimming should be clearly stated in the loading plan.

.3   The quantity remaining on the belt should be accurately known, or else the belts should run off before trimming commences.

.4 Where loading terminals insert empty gaps into the flow of material to allow for changing hatches, these gaps should be adequate and there should be good communications between loader and stockyard to ensure the loader can move safely.

.5 For multi-unloader or loader operations the terminal should inform the master of its procedures for preventing collisions between the loaders/unloaders. The cargo plans should normally ensure that the machines will be separated by at least one unworked hatch.

.6 The actual quantities to be trimmed should be determined by the master in good time as loading completes, and the distribution clearly specified to the terminal representative and to the loader operator.

.7 Due allowance should be made for the belt run-off on completion.

.8 Where load/unload plans are programmed into the computerized control system of loader/unloaders, the operator should monitor these carefully, keep the program updated as the operation progresses, double check if doubt, and be able to revert to a manual tally in event of any problems with the computer program.

.9 The terminal representative should notify the master when cargo conditions have changed due to weather.

4.1.2 The terminal representative is responsible for loading or unloading cargo in accordance with the hatch sequence and tonnages stated on the ship's loading or unloading plan. In addition, the terminal representative should:

.1 complete the checklist in appendix 3 in consultation with the master before loading or unloading is commenced;

.2 not deviate from the loading or unloading plan unless by prior consultation and agreement with the master;

.3 trim the cargo, when loading or unloading, to the master's requirements;

.4 maintain a record of the weight and disposition of the cargo loaded or unloaded and ensure that the weights in the hold do not deviate from the plan;

.5 provide the master with the names and procedures for contacting the terminal personnel or shipper's agent who will have responsibility for the loading or unloading operation and with whom the master will have contact;

.6 avoid damage to the ship by the loading or unloading equipment and inform the master, if damage occurs;

.7 ensure that no hot work is carried out on board or in the vicinity of the ship while the ship is alongside the berth except with the permission of the master and in accordance with any requirements of the port administration; and

.8 ensure that there is agreement between the master and the terminal representative at all stages and in relation to all aspects of the loading or unloading operation.

4.1.2 The terminal representative responsible for loading or unloading cargo should:

.1 Inform the ship of all relevant information regarding:

    .1.1 Cargo operations.

    .1.2 Ship and terminal safety issues and regulations.

    .1.3 Arrangements for safe access to/from the ship.

    .1.4 Arrangements for access for crew members through the terminal premises.

    .1.5 Weather and tidal conditions.

    .1.6 Mooring management recommendations.

.2 Understand and respond to the information provided by the master regarding particular safety and operational issues of concern to the ship.

.3 Have sufficient personnel available to deal with any emergencies likely to affect the safety of its personnel and facilities.

.4 Have details to be specified in the ship/shore checklist, and should also be provided with the terminal's regulations and information booklet.

.5 Have a procedure for checking the origin, nature and extent of damage whether notified by terminal or ship personnel.

.6 Have knowledge of hot work procedures to identify any risks, and be familiar with the control measures and precautions required, noting that it may be necessary to ballast one or more holds to reduce the cargo air draught of the ship. With combination carriers, this is unlikely to introduce hazards if the pipeline system has been well washed. However, if a pump or pipeline has not been adequately washed, the ballasting operation may discharge residual oil into the hold. Atmospheric tests in the hold should therefore be made before any hot work is carried out in, adjacent to, or above a ballasted hold.

4.2   Procedures

4.2.1 The following are considered important procedures in respect of cargo loading:

.1 the master and terminal representative should indicate agreement to the loading plan before commencement of loading by signing the plan in the spaces provided;

.2 the master should state, on the agreed loading plan, the order in which the holds are to be loaded, the weight of each pour, the total weight in each hold and the amount of cargo for vessel trimming purposes, if required;

.3 the terminal representative, on receipt of the ship's initial loading plan (see 3.2.1), should advise the master of the nominal loading rate at which the ship may expect to receive the cargo and the estimated time required to complete each pour;

.4 where it is not practical for the ship to completely discharge its ballast water prior to reaching the trimming stage in the loading process, the master and the terminal representative should agree on the times at which loading may need to be suspended and the duration of such suspensions;

.5 the loading plan should be prepared so as to ensure that all ballast pumping rates and loading rates are considered carefully to avoid overstressing the hull;

.6 the quantities of cargo required to achieve the departure draught and trim should allow for all cargo on the terminal's conveyor systems to be run off and empty on completion of a loading. The terminal representative should advise the master of the nominal tonnage contained on its conveyor system and any requirements for clearing the conveyor system on completion of loading; and

.7 communication arrangements between the ship and terminal should be capable of responding to requests for information on the loading process and of prompt compliance in the event that the master or terminal representative orders loading to be suspended. Consideration should be given to the disposition of cargo on the conveyor systems and to the response time in the event of an emergency stop.

4.2.1 It is the master's responsibility to ensure the loading plan is prepared in accordance with the ship's loading manual.

.1 For each step of the loading operation the loading plan should also show the amount of ballast and the tanks to be deballasted, the ship's draught and trim, and the calculated shear stress and bending moments.

.2 The master should carry out draught checks at regular intervals during the loading, and particularly when between about 75–90% of the cargo is loaded. The tonnage loaded should be compared with the terminal's weight figure, and adjustments to the final trimming figures determined and agreed accordingly.

.3 Any changes to the loading plan required by either terminal or ship should be made known as soon as possible and agreed by the master and terminal representative. Stresses resulting from any changes must remain within the ship's hull stress limitations.

.4 High impact cargo drops and exceeding maximum load limits on tanktops should be avoided.

.5 To avoid over-stressing the ship:

.5.1 Cargo should be distributed evenly within each hold and trimmed to the boundaries of the cargo space to minimize the risk of it shifting at sea.

.5.2 Cargo should not be loaded high against one hold bulkhead or one side, and low against the other.

.5.3 Each hold should be loaded using at least two separate pours per hold.

.5.4 The terminal should maintain an accurate record of the tonnages loaded in each pour into each hold.

.5.5 Sudden increases in the loading rates causing significant overloading should be avoided.

.6 The amount of cargo remaining on the belts depends on the loading rate at the time. This should be known by the loader operator and the terminal representative.

.7 Ship/shore communications arrangements should be confirmed when completing the ship/ shore safety checklist, giving all necessary details and contact details for both ship and terminal including:

.7.1 Language and terminology to be used.

.7.2 Location of telephones and terminal offices, normal communications procedures and telephone numbers.

.7.3 Emergency communications procedures and telephone numbers.

.7.4 Designated port VHF channels

.8 Clarify procedures for providing the duty officer with the tonnage loaded and the loading rate as required.

.9 Clarify arrangements for stops to carry out draught checks.

.10 Clarify arrangements for reporting ship damage by stevedores.

4.2.2 The following are considered important procedures in respect of cargo unloading:

.1 the terminal representative, when proposing or accepting the initial unloading plan, should advise the master of the nominal unloading rate and the estimated time required for each stage of the discharge;

.2 the master should advise the hold order and the weight to be unloaded at each stage of the discharge;

.3 the terminal representative should give the ship the maximum warning when it is intended to increase, or to reduce, the number of unloading heads used; and

.4 communication arrangements between ship and terminal should be capable of responding to requests for information on the unloading process, and of prompt compliance in the event that the master orders unloading to be suspended.

4.2.2 The ship should provide the terminal with its proposed unloading plan in advance of the ship's arrival.

4.2.3 The terminal representative should co-ordinate with the master and agree upon a plan before operations begin.

4.2.4 Agreeing the unloading plan prior to arrival simplifies matters for all concerned when the ship does arrive, as there usually is little time for the master to recalculate the unloading plan after the ship has arrived and is ready to commence unloading.

.1 The master should ensure that the terminal representative is provided with accurate information in good time so that the loader/unloader operator can be notified of the ship's requirements.

4.3 Implementation

4.3.1 The loading or unloading plan should be prepared in a form such as that shown in appendix 2. Worked examples of this form are also shown in appendix 2. A different form may be used, provided it contains the essential information to meet the requirements of this Code. The minimum information for this purpose is that enclosed in the heavy line box on the sample form.

4.3.2 The loading or unloading plan should only be changed when a revised plan has been prepared, accepted and signed by both parties. Loading plans should be kept by the ship and terminal for a period of six months.

4.3.3 A copy of the agreed loading or unloading plan and any subsequent amendments to it should be lodged with the appropriate authority of the port State.

4.3.3 Records should be maintained in accordance with any national requirements.

Section 5
Cargo loading and handling of ballast

5.1 General

5.1.1 When the cargo loading plan is agreed, the master and terminal representative should confirm the method of cargo operations so as to ensure no excessive stresses on the hull, tanktop and associated structures, and exchange information to avoid any structural damage to the ship by cargo handling equipment.

5.1.1 For guidance on avoidance of damage during cargo handling, see annex 2.

5.1.2 The terminal representative should alert the master, when the cargo is heavy, or when the individual grab loads are large, that there may be high, localized impact loads on the ship's structure until the tanktop is completely covered by cargo, especially when high free-fall drops are permitted. As such impacts have the potential for causing structural damage, special care should be taken at the start of the loading operation in each cargo hold.

5.1.2 Special care needs to be taken with heavy cargoes such as iron ore, scrap iron, lead and other concentrates.

   .1 The loader chute, spout or grab should be kept as close to the tanktop as possible and loading should be started at a low rate until the tanktop in the loading area is covered with a layer of cargo. As the pile builds up on that area the cargo will roll down the pile and slowly spread over the rest of the tanktop without any heavy impact.

5.1.3 Monitoring of the cargo handling operation, and effective communication between the terminal and ship, must be maintained at all times, and especially during final trimming of the ship.

5.1.3 Communications may be maintained by all or any of the following:

   .1 Direct verbal contact between the designated ship's officer and the terminal representative.

   .2 Portable radio communication between designated officer, terminal representative and/or loader operator.

   .3 Telephone and/or easily accessible talk-back speakers on loader structure to allow surveyor/ designated ship's officer/terminal representative to speak directly with loader operator during trimming operations.

5.1.4 Any requirement for cargo trimming should be in accordance with the procedures of the IMO Code of Safe Practice for Solid Bulk Cargoes (BC Code) or the International Grain Code, as appropriate.

5.1.4 The master, the terminal representative and the loader operators at the load port should bear the unloading of the cargo in mind while they are loading the ship. They should, where possible, avoid trimming cargo onto beams or ledges from where it will be difficult or unsafe to remove.

5.1.5 In order to effectively monitor the progress of the cargo loading operation it is essential for both the master and terminal representative to have readily accessible information on the total quantity loaded, as well as the quantities per pour.

5.1.5 Trimming pours:

   .1 The loading belts should be run empty before the 90% survey if there is any doubt about the quantity of cargo remaining on them.

.2 Where applicable, scale weights should be checked against the draught survey estimates of cargo loaded and cargo remaining to be loaded, and allowances made for the balance to be loaded.

.3 The quantity of cargo to be trimmed into the fore and aft holds should be delivered exactly as required to ensure the ship finishes with the required fore and aft draughts and trim. This will ensure it will be able to depart from the load port and proceed to and arrive at its unloading port safely and with the required under-keel clearance.

5.1.6 On completion of loading, the master and the terminal representative should agree in writing that the ship has been loaded in accordance with the loading plan, including any agreed variations.

5.1.6 The ship's agent should assist in preparing the necessary documentation on completion of loading.

5.2 Ship duties

5.2.1 The master should advise the terminal representative of any deviation from the deballasting plan or any other matter which may affect cargo loading.

5.2.1 If the ship cannot deballast at the rate agreed in the loading plan, or if deballasting is causing the ship to list or trim incorrectly, the terminal representative should be informed in good time and arrangements made for the suspension of loading until the ship has resolved the problem.

5.2.2 The ship should be kept upright or, if a list is required for operational reasons, it should be kept as small as possible.

5.2.3 The master should ensure close supervision of the loading operation and of the ship during final stages of loading. The master should advise the terminal representative when final trimming of the ship has to commence in order to allow for the conveyor system run-off.

5.2.3 It is prudent that a draught survey is carried out with about 90% of the cargo loaded.

5.3 Terminal duties

5.3.1 The terminal representative should advise the master on any change to the agreed loading rate and, at the completion of each pour, the terminal representative should advise the master of the weight loaded and that cargo loading continues in accordance with the agreed cargo plan.

5.3.1 The weight of the cargo being loaded should be harmonized with the ballast water being pumped out, so that both remain in step.

.1 The rate of loading into the holds should be maintained at a steady flow. The ship should be informed of any changes.

.2 The load plan is normally designed to maintain the ship with a slight trim by the stern in order to strip out the ballast.

5.3.2 The ship should be kept upright with the cargo distributed so as to eliminate any twisting of the ship's structure.

5.3.2 The ship should also ensure that the ballast is discharged in accordance with the loading/unloading plan.

5.3.3 The terminal should use weight meters which are well maintained and provide an accuracy to within 1% of the rated quantity required over the normal range of loading rates. The terminal should frequently monitor the weight of cargo that is being loaded and inform the ship so that it can be compared with the cargo loading plan and the ship's calculation by draught marks.

5.3.3 A one per cent error on a 70,000 tonne cargo is 700 tonnes.

.1 If the weigh scale is reading lower than the actual tonnage loaded, then the scale will be reading 69,300 tonnes when there is 70,000 tonnes on board. If no allowance is made for this, then it may not be possible to complete the trimming of the ship as per cargo plan.

.2   The terminal should co-operate with the master in carrying out the 90% draught survey and determining any weight meter error. Due allowance should then be made when loading the remaining balance of cargo.

Section 6
Unloading cargo and handling of ballast

6.1   General

6.1.1 When the cargo unloading plan is agreed, the master and terminal representative must confirm the method of cargo operations so as to ensure no excessive stresses on the hull, tanktop and associated structures, including any measures to reduce and eliminate any structural damage to the ship by cargo handling equipment.

6.1.1   In addition to the avoidance of structural damage to the ship, the health and safety of ship and shore personnel should not be compromised by the adoption of any unloading practice.

.1   If the ship cannot be unloaded safely by the normal unloading methods due to design features of the particular ship or the way in which the cargo was loaded, then the master and terminal representative should carry out a risk assessment to identify a safe system of work.

.2   Safety issues to be considered include:

.2.1   Safe access for shore personnel; gangways should be secure with safety net fitted, adequately illuminated and with safe access from top of gangway to the deck.

.2.2   Access on deck to be confined to the outboard side only. There should be no access for anyone on the inboard side of the ship where unloading equipment is working overhead.

.2.3   Hold access ladders should be safe, secure and in good condition.

.2.4   Hold access trunks should be adequately lit.

.2.5   Adequate hold lighting. Holds cannot be cleaned properly and personnel cannot work safely if the lighting provided by the ship is inadequate.

.2.6   Adequate ventilation of holds.

.2.7   The risk of overhanging cargo that could fall on personnel working underneath.

.2.8   Provision of safe access to cargo residue requires manual removal from ship's frames, pipes and structures.

.2.9   Arrangements regarding ship's crew entering holds, or lowering clean-up tools/equipment into holds while shore personnel are still working there.

.2.10   Arrangements for safe access to and erection of guard railings around hatch covers, where shore personnel have to remove spillage from top of hatch covers.

.2.11   Ship's crew to ensure that hatch covers are fully opened clear of the line of the hatch coaming and secured in position, so that grab ropes/shackles cannot catch on overhanging lips.

.2.12   Geared ships to have gear swung outboard and lowered as much as possible below the unloader gantry.

.2.13   Hold manhole covers and bilge cover plates should be secured flush with the tanktop. Paint marks on the bulkhead indicating their position are useful to machine drivers.

.2.14   All personnel should keep well clear of the area where the unloader is working.

.2.15   Respiratory protection should be worn by both ship and shore personnel when handling dusty cargo.

.2.16   Reporting of defects – any apparent deficiency or hazard that could affect the safety of unloading operations should in the first instance be reported to the master.

.2.17   All lifting appliances and lifting gear – whether provided by ship or terminal, should be used in a safe and proper manner, and have current test and examination certificates.

6.1.2 Monitoring and effective communication between the terminal and ship must be maintained at all times.

6.1.2 Contact details and procedures should be agreed and noted in the ship/shore safety checklist.

6.1.3 On completion of unloading, the master and the terminal representative should agree in writing that the ship has been unloaded in accordance with the agreed unloading plan, with the holds emptied and cleaned to the master's requirements, and should record any detected damage suffered by the ship.

6.1.3 Hold cleaning requirements are normally specified in the relevant charter party or contract of affreightment. The holds should be cleaned to the master's satisfaction in accordance with the contractual requirements.

.1 Where the ship's crew members have commenced cleaning the holds as the terminal completes unloading in each one; the terminal, when appropriate and in conformance with national regulations, should assist the ship in removing hold sweepings and unloading all the available cargo residue ashore.

6.1.4 In order to maintain an effective monitoring of the progress of the cargo unloading plan, it is essential for both the master and the terminal representative to have readily accessible information on the total unloaded quantity as well as on the quantities unloaded per hatch.

6.1.5 When ballasting one or more holds, master and terminal operator should take account of the possibility of the discharge of flammable vapours from the holds. Suitable precautions* should be taken before any hot work is permitted adjacent to or above that space.

6.1.5 This applies to combination carriers, where holds must be adequately ventilated to ensure that the atmosphere contains no flammable or noxious vapours, and is safe for personnel and heavy machinery to work. Ref: ISGOTT (International Safety Guide for Oil Tankers and Terminals) (chapter 12).

6.1.6 During the unloading of dry bulk cargo it may be necessary to ballast one or more holds to reduce the cargo air draught of the ship. This is unlikely to introduce hazards if the pipeline system has been well washed. However, if a pump or pipeline has not been adequately washed, the ballasting operation may discharge residual oil into the hold. Atmospheric tests in the hold should therefore be made before any hot work is carried out in, adjacent to, or above a ballasted hold.

6.2 Ship duties

6.2.1 The master will advise the terminal representative of any deviation from the ballasting plan or any other matter which may affect cargo unloading.

6.2.2 At the start and during all stages of unloading cargo, the master should ensure that frequent checks are made so that:

.1 cargo spaces and other enclosed spaces are well ventilated, and persons are allowed to enter them only after they have been declared safe for entry in accordance with the guidelines developed by the Organization;

.2 the cargo is being unloaded from each hold in accordance with the agreed unloading plan;

.3 the ballasting operation is proceeding in accordance with the agreed unloading plan;

.4 the ship is securely moored, and that weather conditions are being monitored and local weather forecasts obtained;

.5 the ship's draught is read regularly to monitor the progress of the unloading;

.6 the terminal representative is warned immediately if the unloading process has caused damage, has created a hazardous situation, or is likely to do so;

.7 the ship is kept upright, or, if a list is required for operational reasons, it is kept as small as possible; and

.8 the unloading of the port side closely matches that of the starboard side in the same hold, to avoid twisting the ship.

---

* Refer to the section on the operation of combination carriers in the *International Safety Guide for Oil Tankers and Terminals (ISGOTT)*.

6.2.2   Further guidance is contained in IMO Assembly resolution A.864(20), Recommendations for entering enclosed spaces aboard ships.

Special precautions should be taken and enclosed space entry procedures observed where there is a risk of an unsafe atmosphere in ship's holds, particularly where:

.1   The cargo has been fumigated en passage.

.2   The cargo has oxygen-depleting characteristics.

.3   The cargo is liable to give off flammable or toxic vapours.

The terminal representative should be familiar with the BC Code (Code of Safe Practice for Solid Bulk Cargoes) recommendations for the specific cargoes that the terminal handles, and also with the Material Safety Data Sheets (MSDS) for those materials. When employed on grain-laden ships, the terminal representatives should be familiar with the International Grain Code.

The terminal representative should ensure the master is made aware of:

.1   Any local tidal or current conditions at the berth that could affect the safe mooring of the ship.

.2   Details of any prevailing wind conditions that could affect the safety of operations.

.3   Any forecasts of extreme wind conditions.

.4   Limiting wind or tidal conditions for berthing/unberthing.

.5   Limiting wind conditions for loader/unloader operations.

.6   Other conditions affecting operations, such as wave or swell conditions, visibility, electrical storms.

.7   The effects of either heavy rainfall or drought conditions on the berth or approach channels.

Appropriate safety precautions should be taken while reading ship's draughts, including:

.1   Safe access along jetty edge.

.2   Wearing appropriate personnel protective equipment (including but not limited to lifejacket, safety helmet, safety boots, high visibility clothing, respiratory protection, as necessary).

Hold inspections should be carried out as soon as unloading of a hold is completed and it is safe to enter.

Any stevedore damage reports should be presented to the terminal representative immediately to allow the claim to be verified and agreement reached with the master concerning the arrangements to be made for its repair.

The terminal representative should be informed if the ship is being listed due to the distribution of ballast, or if there are problems on board with pumping ballast.

6.2.3   The master should ensure close supervision of the final stages of the unloading, to ensure that all cargo is unloaded.

6.2.3   The master should also ensure that:

.1   Adequate and proper hold lighting is provided.

.2   Bilge cover plates are properly secured so that they cannot be accidentally dislodged during hold cleaning.

6.3   Terminal duties

6.3.1   The terminal representative should follow the agreed unloading plan and should consult with the master if there is a need to amend the plan.

6.3.1   See annex 5: Guidelines for unloading from the holds so as to minimize listing, twisting, stressing as a result of cargo handling.

6.3.2   The ship is to be kept upright, or, if a list is required for operational reasons, it is to be kept as small as possible.

6.3.2   The cargo should be removed in a methodical pattern across the hold so that any listing to one side and then the other is kept small and is constantly being corrected.

> 6.3.3   The unloading of the port side closely matches that of the starboard side in the same hold, to avoid twisting the ship.

6.3.3   Where grab operations are carried out in automatic or semi-automatic mode the unloader operator should:

.1   Ensure the limits are set correctly for every hold.

.2   That both ship and unloader are monitored constantly for any deviation from these limits.

.3   That the pattern followed by the grab is systematic and even across the hold.

> 6.3.4   Unloading rates and sequences should not be altered by the terminal unless by prior consultation and agreement between the master and the terminal representative.

6.3.4   Where there is significant and unavoidable delay to the unloading, or a reduction in the expected rates due to breakdowns or problems with the terminal materials handling system, the master should be informed and the plan amended as necessary.

> 6.3.5   The terminal representative should advise the master when unloading is considered to be completed from each hold.
>
> 6.3.6   The terminal should make every effort to avoid damage to the ship when using unloading or hold cleaning equipment. If damage does occur, it should be reported to the master and, if necessary, repaired. If the damage could impair the structural capability or watertight integrity of the hull, or the ship's essential engineering systems, the Administration or an organization recognized by it and the appropriate authority of the port State should be informed, so that they can decide whether immediate repair is necessary or whether it can be deferred. In either case, the action taken, whether to carry out the repair or defer it, should be to the satisfaction of the Administration or an organization recognized by it and the appropriate authority of the port State. Where immediate repair is considered necessary, it should be carried out to the satisfaction of the master before the ship leaves the port.

6.3.6   The master should inspect each hold as soon as possible after the completion of unloading of cargo from the hold. Any damage found should be reported to the terminal representative immediately.

> 6.3.7   The terminal representative should monitor the weather conditions and provide the master with the forecast of any local adverse weather condition.

Annex 1

Pre-arrival ship/shore exchange of information

An example of a bulk carrier ship/shore exchange of information

The table below indicates only an example and format for the exchange of information. Terminals may require additional information, especially in the case of part-loaded ships and combination carriers (further details of information to be exchanged may be found in section 3 of the BLU Code). The table may be modified as appropriate by individual terminals.

Information to be provided by the master to the terminal in accordance with relevant IMO guidelines regarding the safe loading and unloading of bulk carriers

	Information	Response
1	Ship name Call sign/IMO Number/Flag Port of registry	Name . . . . Call sign . . . . IMO No. . . . . Flag . . . . Port of registry . . . .
2	ETA sea pilots	Date . . . . Time . . . .
3	Unloading plan/cargo distribution or loading plan	Please attach proposed plan
4	Arrival draughts and proposed departure draughts	Arrival: Forward . . . . /Aft . . . . Departure: Forward . . . . /Aft . . . .
5	Time required for ballasting/ deballasting	
6	Ship's LOA/beam/displacement/ working length from forward coaming of No. 1 hatch to aft coaming of aft hatch	LOA . . . . metres Beam . . . . metres Displacement . . . . tonnes Working length . . . . metres
7	Gangway If shore gangway is provided, can ship provide secure landing place, safety net and bulwark ladder?	
8	Distance from waterline to hatch coaming	
9	Number and kind of mooring lines Number of enclosed fairleads forward and aft	
10	Trimming requirements	

Example of checklist to show suitability for loading/unloading solid bulk cargoes

		Master's comments
1	Cargo holds and hatch openings are suitable for cargo operations	
2	Holds are clearly numbered on hatch covers/coamings	
3	Hatch covers, hatch operating systems and safety devices are in good operational condition	
4	List indication lights, if fitted, have been tested prior to arrival and are operational	
5	If applicable, loading instrument is certified and operational	
6	Propulsion/auxiliary machinery is in good operational order	
7	Mooring equipment is in good functional order	
	Signed: Master	Date:

Example of information to be provided by the terminal to the master in accordance with relevant IMO guidelines regarding the safe loading and unloading of bulk carriers

This may be modified as appropriate by individual terminals.

	Information	Response
1	Name of berth to be used Which side alongside	No. 1 berth: . . . . No. 2 berth: . . . .
1.1	Estimated time of berthing	1. Berthing time . . . .
1.2	Estimated time of completion	2. Estimated completion time . . . .
2	Unloading equipment	1. Number of unloaders . . . . 2. Nominal rate . . . . 3. Estimated times for each stage of unloading to be agreed on arrival. 4. Cargo air draught of unloaders . . . .
2.1	Loading equipment	1. Number of loaders . . . . 2. Expected rate No. 1 berth: . . . . 3. Expected rate No. 2 berth: . . . . 4. Estimated times for each stage of loading to be agreed on arrival. 5. Cargo air draught of loaders . . . .
3	Minimum depth of water alongside	No. 1 berth: . . . . m No. 2 berth: . . . . m Ships arriving on max. draughts to plan unloading so ship raises on even keel for first 12 hours.
3.1	Water density	Depending on tide and weather.

	Information	**Response**
4	Depths in approach and departure channels	Adequate at all times for all ships. Berthing times restricted as follows: No. 1 berth . . . . No. 2 berth . . . .
4.1	Maximum allowable docking speed	. . . . m/s
5	Pilotage anchorage (Pilot station VHF)	Pilots normally board at . . . . Ships awaiting a berth normally proceed direct to the . . . . anchorage.
6	Maximum distance from waterline to top of hatch coaming	Ships loading: . . . . m Ships unloading: . . . . m
7	Arrangements for gangways and access	
8	Tugs:	Number available: . . . . Number normally required: . . . . .type
8.1	Line boat available	Yes/No
9	Main engine immobilization alongside	No. 1 berth: Immobilization permitted/not permitted No. 2 Berth: Immobilization permitted/not permitted
10	Grades of cargo to be loaded	Product A: . . . . tonnes Stowage factor on loading . . . . Product B: . . . . tonnes Stowage factor: . . . . Etc., etc.
11	Any advance information on proposed loading/unloading operations	Draught survey: Ships arriving to load should preferably have ballast tanks either fully pressed up or empty. Slow deballasting: loading continues at normal rate until ship requests loading stop.
11.1	1. Loading plan 2. Unloading plan	1. The terminal's preferred options are: . . . .
12	Travel limits of terminal equipment	Maximum working distance from forward end of No. 1 hatch to aft end of aft hatch: No. 1 berth unloader: . . . . m No. 1 berth loader: . . . . m No. 1 berth unloader: . . . . m No. 1 berth loader: . . . . m
13	Mooring arrangements	Number of headlines or sternlines/breasts/springs: . . . .
14	Unusual mooring requirements	
	Signed: Terminal representative	Date:

Annex 2

Avoidance of damage during cargo handling

The traditional design and configuration of single-side skin bulk carriers presents obstacles to safe and efficient cargo handling, especially discharge with grabs.

The usual types of damage that occur during grab discharge operations are grab and payloader damage in the holds, damage to hatch coamings and covers, and damage to deck fittings and equipment.

Grab damage in the holds can be classified into three categories:

1. Damage to ladders or coamings during free digging.

2. Damage to frames and hopper side during the second phase of digging.

3. Damage to the tanktop during the third phase of digging.

	Procedure	Key point

1	**Prevention of damage to ladders**
	
	.1 When free digging the operator should:
	
	  .1.1 Check for the location of sloping ladders with intermediate platforms extending into the hold space, check if it is going to the outboard or inboard side, and check for the location of platforms.
	
	  .1.2 Check location of vertical ladders and look out for intermediate platforms.
	
	  .1.3 Work carefully across each end of the hold in turn, keeping clear of the ladders until the cargo falls away and the handrails and intermediate platforms can be seen.
		• Ladder may be buried under the cargo with only the top section visible.
		
		• Grab may topple over and strike the ladder, so make due allowances.

2	**Prevention of damage to hoppers and side frames during second phase** .1 Grab evenly over the full area of the hold to avoid development of steep banks in the wings. .2 Do not pendulum swing the grab into the wings so that it could strike the ship's side shell frames. .3 Keep the grab straight and parallel to the ship's side. .4 Do not land the grab on the hopper side where bare steel is visible. .5 Do not attempt to land the grab close to the forward and after bulkheads, as there may be an outward sloping stool plate under the cargo.	• Grab from the highest point of the cargo at all times. • Any damage to the frames may affect the seaworthiness of the ship, and has to be reported to the master. • Avoid swinging the grab in at an angle, as the corner of the grab may strike the hopper tank first. This will cause heavy indents or puncture holes in the tank plate. (See figures A & B)
3	**Prevention of damage to inner bottom plating (tanktop) – third phase** .1 Lower the grab carefully and evenly onto the tanktop. Never drop the grab at speed.	Be particularly careful where there are mounds of cargo on the tanktop. One side of the grab will land safely on the cargo but the other side may drop corner-first onto bare steel. If it lands heavily it can puncture the tanktop.

	Procedure	Key point
4	Prevention of damage to hatch coamings and covers .1 The operator should always check along the line of hatches that the covers are completely opened clear of the coaming. .2 The travel of the grab into the hold should be controlled so that the grab and the grab trolley are in line as the grab is moving out and down into the hold. This will ensure that the swing is under control at all times. .3 When working in the wings the grab trolley should be positioned so that the grab ropes and the grab itself are raised clear of the coaming.	This is caused by grab or rope contact with the coamings or covers. Ship's crew may: • Leave covers slightly closed over the top of the coaming to prevent spillage getting into the drain channels. • Fail to secure the open covers in place, which can allow them to roll closed. • Always be aware that the ship can move in or out, fore and aft, and up and down due to wind, tide, movement of cargo and ballast, or crew adjusting mooring ropes. • Raising or lowering the grab close to the coaming may result in the grab or the grab rope shackles catching on the lips of the hatch cover. This will result in the cover being lifted and dropped heavily, causing major damage to the coaming, the cover and the cover drive mechanism. • Damage to the cross-joint sealing arrangement could also occur.
5	Prevention of damage by payloader to bottoms of ladders, stool plates and bulkheads – fourth phase In co-ordination with the master, the operator should be informed of: .1 Location of the bottoms of ladders. .2 Location of any pipes or pipe guards. .3 Location of bilge cover plates.	Payloader drivers should: • Operate carefully around ladders and projections. Remove material manually where necessary. • Avoid grinding the corners of the payloader bucket along the bottom of the bulkheads and hopper tanks, as this kind of heavy pressure can cause unseen damage. • The master should point out the position of any obstructions on the tanktop. On some ships the locations of bilge cover plates are marked by a line of paint on the bulkhead.
6	Prevention of damage to deck fittings and equipment Before travelling the unloader to a new location: .1 Check that the grab is well clear of all deck fittings and equipment before moving. .2 Check that it is clear for the unloader to move. .3 When working close to the bridge front or foremast make due allowances for aerials and other obstructions to the unloader boom and keep well clear.	Geared ships: • Derrick and crane jibs not in use should be lowered below the level of the unloader boom. • As the ship rises as the cargo is unloaded, the unloader operator should always check that there is safe clearance over all obstructions before attempting to move the unloader. The unloader boom should always be raised before moving if there is any doubt.

Procedure	Key point
7 Error inducing conditions The following conditions may lead to operator error or misjudgement: .1 Overfilled or unevenly filled holds having ladders and platforms buried under the cargo. .2 Environmental conditions – poor lighting, dust, glare, fog. .3 Mechanical or control problems on the unloader – faulty grab controls, slipping winch brakes, slipping long travel brakes. .4 Poor working conditions such as poor conditions in the operator cab, faulty indicators, inadequate means of communications with ship and/or co-workers, faulty seat, dirty windows.	• Never grab from the forward and aft ends of the holds without being sure of where the ladders are. • Do not work unless the cargo in the hold is clearly visible. • All equipment faults should be reported to the terminal representative or relevant maintenance person immediately. • Unloader operation is a demanding job that requires concentration and care. Deficiencies and problems that distract the operator should be rectified immediately.

Figure A *(Section view)*

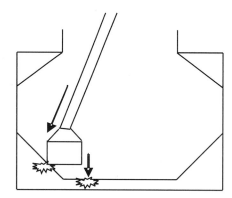

Sides of grab when "across-ship" increase the risk of point impact damage to hopper and tanktop, and this is more likely to happen when the grab is at an angle with the ship as it impacts with the hopper.

Figure B *(Plan view)*

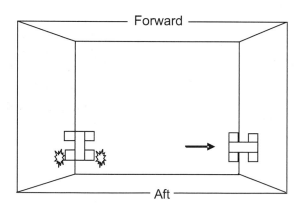

Sides of grab when parallel to ship's side impact more evenly distributed on hopper, but pose more risk to stool plate.

Annex 3

Repair of damage incurred during loading and unloading

Guidelines for terminal representatives in responding to damage incidents

	Procedure	Key point
1	**Reporting** In consultation with the master, report the damage to the relevant authorities as described in the BLU Code.	
2	Inspection procedure .1 Inspect damaged area together with master. .2 Look for signs of fresh metal or freshly broken welds in the impact area. .3 Measure/estimate the damaged area, and length and depth of any indents. .4 Check for signs of previous damage, i.e., rusted broken welds or rusted indents.	Equipment required: Notebook, torch, camera, measuring tape.
3	Minor scrapes and indents .1 Photograph the required repair and estimate the cost. .2 Arrange for repairs if necessary, safe and practicable.	Alternatively agree a mutually acceptable means of resolving the issue with the ship's master. Ensure that such agreement is fully documented.
4	Damage to ladders, handrails and steps which cause safety problems. In consultation with the master and attending representative from the relevant authority, arrange for repairs to be carried out by a competent contractor.	
5	Serious damage This includes holes in tanktops or wing tanks, hatch coaming or hatch cover damage, or damage to decks or fittings essential to maintaining the seaworthiness of the ship. Repairs will have to be carried out in accordance with the requirements of the relevant authorities.	Normally the ship's Classification Society surveyor will be called in.
6	Requirements/procedure In order to avoid or minimize any delays to the ship, the terminal or the specialist repair contractor should have: .1 Steel plate of suitable grade and size for ship repair available. .2 A list of qualified welders, with certificates available.	Plates of 12 mm, 16 mm, 18 mm, or 20 mm grade 50D (or BS 4360/43 D or E) steel, complete with relevant mill certificates will meet most requirements. Have a list of the type of welding rods used.

	Procedure	Key point
7	Work method Carry out the repair in accordance with the procedure and method specified by the surveyor. The following key points will normally have to be observed: .1 Ensure appropriate confined space entry and hot work procedures are followed before personnel begin any activities. .2 Where repair to a hatch cover is required, it should be positively secured in position, and the edges of the hatch cover cordoned off.	Have a competent person carry out an atmosphere test on the tank for explosive vapours/oxygen deficiency before doing any welding/burning or tank entry. Ensure gas detector is properly calibrated.
8	Signing Damage Report Forms All damage reports should be signed and acknowledged. .1 Where the damage is repaired, ensure the master provides appropriate documentation acknowledging that the repair was completed to his satisfaction. .2 If the damage cannot be repaired, duly note estimated cost on the form and attach signed notes of the agreement reached with the master for the completion of the repairs at another port or ship repair facility.	In event of claims for damage which did not occur at this terminal: Record in terms such as "in dispute, old damage, did not occur at this terminal". Acknowledge for "receipt only". Where major damage is concerned the terminal should appoint a competent independent surveyor to act on its behalf.

Annex 4

*Training of terminal personnel involved in loading
and/or unloading bulk carriers*

Loader/unloader operator training should include:

1. The general hazards of loading and/or unloading bulk carriers (ref. *BLU Code (Code of Practice for the Safe Loading and Unloading of Bulk Carriers), BC Code (Code of Safe Practice for Solid Bulk Cargoes)* and the *International Grain Code*, as appropriate).

2. The dangerous effect improper loading and/or unloading can have on a ship.

Practical aspects to be included in the training should include:

-   The BLU Code so that they understand and appreciate both the obligations it places on their terminal, and the limitations of the ships the terminal personnel are loading and/or unloading.

-   The correct operating instructions for the ship loader or unloader they are operating.

-   A basic understanding of the mechanical and electrical components of the loader and/or unloader such as travel drives, braking arrangements, ropes and rope care, grab/trolley winches, conveyors, operating and wind limits, storm anchoring.

-   Emergency procedures such as fire on ship, terminal, or loader and/or unloader; mooring incidents, emergency stops.

-   The correct techniques and patterns to be used to load or unload a ship, depending on the type of and number of loaders or unloaders being used.

To load a ship:

Loader operators should have an appropriate understanding of how to:

-   Distribute the cargo in each hold in accordance with the agreed cargo plan to ensure the ship remains upright, and is neither stressed nor twisted.

-   Ensure no hold is overloaded or overfilled, and that the ship can be safely trimmed on completion.

-   Ensure loading efficiency is maximized, as per the agreed loading/deballasting plan.

-   Ensure safety and environmental protection procedures are followed.

-   Ensure that good communications are maintained between the loader operator and the designated ship's officer, and between master and terminal representative.

To unload a ship:

Unloader operators should have an appropriate understanding of how to:

-   Unload the cargo from each hold in accordance with the agreed unloading plan to ensure that the ship remains upright and is not stressed or twisted.

-   Remove the cargo from the holds by either grab or continuous unloader in a manner that minimizes the risk of damage to the ship's structure.

-   Ensure that good communications are maintained between the unloader operator and the designated ship's officer, and between master and terminal representative.

-   Assess the risks arising from cargo sticking in frames and on hopper sides and facilitate, if possible, its safe removal without risk to the safety of terminal personnel and ship's crew members, or risk of damage to ship.

Terminal representative training

The terminal representative should:

1.   Have a thorough understanding of the underlying principles related to the loading and/or unloading of bulk carriers as described in the BLU Code.

2.   Know how to implement all aspects of the BLU Code.

3.   Understand and manage the ship/shore interface in relation to the operations and limitations of the terminal, its cargo handling equipment and procedures, the planning, control and monitoring of cargoes, relevant properties of the cargoes being handled, berthing/mooring operations and emergency procedures.

The training, assessment and certification of trainees should be carried out by competent persons within the framework of existing training standards and national health and safety legislation.

Annex 5

Hazards

Terminal representatives should be aware that the following hazards may be encountered at the ship/shore interface during the loading and/or unloading of solid bulk cargoes.

Hazard	Possible sources or causes
Fall from heights	• Gangways – typical bulk carrier gangways are unsuitable and unsafe for use at many bulk terminals. • Inadequate fencing of open holds and dangerous edges. • Accessing/egressing ship's holds. • Removing cargo from stairs, ladders and side frames in ship's holds. • Working on top of hatch covers. • Weather conditions and tidal movements.

Moving equipment and vehicles	• Movement of ship loaders and/or unloaders.
	• Movement of mobile plant on terminal:
	   – Payloaders, skid steer loaders, tractors and trailers
	   – Cars, trucks and lorries
	   – Cranes and lift trucks.
	• Operation of mobile plant in ships' holds.
	• Inadequate barriers at terminal edges where mobile plant is operating.

Falling objects	• Lifting and suspension of grabs. • Material falling from grabs. • Personnel on deck walking under the grab. • Lifting and suspension of mobile plant from terminal to ship and from hold to hold. • Lifting and suspension of loading chutes, spouts and arms. • Lifting and suspension of welding and other equipment into hold to carry out damage repairs. • Cargoes falling from ships' hold structures, frames, beams, ledges and ladders. • Personnel lowering or raising equipment in and out of holds with personnel still at work underneath. • Personnel monitoring cargo operations standing too close to where grab is working, and at risk of being struck by grab, or by a breaking grab rope.

Hazard	Possible sources or causes
Slips, trips and falls	• Wet or slippery surface from ice, cargo or oil spillage on ship or terminal. • Badly stowed ropes, hoses and equipment on ship or terminal. • Unmarked obstacles on ship's decks such as manhole covers, securing eyes, safety stanchion sockets. • Climbing and working on and around loose and unstable material in ship's holds. • Personnel handling ship's stores on terminal edge.
Fire or explosion	• Dust created by certain cargoes may constitute an explosion hazard. • Flammable gases emitted by certain bulk cargoes may give rise to a fire or explosion hazard. • Incompatible materials which may react dangerously. • Materials liable to spontaneous combustion. • Bunkering operations. • The use and refuelling of mobile plant in ships' holds. • Smoking and the use of naked flames. • Hot work. • Combination carriers including holds, pumps and pipelines not gas-free when unloading dry bulk, or with slop tanks or wing tanks not inerted.
Hazardous substances	• Dangerous goods. • Cargoes liable to oxidation, oxygen reduction and emission of toxic fumes, particularly when wet. • Cargoes corrosive to skin and eyes, and to ships' structures, particularly when wet. • Cargoes liable to cause oxygen depletion, e.g., metals, vegetable/fruit products, forest products. • Accumulation of dangerous gases in cargo spaces or in adjacent spaces. Failure to observe Confined Space Entry and Atmospheric Testing procedures.
Health hazards due to dust	• Dusty cargoes. • Spillage from loading and/or unloading equipment. • Incorrectly operated and/or maintained loading and/or unloading equipment causing excessive dusting. • Tipping and storage of cargo on terminal.
Strains and sprains	• Manual handling such as shovelling, scraping of cargo in ship's holds. • Operating mobile plant in ship's holds. • Operating grab unloaders and similar equipment. • Handling mooring lines.
Tidal movements and wind conditions	• Gangway becoming unsafe. • Collision between loader and/or unloader and ship's structure or gear. • Failure of unloader and/or loader braking system in high winds, leading to collision with ship. • Runaway of loader and/or unloader and/or transporter cranes in high winds.

Hazard	Possible sources or causes
Berthing and moving ships	• Collision between berthing ship and loader and/or unloader on terminal. • Breaking mooring lines – risk to personnel on ship and terminal from "snap-back" effect. • Passing ships.
Inadequately trained personnel	• Terminal, contractor or temporary employees assigned to work in terminal or on ship without adequate induction or job-specific training. • Ship's personnel unfamiliar with the ship, or with the ship's operations.
Other activities that can occur on and around any terminal	• Failure of persons or organizations controlling different operations to co-operate in ensuring a safe place of work. For example, inadequate control of the activities of personnel, contractors, hauliers, visitors, other ships and port users.

Annex 6

Emergency procedures

Every terminal should always have written procedures for dealing with emergency situations. These should be summarized in the terminal's information and regulation booklet, and should be discussed by the terminal representative and the master of each ship on arrival.

Emergency situations that could occur should be assessed for each terminal, but typically should include:

1.   Fire on board ship.

2.   Fire on the terminal.

3.   Oil spillage and pollution.

4.   Injuries.

The emergency plans should include:

1.   Alarm signals for terminal and for ship.

2.   Notifying the emergency services, including necessary contact points and list of contact numbers.

3.   Location of muster points.

4.   Evacuation procedures.

5.   First aid procedures.

6.   Actions to be taken by both terminal and by ship in the event of:
    .1   Fire or explosion on own ship, on another ship or terminal.
    .2   Oil spillage.
    .3   Ship breaking moorings.
    .4   The necessity to rescue persons from holds, cranes or other plant.
    .5   Other emergency.

7.   Emergency communications procedures.

8.   BC Code Emergency Schedules (EmS) or Material Safety Data Sheets (MSDS) or for any materials possessing chemical hazards which are to be loaded or unloaded.

Uniform method of measurement of the density of bulk cargoes

MSC/Circ.908
(4 June 1999)

4 June 1999

Uniform method of measurement of the density
of bulk cargoes

1   SOLAS regulation XII/10 (Solid bulk cargo density declaration), as adopted by the 1997 SOLAS Conference on Bulk Carrier Safety and interpreted by operative paragraph 4 of resolution MSC.79(70), requires the shipper, prior to loading bulk cargo on a bulk carrier, to declare the density of the cargo which shall be verified by an accredited testing organization.

2   The Maritime Safety Committee, at its seventy-first session (19 to 28 May 1999), recognizing the need for a uniform method of density measurement of the bulk cargoes, adopted the performance specification for the measurement of the density of such cargoes set out at annex.

3   Member Governments are invited to bring this circular to the attention of all parties concerned.

Annex

Performance specification for the measurement
of the density of bulk cargoes*

1   Scope

1.1   This specification may be used to determine the bulk density of bulk cargoes.

1.2   Bulk density is the weight of solids, air and water per unit volume. It includes the moisture content of the cargo and the voids whether filled with air or water.

1.3   The density should be expressed in kilograms per cubic metre (kg/m^3).

2   Apparatus

2.1   This specification provides for the use of a container of known volume and tare weight.

2.2   The container should be sufficiently rigid to prevent deformation or volume changes occurring during the test. Where the material contains lumps, or will not readily flow into corners, the container should be of cylindrical shape and/or of large size in comparison to the size of lumps. Its capacity must be large enough to contain a representative sample of the cargo for which the density is to be determined.

2.3   The internal surfaces of the container should be smooth with any attachments such as handles being fitted to the exterior.

2.4   Weighing should be done using a weighing instrument certificated by an accredited testing organization.

---

* Reference is made to paragraph 1.10 – "Representative test sample" and Appendix D – "Laboratory test procedures, associated apparatus and standards" of the Code of Safe Practice for Solid Bulk Cargoes (BC Code).

3 Procedure

3.1 A sample that is representative of the particle size, compaction and moisture of the material to be loaded on the ship should be selected.

3.2 The container should be filled with a sample of the material so that it is trimmed level with the top of the container. **The material should not be tamped.**

3.3 The weight of the filled container should be measured and the tare weight subtracted to obtain the weight of the sample.

3.4 The density of the sample should be calculated by dividing the weight of the bulk material to be loaded by the volume of the container.

4 Recording results

4.1 The density of the sample should be recorded using the recommended form given in the appendix and made available when requested.

4.2 The result of the density measurement should be signed by a representative of the accredited testing organization.

Appendix

Record of density measurement

The density of the cargo has been measured in accordance with the uniform method of density measurement of bulk cargoes described in the annex to MSC/Circ.908 which refers to SOLAS regulation XII/10.

Cargo (name and relevant reference in the BC Code): . . . .

Shipper (name, address, telephone, etc.): . . . .

Sample origin (stockpile, ship's hold, etc.): . . . .

Date (sampling and density measurement): . . . .

Gross weight (GW) (container plus sample): . . . . .kg

Tare weight (TW) (container): . . . . .kg

Net weight (NW) (sample) (NW = GW – TW): . . . . .kg

Volume (*V*) (container): . . . . m^3

Calculated density (*d*) of the cargo (*d* = NW/*V*): . . . . kg/m^3

**Measurement conducted
by the accredited testing organization**

(Signature, stamp)

Done on . . . .   at . . . .

Lists of solid bulk cargoes for which a fixed gas fire-extinguishing system may be exempted or for which a fixed gas fire-extinguishing system is ineffective

MSC/Circ.1146
(15 December 2004)

MSC/Circ.1146
15 December 2004

Lists of solid bulk cargoes for which a fixed gas fire-extinguishing system may be exempted or for which a fixed gas fire-extinguishing system is ineffective

1   The Maritime Safety Committee, at its sixty-fourth session (5 to 9 December 1994), agreed there was a need to provide Administrations with guidelines regarding the provisions of SOLAS regulation II-2/10 concerning exemptions from the requirements for fire-extinguishing systems.

2   The Committee also agreed to the annexed table 1 providing a list of solid bulk cargoes, for which a fixed gas fire-extinguishing system may be exempted and recommended Member Governments to take into account the information contained in that table when granting exemptions under the provisions of SOLAS regulation II-2/10.7.1.4.

3   The Committee further agreed to the annexed table 2 providing a list of solid bulk cargoes for which a fixed gas fire-extinguishing system is ineffective, and recommended that cargo spaces in a ship engaged in the carriage of cargoes listed in table 2 be provided with a fire-extinguishing system which provides equivalent protection. The Committee also agreed that Administrations should take account of the provisions of SOLAS regulation II-2/19.3.1 when determining suitable requirements for an equivalent fire-extinguishing system.

4   The Maritime Safety Committee, at its seventy-ninth session (1 to 10 December 2004), reviewed the above-mentioned tables as set out in the annex.

5   The annexed tables will be reviewed periodically by the Maritime Safety Committee. Member Governments are requested to provide the Organization, when granting exemptions to ships for the carriage of cargoes not included in table 1, with data on the non-combustibility or fire risk properties of such cargoes. Member Governments are also requested to provide the Organization, when equivalent fire-extinguishing systems are required for the agreed carriage of cargoes not included in table 2, with data on the inefficiency of fixed gas fire-extinguishing systems for such cargoes.

6   The purpose of this circular is to provide guidance to Administrations. It should not, however, be considered as precluding Administrations from their right to grant exemptions for cargoes not included in table 1 or to impose any conditions when granting such exemptions under the provisions of SOLAS regulation II-2/10.7.1.4.

7   This circular supersedes MSC/Circ.671.

Annex

Table 1
List of solid bulk cargoes for which a fixed gas fire-extinguishing system may be exempted

Cargoes including but not limited to those listed in regulation II-2/10

>   Ore
>
>   Coal (COAL and BROWN COAL BRIQUETTES)
>
>   Grain
>
>   Unseasoned timber

Cargoes listed in the Code of Safe Practice for Solid Bulk Cargoes (BC Code), which are not combustible or constitute a low fire risk.

All cargoes not categorized into Group B in the BC Code

The following cargoes categorized into Group B in the BC Code:

ALUMINIUM SMELTING BY-PRODUCTS, UN 3170
ALUMINIUM FERROSILICON POWDER (including briquettes), UN 1395
ALUMINIUM SILICON POWDER, UNCOATED, UN 1398
CALCINED PYRITES (Pyritic ash)
DIRECT REDUCED IRON Briquettes, hot moulded
FERROPHOSPHORUS (including briquettes)
FERROSILICON, with more than 30% but less than 90% silicon (including briquettes), UN 1408
FERROSILICON with 25% to 30% silicon, or 90% or more silicon (including briquettes)
FLUORSPAR (calcium fluoride)
LIME (UNSLAKED)
MAGNESIA (UNSLAKED)
PEAT MOSS
PETROLEUM COKE*
PITCH PRILL
RADIOACTIVE MATERIAL, LOW SPECIFIC ACTIVITY MATERIAL (LSA-I), UN 2912
RADIOACTIVE MATERIAL, SURFACE CONTAMINATED OBJECT(S) (SCO-I), UN 2913
SILICOMANGANESE
SULPHUR (lump and coarse-grained powder), UN 1350
VANADIUM ORE
WOODCHIPS, with moisture content of 15% or more
WOOD PULP PELLETS, with moisture content of 15% or more
ZINC ASHES, UN 1435

Table 2
List of solid bulk cargoes for which a fixed gas fire-extinguishing system is ineffective and for which a fire-extinguishing system giving equivalent protection shall be available

The following cargoes categorized into Group B of the BC Code:

ALUMINIUM NITRATE, UN 1438
AMMONIUM NITRATE, UN 1942
AMMONIUM NITRATE BASED FERTILIZERS UN 2067
AMMONIUM NITRATE BASED FERTILIZERS, UN 2071
BARIUM NITRATE, UN 1446
CALCIUM NITRATE, UN 1454
LEAD NITRATE, UN 1469
MAGNESIUM NITRATE, UN 1474
POTASSIUM NITRATE, UN 1486
SODIUM NITRATE, UN 1498
SODIUM NITRATE AND POTASSIUM NITRATE, MIXTURE, UN 1499

---

* When loaded and transported under the provisions of the BC Code.

Recommendations for entering enclosed spaces aboard ships

Resolution A.864(20)
(adopted on 27 November 1997)

Resolution A.864(20)

adopted on 27 November 1997

Recommendations for entering enclosed spaces aboard ships

THE ASSEMBLY,

RECALLING Article 15(j) of the Convention on the International Maritime Organization concerning the functions of the Assembly in relation to regulations and guidelines concerning maritime safety,

BEING CONCERNED at the continued loss of life resulting from personnel entering shipboard spaces in which the atmosphere is oxygen-depleted, toxic or flammable,

BEING AWARE of the work undertaken in this regard by the International Labour Organization, Governments and segments of the private sector,

NOTING that the Maritime Safety Committee, at its fifty-ninth session, approved appendix F to the Code of Safe Practice for Solid Bulk Cargoes concerning recommendations for entering cargo spaces, tanks, pump-rooms, fuel tanks, cofferdams, duct keels, ballast tanks and similar enclosed spaces,

NOTING FURTHER the decision of the Maritime Safety Committee at its sixty-sixth session to replace appendix F referred to above with the recommendations annexed to this resolution,

HAVING CONSIDERED the recommendation made by the Maritime Safety Committee at its sixty-sixth session,

1.   ADOPTS the Recommendations for entering enclosed spaces aboard ships set out in the annex to the present resolution;

2.   INVITES Governments to bring the annexed Recommendations to the attention of shipowners, ship operators and seafarers, urging them to apply the Recommendations, as appropriate, to all ships;

3.   REQUESTS the Maritime Safety Committee to keep the Recommendations under review and amend them, as necessary.

Annex

Recommendations for entering enclosed spaces aboard ships

Preamble

The object of these recommendations is to encourage the adoption of safety procedures aimed at preventing casualties to ships' personnel entering enclosed spaces where there may be an oxygen-deficient, flammable and/or toxic atmosphere.

Investigations into the circumstances of casualties that have occurred have shown that accidents on board ships are in most cases caused by an insufficient knowledge of, or disregard for, the need to take precautions rather than a lack of guidance.

The following practical recommendations apply to all types of ships and provide guidance to seafarers. It should be noted that on ships where entry into enclosed spaces may be infrequent, for example, on certain passenger ships or small general cargo ships, the dangers may be less apparent, and accordingly there may be a need for increased vigilance.

The recommendations are intended to complement national laws or regulations, accepted standards or particular procedures which may exist for specific trades, ships or types of shipping operations.

It may be impracticable to apply some recommendations to particular situations. In such cases, every endeavour should be made to observe the intent of the recommendations, and attention should be paid to the risks that may be involved.

1 Introduction

The atmosphere in any enclosed space may be deficient in oxygen and/or contain flammable and/or toxic gases or vapours. Such an unsafe atmosphere could also subsequently occur in a space previously found to be safe. Unsafe atmosphere may also be present in spaces adjacent to those spaces where a hazard is known to be present.

2 Definitions

2.1 *Enclosed space* means a space which has any of the following characteristics:

.1 limited openings for entry and exit;

.2 unfavourable natural ventilation; and

.3 is not designed for continuous worker occupancy,

and includes, but is not limited to, cargo spaces, double bottoms, fuel tanks, ballast tanks, pump-rooms, compressor rooms, cofferdams, void spaces, duct keels, inter-barrier spaces, engine crankcases and sewage tanks.

2.2 *Competent person* means a person with sufficient theoretical knowledge and practical experience to make an informed assessment of the likelihood of a dangerous atmosphere being present or subsequently arising in the space.

2.3 *Responsible person* means a person authorized to permit entry into an enclosed space and having sufficient knowledge of the procedures to be followed.

3 Assessment of risk

3.1 In order to ensure safety, a competent person should always make a preliminary assessment of any potential hazards in the space to be entered, taking into account previous cargo carried, ventilation of the space, coating of the space and other relevant factors. The competent person's preliminary assessment should determine the potential for the presence of an oxygen-deficient, flammable or toxic atmosphere.

3.2 The procedures to be followed for testing the atmosphere in the space and for entry should be decided on the basis of the preliminary assessment. These will depend on whether the preliminary assessment shows that:

.1 there is minimal risk to the health or life of personnel entering the space;

.2 there is no immediate risk to health or life but a risk could arise during the course of work in the space; and

.3 a risk to health or life is identified.

3.3 Where the preliminary assessment indicates minimal risk to health or life or potential for a risk to arise during the course of work in the space, the precautions described in 4, 5, 6 and 7 should be followed as appropriate.

3.4 Where the preliminary assessment identifies risk to life or health, if entry is to be made, the additional precautions specified in section 8 should also be followed.

4 Authorization of entry

4.1 No person should open or enter an enclosed space unless authorized by the master or nominated responsible person and unless the appropriate safety procedures laid down for the particular ship have been followed.

4.2 Entry into enclosed spaces should be planned and the use of an entry permit system, which may include the use of a checklist, is recommended. An Enclosed Space Entry Permit should be issued by the master or nominated responsible person, and completed by a person who enters the space prior to entry. An example of the Enclosed Space Entry Permit is provided in the appendix.

5 General precautions

5.1 The master or responsible person should determine that it is safe to enter an enclosed space by ensuring:

.1 that potential hazards have been identified in the assessment and as far as possible isolated or made safe;

.2 that the space has been thoroughly ventilated by natural or mechanical means to remove any toxic or flammable gases, and to ensure an adequate level of oxygen throughout the space;

.3 that the atmosphere of the space has been tested as appropriate with properly calibrated instruments to ascertain acceptable levels of oxygen and acceptable levels of flammable or toxic vapours;

.4 that the space has been secured for entry and properly illuminated;

.5 that a suitable system of communication between all parties for use during entry has been agreed and tested;

.6 that an attendant has been instructed to remain at the entrance to the space whilst it is occupied;

.7 that rescue and resuscitation equipment has been positioned ready for use at the entrance to the space, and that rescue arrangements have been agreed;

.8 that personnel are properly clothed and equipped for the entry and subsequent tasks; and

.9 that a permit has been issued authorizing entry.

The precautions in .6 and .7 may not apply to every situation described in this section. The person authorizing entry should determine whether an attendant and the positioning of rescue equipment at the entrance to the space is necessary.

5.2 Only trained personnel should be assigned the duties of entering, functioning as attendants, or functioning as members of rescue teams. Ships' crews should be drilled periodically in rescue and first aid.

5.3 All equipment used in connection with entry should be in good working condition and inspected prior to use.

6 Testing the atmosphere

6.1 Appropriate testing of the atmosphere of a space should be carried out with properly calibrated equipment by persons trained in the use of the equipment. The manufacturers' instructions should be strictly followed. Testing should be carried out before any person enters the space, and at regular intervals thereafter until all work is completed. Where appropriate, the testing of the space should be carried out at as many different levels as is necessary to obtain a representative sample of the atmosphere in the space.

6.2 For entry purposes, steady readings of the following should be obtained:

.1 21% oxygen by volume by oxygen content meter; and

.2 not more than 1% of lower flammable limit (LFL) on a suitably sensitive combustible gas indicator, where the preliminary assessment has determined that there is potential for flammable gases or vapours.

If these conditions cannot be met, additional ventilation should be applied to the space and re-testing should be conducted after a suitable interval. Any gas testing should be carried out with ventilation to the enclosed space stopped, in order to obtain accurate readings.

6.3 Where the preliminary assessment has determined that there is potential for the presence of toxic gases and vapours, appropriate testing should be carried out using fixed or portable gas- or vapour-detection equipment. The readings obtained by this equipment should be below the occupational exposure limits for the toxic gases or vapours given in accepted national or international standards. It should be noted that testing for flammability does not provide a suitable means of measuring for toxicity, nor vice versa.

6.4 It should be emphasized that pockets of gas or oxygen-deficient areas can exist, and should always be suspected, even when an enclosed space has been satisfactorily tested as being suitable for entry.

7 Precautions during entry

7.1 The atmosphere should be tested frequently whilst the space is occupied, and persons should be instructed to leave the space should there be a deterioration in the conditions.

7.2 Ventilation should continue during the period that the space is occupied and during temporary breaks. Before re-entry after a break, the atmosphere should be re-tested. In the event of failure of the ventilation system, any persons in the space should leave immediately.

7.3 In the event of an emergency, under no circumstances should the attending crew member enter the space before help has arrived and the situation has been evaluated to ensure the safety of those entering the space to undertake rescue operations.

8 Additional precautions for entry into a space where the atmosphere is known or suspected to be unsafe

8.1 If the atmosphere in an enclosed space is suspected or known to be unsafe, the space should only be entered when no practical alternative exists. Entry should only be made for further testing, essential operation, safety of life or safety of a ship. The number of persons entering the space should be the minimum compatible with the work to be performed.

8.2 Suitable breathing apparatus, e.g., of the air-line or self-contained type, should always be worn, and only personnel trained in its use should be allowed to enter the space. Air-purifying respirators should not be used as they do not provide a supply of clean air from a source independent of the atmosphere within the space.

8.3 The precautions specified in 5 should also be followed, as appropriate.

8.4 Rescue harnesses should be worn and, unless impractical, lifelines should be used.

8.5 Appropriate protective clothing should be worn particularly where there is any risk of toxic substances or chemicals coming into contact with the skin or eyes of those entering the space.

8.6 The advice in 7.3 concerning emergency rescue operations is particularly relevant in this context.

9 Hazards related to specific types of cargo

9.1 Dangerous goods in packaged form

9.1.1 The atmosphere of any space containing dangerous goods may put at risk the health or life of any person entering it. Dangers may include flammable, toxic or corrosive gases or vapours that displace oxygen, residues on packages and spilled material. The same hazards may be present in spaces adjacent to the cargo spaces. Information on the hazards of specific substances is contained in the IMDG Code, the Emergency Procedures for Ships Carrying Dangerous Goods (EmS) and Materials Safety Data Sheets (MSDS). If there is evidence or suspicion that leakage of dangerous substances has occurred, the precautions specified in 8 should be followed.

9.1.2 Personnel required to deal with spillages or to remove defective or damaged packages should be appropriately trained and wear suitable breathing apparatus and appropriate protective clothing.

9.2 Bulk liquid

The tanker industry has produced extensive advice to operators and crews of ships engaged in the bulk carriage of oil, chemicals and liquefied gases, in the form of specialist international safety guides. Information in the guides on enclosed space entry amplifies these recommendations and should be used as the basis for preparing entry plans.

9.3 Solid bulk

On ships carrying solid bulk cargoes, dangerous atmospheres may develop in cargo spaces and adjacent spaces. The dangers may include flammability, toxicity, oxygen depletion or self-heating, which should be identified in shipping documentation. For additional information, reference should be made to the Code of Safe Practice for Solid Bulk Cargoes.

9.4 Oxygen-depleting cargoes and materials

A prominent risk with such cargoes is oxygen depletion due to the inherent form of the cargo, for example, self-heating, oxidation of metals and ores or decomposition of vegetable oils, animal fats, grain and other organic materials or their residues. The materials listed below are known to be capable of causing oxygen depletion. However, the list is not exhaustive. Oxygen depletion may also be caused by other materials of vegetable or animal origin, by flammable or spontaneously combustible materials, and by materials with a high metal content:

.1 grain, grain products and residues from grain processing (such as bran, crushed grain, crushed malt or meal), hops, malt husks and spent malt;

.2 oilseeds as well as products and residues from oilseeds (such as seed expellers, seed cake, oil cake and meal);

.3 copra;

.4 wood in such forms as packaged timber, roundwood, logs, pulpwood, props (pit props and other propwood), woodchips, woodshavings, woodpulp pellets and sawdust;

.5 jute, hemp, flax, sisal, kapok, cotton and other vegetable fibres (such as esparto grass/ Spanish grass, hay, straw, bhusa), empty bags, cotton waste, animal fibres, animal and vegetable fabric, wool waste and rags;

.6 fishmeal and fishscrap;

.7 guano;

.8 sulphidic ores and ore concentrates;

.9 charcoal, coal and coal products;

.10 direct reduced iron (DRI)

.11 dry ice;

.12 metal wastes and chips, iron swarf, steel and other turnings, borings, drillings, shavings, filings and cuttings; and

.13 scrap metal.

9.5 Fumigation

When a ship is fumigated, the detailed recommendations contained in the Recommendations on the safe use of pesticides in ships* should be followed. Spaces adjacent to fumigated spaces should be treated as if fumigated.

10 Conclusion

Failure to observe simple procedures can lead to people being unexpectedly overcome when entering enclosed spaces. Observance of the principles outlined above will form a reliable basis for assessing risks in such spaces and for taking necessary precautions.

---

* Refer to the Recommendations on safe use of pesticides in ships, approved by the Maritime Safety Committee of the Organization by circular MSC/Circ.612, as amended by MSC/Circ.689 and MSC/Circ.746.

Appendix

Example of an Enclosed Space Entry Permit

This permit relates to entry into any enclosed space and should be completed by the master or responsible officer and by the person entering the space or authorized team leader.

General

Location/name of enclosed space . . . .

Reason for entry . . . .

This permit is valid   from: . . . . hrs   Date . . . .

                             to: . . . . hrs   Date . . . .
                                    (See note 1)

Section 1 – Pre-entry preparation

(To be checked by the master or nominated responsible person)   Yes   No

- Has the space been thoroughly ventilated?   ☐   ☐

- Has the space been segregated by blanking off or isolating all connecting pipelines or valves and electrical power/equipment?   ☐   ☐

- Has the space been cleaned where necessary?   ☐   ☐

- Has the space been tested and found safe for entry? (See note 2)   ☐   ☐

- Pre-entry atmosphere test readings:

  – oxygen . . . . % vol (21%)   By: . . . .
  – hydrocarbon . . . . % LFL (less than 1%)
  – toxic gases . . . . ppm (specific gas and PEL)   Time: . . . .
                                 (See note 3)

- Have arrangements been made for frequent atmosphere checks to be made while the space is occupied and after work breaks?   ☐   ☐

- Have arrangements been made for the space to be continuously ventilated throughout the period of occupation and during work breaks?   ☐   ☐

- Are access and illumination adequate?   ☐   ☐

- Is rescue and resuscitation equipment available for immediate use by the entrance to the space?   ☐   ☐

- Has a responsible person been designated to be in constant attendance at the entrance to the space?   ☐   ☐

Section 1 – Pre-entry preparation *(continued)*

(To be checked by the master or nominated responsible person)   Yes   No

- Has the officer of the watch (bridge, engine-room, cargo control room) been advised of the planned entry? ☐ ☐

- Has a system of communication between all parties been tested and emergency signals agreed? ☐ ☐

- Are emergency and evacuation procedures established and understood by all personnel involved with the enclosed space entry? ☐ ☐

- Is all equipment used in good working condition and inspected prior to entry? ☐ ☐

- Are personnel properly clothed and equipped? ☐ ☐

Section 2 – Pre-entry checks

(To be checked by the person entering the space or authorized team leader)   Yes   No

- I have received instructions or permission from the master or nominated responsible person to enter the enclosed space ☐ ☐

- Section 1 of this permit has been satisfactorily completed by the master or nominated responsible person ☐ ☐

- I have agreed and understand the communication procedures ☐ ☐

- I have agreed upon a reporting interval of . . . . minutes ☐ ☐

- Emergency and evacuation procedures have been agreed and are understood ☐ ☐

- **I am aware that the space must be vacated immediately in the event of ventilation failure or if atmosphere tests show a change from agreed safe criteria** ☐ ☐

Section 3 – Breathing apparatus and other equipment

(To be checked jointly by the master or nominated responsible person and the person who is to enter the space)   Yes   No

- Those entering the space are familiar with the breathing apparatus to be used ☐ ☐

- The breathing apparatus has been tested as follows:
  - gauge and capacity of air supply . . . .
  - low pressure audible alarm . . . .
  - face mask – under positive pressure and not leaking . . . .

- The means of communication has been tested and emergency signals agreed ☐ ☐

- All personnel entering the space have been provided with rescue harnesses and, where practicable, lifelines ☐ ☐

Signed upon completion of sections 1, 2 and 3 by:

Master or nominated responsible person. . . . . Date. . . . . Time . . . .

Responsible person supervising entry. . . . . Date. . . . . Time . . . .

Person entering the space or
authorized team leader. . . . . Date. . . . . Time . . . .

Section 4 – Personnel entry
(To be completed by the responsible person supervising entry)

Names	Time in	Time out
. . . .	. . . .	. . . .
. . . .	. . . .	. . . .
. . . .	. . . .	. . . .
. . . .	. . . .	. . . .

Section 5 – Completion of job
(To be completed by the responsible person supervising entry)

- Job completed   Date . . . . Time . . . .

- Space secured against entry   Date . . . . Time . . . .

- The officer of the watch has been duly informed   Date . . . . Time . . . .

Signed upon completion of sections 4 and 5 by:

Responsible person supervising entry . . . . Date . . . . Time . . . .

THIS PERMIT IS RENDERED INVALID SHOULD VENTILATION OF THE SPACE STOP OR IF
ANY OF THE CONDITIONS NOTED IN THE CHECKLIST CHANGE

Notes:

1   The permit should contain a clear indication as to its maximum period of validity.

2   In order to obtain a representative cross-section of the space's atmosphere, samples should be taken from several levels and through as many openings as possible. Ventilation should be stopped for about 10 minutes before the pre-entry atmosphere tests are taken.

3   Tests for specific toxic contaminants, such as benzene or hydrogen sulphide, should be undertaken depending on the nature of the previous contents of the space.

RECOMMENDED POSTER FOR DISPLAY ON BOARD SHIPS
IN ACCOMMODATION OR OTHER PLACES, AS APPROPRIATE
(reduced format)

Enclosed spaces can kill!

Do not ignore or forget it –

you may end up like this . . . . . .

You should NEVER enter any enclosed space unless an Enclosed Space Entry Permit has been issued

Recommendations on the safe use of pesticides in ships applicable to the fumigation of cargo holds

MSC.1/Circ.1264
(27 May 2008)

MSC.1/Circ.1264
27 May 2008

Recommendations on the safe use of pesticides in ships
applicable to the fumigation of cargo holds

1   The Maritime Safety Committee, at its sixty-second session (24 to 28 May 1993), approved the Recommendations on the safe use of pesticides in ships (MSC/Circ.612), proposed by the Sub-Committee on Containers and Cargoes at its thirty-second session.

2   The Maritime Safety Committee, at its eighty-fourth session (7 to 16 May 2008), approved the Recommendations on the safe use of pesticides in ships applicable to the fumigation of cargo holds, which apply to carriage of solid bulk cargoes including grain in pursuance of the requirement of SOLAS regulation VI/4, proposed by the Sub-Committee on Dangerous Goods, Solid Cargoes and Containers at its twelfth session, set out in the annex.

3   The Committee agreed that the Recommendations should not apply to the carriage of fresh food produce under controlled atmosphere.

4   Member Governments are invited to bring the Recommendations to the attention of competent authorities, mariners, fumigators, fumigant and pesticide manufacturers and others concerned.

5   The present circular supersedes MSC/Circ.612, as amended by MSC/Circ.689 and MSC/Circ.746 with regard to the fumigation of cargo holds.

Annex

Recommendations on the safe use of pesticides in ships
applicable to the fumigation of cargo holds

1   Introduction

1.1   Insect and mite pests of plant and animal products may be carried into the cargo holds with goods (introduced infestation); they may move from one kind of product to another (cross-infestation) and may remain to attack subsequent cargoes (residual infestation). Their control may be required to comply with phytosanitary requirements to prevent spread of pests and for commercial reasons to prevent infestation and contamination of, or damage to, cargoes of human and animal food both raw and processed materials. Although fumigants may be used to kill rodent pests, the control of rodents on board ships is dealt with separately. In severe cases of infestation of bulk cargoes such as cereals, excessive heating may occur.

1.2   The following sections provide guidance to shipmasters in the use of pesticides* with a view to safety of personnel. They cover pesticides used for the control of insect† and rodent pests in empty and loaded cargo holds.

---

* The word *pesticide* as used throughout the text means fumigants. Examples of some commonly used pesticides are listed in appendix 1.
† The word *insect* as used throughout the text includes mites.

---

2 Prevention of infestation

2.1 Maintenance and sanitation

2.1.1 Ship cargo holds, tanktop ceilings and other parts of the ship should be kept in a good state of repair to avoid infestation. Many ports of the world have rules and by-laws dealing specifically with the maintenance of ships intended to carry grain cargoes; for example, boards and ceilings should be completely grain-tight.

2.1.2 Cleanliness, or good housekeeping, is as important a means of controlling pests on a ship as it is in a home, warehouse, mill or factory. Since insect pests on ships become established and multiply in debris, much can be done to prevent their increase by simple, thorough cleaning. Box beams and stiffeners, for example, become filled with debris during discharge of cargo and unless kept clean can become a source of heavy infestation. It is important to remove thoroughly all cargo residue from deckhead frames and longitudinal deck girders at the time of discharge, preferably when the cargo level is suitable for convenient cleaning. Where available, industrial vacuum cleaners are of value for the cleaning of cargo holds and fittings.

2.1.3 The material collected during cleaning should be disposed of, or treated, immediately so that the insects cannot escape and spread to other parts of the ship or elsewhere. In port it may be burnt or treated with a pesticide, but in many countries such material may only be landed under phytosanitary supervision. If any part of the ship is being fumigated the material may be left exposed to the gas.

2.2 Main sites of infestation

2.2.1 *Tanktop ceiling:* If, as often happens, cracks appear between the ceiling boards, food material may be forced down into the underlying space and serve as a focus of infestation for an indefinite period. Insects bred in this space can readily move out to attack food cargoes and establish their progeny in them.

2.2.2 *'Tween-deck centre lines, wooden feeders and bins* are often left in place for several voyages and because of their construction are a frequent source of infestation. After unloading a grain cargo, burlap and battens covering the narrow spaces between the planks should be removed and discarded before the holds are cleaned or washed down. These coverings should be replaced by new material in preparation for the next cargo.

2.2.3 *Transverse beams and longitudinal deck girders* which support the decks and hatch openings may have an L-shaped angle-bar construction. Such girders provide ledges where grain may lodge when bulk cargoes are unloaded. The ledges are often in inaccessible places overlooked during cleaning operations.

2.2.4 *Insulated bulkheads near engine-rooms:* When the hold side of an engine-room bulkhead is insulated with a wooden sheathing, the airspace and the cracks between the boards often become filled with grain and other material. Sometimes the airspace is filled with insulating material which may become heavily infested and serves as a place for insect breeding. Temporary wooden bulkheads also provide an ideal place for insect breeding, especially under moist conditions, such as when green lumber is used.

2.2.5 *Cargo battens:* The crevices at the sparring cleats are ideal places for material to lodge and for insects to hide.

2.2.6 *Bilges:* Insects in accumulations of food material are often found in these spaces.

2.2.7 *Electrical conduit casings:* Sometimes the sheet-metal covering is damaged by general cargo and when bulk grain is loaded later, the casings may become completely filled. This residual grain has often been found to be heavily infested. Casings that are damaged should be repaired immediately or, where possible, they should be replaced with steel strapping, which can be cleaned more easily.

2.2.8   Other places where material accumulates and where insects breed and hide include:

The area underneath burlap, which is used to cover limber boards and sometimes to cover tanktop ceilings.

Boxing around pipes, especially if it is broken.

Corners, where old cereal material is often found.

Crevices at plate landings, frames and chocks.

Wooden coverings of manholes or wells leading to double-bottom tanks or other places.

Cracks in the wooden ceiling protecting the propeller shaft tunnel.

Beneath rusty scale and old paint on the inside of hull plates.

Shifting boards.

Dunnage material, empty bags and used separation cloths.

Inside lockers.

3   Chemical control of insect infestation

3.1   Methods of chemical disinfestation

3.1.1   *Types of pesticides and methods of insect control*

3.1.1.1   To avoid insect populations becoming firmly established in cargo holds and other parts of a ship, it is necessary to use some form of chemical toxicant for control. The materials available may be divided conveniently into two classes: contact insecticides and fumigants. The choice of agent and method of application depend on the type of commodity, the extent and location of the infestation, the importance and habits of the insects found, and the climatic and other conditions. Recommended treatments are altered or modified from time to time in accordance with new developments.

3.1.1.2   The success of chemical treatments does not lie wholly in the pesticidal activity of the agents used. In addition, an appreciation of the requirements and limitations of the different available methods is required. Crew members can carry out small scale or "spot" treatments if they adhere to the manufacturer's instructions and take care to cover the whole area of infestation. However, extensive or hazardous treatments including fumigation and spraying near human and animal food should be placed in the hands of professional operators, who should inform the master of the identity of the active ingredients used, the hazards involved and the precautions to be taken.

3.1.2   *Fumigants*

3.1.2.1   Fumigants act in a gaseous phase even though they may be applied as solid or liquid formulations from which the gas arises. Effective and safe use requires that the space being treated be rendered gastight for the period of exposure, which may vary from a few hours to several days, depending on the fumigant type and concentration used, the pests, the commodities treated and the temperature. Additional information is provided on two of the most widely used fumigants, methyl bromide and phosphine, in appendix 1.

3.1.2.2   Since fumigant gases are poisonous to humans and require special equipment and skills in application, they should be used by specialists and not by the ship's crew.

3.1.2.3   Evacuation of the space under gas treatment is mandatory and in some cases it will be necessary for the whole ship to be evacuated (see 3.3.1 and 3.3.2 below).

3.1.2.4   A "fumigator-in-charge" should be designated by the fumigation company, government agency or appropriate authority. He should be able to provide documentation to the master proving his competence and authorization. The master should be provided with written instructions by the fumigator-in-charge on the type of fumigant used, the hazards to human health involved and the precautions to be taken, and, in view of the highly toxic nature of all commonly used fumigants, these should be followed carefully. Such instructions should be written in a language readily understood by the master or his representative.

3.2   Disinfestation of empty cargo holds

3.2.1   An empty cargo hold may be fumigated. Examples of some commonly used pesticides are listed in appendix 1. (For precautions before, during and after fumigation of cargo holds see 3.3 below.)

3.3   Disinfestation of cargoes and surrounds

3.3.1   *Fumigation with aeration (ventilation) in port*

3.3.1.1   Fumigation and aeration (ventilation) of empty cargo holds should always be carried out in port (alongside or at anchorage). Ships should not be permitted to leave port until gas-free certification has been received from the fumigator-in-charge.

3.3.1.2   Prior to the application of fumigants to cargo holds, the crew should be landed and remain ashore until the ship is certified "gas-free", in writing, by the fumigator-in-charge or other authorized person. During this period a watchman should be posted to prevent unauthorized boarding or entry, and warning signs should be prominently displayed at gangways and at entrances to accommodation. A specimen of such a warning sign is given in appendix 2.

3.3.1.3   The fumigator-in-charge should be retained throughout the fumigation period and until such time as the ship is declared gas-free.

3.3.1.4   At the end of the fumigation period the fumigator will take the necessary action to ensure that the fumigant is dispersed. If crew members are required to assist in such actions, for example in opening hatches, they should be provided with adequate respiratory protection and adhere strictly to instructions given by the fumigator-in-charge.

3.3.1.5   The fumigator-in-charge should notify the master in writing of any spaces determined to be safe for re-occupancy by essential crew members prior to the aeration of the ship.

3.3.1.6   In such circumstances the fumigator-in-charge should monitor, throughout the fumigation and aeration periods, spaces to which personnel have been permitted to return. Should the concentration in any such area exceed the occupational exposure limit values set by the flag State regulations, crew members should be evacuated from the area until measurements show re-occupancy to be safe.

3.3.1.7   No unauthorized persons should be allowed on board until all parts of the ship have been determined gas-free, warning signs removed and clearance certificates issued by the fumigator-in-charge.

3.3.1.8   Clearance certificates should only be issued when tests show that all residual fumigant has been dispersed from empty cargo holds and adjacent working spaces and any residual fumigant material has been removed.

3.3.1.9   Entry into a space under fumigation should never take place except in the event of an extreme emergency. If entry is imperative the fumigator-in-charge and at least one other person should enter, each wearing adequate protective equipment appropriate for the fumigant used and a safety harness and lifeline. Each lifeline should be tended by a person outside the space, who should be similarly equipped.

3.3.1.10   If a clearance certificate cannot be issued after the fumigation of cargo in port, the provisions of 3.3.2 should apply.

3.3.2   *Fumigation continued in transit*

3.3.2.1   Fumigation in transit should only be carried out at the discretion of the master. This should be clearly understood by owners, charterers, and all other parties involved when considering the transport of cargoes that may be infested. Due consideration should be taken of this when assessing the options of fumigation. The master should be aware of the regulations of the flag State Administration with regard to in-transit fumigation. The application of the process should be with the agreement of the port State Administration. The process may be considered under two headings:

.1   fumigation in which treatment is intentionally continued in a sealed space during a voyage and in which no aeration has taken place before sailing; and

.2   in-port cargo fumigation where some aeration is carried out before sailing, but where a clearance certificate for the cargo hold(s) cannot be issued because of residual gas and the cargo hold(s) has been re-sealed before sailing.

3.3.2.2   Before a decision on sailing with a fumigated cargo hold(s) is made it should be taken into account that, due to operational conditions, the circumstances outlined in 3.3.2.1.2 may arise unintentionally, e.g., a ship may be required to sail at a time earlier than anticipated when the fumigation was started. In such circumstances the potential hazards may be as great as with a planned in-transit fumigation and all the precautions in the following paragraphs should be observed.

3.3.2.3   Before a decision is made as to whether a fumigation treatment planned to be commenced in port and continued at sea should be carried out, special precautions are necessary. These include the following:

.1   at least two members of the crew (including one officer) who have received appropriate training (see 3.3.2.6) should be designated as the trained representatives of the master responsible for ensuring that safe conditions in accommodation, engine-room and other working spaces are maintained after the fumigator-in-charge has handed over that responsibility to the master (see 3.3.2.12); and

.2   the trained representatives of the master should brief the crew before a fumigation takes place and satisfy the fumigator-in-charge that this has been done.

3.3.2.4   Empty cargo holds are to be inspected and/or tested for leakage with instruments so that proper sealing can be done before or after loading. The fumigator-in-charge, accompanied by a trained representative of the master or a competent person, should determine whether the cargo holds to be treated are or can be made sufficiently gastight to prevent leakage of the fumigant to the accommodation, engine-rooms and other working spaces in the ship. Special attention should be paid to potential problem areas such as bilge and cargo line systems. On completion of such inspection and/or test, the fumigator-in-charge should supply to the master for his retention a signed statement that the inspection and/or test has been performed, what provisions have been made and that the cargo holds are or can be made satisfactory for fumigation. Whenever a cargo hold is found not to be sufficiently gastight, the fumigator-in-charge should issue a signed statement to the master and the other parties involved.

3.3.2.5   Accommodation, engine-rooms, areas designated for use in navigation of the ship, frequently visited working areas and stores, such as the forecastle head spaces, adjacent to cargo holds being subject to fumigation in transit should be treated in accordance with the provisions of 3.3.2.13. Special attention should be paid to gas concentration safety checks in problem areas referred to in 3.3.2.4.

3.3.2.6   The trained representatives of the master designated in 3.3.2.3 should be provided and be familiar with:

.1   the information in the relevant Safety Data Sheet; and

.2   the instructions for use, e.g., on the fumigant label or package itself, such as the recommendations of the fumigant manufacturer concerning methods of detection of the fumigant in air, its behaviour and hazardous properties, symptoms of poisoning, relevant first aid and special medical treatment and emergency procedures.

3.3.2.7 The ship should carry:

.1 gas-detection equipment and adequate fresh supplies of service items for the fumigant(s) concerned as required by 3.3.2.12, together with instructions for its use and the occupational exposure limit values set by the flag State regulations for safe working conditions;

.2 instructions on disposal of residual fumigant material;

.3 at least four sets of adequate respiratory protective equipment; and

.4 a copy of the latest version of the *Medical First Aid Guide for Use in Accidents Involving Dangerous Goods (MFAG)*, including appropriate medicines and medical equipment.

3.3.2.8 The fumigator-in-charge should notify the master in writing of the spaces containing the cargo to be fumigated and also of any other spaces that are considered unsafe to enter during the fumigation. During the application of the fumigant the fumigator-in-charge should ensure that the surrounding areas are checked for safety.

3.3.2.9 If cargo holds are to be fumigated in transit:

.1 After application of the fumigant, an initial check should be made by the fumigator-in-charge together with trained representatives of the master for any leak which, if detected, should be effectively sealed. When the master is satisfied that all precautions detailed in 3.3.2.1 to 3.3.2.12 have been fulfilled (refer to model checklist in appendix 3) then the vessel may sail. Otherwise, provisions outlined in 3.3.2.9.2 or 3.3.2.9.3 are to be followed.

If the provisions of 3.3.2.9.1 are not satisfied,

either:

.2 After application of fumigants, the ship should be delayed in port alongside at a suitable berth or at anchorage for such a period as to allow the gas in the fumigated cargo holds to reach sufficiently high concentrations to detect any possible leakage. Special attention should be paid to those cases where fumigants in a solid or liquid form have been applied which may require a long period (normally from 4 to 7 days unless a recirculation or similar distribution system is used) to reach such a high concentration that leakages can be detected. If leakages are detected, the ship should not sail until the source(s) of such leakages is (are) determined and eliminated. After ascertaining that the ship is in a safe condition to sail, i.e. no gas leakages are present, the fumigator-in-charge should furnish the master with a written statement that:

.2.1 the gas in the cargo hold(s) has reached sufficiently high concentrations to detect any possible leakages;

.2.2 spaces adjacent to the treated cargo hold(s) have been checked and found gas-free; and

.2.3 the ship's representative is fully conversant with the use of the gas-detection equipment provided.

or:

.3 After application of the fumigants and immediately after the sailing of the ship, the fumigator-in-charge should remain on board for such a period as to allow the gas in the fumigated cargo hold or spaces to reach sufficiently high concentrations to detect any possible leakage, or until the fumigated cargo is discharged (see 3.3.2.20), whichever is the shorter, to check and rectify any gas leakages. Prior to his leaving the ship, he should ascertain that the ship is in a safe condition, i.e. no gas leakages are present, and he should furnish the master with a written statement to the effect that the provisions of 3.3.2.9.2.1, 3.3.2.9.2.2 and 3.3.2.9.2.3 have been carried out.

3.3.2.10 On application of the fumigant, the fumigator-in-charge should post warning signs at all entrances to places notified to the master as in 3.3.2.8. These warning signs should indicate the identity of the fumigant and the date and time of fumigation. A specimen of such a warning sign is given in appendix 2.

3.3.2.11 At an appropriate time after application of the fumigant, the fumigator-in-charge, accompanied by a representative of the master, should check that accommodation, engine-rooms and other working spaces remain free of harmful concentrations of gas.

3.3.2.12 Upon discharging his agreed responsibilities, the fumigator-in-charge should formally hand over to the master in writing responsibility for maintaining safe conditions in all occupied spaces. The fumigator-in-charge should ensure that gas-detection and respiratory protection equipment carried on the ship is in good order, and that adequate fresh supplies of consumable items are available to allow sampling as required in 3.3.2.13.

3.3.2.13 Gas concentration safety checks at all appropriate locations, which should at least include the spaces indicated in 3.3.2.5, should be continued throughout the voyage at least at eight-hour intervals or more frequently if so advised by the fumigator-in-charge. These readings should be recorded in the ship's log-book.

3.3.2.14 Except in extreme emergency, cargo holds sealed for fumigation in transit should never be opened at sea or entered. If entry is imperative, at least two persons should enter, wearing adequate protection equipment and a safety harness and lifeline tended by a person outside the space, similarly equipped with protective, self-contained breathing apparatus.

3.3.2.15 If it is essential to ventilate a cargo hold or holds, every effort should be made to prevent a fumigant from accumulating in accommodation or working areas. Those spaces should be carefully checked to that effect. If the gas concentration in those areas at any time exceeds the occupational exposure limit values set by the flag State regulations, they should be evacuated and the cargo hold or cargo holds should be re-sealed. If a cargo hold is re-sealed after ventilation it should not be assumed that it is completely clear of gas and tests should be made and appropriate precautions taken before entering.

3.3.2.16 Prior to the arrival of the ship, generally not less than 24 hours in advance, the master should inform the appropriate authorities of the country of destination and ports of call that fumigation in transit is being carried out. The information should include the type of fumigant used, the date of fumigation, the cargo holds which have been fumigated, and whether ventilation has commenced. Upon arrival at the port of discharge, the master should also provide information as required in 3.3.2.6.2 and 3.3.2.7.2.

3.3.2.17 On arrival at the port of discharge the requirements of receiving countries regarding handling of fumigated cargoes should be established. Before entry of fumigated cargo holds, trained personnel from a fumigation company or other authorized persons, wearing respiratory protection, should carry out careful monitoring of the spaces to ensure the safety of personnel. The monitored values should be recorded in the ship's log-book. In case of need or emergency the master may commence ventilation of the fumigated cargo holds under the conditions of 3.3.2.15, having due regard for the safety of personnel on board. If this operation is to be done at sea, the master should evaluate weather and sea conditions before proceeding.

3.3.2.18 Only mechanical unloading that does not necessitate entry of personnel into the cargo holds of such fumigated cargoes should be undertaken. However, when the presence of personnel in cargo holds is necessary for the handling and operation of unloading equipment, continuous monitoring of the fumigated spaces should be carried out to ensure the safety of the personnel involved. When necessary, these personnel should be equipped with adequate respiratory protection.

3.3.2.19 During the final stages of discharge, when it becomes necessary for personnel to enter the cargo holds, such entry should only be permitted subsequent to verification that such cargo holds are gas-free.

3.3.2.20 Upon completion of discharge and when the ship is found free of fumigants and certified as such, all warning signs should be removed. Any action in this respect should be recorded in the ship's log-book.

4 Regulations for the use of pesticides

4.1 National and international controls on pesticide usage

4.1.1 In many countries the sale and use of pesticides are regulated by governments to ensure safety in application and prevention of contamination of foodstuffs. Among the factors taken into account in such regulations are the recommendations made by international organizations such as FAO and WHO, especially in regard to maximum limits of pesticide residues in food and foodstuffs.

4.1.2 Examples of some commonly used pesticides are listed in appendix 1. Pesticides should be used strictly in accordance with the manufacturer's instructions as given on the label or package itself. National regulations and requirements vary from one country to another; therefore particular pesticides which may be used for treatment of cargo holds and accommodation in ships may be limited by the regulations and requirements of:

.1 the country where the cargo is loaded or treated;

.2 the country of destination of the cargo, especially in regard to pesticide residues in foodstuffs; and

.3 flag State of the ship.

4.1.3 Ships' masters should ensure that they have the necessary knowledge of the above regulations and requirements.

5 Safety precautions – general

5.1 Fumigation

5.1.1 Ship's personnel should not handle fumigants and such operations should be carried out only by qualified operators. Personnel allowed to remain in the vicinity of a fumigation operation for a particular purpose should follow the instructions of the fumigator-in-charge implicitly.

5.1.2 Aeration of treated cargo holds should be completed and a clearance certificate issued as in 3.3.1.8 or 3.3.1.10 before personnel are permitted to enter.

5.2 Exposure to pesticides resulting in illness

5.2.1 In the case of exposure to pesticides and subsequent illness, medical advice should be sought immediately. Information on poisoning may be found in the *Medical First Aid Guide for Use in Accidents Involving Dangerous Goods (MFAG)* or on the package (manufacturer's instructions and safety precautions on the label or the package itself).

Appendix 1

Fumigants suitable for shipboard use

The materials listed should be used strictly in accordance with the manufacturer's instructions and safety precautions given on the label or package itself, especially in respect of flammability, and with regard to any further limitations applied by the law of the country of loading, destination or flag of the ship, contracts relating to the cargo, or the shipowner's instructions.

1   Fumigants against insects in empty cargo holds

TO BE APPLIED ONLY BY QUALIFIED OPERATORS

> Carbon dioxide
>
> Nitrogen
>
> Methyl bromide and carbon dioxide mixture
>
> Methyl bromide
>
> Hydrogen cyanide
>
> Phosphine

2   Fumigants against insects in loaded or partially loaded cargo holds

CARE IS NEEDED IN SELECTING TYPES AND AMOUNTS OF FUMIGANTS FOR TREATMENT OF PARTICULAR COMMODITIES

> Carbon dioxide
>
> Nitrogen
>
> Methyl bromide and carbon dioxide mixture
>
> Methyl bromide
>
> Phosphine

3   Fumigant information

3.1   Methyl bromide

Methyl bromide is used in situations where a rapid treatment of commodities or space is required. It should not be used in spaces where ventilation systems are not adequate for the removal of all gases from the free space. In-ship in-transit fumigations with methyl bromide should not be carried out. Fumigation with methyl bromide should be permitted only when the ship is in the confines of a port (either at anchor or alongside) and to disinfest before discharge, once crew members have disembarked (see 3.1.2.3). Prior to discharge, ventilation must be done, forced if necessary, to reduce the gaseous residues below the occupational exposure limit values set by the flag State regulations in the free spaces. (See procedures for ventilation in 3.3.2.17 to 3.3.2.19).

3.2   Phosphine

3.2.1   A variety of phosphine-generating formulations are used for in-ship in-transit or at-berth fumigations. Application methods vary widely and include surface-only treatment, probing, perforated tubing laid at the bottom of spaces, recirculation systems and gas-injection systems or their combinations. Treatment times will vary considerably depending on the temperature, depth of cargo and on the application method used.

3.2.2   Any discharge of active packages producing phosphine gas represents a significant risk to the public who may encounter them at sea. It should therefore be ensured that all waste and residues are disposed of in an appropriate manner, either by incineration or by disposal on shore, as recommended by the manufacturer. **Clear written instructions must be given to the master of the ship, to the receiver of the cargo and to the authorities at the discharging port as to how any powdery residues are to be disposed of.**

3.2.3   These will vary with each formulation and the method of application. Prior to discharge, ventilation must be done, forced if necessary, to reduce the gaseous residues below the occupational exposure limit values set by the flag State regulations in the free spaces (see procedures for ventilation in 3.3.2.17 to 3.3.2.19). For safety aspects during the voyage see 3.3.2.3.

Appendix 2

Fumigation warning sign

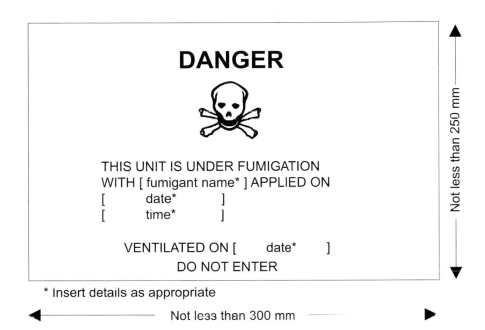

* Insert details as appropriate

Appendix 3

Model checklist for in-transit fumigation

Date: . . . .

Port: . . . .   Terminal/Quay: . . . .

Ship's name: . . . .

Type of fumigant: . . . .   Method of application: . . . .

Date & time fumigation commenced: . . . .

Name of fumigator/company: . . . .

The master and fumigator-in-charge, or their representatives, should complete the checklist jointly. The purpose of this checklist is to ensure that the responsibilities and requirements of 3.3.2.11 and 3.3.2.12 are carried out fully for in-transit fumigation under section 3.3.2.9.

Safety of operations requires that all questions should be answered affirmatively by ticking the appropriate boxes. If this is not possible, the reason should be given and agreement reached upon precautions to be taken between ship and fumigator-in-charge. If a question is considered to be not applicable, write "n/a", explaining why, if appropriate.

PART A: BEFORE FUMIGATION

		SHIP	FUMIGATOR-IN-CHARGE
1	The inspection required before loading has been performed (3.3.2.4)	☐	☐
2	All the cargo holds to be fumigated are satisfactory for fumigation	☐	☐
3	Spaces, where found not to be satisfactory, have been sealed	☐	☐
4	The master or his trained representatives have been made aware of the specific areas to be checked for gas concentrations throughout the fumigation period	☐	☐
5	The master or his trained representatives have been made familiar with the fumigant label, detection methods, safety procedures and emergency procedures (refer to 3.3.2.6)	☐	☐
6	The fumigator-in-charge has ensured that gas-detection and respiratory protection equipment carried on the ship is in good order, and that adequate fresh supplies of consumable items for this equipment are available to allow sampling as required by 3.3.2.13	☐	☐
7	The master has been notified in writing of:		
	(a) the spaces containing cargo to be fumigated	☐	☐
	(b) any other spaces that are considered unsafe to enter during the fumigation	☐	☐

PART B: AFTER FUMIGATION

The following procedure should be carried out after application of fumigant and closing and sealing of cargo holds.

		SHIP	FUMIGATOR-IN-CHARGE
8	Presence of gas has been confirmed inside each hold under fumigation	☐	☐
9	Each hold has been checked for leakage and sealed properly	☐	☐
10	Spaces adjacent to the treated cargo holds have been checked and found gas-free	☐	☐
11	The responsible crew members have been shown how to take gas readings properly when gas is present and they are fully conversant with the use of gas-detection equipment provided	☐	☐
12	Methods of application:		
	(a) *Surface application method* Initial rapid build-up of the gas in the upper regions of hold airspace with subsequent penetration downward of the gas over a longer period or	☐	☐
	(b) *Deep probing* More rapid dispersion of gas than in (a) with lower concentrations in upper regions of airspace in the hold or	☐	☐
	(c) *Recirculation* Rapid dispersion of gas throughout hold but at lower initial gas levels with subsequent build-up of gas levels which, however, may be lower due to even distribution or	☐	☐
	(d) *Other*	☐	☐
13	The master or trained representatives have been briefed fully on the method of application and the spread of the gas throughout the hold	☐	☐
14	The master or trained representatives have been made:		
	(a) aware that even though the initial check may not indicate any leaks, it is essential that monitoring is to be continued in the accommodation, engine-room, etc. because gas concentrations may reach their highest levels after several days	☐	☐
	(b) aware of the possibility of the spreading of gas throughout the duct keel and/or ballast tanks	☐	☐
15	The fumigator-in-charge has supplied a signed statement to the master conforming to the requirements of 3.3.2.12 for his retention	☐	☐

The above has been agreed:

Time: . . . .   Date: . . . .

For ship: . . . .   Fumigator-in-charge: . . . .

Rank: : . . . .

Contact names and addresses of the offices of designated national competent authorities responsible for the safe carriage of grain and solid bulk cargoes

BC.1/Circ.66
(6 February 2009)

Contact names and addresses of the offices of designated national competent authorities responsible for the safe carriage of grain and solid bulk cargoes

1   Annexed is a revised list of contact names and addresses of the offices of designated national competent authorities of Member States' Administrations responsible for matters relating to the carriage of grain and solid bulk cargoes.

2   Member Governments, which have not yet done so, are invited to inform the Secretariat of the names and addresses as well as telephone, telex and telefax numbers and e-mail addresses of their authorities responsible for the carriage of grain and solid bulk cargoes.

3   To keep the list as up to date as possible, Member Governments which have previously submitted relevant information (BC.1/Circ.65) are invited to review the information provided in the annex and notify the Secretariat of any changes.

4   This circular replaces BC.1/Circ.65, which is hereby revoked.

Annex

List of contact names and addresses of the offices of designated national competent authorities responsible for the safe carriage of grain and solid bulk cargoes

ALBANIA

Ministry of Transport and Telecommunication
Directory of Maritime Transport
Tirana
Albania

Telephone:	+355 42 20479
Telex:	+355 42 204 79
E-mail:	shxhaxhiu@yahoo.com

ANGOLA

Instituto Marítimo e Portuário de Angola
Rua Rainha Ginga No. 74
4 Andar
Luanda
Angola

Telephone:	+244 222 390 034
Fax:	+244 222 390 034
E-mail:	ispscode_angola@snet.co.ao

ARGENTINA

Prefectura Naval Argentina
Dirección de Policía de Seguridad de la Navegación
División Técnica Naval
Sección Franco Bordo y Arqueo
Avda. E. Madero 235 – 1° piso – Of. 1.44
Buenos Aires
Republica Argentina (CP. 1106)

| Telephone: | + 54 1 34 3991 |
| Telex: | 18581 PREFC AR |

AUSTRALIA

Head Office Administration:
Manager – Ship Inspection Group
Maritime Operations
Australian Maritime Safety Authority
GPO Box 2181
Canberra ACT 2601
Australia

Telephone:	+ 61 2 6279 5048
Telefax:	+ 61 2 6279 5058
E-mail:	mocbrshipman@amsa.gov.au

BAHAMAS

Bahamas High Commission
(Maritime Division, Ministry of Transport)
10 Chesterfield Street
London W1Y 8AH
United Kingdom

Telephone:	+ 44 20 7493 5515
Telefax:	+ 44 20 7491 0587
Telex:	892617 BAHREG G

Kenneth D. McLean
Director & CEO of Maritime Affairs
The Bahamas Maritime Authority
120 Old Broad Street
London EC2N 1AR
United Kingdom

| Telephone: | +44 20 7562 1300 |
| Fax: | +44 20 7614 0675 |

BANGLADESH

Department of Shipping
141–143, Motijheel Commercial Area
BIWTA Bhaban (8th Floor)
Dhaka-1000
Bangladesh

Telephone:	+880 2 9555128
Telefax:	+880 2 7168363
E-mail:	dosdgdbd@bttb.net.bd

BELGIUM

Frans Van Rompuy
Director-General
Federal Public Service Mobility and Transport
Directorate-general Maritime transport
Rue du Progrés 56
1210 Brussels
Belgium

Telephone:	+32 2 277 35 00
	+32 2 277 40 51
E-mail:	info.mar@mobilit.fgov.be

BELIZE

Major (Ret'd) Lloyd Jones
Ports Commissioner
Belize Ports Authority
Caesar Ridge Road, Customs Building
Belize City
Belize
Central America

Telephone:	+501 227 2480
	+501 227 2540
Telefax:	+501 227 2500
E-mail:	Bzportauth@btl.net

BENIN

Direction de la Marine Marchande
Bvd de la Marine – Zone Portuaire
01 BP 1234 Cotonou
République du Bénin

Telephone:	+229 2131 5845/4669
	+229 9505 6752
Telefax:	+229 2131 5845
E-mail:	marimarc@intnet.bj

BRAZIL

Directoria de Portos e Costas (DPC-20)
Rua Teófilo Otoni N° 04
Centro
Rio de Janeiro
CEP 20090-070
Brazil

Telephone:	+55 21 2104 5203
Telefax:	+55 21 2104 5202
E-mail:	secom@dpc.mar.mil.br

BRUNEI DARUSSALAM

Director of Marine
Marine Department
Jalan McArthur
Bandar Seri Begawan 2053
Brunei Darussalam

Telephone:	+673 2 222293
Telefax:	+673 2 222861
Telex:	BU2650

BULGARIA

Head Office:
Bulgarian Maritime Administration
Ministry of Transport and Communications
9, Vassil Levski str.
Sofia 1000
Republic of Bulgaria

Telephone:	+359 2 930 09 10
Telefax:	+359 2 930 09 20
E-mail:	bma@marad.bg

Regional offices:
Varna Regional Office of the Bulgarian Maritime Administration
5, Primorski bvd.
Varna 9000
Republic of Bulgaria

| Telephone: | +359 52 684 920 |
| Telefax: | +359 52 602 378 |

Bourgas Regional Office of the Bulgarian Maritime Administration
3, Kniaz Batemberg str. 3rd Floor
Bourgas 8000
Republic of Bulgaria

| Telephone: | +359 56 844 339 |
| Telefax: | +359 56 840 064 |

CAMEROON

Mr. PONDY OTTO Simon Emmanuel
Sous Directeur de la Navigation, de la Sécurité et de la Protection de L'Environnement Maritime, Fluvial et Lacustre
BP 416 Douala
Cameroun

Telephone:	+237 99 394 406
Fax:	+237 33 428 956
E-mail:	otto_sim@yahoo.fr

Mme Mouelle Ndoh Mimosette Marceline
Direction des Affaires Maritimes du Cameroun
BP 416 Douala
Cameroun

Telephone:	+237 342 8956
Fax:	+237 342 8956
E-mail:	mouellen@yahoo.fr

CAMEROON *(continued)*

Mr. Wepandje Emmanuel
Direction des Affaires Maritimes et des Voies Navigables du Cameroun
BP 416 Douala
Cameroun

Telephone:	+237 342 8956/777 5293
Fax:	+237 342 8959
E-mail:	ewepandje@yahoo.fr

CANADA

The Chairman
Marine Technical Review Board
Contact: Director, Operations & Environmental Programs
Marine Safety, Transport Canada
Tower C, Place de Ville
330 Sparks Street, 10th Floor
Ottawa, Ontario, K1A 0N5
Canada

Telephone:	+1 613 991 3132
	+1 613 991 3143
	+1 613 991 3139
	+1 613 991 3140
Telefax:	+1 613 993 8196

CAPE VERDE

Companhia Nacional de Navegacão "Arca Verde" – E.P.
Rua Guerra Mendes
Praia
PO Box 41
Cape Verde

Telephone:	+238 545 and 592
Telegram:	Arca Verde
Telex:	60 M.T.C. CV

NAGUICAVE – Companhia Maritime de Navegacão Guiné-Cabo Verde, S.A.R.L.
Avenida 5 de Julho – Cidade do Mindelo
PO Box 142
Cape Verde

Telephone:	+238 2652
Telegram:	NAGUICAVE
Telex:	81 BANCO SV CV

Directorate General of Marine and Ports or Harbour Master
S. Vicente
PO Box 7
Cape Verde

Telex:	32 Marpor CV

CHILE

Dirección General del Territorio Marítimo y de Marina Mercante
Errazuriz 537
Correo Naval
Valparaíso
Chile

Telephone:	+56 32 258091/94
Telex:	230602 DGTMM CL

CHINA

Maritime Safety Administration of the People's Republic of China
11 Jianguomennei Avenue
Beijing, 100736
China

Telephone:	+86 10 65292873
Telefax:	+86 10 65292875
Telex:	222258 CMSASR CN
E-mail:	xujixiang@msa.gov.cn

COLOMBIA

Dirección General Marítima
Transversal 41 No. 27-50 CAN
Bogotá
Colombia

Telephone:	+57 1 2200490
Telefax:	+57 1 2222636

CONGO

Mr. SOUINGUISSA Gabriel
Directeur de la Sécurité Maritime
Direction Générale de la Marine Marchande
BP 1107 Pointe Noire
Congo

Telephone:	+242 661 5321
E-mail:	gabrielsouina@yahoo.fr

BOUKONO Jean Claude
Directeur de la Navigation Maritime
Direction Générale de la Marine Marchande
BP 1107 Pointe Noire
Congo

Telephone:	+242 539 0493
E-mail:	jcboukono@yahoo.fr

CÔTE D'IVOIRE

Commandant Tano Koffi Bertin
Directeur de la Navigation de la Sécurité et de la Garde Côtière
Administration Maritime (Affaires Maritimes)
BP V67
Abidjan
Côte d'Ivoire

Telephone:	+225 2022 1630
Mobile:	+225 (0)785 8529
Fax:	+225 2021 5317
E-mail:	tkoffibertin@yahoo.fr

CROATIA

Ministry of the Sea, Tourism, Transport and Development
Maritime Safety Department
Zagreb, Prisavlje 14
Croatia

Telephone:	+385 1 6169 070
Telefax:	+385 1 6195 956

CUBA

Dirección de Seguridad e Inspección Marítima
Ministerio del Transporte
Boyeros y Tulipán, 4to. piso
Ciudad de la Habana
Cuba

Telephone:	+53 7 816607 & 819498
Telex:	511135 MITRANS CU

CYPRUS

Department of Merchant Shipping
Address: Kyllinis Street
Mesa Geitonia
CY-4007 Lemesos
Cyprus

Mailing Address: Department of Merchant Shipping
PO Box 56193
CY-3305 Lemesos
Cyprus

Telephone:	+357 25 848100
Telefax:	+357 25 848200
Telex:	2004 MERSHIP CY
E-mail:	maritimeadmin@dms.mcw.gov.cy

DEMOCRATIC PEOPLE'S REPUBLIC OF KOREA

Maritime Administration of the Democratic People's Republic of Korea
Tonghung-dong, Central District
PO Box 416
Pyongyang
Democratic People's Republic of Korea

Telephone:	+850 2 18111, Ext. 8059
Telefax:	+850 2 381 4410
E-mail:	mab@silibank.com

DEMOCRATIC PEOPLE'S REPUBLIC OF KOREA *(continued)*

Local Office:
MAB Bangkok
310/4, Phatthanakan Road, Soi 57
Prawet District,
Bangkok Metropolis 10250
Thailand

Telephone: +66 1 926 2472
Telefax: +66 2 722 3657
E-mail: haesaguk@mweb.co.th

DEMOCRATIC REPUBLIC OF THE CONGO

Mr. Mbuangi-Mbuku Lelo Joachin-Egide
Ministère des Transports et Communications
BP 3683 Kinshasa Gombé
R D Congo

Telephone: +24 3 816 914 754
E-mail: jmmle@yahoo.fr

Mr. Mambuma Nsungu Theodore
Ministère des Transports et Communications: OEBK
BP 8091 Kinshasa I
R D Congo

Telephone: +243 998 379 865
E-mail: theomambu@yahoo.fr
                    oebkmat@bulamatadi.net

DENMARK

Mr. Arne Ulstrup
Chief Ship Surveyor
Danish Maritime Authority
Vermundsgade 38 C
DK-2100 Copenhagen
Denmark

Telephone: +45 39 17 4400
Telefax: +45 39 17 4401
E-mail: sfs@dma.dk

DOMINICAN REPUBLIC

Autoridad Portuaria Dominicana (APORDOM)
PO Box 259-2
Ave. Máximo Gómez Esq. México No. 70
Santo Domingo
República Dominicana

Telephone: +1 809 688 4481
Telex: +809 346 0699

ECUADOR

Dirección General de la Marina Mercante y del Litoral
Dirección de Transporte Marítimo
Malecón y Clemente Ballén
PO Box 7412
Guayaquil
Ecuador

Telephone:	+593 4 324 231
Telefax:	+593 4 324 246
Telex:	043325 DGMER ED

EGYPT

Rear-Admiral/Mokhtar Adel Wahed Ammar
Head of Maritime Transport Sector
Ministry of Transport
4, Ptolemy Street
Alexandria, 21514
Egypt

Telephone:	+20 3 484 2119 (24 hours)
	+20 3 484 2058 (24 hours)
	+20 3 484 3631 (personal)
Telefax:	+20 3 484 2041
	+20 3 484 2096
E-mail:	mmt@idsc.net.eg

EL SALVADOR

Viceministerio de Transporte
Dirección General de Transporte Terrestre
1a Avenida Sur No. 630
San Salvador
El Salvador, C.A.

Telephone:	+503 2221 0601

Comisión Ejecutiva Portuaria Autónoma (CEPA)
Bulevar de los Héroes
Edificio Torre Roble
San Salvador
El Salvador, C.A.

Telephone:	+503 2218 1300

EQUATORIAL GUINEA

Mr. Pedro Mensuy Asumu
Director General de Transportes, Terrestre y Fluvial
Ministerio de Transportes, Tecnologia, Correos y Comunicaciones
Malabo
Guinea Equatoriale

Telephone:	+240 278 646
Mobile:	+240 099 517
Fax:	+240 093 999
E-mail:	mensuyasumu@yahoo.com

EQUATORIAL GUINEA *(continued)*

Mr. Fernando Biahute Mateu
Expert/Conseiller Technique Portuaire Maritime National
Administration des ports Guinée Equatoriale
APGE, BP 563
Malabo
Guinea Equatoriale

Telephone: +240 259 763
Fax: +240 091 184
E-mail: ferbiahute@yahoo.es
                    biahute@lubrafreeport.com

ESTONIA

Estonian National Maritime Board
Maritime Safety Department
Lume 9
10416 Tallinn
Estonia

Telephone: +372 6205 700
Telex: +372 6205 706

FINLAND

Finnish Maritime Administration
POB 171
FIN-00181 Helsinki
Finland

Telephone: +358 (0)2044840
Telex: +358 (0)204484500
E-mail: pertti.haatainen@fma.fi
                    bo.fagerholm@fma.fi

FRANCE

Ministère de l'Equipement, des Transports et du Logement
3 Place de Fontenoy
75700 Paris 07 SP
France

Telephone: +33 1 44 49 86 41
Telefax: +33 1 44 49 86 40

GABON

Mr. AUBAME Gérard Philippe Alain
Directeur des Gens de Mer, de la Navigation et de la Sécurité Maritimes
Direction Générale de la Marine Marchande
BP 803 Libreville
Gabon

Telephone: +241 72 00 42/06 24 71 11
Fax: +241 76 01 85/77 52 56
E-mail: gaubame@yahoo.fr

GABON *(continued)*

Mr. Nkoulou-Mezui Claver
Direction Générale de la Marine Marchande
BP 803 Libreville
Gabon

Telephone: +241 745 307/0736 0279
Fax: +241 76 01 85

Cdt. Major Mouenzi-Mouenzi Allyanoh
Direction de la Réglementation Maritime et de la Coopération Ministère
de la Marine Marchande et des Equipments Portuaires
BP 803 Libreville
Gabon

Telephone: +241 760 185/+0625 0459 /0729 3348
Fax: +241 760 185
E-mail: allyano@yahoo.fr

GAMBIA

Mr. Dembo Jarju
Gambia Ports Authority
Gambia Navy
PMB 49 Banjul
Gambia

Telephone: 1 220 993 3787/422 7266/9940
E-mail: dejarju68@yahoo.com

Mr. Mboob Momodou A. B. S.
Gambia Ports Authority
Liberation Avenue
PO Box 617 Banjul
Gambia

Telephone: +220 422 7266/9940
Fax: +220 422 7268
E-mail: modouamie@yahoo.com

GEORGIA

Maritime Transport Administration
4, Shavsheti Str.
Batumi 6017
Georgia

Telephone: +995 222 7 49 25/ 7 39 17/ 7 39 09
Telefax: +995 222 7 39 29
E-mail: magheadof@fsc.gov.ge
               magheadof@gol.ge

GERMANY

Bundesminister für Verkehr, Bau- und Wohnungswesen
Abteilung Luft- und Raumfahrt, Schifffahrt
Robert-Schuman-Platz 1
53175 Bonn
Germany

Telephone:	+49 228 300 0 or 300-Extension
Telefax:	+49 228 300 34 28
E-mail:	poststelle@bmvbw.bund.de

See-Berufsgenossenschaft
Ship Safety Division
Postfach 11 04 89
20404 Hamburg
Germany

Telephone:	+ 49 40 361370
Telefax:	+ 49 40 36137770
E-mail:	schiffssicherheit@see-bg.de

Germanischer Lloyd
Vorsetzen 35
Postfach 111606
20459 Hamburg
Germany

Telephone:	+49 40 361490
Telefax:	+49 40 36149200
E-mail:	headoffice@gl-group.com

GHANA

Director-General
Ghana Maritime Authority
PMB 34, Ministries Post Office
Ministries-Accra
Ghana

Telephone:	+233 21 662122/684392
Telefax:	+233 21 677702
E-mail:	info@ghanamaritime.org

GREECE

Ministry of Mercantile Marine
Merchant Ships General Inspections Directorate
Design & Construction Directorate
MARPOL & Cargoes Department
Konstantinou Paleologou 1 st.
Piraeus
Greece

Telephone:	+30 210 419 1800
Telefax:	+30 210 413 7997
E-mail:	dmk@mail.yen.gr

GUINEA

Mr. Mohamed Cheick Fofana
Direction Nationale de la Marine Marchande
BP 6
Conakry
Guinea

Telephone: +224 3045 2343/3539
Fax: +224 3041 3577
E-mail: dnmmgn@yahoo.fr

Mr. Cissoko Mamadou
Chef de la section Navires et navigabilité
Direction Nationale de la Marine Marchande
BP 6
Conakry
Guinea

Telephone: +224 642 481 69
Fax: +224 3041 3577

Mr. Diallo Mamadou Sïdou
Direction Nationale de la Marine Marchande
BP 6
Conakry
Guinea

Telephone: +224 6033 6417
Fax: +224 413 577
E-mail: cfofana23@yahoo.fr

GUINEA-BISSAU

Mr. Mendonça Mario
Ministère des Transports et Communications
Guinea-Bissau

Telephone: +245 666 2925
Fax: +245 207 323
E-mail: mariomendon@hotmail.com

Mr. Mario Musante da Silva Loureiro
Direction Générale de la Marine Marchande
C/P 25 Bissau
Guinea-Bissau

Telephone: +245 665 2152
Fax: +245 204 114

ICELAND

Directorate of Shipping
PO Box 484
121 Reykjavik 101
Iceland

Telephone: +354 1 91 25844

INDIA

The Secretary of the Government of India
Ministry of Shipping, Road Transport & Highways
Department of Shipping
Transport Bhavan
1, Parliament Street
New Delhi – 110 001
India

Telephone:	+91 11 2371 4938 (direct)
Telefax:	+91 11 2371 6656
E-mail:	secyship@hub.nic.in

The Director-General of Shipping
Directorate General of Shipping
Jahaz Bhavan
Walchand Hirachand Marg
Mumbai – 400 001
India

Telephone:	+91 22 2261 3156 (direct)/26136 5154 (operator)
Telex:	+91 22 2262 6756
E-mail:	dgship@dgshipping.com
Website:	www.dgshipping.com

The Principal Officer
Mercantile Marine Department
Old C.G.O. Building
101, Maharshi Karve Road
Post Box No. 11096
Mumbai – 400 020
India

Telephone:	+91 22 2201 4671/2207 6881 (direct)
	+91 22 2203 9881 (operator)
Telefax:	+91 22 2201 3307
E-mail:	mmdmt498@bom3.vsnl.net.in

The Principal Officer
Mercantile Marine Department
Marine House
Hastings
Kolkata – 700 022
India

Telephone:	+91 33 2223 0167 (direct)
	+91 33 2223 0236/37/38 (operator)
Telefax:	+91 33 2223 0853
E-mail:	pommdcal@vsnl.com
	pommdkol@sify.com

INDIA *(continued)*

The Principal Officer
Mercantile Marine Department
Anchor Gate Building, 2nd Floor
Post Box No. 5004
Rajaji Salai
Chennai – 600 001
India

Telephone:	+91 44 2523 3336 (direct)
	+91 44 2525 1107/08 (operator)
Telefax:	+91 44 2523 2929
E-mail:	mmdchennai@vsnl.net

IRAN (ISLAMIC REPUBLIC OF)

Director General Port Affairs
Ports and Maritime Organization (PMO)
PMO Headquarter
South Didar St.
Haghani Exp way
Vanak Sq.
Tehran
Islamic Republic of Iran

Telephone:	+98 21 849 32201
Telefax:	+98 21 849 32227
E-mail:	J_Eslami@pmo.ir

IRELAND

The Chief Surveyor
Marine Survey Office
Department of Communications, Marine and Natural Resources
Leeson Lane
Dublin 2
Ireland

Telephone:	+353 1 678 3400
Telefax:	+353 1 678 3409
E-mail:	mso@dcmnr.gov.ie
Website:	www.dcmnr.gov.ie/mso

ISRAEL

Capt. E. Sternberg – Deputy Director
Capt. E. Gerson – Senior Shipping Inspector
Administration of Shipping and Ports
PO Box 806
Haifa 31077
Israel

Telephone:	+972 4 8632 080/087
Telefax:	+972 4 8632 118
E-mail:	alexg@mot.gov.il

ITALY

Italian Coast Guard Headquarters
Viale Dell'Arte 16
Rome 00144
Italy

Telephone:	+39 06 5908 4919
Telefax:	+39 06 5908 4918
E-mail:	uffl.rep6cogecap@infrastrutturetrasporti.it

Italian Coast Guard Headquarters
Ponte Dei Mille
Genoa 16100
Italy

Telephone:	+39 010 24 12 797
Telefax:	+39 010 24 78 245
E-mail:	001@sicnavge.it

JAMAICA

Jamaica Merchant Marine Limited
7th Floor, Dyoll Building
40/46 Knutsford Boulevard
PO Box 952
Kingston
Jamaica
West Indies

Telephone:	+1 809 92 91982/6
Telex:	2483 & 2295 JMM JA
Cable:	Jamerine

Jamaica Commodity Trading Company Limited
8 Ocean Boulevard
Kingston Mall
Jamaica
West Indies

Telephone:	+1 809 92 20971/9
Telex:	2318 Januhold Ja.

Alcan Jamaica Limited
4 St. Lucia Avenue
Kingston 5
Jamaica
West Indies

Telephone:	+1 809 92 64011/4

Alcoa Minerals of Jamaica Incorporated
10 Grenada Crescent
Kingston 5
Jamaica
West Indies

Telephone:	+1 809 926 3390
Telex:	2116 Alcoamin, Ja.

JAMAICA *(continued)*

Kaiser Bauxite Company
Imperial Life Building
Kingston 5
Jamaica
West Indies

Telephone:	+1 809 926 4723
Telex:	Kaisbaux Co. 2256

Alumina Partners of Jamaica
64 Knutsford Boulevard
Kingston 5
Jamaica
West Indies

Telephone:	+1 809 926 1650 or
	(Head Office-Main) 962 3251

Jamaica Gypsum and Quarries Limited
Harbour Head
PO Box 11
Kingston
Jamaica
West Indies

Telephone:	+1 809 928 6102
Telex:	NIBJ 2487 (Janico)

Bauxite and Alumina Trading Company
11 Trinidad Terrace
Kingston 5
Jamaica
West Indies

Telephone:	+1 809 926 4553
	+1 809 926 4602
	+1 809 926 4555
Telex:	2436

JAPAN

Inspection and Measurement Division
Maritime Bureau
Ministry of Land, Infrastructure and Transport
2-1-3 Kasumigaseki, Chiyoda-ku
Tokyo
Japan

Telephone:	+81 3 5253 8639
Telex:	+81 3 5253 1644
E-mail:	MRB_KSK@mlit.go.jp

KENYA

The Director
Shipping & Maritime Affairs
Ministry of Transport
Nairobi
Kenya

Telephone:	+254 20 2729200
Telefax:	+254 20 2724553
E-mail:	info@transport.go.ke

LATVIA

Maritime Administration of Latvia
Trijādības iela 5
Rīga LV-1048
Latvia

Telephone:	+371 67 062 100
Telefax:	+371 67 860 082
E-mail:	lja@lja.lv

LEBANON

Ministry of Public Works & Transport
Directorate General of Land & Maritime Transport
George Picot St., Starco Bldg., 3rd Floor
Beirut
Lebanon

Telephone:	+961 1 371 644
	+961 1 371 645
Fax:	+961 1 371 647
E-mail:	ministry@transportation.gov.lb

LIBERIA*

The Office of the Deputy Commissioner of Maritime Affairs, R.L.
c/o Liberian International Ship and Corporate Registry, LLC (LISCR)
8619 Westwood Center Drive
Suite 300
Vienna, Virginia 22182
United States of America

Telephone:	+1 703 790 3434
Telefax:	+1 703 790 5655
E-mail:	info@liscr.com

LITHUANIA

Lithuanian Maritime Safety Administration
J. Janonio str. 24
LT-92251, Klaipeda
Lithuania

Telephone:	+370 46 469 602
Telefax:	+370 46 469 600
E-mail:	msa@msa.lt

---

* A duty officer arrangement covers all periods outside normal office hours.

MALTA

Mr. Vincent Spiteri Staines
Manager
Midigrain Limited
4 Mill Street
Marsa
Malta

Telephone: +356 605190

MARSHALL ISLANDS

The Maritime Administrator,
Republic of the Marshall Islands
c/o Marshall Islands Maritime and Corporate Administrators, Inc.
11495, Commerce Park Drive
Reston, Virginia, 20191-1507
United States of America

Telephone: +1 703 620 4880
Telefax: +1 703 476 8522
E-mail: maritime@register-iri.com

MAURITANIA

Mr. Mohamed Lemine Ould Sidbrahim
Directeur de la Marine Marchande
BP 6808
Nouakchott
Mauritania

Telephone: +222 525 7893
Fax: +222 525 6104
E-mail: alysidi@yahoo.fr

Mr. Ould Ali Sidi
Directeur Adjoint CCSM/MT
BP 6808
Nouakchott
Mauritania

Telephone: +222 524 2592
Fax: +222 524 2593
E-mail: alysidi@yahoo.fr

MAURITIUS

Director of Shipping
Level IV, New Government Centre
Port Louis
Mauritius

Telephone: +230 201 2115
Telefax: +230 201 3417 / 211 7699
E-mail: transmau@intnet.mu

MEXICO

Lic. Alejandro Chacón Dominguez
Coordinador General de Puertos y Marina Mercante
Secretaría de Comunicaciones y Transportes
Avenida Nuevo León no. 210, Piso 19
Colonia Hipódromo Condesa, C.P. 06100
México, Distrito Federal

Telephone:	+52 55 5265 3110
Telefax:	+52 55 5265 3108
E-mail:	achacon@sct.gob.mx

Lic. Adolfo Xavier Zagal Olivares
Director General de Marina Mercante
Secretaría de Comunicaciones y Transportes
Avenida Nuevo León no. 210, Piso 3
Colonia Hipódromo Condesa, C.P. 06100
México, Distrito Federal

Telephone:	+52 55 5265 3220
Telefax:	+52 55 5265 3233
E-mail:	azagalol@sct.gob.mx

Cap. Alt. Francisco Riveros García
Director General Adjunto de Marina Mercante
Secretaría de Comunicaciones y Transportes
Avenida Nuevo León no. 210, Piso 7
Colonia Hipódromo Condesa, C.P. 06100
México, Distrito Federal

Telephone:	+52 55 5265 3222
Telefax:	+52 55 5265 3235
E-mail:	friverog@sct.gob.mx

MOROCCO

Direction de la Marine Marchande
Boulevard Félix Houphouet Boigny
Casablanca
Morocco

Telephone:	+212 2 221 93
Telefax:	+212 2 273 340
Telex:	24613

NETHERLANDS

Head of the Netherlands Shipping Inspectorate
Bordewijkstraat 4
Postbus 5817
2280 HV Rijswijk
The Netherlands

Telephone:	+31 70 395 5555
Telefax:	+31 70 319 1456
Telex:	31040 DGSM NL

NEW ZEALAND

Director of Maritime New Zealand
Maritime New Zealand
PO Box 27006
Wellington
New Zealand

Telephone:	+64 4 473 0111
Telefax:	+64 4 494 1263
E-mail:	manager.rules@maritimenz.govt.nz

NIGERIA

The Government Inspector of Shipping
Federal Ministry of Transport
(Marine Inspectorate Division)
Marina
Lagos
Nigeria

Telephone:	+234 1 631208 or 652120 Ext. 281

NORWAY

Norwegian Maritime Directorate
Smedasundet 50A
PO Box 2222
N-5509 Haugesund
Norway

Telephone:	+47 52 745 000
Telefax:	+47 52 745 001
E-mail:	postmottak@sjofartsdir.no

PAKISTAN

Captain M Aslam Shaheen
Chief Nautical Surveyor and Principal Examiner of Master & Mates
Government of Pakistan
Ministry of Communications,
Ports & Shipping Wing
Plot No.12, Misc. Area
Mai Kolachi Bye Pass
Karachi – 74200
Pakistan

Telephone:	+92 21 920 4191
Telefax:	+92 21 920 6407/4191
Telex:	29822 DGPS PK

PAKISTAN *(continued)*

Captain M. Saleem Baloch
Principal Officer
Mercantile Marine Department
Ministry of Communications,
Ports & Shipping Wing
70/4, Timber Pond
N M Reclamation, Keamari
Karachi – 74000
Pakistan

Telephone:	+92 21 2851 307
PABX:	+92 21 2851 306 & 2852703–4
Telefax:	+92 21 2851 307
Telex:	29822 DGPS PK

PANAMA

Director
Department of Maritime Safety
Directorate of Consular and Maritime Affairs
Republic of Panama
1180 Avenue of the Americas, 23rd floor
New York, NY 10036
United States of America

Telephone:	+1 212 869 6440
Telefax:	+1 212 575 2285

Mr. Celedonio Moncayo
Dirección General de Consular y Naves
Apartado postal 5245
Panama 5
Republic of Panama

Telephone:	+507 25 6693
Telex:	3367 Secnaves P G

PERU

Dirección General de Capitanías y Guardacostas
Marina de Guerra del Perú
Jr. Constitución No. 150
Callao
Perú

Telephone:	51 1 613 6857
Telefax:	51 1 613 5657/6726
Telex:	26042 PE COSTCAL
E-mail:	dicapi.medioambiente@dicapi.mil.pe

PHILIPPINES

Commander, Maritime Safety Office
Philippine Coast Guard
Coast Guard Station Farola
Binonda
Manila
Philippines

PHILIPPINES *(continued)*

The Administrator
Maritime Industry Authority
5th Floor, PPL Bldg.
UN Avenue
Manila
Philippines

Telephone:	+ 63 2 582711
Telex:	27267 MIA

General Manager
Philippine Ports Authority
Marsman Bldg., Gate 1
South Harbor, Port Area
Manila
Philippines

Telephone:	+63 2 479 204
Telex:	(ITT) 40404
TX Box:	(0203)

Assistant General Manager
Port Services Office
Philippine Ports Authority
Marsman Bldg., Gate 1
South Harbor, Port Area
Manila
Philippines

Telephone:	+63 2 476 117
Telex:	(ITT) 40404
TX Box:	(0203)

POLAND

Ministry of Transport and Maritime Economy
Department of Maritime and Inland Waters Administration
ul. Chałubinskiego 4–6
00-928 Warszawa
Poland

Telephone:	+48 22 6 211 448
Telefax:	+48 22 6 288 515
Telex:	816651 PKP PL

Polski Rejestr Statków
al. Gen. J. Hallera 126
80-416 Gdansk
Poland

Telephone:	+48 58 412 068/412 069/416 482
Telefax:	+48 58 316 636
Telex:	512373 PRS PL
	512952 PRS PL

PORTUGAL

Instituto Portuário e dos Transportes Marítimos
Edifício Vasco da Gama
Rua General Gomes Araújo
1399-005 Lisboa
Portugal

Telephone: +351 21 391 4500
Telefax: +351 21 391 4600
E-mail: imarpor@mail.telepac.pt

REPUBLIC OF KOREA

Safety Policy Division of Safety Management Bureau
Ministry of Maritime Affairs & Fisheries
139 Chungjong-no 3, Seodaemun-gu
Seoul 120-715
Republic of Korea

Telephone: +82 2 3148 6312
Telefax: +82 2 3148 6317
E-mail: lsjin@mamaf.go.kr

RUSSIAN FEDERATION

Mr. V. Kourilenko
Deputy Head
Main Department for Shipping and Port Operations (Glavflot)
Ministry of Merchant Marine
1/4, Zhdanova Str.
Moscow 103759
The Russian Federation

Telephone: +7 095 926 15 09
Telex: 411197 MMF SU

Mr. M. Baranovskiy
Central Merchant Marine Institute
Bulk Cargoes Laboratory
6, Kr. Konnitsa Str.
Leningrad 193015
The Russian Federation

Telephone: +7 812 216 9169

SAO TOME AND PRINCIPE

Mr. D'Alva Costa Alegre Filinto Guilherme
Ministério dos Assuntos Marítimos e Ambiente

PO Box 13
São Tomé et Principe

Telephone: +239 221 904
Fax: +239 227 150
E-mail: filintocalegre@hotmail.com

SAO TOME AND PRINCIPE *(continued)*

Mr. Deodato Gomes Rodrigues
Empresa Nacional de Administração dos Portos
"ENAPORT – CARGO" das Alfândegas 437
São Tomé et Principe

Telephone:	+239 221 841/224841
Fax:	+239 227 4949/224949
E-mail:	enaport@cstome.net

SAINT VINCENT AND THE GRENADINES

Ms. N. Dabinovic
Commissioner for Maritime Affairs
St. Vincent and the Grenadines
8 Avenue de Frontenex
CH-1207 Geneva
Switzerland

Telephone:	+41 22 707 6300
Telefax:	+41 22 707 6350
E-mail:	geneva@svg-marad.com

SENEGAL

Direction Marine Marchande
Ministère de l'Economie Maritime et des Transports Maritimes Internationaux
Building Administratif
BP 4050
Dakar
Senegal

Telephone:	+221 33 823 3426
Fax:	+221 33 823 8720

Mr. Thioub Yerim
Directeur Général
Direction Marine Marchande
12 Avenue Faidherbe x Rue Vincens
BP 4032
Dakar
Senegal

Telephone:	+221 821 3643
Fax:	+221 823 6869

Mr. S. Y. Ibrahima
Administrateur des Affaires Maritimes
Direction de la Marine Marchande
BP 4032
Dakar
Senegal

Telephone:	+221 650 4104/821 3643
Fax:	+221 823 6862
E-mail:	isiba@hotmail.com

SIERRA LEONE

Sierra Leone International Ship Registry
1010 Common Street, Suite 2533
New Orleans, LA 70112
United States of America

Telephone: +504 636 1387
Telefax: +504 636 1388
E-mail: registrar@sierraleoneship.com

SINGAPORE

Shipping Division
Maritime and Port Authority of Singapore
21-00 PSA Building
460 Alexandra Road
Singapore 119963

Telephone: +65 6375 1600
Telefax: +65 6375 6231
E-mail: shipping@mpa.gov.sg

SLOVENIA

Slovenian Maritime Administration
Ukmarjev trg 2
6000 Koper
Slovenia

Telephone: +386 5 663 2100
Telefax: +386 5 663 2102
E-mail: ursp.box@gov.si

SOUTH AFRICA

The Chief Executive Officer
South African Maritime Safety Authority
Hatfield Gardens Block E
333 Grosvenor Street
Hatfield
Pretoria 0083
South Africa

PO Box 13186
Hatfield
Pretoria 0028
South Africa

Telephone: +27 (0)12 342 3049
Telefax: +27 (0)12 342 3160

The Executive Manager: Operations
South African Maritime Safety Authority
Private Bag X7025
Roggebaai 8012
Cape Town
South Africa

Telephone: +27 (0)21 402 8986
Telefax: +27 (0)21 421 6109

SPAIN

Dirección General de la Marina Mercante
Subdirección General de Seguridad Marítima y Contaminación
C. Ruiz de Alarcón 1
28071-Madrid
Spain

Telephone: +34 91 597 9269
Telefax: +34 91 597 9235

SUDAN

Abu Bakr M. Abu Bakr
Sudan Shipping Line Ltd.
PO Box 1731, Chartering Dept.
Khartoum
Sudan

Telephone: +249 11 77902/77058
Telex: 301 SUDSHIP KM
                      332 OSTOOL KM

SWEDEN

Swedish Transport Agency
Maritime Department
Box 653
SE-601 15 Norrköping
Sweden

Telephone: +46 771 503 503
Telefax: +46 11 239 934
E-mail: sjofart@transportstyrelsen.se

SWITZERLAND

Swiss Maritime Navigation Office
Nauenstrasse 42
CH 4002 Basel
Switzerland

Telephone: +41 61 270 9120
Telefax: +41 61 270 9129
Telex: 965514

THAILAND

Marine Department
Ministry of Transport
1278 Thanon Yothi
Bangkok 10100
Thailand

Telephone: +662 233 1311–8
Telefax: +662 236 7248
E-mail: hmd@mail.md.go.th

TOGO

Mr. Fatonzoun Mawutoe
Directeur des Affaires Maritimes
BP 8533 Lomé
Togo

Telephone:	+228 221 2805/4161
Fax:	+228 222 2806
E-mail:	fatonzoun@yahoo.com

TRINIDAD AND TOBAGO

Director of Maritime Services
Maritime Services Division
Ministry of Works and Transport
48–50 Sackville Street
Port of Spain
Republic of Trinidad and Tobago

Telephone:	+1 809 625 3858
Telefax:	+1 809 625 3858

Mr. Feeraz Ali
Metallurgist
Quality Control Department
Caribbean ISPAT Trinidad & Tobago Ltd.
Point Lisas Industrial Estate
Couva
Republic of Trinidad and Tobago

Telephone:	+1 809 636 2381
Telefax:	+1 809 679 3708

TURKEY

Turkish Embassy in London
43 Belgrave Square
London SW1X 8PA
United Kingdom

Telephone:	+44 20 7393 0202/226
	+44 20 7201 7062
Telefax:	+44 20 7393 0066
E-mail:	fikrethakguden@turkishnavy.com

Prime Ministry of the Republic of Turkey
Undersecretariat for Maritime Affairs
Head of Foreign Relations Department
GMK Bulvari, No. 128
Maltepe 06570
Ankara
Turkey

Telephone:	+90 312 232 38 49/50
	+90 312 231 3052
Telefax:	+90 312 231 1379
E-mail:	disiliskiler@denizcilik.gov.tr

UNITED KINGDOM

Treatment of Bulk Cargoes including the Carriage of Grain and Minerals
Department of Transport
Marine Division DSG1c
Sunley House
90–93 High Holborn
London WC1V 6LP
United Kingdom

Telephone:	+44 20 7405 6911
Telefax:	+44 20 7405 1145
Telex:	264084

UNITED STATES

Stability of Ships with Grain or Bulk Cargoes
Commandant (G-MSE-2)
U.S. Coast Guard
Attention: Chief, Naval Architecture Division
2100 Second Street, SW
Washington, DC 20593-0001
United States of America

Telephone:	+1 202 267 2988
Telefax:	+1 202 267 4816
Telex:	892427

Chemical Aspects of Bulk Cargoes
Commandant (G-MSO-3)
U.S. Coast Guard
Attention: Chief, Hazardous Materials Standards Division
2100 Second Street, SW
Washington, DC 20593-0001
United States of America

Telephone:	+1 202 267 1217
Telefax:	+1 202 267 4570
Telex:	892427

Grain and Bulk Cargoes
National Cargo Bureau Inc.
17 Battery Place, Suite 1232
New York, NY 10004-1110
United States of America

Telephone:	+1 212 785 8300
Telefax:	+1 212 785 8333
E-mail:	ncbnyc@natcargo.org

URUGUAY

Prefectura Nacional Naval
Dirección Registral y de Marina Mercante
Edificio Aduana 1er piso, CP 11.000
Montevideo
Uruguay

Telephone:	+598 2 915 79 13
	+598 2 916 49 14
Telefax:	+598 2 915 79 13
	+598 2 916 49 14
E-mail:	delea@armada.gub.uy
	pnndirme@adinet.com.uy

VANUATU

Deputy Commissioner of Maritime Affairs
Vanuatu Maritime Services Limited
42 Broadway, Suite 1200-18
New York, NY 10004
United States of America

Telephone:	+1 212 425 9600
Telefax:	+1 212 425 9652
E-mail:	email@vanuatuships.com

ASSOCIATE MEMBER

HONG KONG, CHINA

The Director of Marine
Marine Department
21/F–24/F, Harbour Building
38 Pier Road
Hong Kong, China

Telephone:	+(852) 2852 4510
Telefax:	+(852) 2545 0556
E-mail:	ss_css@mardep.gov.hk

INTERNATIONAL ORGANIZATIONS

INTERNATIONAL CHAMBER OF SHIPPING (ICS)

12 Carthusian Street
London EC1M 6EZ
United Kingdom

Telephone:	+44 (0)20 7417 8844
Telefax:	+44 (0)20 7417 8877

BIMCO

Bagsvaerdvej 161
DK-2880 Bagsvaerd
Denmark

Telephone:	+45 44 444 500
Telefax:	+45 44 444 450 (national)
Telex:	19086 bimco dk
Telegraphic address:	BIMCOSHIP COPENHAGEN

Related IMO Publishing Titles

The following publications might be of interest to you. They may be purchased from authorized distributors. Please visit our website (www.imo.org) for further details.

INTERNATIONAL MARITIME DANGEROUS GOODS (IMDG) CODE
2010 Edition (incorporating amendment 35-10)

The International Convention for the Safety of Life at Sea, 1974 (SOLAS), as amended, deals with various aspects of maritime safety and contains in chapter VII the mandatory provisions governing the carriage of dangerous goods in packaged form or in solid form in bulk. The carriage of dangerous goods is prohibited except in accordance with the relevant provisions of chapter VII, which are amplified by the International Maritime Dangerous Goods (IMDG) Code.

From 1 January 2011, the provisions of the IMDG Code, 2010 Edition may be applied on a voluntary basis, pending their official entry into force on 1 January 2012 without any transitional period. The provisions of the 2008 edition may no longer be applied after that date.

This is a two-volume set. Volumes 1 and 2 are not sold separately

English	IH200E	ISBN 978-92-801-15130
French	IH200F	978-92-801-24378
Spanish	IH200S	978-92-801-35862

IMDG CODE SUPPLEMENT
2010 Edition

The International Maritime Dangerous Goods Code relates to the safe carriage of dangerous goods by sea, but does not include all details of procedures for packing of dangerous goods or actions to take in the event of an emergency or accident involving personnel who handle goods at sea. These aspects are covered by the publications that are associated with the IMDG Code, which are included in this Supplement.

The Supplement also includes texts of the Medical First Aid Guide, descriptions of the reporting procedures for incidents involving dangerous goods, harmful substances and/or marine pollutants, the IMO/ILO/UNECE Guidelines for Packing of Cargo Transport Units, the Recommendations on the Safe Use of Pesticides in Ships and other appropriate Assembly resolutions, resolutions and Circulars of the Maritime Safety Committee and Circulars of the Facilitation Committee and of the Sub-Committee on Dangerous Goods, Solid Cargoes and Containers.

English	IH210E	ISBN 978-92-801-15147
French	IH210F	978-92-801-24385
Spanish	IH210S	978-92-801-35855

IMDG CODE ON THE WEB

This product is a yearly subscription to the IMDG Code in English for the single user only.

It provides users with access to:

- The texts of the IMDG Code, 2008 and 2010 Editions, and the IMDG Code Supplement, 2008 and 2010 Editions

- Search by substance or UN Number
- Search by French and Spanish language Proper Shipping Names
- Extensive cross-referencing
- Online colour displays of hazard labels, signs and marks
- Medical First Aid Guide illustrations
- Easy-to-use menus and navigation features

English   S200E

IMDG CODE FOR WINDOWS, VERSION 10 (2010)

Features unique to the IMDG Code for Windows include:

- Contains the full text of the IMDG Code (35-10) and IMDG Code Supplement
- Searchable by Proper Shipping Name, UN Number and IMDG Code references
- Easy-to-use menus, on-screen user manual and help screens
- Search by French and Spanish language Proper Shipping Names
- Multiple windows (MDI) for viewing multiple pages or substances
- Extensive cross-referencing
- On-screen colour displays of hazard labels, signs and marks
- Medical First Aid Guide and Emergency Schedules
- Easy generation and printing of a Dangerous Goods Note
- New in V10; improved text searching and label displays
- Includes optional V9 Amdt 34-08 for use during transition period

English DH200E/ZH200E   ISBN 978-92-801-70337

Wall Chart: IMO DANGEROUS GOODS LABELS, MARKS AND SIGNS
2010 Edition

This updated full-colour wall chart illustrates the labels, marks and signs required under SOLAS and detailed in the IMDG Code.

English   ID223E   ISBN 978-92-801-15246

GUIDELINES ON THE ENHANCED PROGRAMME OF INSPECTIONS DURING SURVEYS OF BULK CARRIERS AND OIL TANKERS
2008 Edition

The Guidelines became mandatory in 1996, under SOLAS regulation XI/2, which requires that bulk carriers and oil tankers be subject to an enhanced programme of inspections in accordance with the Guidelines. Since their adoption, the Guidelines have been frequently updated and brought in line with regulatory and technological developments as well as with current practice, in particular with the relevant IACS Unified Requirements. In this edition, the Guidelines have been amended.

English	IA265E	ISBN 978-92-801-14966
French	IA265F	978-92-801-24248
Spanish	IA265S	978-92-801-01645

THE IMO-Vega DATABASE, Version 15
2010 Edition

IMO-Vega, developed jointly by IMO and Det Norske Veritas (DNV), is an essential tool for anyone involved in shipping: ship-owners and operators, shipbuilders, classification societies, casualty investigators, governments, insurers and underwriters, port authorities, surveyors and many others. Given year of build, ship type, ship size, cargo, trade area and flag, IMO-Vega will quickly identify the requirements applicable to the ship in question.

Unlike other, similar products, IMO-Vega contains historical data – including regulations which have been superseded. In the context of Port State Control, for example, access to the correct historical regulations is essential.

English   D15A   ISBN 978-92-801-70368

IMO-Vega ON THE WEB

This product is a yearly subscription to IMO-Vega and is updated regularly.

English   SVEGA

4 Albert Embankment • London SE1 7SR • United Kingdom

Tel: +44 (0)20 7735 7611 • Fax: +44 (0)20 7587 3241 • Email: sales@imo.org

www.imo.org

IMO INTERNATIONAL MARITIME ORGANIZATION

PUBLISHING

Notes

Notes

Notes

Notes

Notes